NEW HAMPSHIRE

AN EXPLORER'S GUIDE

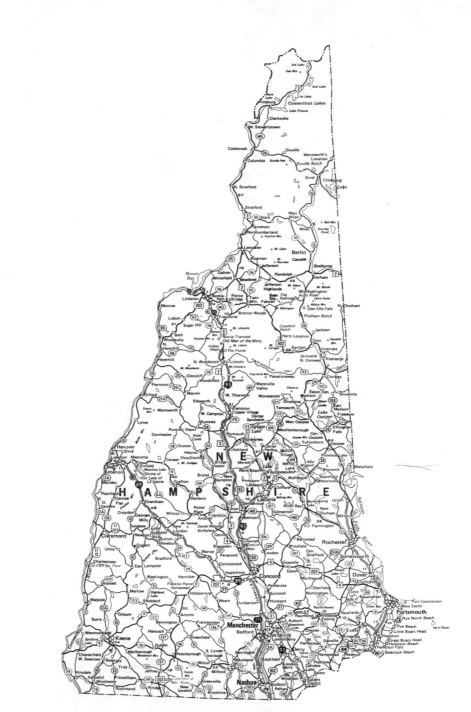

Copyright, THE NATIONAL SURVEY, 1991

New Hampshire

AN EXPLORER'S GUIDE

Christina Tree
Peter Randall

The Countryman Press
Woodstock, Vermont

No entries for any of the establishments listed in the Explorer's Guide
Series have been solicited or paid for.

The Countryman Press, Inc.
P.O. Box 175
Woodstock, Vermont 05091

Library of Congress Cataloging-in-Publication Data

Tree, Christina
    New Hampshire : an explorer's guide / Christina Tree, Peter
Randall.
        p.   cm.
    Includes index.
    ISBN 0-88150-200-6 : $16.95
    1. New Hampshire — Description and travel — 1981- —Guide-books.
I. Randall, Peter, 1940- .   II. Title.
    F32.3.t74   1991
    917.4204'43—dc20   91-8210
                                                              CIP

Printed in the United States of America

10 9 8 7 6 5 4 3 2 1

Series design by Frank Lieberman

Maps by Alex Wallach

Cover design by Leslie Fry

Cover photograph of Harrisville, New Hampshire, by Peter E. Randall

To Martha Rudneski Tree, my mother

— C.T.

To the memory of my mother, Virginia Chase Randall

— P.E.R.

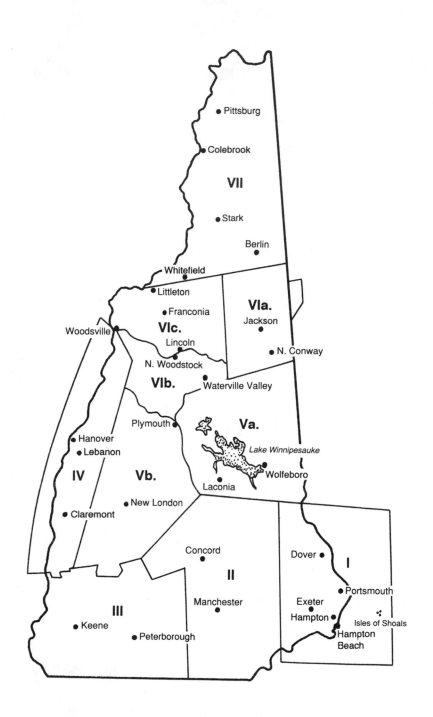

- Pittsburg
- Colebrook

VII

- Stark
- Berlin
- Whitefield
- Littleton
- Franconia

VIc.

Woodsville

- Lincoln
- N. Woodstock

VIa.
- Jackson
- N. Conway

VIb.
- Waterville Valley

- Plymouth
- Hanover
- Lebanon

Va.

Lake Winnipesauke
- Wolfeboro
- Laconia

IV   **Vb.**

- New London
- Claremont

- Concord

II

- Dover
- Manchester

I
- Portsmouth

III
- Keene
- Peterborough

- Exeter
- Hampton
- Isles of Shoals
- Hampton Beach

Contents

Introduction   1
What's Where in New Hampshire   5

I.   **THE SEACOAST   21**
Portsmouth and vicinity   25
Hampton, Hampton Beach, Exeter, and vicinity   46
Durham, Dover, and vicinity   59

II.   **THE MERRIMACK VALLEY   65**
The Manchester Area   68
The Concord Area   81

III.   **THE MONADNOCK REGION   93**
Peterborough, Keene, and surrounding villages   94

IV.   **THE UPPER CONNECTICUT RIVER VALLEY   131**
Upper Valley Towns   132

V.   **CENTRAL NEW HAMPSHIRE LAKES   159**
The Lake Winnipesauke Region   160
A Country Road Alternative
The Western Lakes   201

VI.   **THE WHITE MOUNTAINS   225**
White Mountain National Forest   226
Mt. Washington's Valleys   234
North Conway and vicinity / Jackson and Bartlett / Mt.
Washington and Pinkham Notch / Crawford Notch and
Bretton Woods / Evans Notch
The Western Whites   282
Lincoln and North Woodstock / The Waterville Valley /
Plymouth and the Baker River Valley
Franconia and North of the Notches   310
Franconia, Bethlehem, Sugar Hill / Lisbon to Littleton

VII.   **THE NORTH COUNTRY   327**
Along Route 2   331
Berlin and Route 16 North   336
Littleton, Whitefield, Lancaster, Groveton, and Stark   341
Colebrook, Pittsburg and vicinity   346

Index   353
Lodging Index   361

Isles of Shoals.

Introduction

This all-new Explorer's Guide marks the first comprehensive guide to New Hampshire since the 1930s.

New Hampshire had more lodgings for visitors back in the 1800s, when it was the most-touristed state in New England, than it did for most of the twentieth century. From the seacoast through the lakes region to the White Mountains, hundreds of wooden hotels were built during the last half of the nineteenth century for summer visitors who came to enjoy dramatic scenery, cool breezes, and genteel hospitality. Most tourists came by train and stayed at one hotel for a week, a month, or for the entire summer season.

The automobile changed this vacation pattern because it gave the traveler more mobility. Most of the big, wooden hotels were destroyed by fire, while others were closed and razed, unable to compete with the more economical cabin colonies and, later, motels. For New Hampshire there was a real decline in the number of accommodations available for visitors.

This situation changed during the 1980s, however, when the state experienced an explosion of new lodgings. Within the past decade the number of visitors who can be accommodated in New Hampshire on any one night has more than doubled. Many of these new "beds" (a travel industry buzz word) are in the condominium complexes that have sprouted around ski areas and lakes. Some are in large new hotels that have appeared in old tourist towns like North Conway. Others are in the hundreds of new inns, bed & breakfasts, and lodgings that have opened off the beaten path in recent years.

For the tourist, as well as the native, finding those places has not been easy; thus, *New Hampshire: An Explorer's Guide*—a book intended for New Hampshire residents *and* visitors. No other portrait of the state gathers so much practical information between two covers. All listings in this book are free; there is no paid advertising.

The book's chapters are organized into areas that coincide with those covered by local chambers of commerce. Each section begins with a "verbal snapshot" of the landscape and historic background. Sources of information, how to get around, and descriptions of everything to see and do—from winter sports to places to swim and pic-nic—follow. Then come capsule descriptions of places to stay. Our focus is on inns and bed & breakfasts because we feel that the Mobil and AAA guides do a fine job with motels. We have personally visited more than 90 percent of the lodgings included (that other 10 percent has been highly recommended, and we have contacted them by phone). We include prices because categories like "moderate" and "expensive" can be misleading, depending on what they include. Please allow for inflation and add the state room and meals tax. Some inns also add a service charge; be sure to inquire.

After lodging comes critiques of local upscale restaurants (Dining Out) and of the everyday options (Eating Out). We also describe shops worth seeking out and the special events of that area.

This book has been ten years in the making. In 1981 Chris spent much of a summer exploring New Hampshire with three small boys in tow. At the time, however, New Hampshire didn't seem ready for an Explorer's Guide. A decade ago lodging was pretty much limited to well-defined resort areas like Lake Sunapee, Lake Winnipesaukee, Hampton Beach, and the Mt. Washington Valley. Of course, New Hampshire still has its clearly defined "tourist track"—and there's nothing wrong with that—and though we personally never tire of the seashore and Portsmouth, North Conway, or Lake Winnipesaukee, there's more. Much more.

The Monadnock region used to be a place to go day hiking or to a concert or play. Now, almost every picturesque town offers an inn or B&B and sources of information about swimming, hiking, and biking. In the Upper Valley region you can take in a concert and some fine art at Dartmouth's Hood Museum, then canoe the Connecticut River from inn to inn. And in the area we've called the Western Lakes (because it harbors so many lakes, not just Sunapee), myriad, widely scattered lodging places offer access to swimming, sailing, summer theater, fine dining, and hiking up the mountains of Sunapee, Kearsarge, and Cardigan.

Less developed than the western side of Lake Winnipesaukee are the northern and eastern sections of the region—perfect places for those who enjoy country drives, roadside vegetable stands, and just poking around in antiques shops. Center Sandwich, Tamworth, Eaton, and Wakefield, for example, are less visited; yet they have comfortable inns and plenty to explore.

Surprisingly, only in the past decade have the state's largest ski resorts—Loon Mountain and Waterville Valley—become full-fledged, year-round resorts. They are part of the Western Whites, a rugged part of the White Mountains that is relatively untouristed beyond the spec-tacular natural sites in Franconia Notch.

The least-touristed section of the state is the North Country, the vast forested area north of the White Mountains. Fast-running rivers are perfect for fishing or canoeing. You can camp on picturesque wilderness lakes and fall asleep to the calls of loons, watch moose grazing beside the road, or ride to Canada on your snowmobile.

The urban communities of the Merrimack Valley, the state's industrial heartland, also have long been ignored by visitors; yet here are several of the best museums, two of the largest state parks, and a growing number of fine restaurants.

One author of this book is a "visitor" and the other, a "native." Chris Tree has explored the Granite State for more than 20 years as a travel writer whose New England stories appear regularly in the *Boston Globe* Sunday travel section. She is the author of *How New England Happened* (a historical guide to the region); co-author of *Best Places to Stay in New England* and the Explorer's Guides to Maine and Vermont. She is also the contributing travel editor to the magazine *New England Living* and a contributing editor to the annual *Original New England Guide*.

Peter Randall was born in New Hampshire and lives in the same seacoast town where his first American ancestor arrived in 1640. Educated at the University of New Hampshire, Peter is a former editor of *New Hampshire Profiles* magazine and worked for several daily and weekly newspapers before starting a small publishing company in 1976. Concentrating on local and town histories, his company has published more than 200 titles. An accomplished photographer, he has authored nine other books, including guides, works of history, and collections of photographs.

The authors wish to thank the staffs of the New Hampshire Office of Vacation Travel, especially Ann Kennard and Betty Lund, and the local chambers of commerce who helped provide and check information for the book. Others who have assisted include John Harrigan, Steve Smith, Ann Keefe, and Mildred Beach. We would also like to thank our editors, Jeanie Levitan and Valerie F. Levitan, for their encouragement, support, and patience.

We welcome comments and suggestions. Please direct them to: Editor, *New Hampshire: An Explorer's Guide*, The Countryman Press, PO Box 175, Woodstock, Vermont 05091.

Christina Tree
Peter E. Randall

The Pierce Homestead was built in 1804 by Benjamin Pierce, a general in the American Revolution, twice governor of New Hampshire (1827-28, 1829-30), and father of Franklin Pierce, the 14th President of the United States (1853-57). Franklin Pierce was born in Hillsboro November 23, 1804 and the family occupied this dwelling shortly thereafter.

President Franklin Pierce's childhood home, Hillsborough.

What's Where in New Hampshire

AGRICULTURAL FAIRS   New Hampshire boasts a baker's dozen summer and fall country fairs. Part of the social fabric of the nineteenth century, and still popular today, the country fair is the place where farm families meet their friends and exhibit their best home canned and fresh vegetables, livestock, and handwork such as quilts, baked goods, and needlework. Horse and cattle pulling, 4-H competitions, horse shows, and woodsmen's competitions are joined by midways, food stalls, and exhibits of farm implements, home furnishings, and a host of other items. The "New Hampshire's Rural Heritage," pamphlet from the New Hampshire Department of Agriculture (271-3788), Box 2042, Concord 03302-2042, lists the dates and locations of all fairs. These events are also mentioned in the Special Events sections of this book. The largest fair is Deerfield, held annually at the end of September, but other popular fairs include Hopkinton and Lancaster, both held on Labor Day weekend; Cheshire Fair in Swanzey, held early August; and Sandwich on Columbus Day weekend. Additionally, many local towns and organizations hold annual one-day fairs. Check with local chambers of commerce for exact dates.

AIR SERVICE   Manchester Airport is the state's major airport, served by United, USAir, Northwest Airlink, Continental, and Business Express. Lebanon is served by Northwest Airlink and by Business Express and Laconia by Sky Master (three flights a day to Boston). In addition, the state offers 20 airfields without scheduled service. Flying schools are located at Lebanon, Keene, Manchester, Laconia, Rochester, and Claremont. For details contact the New Hampshire Division of Aeronautics (271-2251), 65 Airport Road, Concord 03301.

ANTIQUARIAN BOOKSHOPS   It's hard to resist a good old book and New Hampshire has enough dealers in used, rare, and antiquarian books to keep any bibliophile busy just looking for bargains, to say nothing of actually sitting down and reading newly found treasures. Among the specialty dealers are shops selling first editions and books related to espionage, gardening, the White Mountains, hot-air ballooning, and women's studies. One shop has only 750 volumes while several others approach 100,000 titles to search. For a list of dealers, write the New Hampshire Antiquarian Booksellers

Association, c/o The Portsmouth Bookshop, 110 State Street, Portsmouth 03801. The association sponsors an annual mid-September book show and fair in Concord. This event attracts some 85 dealers from 10 states.

ANTIQUES   The New Hampshire Antiques Dealers Association (RFD 1, Box 305 C, Tilton 03276), lists some 170 dealers and nearly 20 group shops in this state, more than enough to keep the antiques buff happy. From the seacoast to the mountains and from the lakes region to Monadnock there are dealers in nearly every community, and the diversity of items offered equals any to be found in New England. Perhaps the largest concentration of shops is along Route 4 in Northwood and Epsom, but nearby Concord, Hopkinton, and Contoocook have nearly as many shops. Meredith, Centre Harbor, and Center Sandwich also have many shops as does Hillsboro, Peterborough, Fitzwilliam, and Route 1 in the seacoast area. The association's annual show is held in early August in Manchester, but several other annual shows are listed elsewhere in this book.

APPLE AND FRUIT PICKING   New Hampshire has many orchards and farms where you can pick your own apples, pears, peaches, and berries and press cider. The vegetable- and fruit-picking season begins in the early summer, while apples and other tree fruits ripen as fall begins. Many orchards have weekend festivals with fresh baked apple pies, donuts and cider, pumpkins, tractor-pulled wagon rides, music, and other activities aimed at making a perfect family outing. Don't forget to visit the orchards in the spring when the trees are blossoming. Write the New Hampshire Department of Agriculture, Box 2042, Concord 03302-2042, and ask for the "New Hampshire's Rural Heritage," "Harvest New Hampshire,"and the "Apple Growers Association" brochures.

AREA CODE   603 covers all of New Hampshire.

ART MUSEUMS AND GALLERIES New Hampshire's two major art museums are the Currier Gallery of Art in Manchester and the Hood Museum of Art at Dartmouth College. The Currier's collection includes some outstanding nineteenth- and twentieth-century European and American works and is departure point for tours to the Zimmerman House, designed by Frank Lloyd Wright. The Hood Museum's permanent collection ranges from some outstanding ancient Assyrian bas-relief to a huge abstract piece by Frank Stella. Both museums stage changing exhibits. (See Manchester and Upper Valley Towns for descriptions of each museum.) "The New Hampshire Visual Arts Map," published by the League of New Hampshire Craftsmen Foundation (see Crafts), includes a descriptive listing of more than a dozen galleries scattered around the state. Another important source of coltural information is the New Hampshire State Council on the Arts, 40 N. Main Street, Concord 03301 (271-2789).

AUTOMATIC TELLER MACHINES The official New Hampshire Highway lists locations of the following ATMs: Mac, Pocketbank, Cirrus, and

American Express. For more information call 800-523-4175.

BANDS Town bands are still popular in New Hampshire, and many hold summer concerts in outdoor bandstands. Schedules change yearly so check with local chambers of commerce. Conway, North Conway, Alton, Wolfeboro, Exeter, and Hampton Beach are among the places with regular band concerts.

BED & BREAKFASTS B&Bs appear under their own listing within the Lodging section of each chapter. It seems like there is a new B&B opening everyday in New Hampshire. We don't list everyone, but our selection ranges from working farms to historic mansions and from two-guest-room, private homes to larger places with a score or more of rooms. B&B rates in this book are for two persons (unless otherwise specified); single rates are somewhat less.

BICYCLING The Monadnock region is the state's liveliest bicycling scene. Monadnock Bicycle Touring offers self-guided inn-to-inn tours. *Peterborough Bike Tours* by Ann Harrison of the Peterborough AYH describes 10 local one-day tours. Rental mountain and touring bikes are available in Peterborough (see the Monadnock section for details). Also see Bicycling in the Western Lakes Region, where self-guided, inn-to-inn tours are offered. The New England Bicycling Center in Danbury offers bikes, maps, room and board. Loon Mountain Bike Center in Lincoln (see the Western Whites) offers mountain bike rentals and guided tours. The guide to the state's best bike routes is *30 Bicycle Tours in New Hampshire* by Adophe Bernotas (Backcountry). The Biking Expedition in Henniker (see the Merrimack Valley) offers guided biking tours geared to 7th–12th graders throughout New England and in other parts of the country, in Canada, and in Europe. The Granite State Wheelmen, for resident bicycling enthusiasts, schedules frequent rides throughout the state. Contact K. Lachairte, 83 Londonderry Road, Windham 03087.

BIRDING New Hampshire is not a bird-watcher's paradise like the Everglades, but there are several places that should be visited. Coastal Route 1A from Seabrook to New Castle provides numerous ocean, harbor, and salt marsh vantage points to observe shorebirds and sea fowl of all types, as well as various ducks and larger wading birds, especially in the summer when snowy egrets, great and little blue heron, glossy ibis, and black-crowned night heron are common. Lake Umbagog, described in the North Country chapter, has nesting eagles and osprey, loons, and other freshwater birds. Visit or contact Audubon House, the headquarters of the New Hampshire Audubon Society, 3 Silk Farm Road (Box 528), Concord 03302-0516, for more birding information. The Audubon Society's various regional chapters offer bird walks throughout the year. See a full listing in the Merrimack Valley chapter for more information.

BOATING New Hampshire law requires all boats used in fresh water to be registered, a formality which most marinas can provide. Or contact the

Department of Safety, Motor Vehicle Division (271-2251), Hazen Drive, Concord 03301, or the Division of Safety Services (271-3336). In the Lake Winnipesaukee area, contact the Safety Services Marine Division (293-2037), Route 11, Glendale. Boats used in tidal waters must be registered with the United States Coast Guard. Contact the USCG Portsmouth Harbor Station (436-0171), New Castle 03854; the New Hampshire Port Authority (436-8500), Box 506, 555 Market Street, Portsmouth 03802; or the New Hampshire Department of Safety, Marine Services Division (431-1170), Portsmouth State Fish Pier, Box 1355, Portsmouth 03802. Also contact the New Hampshire Marine Dealers Association (524-6661), 958 Union Avenue, Laconia 03246.

BOOKS   Many New Hampshire books are mentioned throughout this guide. For a general history of the state, try *New Hampshire* by Elting and Elizabeth Morison (Norton). A general good history is Jere Daniell's *Colonial New Hampshire, A History* (Kraus International), while another favorite is Ralph Nading Hill's, *Yankee Kingdom: Vermont and New Hampshire* (Countryman). *New Hampshire Four Seasons* (Downeast) by Peter E. Randall is a collection of 180 color photographs of New Hampshire, while William Schaller's *New Hampshire Backroads* (American Geographic Society) is a collection of photographs and text. The latter publisher has also released *New Hampshire: Portrait of the Land and its People. The New Hampshire Atlas & Gazetteer* (DeLorme Publishing), has maps of all major communities in the state. Check with independent bookstores, most of which have strong local

book sections and should be checked for titles that might not be available elsewhere.

BUS SERVICE   New Hampshire enjoys better bus service than any other New England state. **Concord Trailways** (in NH 800-852-3317; outside NH 800-258-3722) serves Manchester and Concord; Laconia, Meredith, and Centre Harbor in the Lake Winnipesaukee Region; Franconia, North Conway, and Jackson in the White Mountains; and north to Colebrook and Dixville Notch (The Balsams).**Greyhound Bus Lines** (436-0163) stops daily in Portsmouth's Market Square, connecting the seacoast with nationwide bus service. **C&J Trailways** (431-2424, 742-2990) provides many trips daily, connecting Logan Airport and downtown Boston with Dover, Durham, and Portsmouth, New Hampshire; Newburyport, Massachusetts; and Portland, Maine. **Vermont Transit** (802-864-6811) stops in Newport, Mt. Sunapee, Newbury, Bradford, Henniker, Warner, Concord, Manchester, and Nashua en route from White River Junction (VT) to Boston. It also stops in Keene and Fitzwilliam en route from Brattleboro (VT) to Boston; another route includes stops in Charlestown and Walpole. See the Merrimack Valley for limo service connecting with Boston's Logan Airport.

CAMPGROUNDS   For many people, camping offers the best way to visit a state. New Hampshire has a wide variety of camping opportunities, ranging from primitive sites with few amenities to full-service areas with water and sewer hookups, electricity, TV, stores, recreation buildings, playgrounds, swimming pools, and boat launching. The most complete information is available from the New Hampshire Campground Owners' Association (846-5511), Box 320, Twin Mountain 03595. Their free directory lists 171 private, state, and White Mountain National Forest (WMNF) campgrounds. State and WMNF campgrounds are also listed in this book. Most private areas take reservations and some are completely booked by the end of one summer for the next. The state-owned campgrounds operate on a first-come, first-served basis only and offer few amenities, but many are on lakes with sandy beaches. Most WMNF sites are also on a first-come, first-served basis, however, a toll-free reservation system (800-283-2267) operates for some sites in the following campgrounds: White Ledge (Conway); Covered Bridge (Kancamagus); Sugarloaf I and II (Twin Mountain); Basin, Cold River, and Hastings (Evans Notch); Dolly Copp (Pinkham Notch); and Campton, Russell Pond, and Waterville (near I-93). The reservation service operates March through September (Monday to Friday 12–9, weekends 12–5) and costs $6 in addition to the camping fee. Reservations may be made 120 days before arrival, but 10 days before arrival is the minimum time.

CANOEING   New Hampshire offers many miles of flat-water and white-water canoeing opportunities. The Androscoggin, Connecticut, Saco, and Merrimack rivers are perhaps the most popular waters for canoeing, but there are many other smaller rivers as well. Many folks also like to paddle the numerous lakes and ponds of New Hampshire. Since spring runoffs have an impact on the degree of paddling difficulty to be found on a river, make sure you know what your river offers before heading downstream. The best source of information is the *AMC River Guide: New Hampshire and Vermont*, published by the Appalachian Mountain Club, 5 Joy Street, Boston, MA 02108. Also see *Canoe Camping Vermont and New Hampshire Rivers* (Backcountry). Also contact the Merrimack Watershed Council (224-8322), 54 Portsmouth Street, Concord 03301, for information on the Merrimack River; and Saco Bound (447-2177), Box 119, Route 302, Center Conway 03813, for information on the Saco and Androscoggin rivers.

CHILDREN, FOR   Children's museums are described in the Portsmouth, Upper Valley Towns, Manchester, and Concord and in the Monadnock Region. The White Mountain Attractions is the state's single largest family-geared magnet. Ranging from the excursion vessel *M/S Mt. Washington* on Lake Winnipesaukee to the gondola at Wildcat Mountain, from natural phenomena like Lost River in North Woodstock to theme parks like Story Land in Glen and Six Gun City and Santa's Village (both in Jefferson), this is a highly organized promotional association with a helpful Visitors Center just off Exit 32 of I-93 in North Woodstock. Phone 745-8720 or 800-FIND MTS, or write Box 10, North Woodstock 03262. Other attractions with child appeal range from Friendly Farm in Dublin to New England's biggest video center in Weirs Beach. All are described as they appear, region by region.

CHILDREN'S SUMMER CAMPS More than 100 summer camps are located in New Hampshire. For a free brochure contact the New Hampshire Camp Director's Association (437-2121), Box 427, Londonderry 03053.

CHRISTMAS TREES Plantation-grown New Hampshire Christmas trees are the perfect accent for the holidays. These trees have been planted specifically to be harvested at about 10 years of age. Some growers allow you to come early in the season to tag your own tree, which you can cut at a later time for the holidays; others allow choose-and-cut only in December. Write the New Hampshire Department of Agriculture, Box 2042, Concord 03302-2042, and ask for the "Harvest New Hampshire" brochure, or get the list from the New Hampshire-Vermont Christmas Tree Growers' Association, RD 1, Box 470, Wolcott, VT 05680.

COLLEGES AND UNIVERSITIES While everybody can't live in New Hampshire year-round, many students do the next best thing by getting their education in this state. Among a number of preparatory schools, New Hampshire has two of the country's best (Phillips Exeter and St. Paul's), and higher education opportunities ranging from two-year schools to the highly regarded University of New Hampshire and Dartmouth College. A descriptive brochure of 13 accredited, four-year institutions is available from the New Hampshire College and University Council (669-3432), 2321 Elm Street, Manchester 03104.

CONSERVATION GROUPS The **Society for the Protection of New Hampshire Forests** (SPNHF) was founded in 1901 to fight the systematic leveling of the state's forests by lumber firms. They were instrumental in the passage of the 1911 Weeks Act, authorizing (for the first time) the federal purchase of lands to create national forests. One direct result is the 729,353-acre White Mountain National Forest. The group is also largely responsible for Mt. Monadnock's current public status, and it now holds 57 properties for public use which total more than 18,000 acres. Many are described within this book, especially within the Monadnock Region, which harbors a large percentage. Stop by SPNHF headquarters in East Concord (just off I-93 Exit 15) or write SPNHF (224-9945), 54 Portsmouth Street, East Concord, to obtain a copy of the society's "Lands Map & Guide" to their properties. If you are a hiker, fisherman, or cross-country skier it is a valuable key to real treasure.

The **Appalachian Mountain Club**, founded in 1876 to blaze and map hiking trails through the White Mountains, was also a crucial lobbying group for the passage of the Weeks Act. Today, like SPNHF, it continues to support environmental causes and cater to hikers, maintaining hundreds of miles of trails and feeding and sheltering hikers in a chain of eight "high huts" in the Presidential Range, each a day's hike apart (see High Huts of the White Mountains). Pinkham Notch Camp, a comfortable complex at the eastern base of Mt. Washington, serves as headquarters for the high huts and as a year-round center for a wide variety of workshops in subjects ranging from nature drawing to North Country literature as well as camping and cross-country skiing. The AMC also maintains a hostel-like camping and lodging facility at Cardigan, runs shuttle buses for hikers around Mt. Washington, and much more. Their guidebooks remain the hikers' bibles.

The Audubon Society of New Hampshire maintains 31 wildlife sanctuaries throughout the state. Within this book we have described a number but you might like to request the free pamphlet "Guide to ASNH Wildlife Sanctuaries" by writing to the Audubon Society of New Hampshire Headquarters (224-9909), 3 Silk Farm Road (Box 528), Concord 03302-0516.

COVERED BRIDGES   New Hampshire harbors more than 60 covered bridges. These are marked on the official state highway map and we have tried to describe them within each chapter. The country's longest covered bridge, rebuilt in 1990, connects Cornish with Windsor,VT (technically the New Hampshire line runs to the Vermont shore so it's all in New Hampshire). The state's oldest authenticated covered bridge (1827) links Haverhill and Bath. The Swanzey area near Keene (see the Monadnock Region) boasts the state's greatest concentration of covered bridges: six within little more than a dozen miles.

CRAFTS   The League of New Hampshire Craftsmen, with headquarters at 205 N. Main Street, Concord 03301 (224-2471), is one of the country's oldest, most effective statewide crafts groups. It maintains a half dozen shops displaying work by members, sponsors the outstanding annual Craftsmen's Fair in early August at Mt. Sunapee State Park in Newbury, and publishes the New Hampshire Visual Arts Map, an extremely useful free pamphlet/guide to museums, galleries, and studios throughout the state. Two of these galleries, the Sharon Arts Center in the Monadnock Region and Sandwich Home Industries in the Lake Winnipesaukee Area, are themselves worth a trip. The league can also furnish information about crafts workshops throughout the state.

CRUISES   Few summer activities are as relaxing as a boat ride, and New Hampshire has many trips available from the ocean to the lakes. The two most popular cruises are the *M/V Thomas Laighton* (Isles of Shoals Steamship Company), which sails several times daily from Portsmouth to the off-shore Isles of Shoals, and the *M/S Mt. Washington* on Lake Winnipesaukee. Squam Lake has two small boat cruises, and Lake Sunapee has several also. For details see the chapters on the Seacoast, Lake Winnipesaukee, and the Western Lakes.

EMERGENCIES   New Hampshire's telephone books have full listings of local emergency numbers inside the front cover. The State Police can be called at 800-852-3411. The New Hampshire Poison Center number is 800-652-8236. Hospital and ambulance numbers are also included at the beginning of each chapter in this book.

EVENTS   The Official New Hampshire Guidebook (see Information) lists current events, and in each chapter we have listed Special Events that occur year after year.

FACTORY OUTLETS   Several areas of New Hampshire have become tourist destinations just because of their shopping opportunities. The best known region is North Conway where some 200 shops, discount stores, and factory outlets have given the term "shopping trip" a new meaning. If you can't find what you want to buy there, you probably don't need it. North Hampton also has a large outlet shopping complex, but seacoast shoppers often drive across the Piscataqua River to Kittery, Maine, where outlets are nearly as numerous as in North Conway. Remember, Maine has a sales tax, New Hampshire does not.

FARMER'S MARKETS   Many farms used to have roadside stands where they sold their produce, and many still operate in New Hampshire, but the current trend is to sell through farmer's markets—once-a-week gatherings of many farmers. Open mainly from late June through Columbus Day, markets operate in the Concord, Conway, Dover, Exeter, Hampton, Portsmouth, Laconia, Manchester, Milford, and Warner. Fresh fruits and vegetables, baked goods, honey, and crafts are among the items for sale. Many of the state's organic farmers sell their produce at these markets. "New Hampshire's Rural Heritage," lists farmer's markets locations and hours and is available from the New Hampshire Department of Agriculture (271-3788), Box 2042, Concord 03302-2042. Also see listings in this book.

FISHING   Freshwater fishing requires a license for anyone age 12 and older. Some 450 sporting goods and country stores sell licenses, or contact the New Hampshire Fish and Game Department (271-3421), 2 Hazen Drive, Concord 03301. The White Mountain National Forest issues a special brochure on trout fishing in the forest. No license is required for saltwater fishing. Party boats leave several times daily from April until October from docks at Rye, Hampton, and Seabrook harbors. Most of these boats have full tackle for rent.

FOLIAGE   Color first appears on hillsides in the North Country in mid-September, and by the end of that month Crawford and Pinkham notches are usually spectacular. The colors spread south and through lower elevations during the first two weeks in October. Columbus Day weekend is traditionally the time New England residents come "leaf peeping," and it's the period we suggest you avoid, if possible. At least avoid the traditional foliage routes—the Kancamagus Highway, Route 3 through Franconia Notch, and Route 16 to North Conway—on those three days. Come the first weekend in October instead and try to get off the road entirely. This is prime hiking weather (no bugs). The state maintains a Fall Foliage hotline (800-258-3608) with "conditions" updated regularly. The wise traveler will make reservations for overnight accommodations well in advance for the foliage season since even such areas as Lincoln or North Conway, with hundreds of rooms, are fully booked on key weekends.

GOLF   We describe golf courses as they appear region by region. They are also listed in **The Official New**

Hampshire   Guidebook   (see Information).

HIGH HUTS OF THE WHITE MOUNTAINS   The most unusual lodging opportunities in the state are found in the White Mountains where the Appalachian Mountain Club operates eight, full-service high mountain huts. Generally the huts are open from June through Labor Day, but several welcome hikers through September and two are open on a caretaker-basis all year. Guests hike to the huts, most of which are located a day's walk apart so that you can walk for several days and stay in a different hut each night. You sleep in co-ed bunk rooms equipped with mattresses and blankets. Meals are huge and varied. Reservations are required. A shuttle service allows you to park at the trailhead for one hut, then ride back to your vehicle after your hike. Contact Appalachian Mountain Club Pinkham Notch Camp (466-2727, for overnight or workshop reservations), Route 16, Box 298, Gorham 03518.

HIKING   New Hampshire offers the most diverse hiking in New England. The White Mountain National Forest alone has some 1,200 miles of hiking trails, and there are additional miles in state parks. A long difficult section of the Appalachian Trail cuts through New Hampshire, entering the state near Hanover, crossing the highest peaks, including Mt. Washington, and exiting along the rugged Mahoosuc Range on the Maine border. The White Mountains is the most popular hiking area, and the many trails offer easy to challenging routes.

The most spectacular climbs are on the Franconia Ridge and over the Presidential Range which includes Mt. Washington, at 6,288 feet the highest peak in the northeast. Although relatively low compared to the Rockies, for example, Mt. Washington records the worst weather for any surface station outside of the polar regions. Hikers are urged to use caution and to consult weather forecasts before venturing onto the exposed areas above treeline. About 100 people have died on Mt. Washington; some of them in the summer when caught unprepared by extreme changes in weather conditions. White Mountain hiking information is available from the Appalachian Mountain Club Pinkham Notch Camp (466-2725 for weather, trail, or general information; 466-2727 for overnight or workshop reservations) Route 16, Box 298, Gorham 03518, or from the White Mountain National Forest (for details see the Mt. Washington's Valleys chapter).

There is plenty of hiking elsewhere in New Hampshire as well. Mt. Monadnock in southern New Hampshire is one of the most climbed peaks in the world, and Kearsarge in central New Hampshire offers a relatively easy walk to its summit and nice views. Several lower mountains in the Lake Winnipesaukee region are easily climbed. Mt. Major, in particular, is easy and has a fine view across the lake. These hikes are described elsewhere in this book, but for more details one of the following books is recommended. The *AMC White Mountain Guide* has the most comprehensive trail information available for hiking anywhere in New Hampshire, but also see *Fifty Hikes in the White Mountains, Fifty Hikes in New Hampshire, Waterfalls of*

New Hampshire, and *Walks and Rambles in the Upper Connecticut Valley* (all Backcountry books), the *Monadnock Guide* (Society for the Protection of New Hampshire Forests, Concord), and the guidebook of the Squam Lakes Association of Holderness.

An exciting hiking project now underway is the creation of the Heritage Trail which will run the length of the state following the banks of the Merrimack, Pemigewasset, and Connecticut rivers. Many segments of the trail are in place and new sections are added annually. For details call 271-3627.

HISTORIC HOUSES AND SITES   New Hampshire residents have a strong appreciation for the state's history. Most communities have historical societies, and throughout the state are many historic buildings and sites open to the public. Most are listed in this guide. The largest concentration of historical houses is in Portsmouth, home of the large Strawbery Banke restoration and eight other houses open to the public. Along New Hampshire highways are roadside markers with short tidbits of local history. A copy of the roadside marker guide is available from the Division of Historic Resources (271-3483). *New Hampshire Architecture* (University Press of New England), is a fine guide to historical and significant buildings.

HONEY   More than 200 members of the New Hampshire Beekeepers Association have hives throughout the state, and their honey is usually for sale at farmer's markets, some country stores, and at roadside stands.

HORSEBACK RIDING   Rising insurance costs are narrowing trail riding options, but you can still ride a horse through the woods at Morning Mist Farm in Henniker (see the Merrimack Valley), at the Castle in the Clouds in Meredith (see the Lake Winnipesaukee Area), at both Waterville Valley and Loon Mountain in the Western Whites, at the Mt. Washington Hotel in Bretton Woods (see Mt. Washington's Valleys), and at Philbrook Farm Inn in Shelburne (see The North Country: Along Route 2).

HUNTING   New Hampshire has long been a popular state for hunting. Licenses are required and are available from some 450 sporting goods and country stores, or contact the New Hampshire Fish and Game Department (271-3421), 2 Hazen Drive, Concord 03301.

ICE CREAM   It's hard to beat Annabelle's Ice Cream, located on Ceres Street in Portsmouth, open from spring through late fall. President George Bush liked their flavors so much that he had them make and serve red, white, and blueberry ice cream at the White House for Fourth of July. Another popular homemade brand of ice cream is served at Lagos' Lone Oak Dairy Bars on old Route 16 in Rochester and Route 1 in Rye.

INFORMATION   We describe regional information sources at the head of each chapter. Ask toll-free information (800-555-1212) for the current listing for the state-maintained New Hampshire Office of Vacation Travel. You can also call 271-2343 or write to the Office of Vacation Travel, Department of Resources and Economic Development, PO Box 856, Concord 03301. Request a copy of **The New Hampshire Guidebook** and a highway map. The guidebook includes year-round listings of the basics: golf courses, alpine and cross-country ski areas, covered bridges, scenic drives, events, fish and game rules, State Parks, and State Liquor Stores. It also includes paid dining and lodging listings. Maps and pamphlets are also available in the state's full-service rest areas (see Rest Areas).

LAKES   Central New Hampshire is open, rolling country, spotted with lakes. Winnipesaukee is by far the state's largest, most visitor-oriented lake, and it is surrounded by smaller lakes: Winnesquam, Squam, Wentworth, Ossipee. Traditionally this has been New Hampshire's Lakes Regions but we've added the Western Lakes because there are so many west of I-93 as well: Sunapee and Newfound for starters, Little Sunapee, Massasecum, Pleasant, Highland, and Webster when you start looking for places to swim. Outdoorsmen are also well aware of the grand expanses of Umbagog Lake in Errol and of the Connecticut Lakes in New Hampshire's northernmost North Country.

LIBRARIES   Every New Hampshire city and town has a public library, and there are many college and private libraries as well. In the seacoast, the Portsmouth Public Library and the Portsmouth Athenaeum, and the Exeter Public Library and Exeter Historical Society are centers for regional history and genealogical research. The University of New Hampshire's Dimond Library has an extensive New Hampshire special collections section and all of the resources one would expect to find in a major educational institution. In Concord, the State Library and the New Hampshire Historical Society, located side-by-side on Park Street, are centers for New Hampshire research. Peterborough's public library was the first in New Hampshire, and it and the nearby Peterborough Historical Society library have important regional collections. In Keene, the Historical Society of Cheshire County Archive Center and the Keene State Library are the best sources for local research. Baker Library at Dartmouth College is one of the fine institutions in the east. Among its many resources is an extensive White Mountain collection.

LLAMA TREKS   White Mountain Llamas in Jefferson (see The North Country) is a source of one- to four-day treks. Similar treks in the Evans Notch area of the White Mountains, just over the Maine border, are offered by the Telemark Inn & Llama Farm in West Bethel.

LOTTERY   New Hampshire's is the oldest legal lottery in the country. Since 1964 it has funded more than $186 million to local education. For details phone 271-2825.

MAGAZINES AND NEWSPAPERS   For such a small state, New Hampshire has an abundance of periodicals. The *Manchester Union-Leader* (Box 780, Manchester 03105), is the largest daily, and its strong conservative editorial policy has made it well known throughout the country. It is the best source of statewide news, but there are also dailies in Portsmouth, Dover, Laconia, Concord, Claremont, Lebanon, Keene, Nashua, and Concord. Many of the larger towns also have weekly newspapers. The *Granite State Vacationer* (Box 519, Dover 03820) is a recreation newspaper, published 27 times each year and distributed free at roadside rest areas and information centers. It and several regional, free, tourist-oriented periodicals are good sources of information about local events and activities. *New Hampshire Profiles* (Box 370, Stratham 03885), founded in 1951, is the oldest general-interest New Hampshire magazine. Among its competitors are *New Hampshire Premier* (20 Ladd Street, Portsmouth 03801) and *The Spectator* (Box 896, Concord 03302), the latter a journal of news and opinion.

MAPLE SUGARING   When cool nights and warm days during late February through April start the sap running in maple trees, maple syrup producers fire up their evaporators to begin making the sweet natural treat. Most producers welcome visitors and many offer tours, sugar on snow parties, and breakfast (pancakes with maple syrup, of course). For a list of maple syrup producers, contact the New Hampshire Department of Agriculture (271-3788), Box 2042, Concord 03302-2042.

MOUNTAINTOPS   The summits of some New Hampshire mountains are more popular than others mainly because they offer better views, great hiking trails, or ways to ride to the top. The most popular, of course, is Mt.

Washington, at 6,288 feet the highest peak in the northeast. The Mt. Washington Auto Road is an 8-mile graded road on which you can drive your own car or ride in a chauffeured van. The Mt. Washington Cog Railway offers an unusual steam-powered ride to the summit. Across Route 16 from Mt. Washington, the Wildcat Mountain gondolas whisk you to the top of that wooded peak for a spectacular view of the Presidential Range. The Cannon Mountain tramway in Franconia offers its riders a view of the Franconia Range, the state's second highest group of mountains. Mt. Lafayette is one of the popular hikes from Franconia Notch. Lower mountains also provide worthy views. Mt. Chocorua rises beside Route 16 in Tamworth; although only 3,400 feet high, it is a challenging hike, but with a great vista from its summit. Although it is not a mountaintop, Castle in the Clouds (Route 109, Moultonborough), gives nonhikers the best view of Lake Winnipesaukee. Mt. Major (Route 11, Alton), has an easy walk to its open summit. Mt. Monadnock dominates the view throughout southwestern New Hampshire, but if you are not up to the hike, drive to the top of nearby Pack Monadnock (Miller State Park), Route 101, Peterborough. For those who like a challenge, the Appalachian Mountain Club has an informal 4,000 Footer Club; become a member by climbing all 48 New Hampshire mountains over 4,000 feet high. The peaks are listed in the *AMC White Mountain Guide*. Some rugged folks have climbed all 48 in the winter; others have done it twice, with their dogs, or some other unique way.

MUSEUMS   Aside from art museums and children's museums (see Art

Photo by Stuart Bratesman

The Hopkins Center, Dartmouth College.

Museums and Galleries and For Children), New Hampshire offers historical museums and houses (described here region by region). Canterbury Shaker Village in Canterbury (see the Concord Area) is an outstanding museum village. The New Hampshire Farm Museum in Milton tells the history of farming in the state.

MUSIC   Music festivals are described under Entertainment and/or Special Events. Check out the New Hampshire Music Festival in Centre Harbor (see the Lake Winnipesaukee Area), year-round performances at the North Country Center for the Arts in Lincoln, summer concerts at Waterville Valley's Music Festival Concert Series, the Prescott Park Festival in Portsmouth,

the Mt. Washington Valley Arts Festival, and the Cochico Arts Festival in Dover. The Monadnock Region is a traditional center for outstanding music; Monadnock Music is a series of two dozen summer concerts, operas, and orchestra performances staged in town halls, churches, and schools, and the Apple Hill Chamber Players in Nelson offers free faculty concerts. Band music is another sound of summer in New Hampshire. The Temple Band, also based in the Monadnock Region, claims to be the oldest town band in the country.

PARKS   New Hampshire has one of the oldest and best state park systems in the country. High mountains; lake, ocean, and river shores; unique stands of flowering shrubs and trees; historic buildings; geological and archaeological sites comprise the diverse locations of the nearly 50 parks. Swimming, fishing, picnicking, camping, and hiking are among the many activities enjoyed in these parks. See Campgrounds for camping information or contact the New Hampshire Division of Parks (271-3254), 105 Loudon Road, Concord 03301. The 768,000-acre White Mountain National Forest runs through the middle of New Hampshire from east to west. The largest national forest in the east, it is managed for multiple-use activities including lumbering as well as recreation. Several ranger stations are located along major highways to provide information and assistance for forest users. The Saco Ranger Station (447-5448), at the Conway of the Kancamagus Highway, is open seven days a week, 8–4:30, or contact WMNF headquarters (528-8721), Box 638, 719 Main Street, Laconia

Photo by Dick Smith

Mount Washington State Park.

03247. Almost all cities and towns have parks, many of which include tennis courts open to the public.

PICK YOUR OWN   (See Apple and Fruit Picking.)

RENTAL COTTAGES, CONDOMINI-UMS   Cottages are particularly plentiful and available in the Lake Winnipesaukee and the Western Lakes areas (contact the local chambers) and the same condominiums that cost $150 plus per night at Waterville Valley and Loon Mountain during ski season, are a fraction of the price in summer—when golf, horseback riding, hiking, and a variety of other activities make them increasingly attractive. The Mt. Washington Valley Chamber of Commerce also keeps year-round tabs on condominiums and other family lodging.

REST AREAS   The state operates 17 highway rest areas. Three are open 24 hours a day: Hooksett (I-93 northbound and southbound) and Seabrook (northbound on I-95). The complete list of rest areas is printed on the official New Hampshire Highway Map, which is available at any information center or from the New Hampshire Office of Vacation Travel (271-2666), Box 856, Concord 03302.

ROCK HOUNDING   Ruggles Mine in Grafton (see the Western Lakes) is said to offer 150 kinds of minerals and gem stones. Commercial production of mica began here in 1803, and it's an eerie, interesting place that has gotten many a rock hound hooked.

SKI CONDITIONS   For alpine ski conditions call 224-2525 (outside NH 800-258-3608). For cross-country conditions call 224-6363 (outside NH 800-262-6660).

SKIING, CROSS-COUNTRY   New Hampshire offers more than 30 touring centers with a total of over 1,200 kilometers of trails. The Jackson Ski Touring Foundation is the state's largest, with 150 kilometers of varied trails including a run down the backside of Wildcat Mountain (accessible from the alpine summit via a single ride on its gondola). Bretton Woods Ski Touring Center offers a similar run from the top of its alpine area and a total of 88 kilometers of trails. The Mt. Washington Valley Ski Touring Foundation offers another 60 kilometers, and the AMC in Pinkham Notch offers cross-country workshops and guided tours on national forest trails, too. Farther south both Loon Mountain and Waterville Valley offer major cross-country centers which tie into national forest trails. Norsk in New London is the outstanding cross-country center in central New Hampshire (in terms of size, elevation, and grooming) and Windblown Ski Touring Center in New Ipswich is favored by Bostonians—it's high, handy, and quite beautiful. In '91 the Office of Vacation Travel's cross-country snow report line is 224-6363 or 800-262-6660. The centers are described region by region within this book. Also look for the state's free SKI MAP (see Downhill Skiing), available from the NH Office of Vacation Travel (see Information).

SKIING, DOWNHILL   New Hampshire boasts 25 downhill ski areas with a total of over 500 trails and 130 lifts. It's worth noting that on weekends their proximity to Boston puts these lifts (and lift tickets) at a real premium, but on weekdays they tend to be relatively empty. This pattern is beginning to alter as many of the "areas" become full-fledged "resorts." Loon Mountain in Lincoln and Waterville Valley (see the Western Whites), the state's largest areas, now offer a variety of activities to attract "ski-weekers" as well as day-trippers and weekenders. New Hampshire's areas may also just represent the world's largest concentration of snowmaking. The quality of the snowmaking itself varies but most of New Hampshire's alpine slopes are now dependably white from Christmas through Easter. There's some discussion between Vermont and New Hampshire about whether alpine skiing was first introduced to this country in Woodstock (VT) or in Jackson (NH) but New Hampshire has New England's only ski museum (see Franconia and North of the Notches). We have described each ski area as it appears, region by region. In '91 the statewide snow phone is 224-2525 or 800-258-3608. Request a copy of the free New Hampshire Ski Map; it profiles the ski areas and includes winter events and attractions.

SLED DOG RACES   The world championships are in Laconia in February and climax in a series of colorful local meets.

SLEIGH RIDES   A number of New Hampshire inns and farms offer sleigh rides and hayrides in-season. Several are listed in this guide and others are found in "New Hampshire's Rural Heritage," a pamphlet from the New Hampshire Department of Agriculture (271-3788), Box 2042, Concord 03302-2042.

SNOWMOBILING   With some 6,000

miles of trails, New Hampshire offers the snowmobiler vast opportunities for winter fun. Note: large portions of the WMNF are off limits to snowmobiling, trail bikes, or off-road vehicles, but most state parks do permit off-road vehicles on marked trails. For maps and regulations, contact the Bureau of Off-Road Vehicles (271-3254), Box 856, Concord 03302; the New Hampshire Snowmobile Association (224-8906), Box 38, Concord 03301; or chambers of commerce in Twin Mountain, Colebrook, Lincoln-North Woodstock, or North Conway. For snowmobile snow conditions call 244-4666 or (outside NH) 800-258-3609.

SOARING   Glider lessons and rides are offered in Franconia at North Country Flying Service (North of Franconia Notch) and by New England Light Aircraft in Salem (253-9526).

SUMMER THEATER   New Hampshire offers some outstanding summer theater. The Barnstormers in Tamworth, the Peterborough Players in Peterborough, and the New London Barn Playhouse in New London all rank among New England's oldest, best respected "straw hat" theaters. The Weathervane Theater in Whitefield, the American Stage Festival in Milford, the Hopkins Center at Dartmouth College in Hanover, the Arts Center at Brickyard Pond in Keene, and the Prescott Art Festival in Portsmouth also stage lively summer productions. Children's performances are staged at Andy's Summer Playhouse in Wilton Center, at the Actors Theater Playhouse in West Chesterfield, and at Waterville Valley during its Summer Concert Series. All are described region by region under Entertainment.

TRAILS, LONG DISTANCE   New Hampshire from the road is beautiful but unless you see its panoramas from a high hiking trail you miss its real magnificence. Long-distance hiking trails now cross-cross the state. The longest, most spectacular, and most famous, the Appalachian Trail cuts diagonally across the White Mountains, entering the state in Hanover on the west and traversing Franconia Notch, Mt. Washington, and Pinkham Notch on its way into Maine. Detailed maps and guides as well as a free pamphlet guide "The Appalachian Trail in New Hampshire and The White Mountains" is available from the Appalachian Mountain Club Headquarters (617-523-0636), 5 Joy Street, Boston, MA 02108; also from the AMC Pinkham Notch Camp (see Hiking). The Metacomet Trail, running 14 miles south from Little Monadnock; the Wapack Trail, which heads south along ridges from North Pack Monadnock; and the Monadnock-Sunapee Trail, a 47-mile footpath, are also well mapped. Also see Hiking within each region.

WATERFALLS   The White Mountains have the best waterfalls to view and all are described in *Waterfalls of the White Mountains* (Backcountry), which lists 30 trips to some 100 waterfalls.

I. The Seacoast

Pittsburg

Colebrook

VII

Stark

Berlin

Whitefield

Littleton

VIa.

Franconia

Jackson

Woodsville

VIc.

Lincoln

N. Conway

N. Woodstock

VIb.

Waterville Valley

Plymouth

Va.

Hanover

Lebanon

Lake Winnipesauke

IV

Vb.

Wolfeboro

Laconia

New London

Claremont

Concord

Dover

I

II

Portsmouth

Manchester

Exeter

III

Hampton

Isles of Shoals

Keene

Hampton Beach

Peterborough

Introduction

With only 18 miles of oceanfront, New Hampshire's seacoast is often overlooked by visitors who are more impressed with neighboring Maine's more than 2,500 miles of coastline. In its small coastal area, however, New Hampshire has more than enough historical sites, beaches, restaurants, and events and attractions to keep her guests busy for many days and returning again and again for more.

At opposite ends of the seacoast are Portsmouth and Hampton Beach, near to each other in mileage but much farther apart in ambience and style.

Settled in 1630, Portsmouth was the colonial capital and an important seaport during the Georgian and Federal eras, periods which have given the city its distinctive architectural character. With fine inns and restaurants, a number of original and restored historical houses open to the public, theater, dance, music, and a superb waterfront park, Portsmouth is New Hampshire's most delightful and interesting city, loved and appreciated by its residents and visitors alike.

Hampton Beach has been one of New England's most popular seaside resorts since the development of the electric trolley at the turn of the century. Too bad the trolleys don't operate any more since the automobile traffic, especially on weekends, is one long snarl. Sand and sun, pizza and fried dough, and lively entertainment characterize Hampton Beach, where over 200,000 people can be found on a summer holiday weekend. For many people, a week at Hampton Beach has been an annual family tradition for half a century or more.

Between these two extremes are mostly small towns (less than 1,000 to 12,000 population) with white churches, town commons, colonial architecture, and an ambience that is attracting many new residents and straining the capacity of these towns to manage the growth that has characterized this area since the end of World War II. With the recent closure of Pease Air Force Base and the decline in activity at the Portsmouth Naval Shipyard, the seacoast is facing an uncertain economic future, but its superb location and abundant educational, cultural, physical, and human resources seem to be more than adequate to continue the region's reputation as one of the top places in the country to live and work (and vacation).

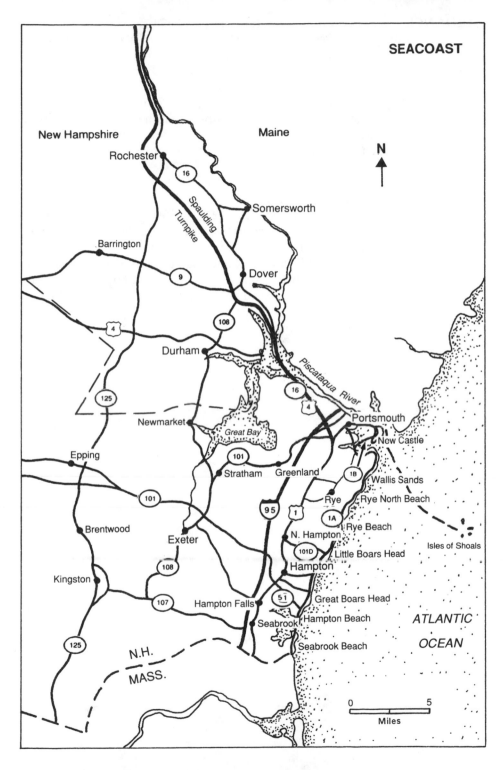

SEACOAST

N

New Hampshire

Maine

Rochester

16

Spaulding Turnpike

Somersworth

Barrington

9

Dover

108

4

Durham

125

16

4

Piscataqua River

Newmarket

Portsmouth

Great Bay

New Castle

Epping

101

Stratham   Greenland

18

Wallis Sands

101

Rye   Rye North Beach

95

1

Brentwood

1A

Rye Beach

N. Hampton

Exeter

101D

Little Boars Head

108

Hampton

Isles of Shoals

Kingston

107

Hampton Falls

51

Great Boars Head

125

N.H.

Seabrook   Hampton Beach

ATLANTIC

MASS.

Seabrook Beach

OCEAN

0   5

Miles

GUIDANCE   Seacoast Council on Tourism (436-7678, outside NH 800-221-5623), 1000 Market Street, Portsmouth 03801. Publishes a handy guide. (Also see chambers of commerce under sectional listings.)

GETTING THERE   By plane: **Boston's Logan Airport, Portland's Jetport,** and **Manchester Airport** are each an hour's drive from the seacoast.

By car: I-95, the state's first super highway, built in the 1950s, bisects the seacoast, connecting New Hampshire to the seacoast regions of Massachusetts and Maine. From the west, Routes 4 and 101 connect the seacoast with the central regions of the state while Route 16 is the road from the mountains.

By bus: **Greyhound Bus Lines** (436-0163) stops daily in Portsmouth's Market Square, connecting the seacoast with nationwide bus service. **C&J Trailways** (431-2424, 742-2990) provides many trips daily, connecting Logan Airport and downtown Boston with Dover, Durham, and Portsmouth, New Hampshire; Newburyport, Massachusetts; and Portland, Maine. **Hampton Shuttle** (926-4432), a reservation-only shuttle service makes eight trips daily from Hampton, Exeter, and Seabrook to Logan Airport. **Meadowbrook Inn** (436-2700), Portsmouth Traffic Circle, Portsmouth, runs several van trips daily between Portsmouth and Logan Airport.

Portsmouth and vicinity

For more than 300 years, the seacoast's largest community has been influenced by its maritime location. "We came to fish," announced Portsmouth's first residents in 1630, but soon the community (first called Strawbery Banke) became a center for the mast trade, supplying long straight timbers for the Royal Navy. Portsmouth's captains and crews soon roamed the entire world, in locally built vessels, hauling cargoes to and from New England, the Caribbean, Europe, and the Far East. In the years before and after the Revolutionary War, wealthy captains and merchants built many of the fine homes and commercial buildings which characterize Portsmouth today.

Unhappy with the demands of the British government, Portsmouth residents were quick to voice opposition to the crown. Before Paul Revere rode to Lexington and Concord, he first galloped to Portsmouth, warning the patriots to raid nearby Fort William and Mary and to remove the gunpowder before the British came from Boston to strengthen the undermanned fort. John Paul Jones lived in Portsmouth while overseeing the construction of two major warships during the revolution. Built on the banks of the Piscataqua River were 28 clippers, unrivaled in construction, beauty, and speed as they hauled passengers and merchandise around the world.

The Portsmouth Naval Shipyard, founded in 1800, has long been associated with submarines, turning out 100 vessels to aid the Allied cause in World War II. Portsmouth's red and green tugboats symbolize the city's current maritime activity. Oil tankers and bulk cargo vessels continue to ply the river, halting traffic as they pass through bridges, creating a bustle of activity now missing from so many other old New England seaports which have lost their commercial ship traffic.

The result of this 300-year maritime heritage is present in the city's architecture; in its active waterfront which is used for international, commercial, and recreational boating; and in the many cultural activities that involve its riverfront location. Once an old swabby town, complete with rundown bars and a decaying city center and surrounding neighborhoods, Portsmouth has been transformed into an exciting city as its residents have begun to appreciate its historical traditions and classic architecture. Portsmouth's renaissance continues,

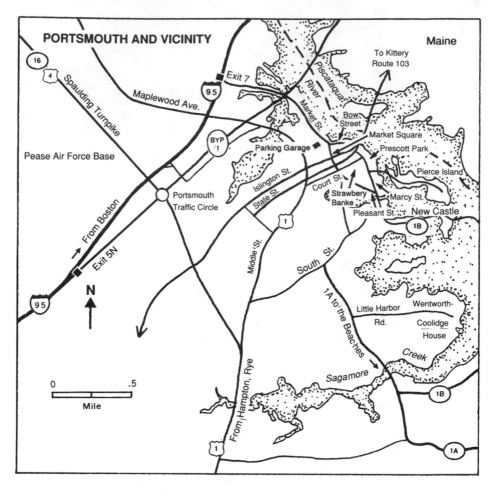

PORTSMOUTH AND VICINITY   Maine

To Kittery
Route 103

16

4

Spaulding Turnpike

Maplewood Ave.

Exit 7

95

Piscataqua River

Market St.

Bow Street

Market Square

BYP 1

Parking Garage

Prescott Park

Pease Air Force Base

Pierce Island

Islington St.

Court St.

From Boston

Portsmouth
Traffic Circle

State St.

Strawbery Banke

Marcy St.

Pleasant St.

New Castle

1B

Exit 5N

1

Middle St.

South St.

95

N

1A to the Beaches

Little Harbor
Rd.

Wentworth-
Coolidge
House

Creek

0   .5

Mile

From Hampton, Rye

Sagamore

1B

1

1A

fueled by fine restaurants (the best north of Boston, and some would say "including" Boston), inns, music, dance, theater, and, seemingly, a festival every month of the year.

The Piscataqua River, one of the fastest flowing navigable rivers in the world, separates New Castle, Portsmouth, and Newington, New Hampshire, from Kittery and Eliot, Maine. It is crossed by three main bridges. The lowest is Memorial Bridge, near the center of town, which raises its draw many times daily for commercial and recreational vessels. Residents and visitors alike usually stop to watch as the little tugs shepherd huge ocean-going vessels past this bridge. Next upstream is the Sarah Mildred Long Bridge, once the busiest bridge for motor vehicles, but no longer now that the I-95 bridge just upriver carries most of the through traffic. The Piscataqua drains the Great Bay, a large, relatively shallow tidal bay known for its wildlife and winter ice fishing.

GUIDANCE   Greater Portsmouth Chamber of Commerce (436-1118), 500 Market Street, Box 239, Portsmouth 03802. A busy and active promoter of local tourism, the chamber has a year-round information center on Market Street, a short walk west of downtown. It serves Portsmouth and adjacent communities on both sides of the Piscataqua River. There is also a summer information kiosk in Market Square.

GETTING AROUND   By taxi: There are taxi stands on Market Square, across the street from the church. **A-1 Taxi** (436-7500), **Allied Taxi** (436-7111), **City Cab** (431-2345), and **Colonial Taxi** (436-0008) are among the several companies available.

By bus: **COAST** (Cooperative Alliance for Seacoast Transportation) (862-1931), the local bus transportation, connects Portsmouth and major outlying shopping centers with Durham, Dover, Newmarket, Rochester, Somersworth, and Berwick, Maine. A main stop is in Market Square.

By car: When traveling on I-95, take Exit 7, Market Street, which leads directly downtown, past the Chamber of Commerce Information Center, to Market Square.

PARKING   Although Portsmouth's traffic is not worse than any other city, it does have limited on-street parking, and its meter maids are super-efficient in providing a written welcome to the city. Meter parking is limited to two hours so seek out the parking garage, situated just off Market Square in the middle of town, or the large lot off Pleasant Street, adjacent to the South Mill Pond. All of Portsmouth's points of interest and finest restaurants are within an easy walk of both places. Portsmouth is best enjoyed on foot, anyway.

MEDICAL EMERGENCY   Portsmouth Regional Hospital (436-5110), 33 Borthwick Avenue, Portsmouth 03801. 24-hour emergency walk-in service. Portsmouth ambulance: 436-1127. Rye ambulance: 964-8683.

TO SEE AND DO   Water Country (436-3556), Route 1, one mile south of town, Portsmouth 03801. Open weekends Memorial Day to mid-June, then daily until Labor Day. June and September, 11–6, July and August, 9:30–8. Called New England's largest water park, this complex has seven large water slides, a huge wave pool, and a new Raging Rapids ride plus Adventure River ride, bumper boats, fountains, and a kiddie pool. One admission covers all day for all rides; tube and boat rentals, additional. Discount admission after 4:30 PM.

The Children's Museum of Portsmouth (436-3853), 280 Marcy Street, Portsmouth 03801. Open Tuesday–Saturday 10–5, Sundays 1–5, Mondays during school vacations and the summer 10–5. Housed in an old meetinghouse in the city's historic South End, this colorful museum is exciting for children of all ages. Many of its exhibits reflect the area's maritime heritage. Kids can explore the yellow submarine or ride in the lobster fishing boat plus there are many other hands-on exhibits, changing displays, and organized activities. Children and adults, $3.50. Children under 9 must be accompanied by someone age 12 or older. Memberships also available.

Piscataqua Gundalow Project (Box 1522, Portsmouth 03802), Prescott Park, Marcy Street, Portsmouth. From the mid-1600s through the mid-nineteenth century, unique flat-bottomed workboats called gundalows hauled cargo between Portsmouth and upriver ports such as Exeter, Newmarket, Durham, Dover, and Berwick. Powered by the tides and lanteen sails, which could be lowered quickly to pass under bridges, the gundalows were important to the local economy and became familiar vessels on the river. Replaced by the railroad, the gundalow passed into history until the 1980s when a nonprofit organization constructed this reproduction vessel for use as an educational tool to focus attention on the heritage of the river, Great Bay, and the seacoast environment. During July the gundalow is tied up at Prescott Park and is open for tours on weekends. At other times, it travels to surrounding ports. The tour schedule is posted at the Sheafe Warehouse. Fee charged for tour.

Port of Portsmouth Maritime Museum and Albacore Park (436-3680), Market Street, Box 4367, Portsmouth 03802. Open daily March–November, 9:30–4. Tour the *U.S. Albacore,* an important experimental submarine built in the 1950s at the nearby Portsmouth Naval Shipyard. This 205-foot submarine was used for 20 years as the design model for the contemporary nuclear United States fleet. The tour includes a memorial park and gardens, a short film, picnic area, gift shop, and the submarine. Fee charged.

Portsmouth Athenaeum (431-2538), 9 Market Square, Portsmouth 03801. Research library open Tuesdays and Thursdays 1–4, Saturdays 10–4, and by appointment. Reading Room open to the public for tours Thursdays 1–4. This three-story brick Federal building, with its four white pilasters, is the architectural anchor for Market Square. Built in 1805, after one of Portsmouth's disastrous fires, the building has, since 1823, been the home of the Athenaeum, a private library and museum. Genealogy, maritime history, biographies, and Civil War memorabilia are among its important holdings. Throughout the building are fully rigged ship models, half models, and paintings. Free.

Strawbery Banke (433-1100), ticket office off Marcy Street, Box 300, Portsmouth 03802. Open May–October and first two weekends in December, plus special winter and off-season group tours available. In the early 1960s the 10-acre site, which is now this nationally known and respected restoration project, was supposed to be razed for an urban renewal project. Local protests stopped the demolition, saving more than 30 historically significant buildings. The museum now has 42 buildings, including several moved to this site to protect them from demolition elsewhere in the city. Most of the buildings are on their original foundations, which makes this a unique project when compared to other historical restorations composed of new re-creations or buildings assembled from many places. As the location of Portsmouth's first settlement in 1630 and a residential area until the early 1960s, Strawbery Banke reflects the living 300-year history of this neighborhood, not just one era. Furnished houses have rooms reflecting life from the seventeenth through the mid-twentieth centuries, depicting a variety of lifestyles, from wealthy merchants and professional people, to sea captains, poor widows, and ordinary working families. Other houses have exhibits, displays, and craftspeople who offer their work for sale. The December candlelight stroll is a popular holiday attraction, and there are other special events throughout the year, including militia musters, horticulture and fabric workshops, and small craft displays—the latter complementing the institution's wooden boat shop. Extensive eighteenth- and nineteenth-century gardens enhance the grounds. The Washington Street Eatery, one of the city's best spots for gourmet sandwiches, soups, and light meals, is on the grounds. Picnic area and gift shop.

    Farmer's Market, Parrott Avenue, Portsmouth. Saturdays 9–1, June through mid-October. Fresh, locally grown veggies and fruits in season, homebaked goods, and crafts. Seacoast Grower's Association, 778-3702.

BUGGY RIDES   **The Portsmouth Livery Company** (427-0044), 319 Lincoln Avenue, Portsmouth 03801. Open daily May–October; November–April open Friday–Sunday and Monday holidays, weather permitting. You will find Ray Parker and his horse and buggy in Market Square next to the North Church. Day and evening sightseeing tours are offered, ranging in length from 15 minutes to 35 minutes. The latter includes a ride through historic Strawbery Banke. A gourmet picnic ride for two with lunch served at a scenic picnic area, then a return ride is also offered.

HISTORIC HOUSES   **John Paul Jones House** (436-8240), Middle and State streets, Portsmouth 03801. Open May 15–October 15, Monday–Saturday 10–4, Sundays in July and August 2–4. The museum house of the Portsmouth Historical Society, this home was the residence of Captain John Paul Jones when he lived in Portsmouth overseeing the construction of two Revolutionary War frigates, *Ranger* and *America*. A traditional Georgian house, built in 1758, it has furnished period rooms and a small museum. Fee charged.

    Governor John Langdon Memorial (436-3205), 143 Pleasant Street, Portsmouth 03801. Open June–October 15, Wednesday–Sunday 12–5. One of New England's finest Georgian mansions, the house was built in 1784 by John Langdon, a wealthy merchant who was an important figure in the revolution and later a United States senator and governor of New Hampshire. George Washington was entertained in this house, which is now owned by the Society for the Preservation of New England

Antiquities. Extensive gardens are behind the house. Fee charged.

Moffat-Ladd House (436-8221), 154 Market Street, Portsmouth 03801. Open June through mid-October, Tuesday–Saturday 10–4, Sunday 2–5. Built in 1763, this house was the residence of wealthy eighteenth-century shipowners and merchants and is furnished in that period to reflect the family's lifestyle. William Whipple, a signer of the Declaration of Independence, lived here. Its great hall is a masterpiece of detailed woodworking. Internationally famous gardens fill the backyard, and don't miss the summer-long book sale in the carriage house. Owned by the Society of Colonial Dames. Fee charged.

Rundlett-May House (436-3205), Middle Street, Portsmouth 03801. Open June through mid-October, Wednesday–Sunday 12–5. Built in 1807, this Federal mansion remained in the builder's family until just a few years ago when it was acquired by the Society for the Preservation of New England Antiquities. Although it has many fine Federal pieces built especially for the house, it does reflect the continuous ownership of successive generations of a family who valued the original features of the house and adapted their lifestyle with an appreciation for the past. The stable is impressive as are the extensive gardens and grounds, which retain much of their original layout. Fee charged.

Warner House (436-5909), 150 Daniel Street, Portsmouth 03801. Open June through mid-October, Tuesday–Saturday 10–4, Sunday 1–4. The finest New England example of an eighteenth-century urban brick dwelling, this house was built in 1716 and during its early years was the home of leading merchants and officials of the royal provincial government. It has outstanding murals painted on the staircase walls, splendid paneling, and period furnishings. Benjamin Franklin was said to have installed the lightning rod on the west wall. Owned by the Warner House Association. Fee charged.

Wentworth-Gardner and Tobias Lear Houses (436-4406), Gardner and Mechanic streets, Portsmouth 03801. Open mid-June through mid-October. Tuesday–Sunday 1–4. Built in 1760, the Wentworth-Gardner House is one of the perfect examples of Georgian architecture found in America. Built by Madam Mark Hunking as a gift to her son Thomas (brother of the last royal governor), its exquisite carving took 14 months to complete. It has been beautifully restored and furnished. Adjacent is the Tobias Lear House, built in 1740, the childhood home of George Washington's private secretary. The president enjoyed tea in the parlor in 1789. Not completely restored, the Lear House occasionally is open to the public. Both houses are owned by the Wentworth-Gardner and Tobias Lear Houses Association. Fee charged.

Richard Jackson House (431-3205), Northwest Street, Portsmouth. Open by appointment only; allow one-day notice. This is New

Portsmouth waterfront, Wentworth-Gardner house at right.

Hampshire's oldest house, built in 1664 with later additions. It has few furnishings and is of interest primarily for its seventeenth-century architectural details. It is most picturesque in May when its apple orchard is in bloom. Owned by the Society for the Preservation of New England Antiquities.

St. John's Episcopal Church (436-6902), Chapel Street, Portsmouth. Open Sundays and other times by applying at the church office in the adjacent building. Built in 1807, this church is a prominent city landmark, located beside the river. Its classic interior has wall paintings, religious objects, and interesting plaques. Its adjacent 1754 graveyard is the resting place of many of the city's colonial leaders, including Benning Wentworth, Royal Governor, 1741–1766.

Wentworth-Coolidge Mansion Historic Site (436-6607), Little Harbor Road (off Route 1A), Portsmouth 03801. Open weekends Memorial Day–late June, then daily until Labor Day. Owned by the state, this rambling 40-room mansion is one of the most interesting and historic buildings in New Hampshire. It was the home of Royal Governor Benning Wentworth, whose term from 1741 until 1766 was the longest of any royal governor in America. Council meetings were held in an ornately paneled room overlooking the channel between Portsmouth and Little harbors. Its lilacs, which bloom in late May, are said to be the first planted in America. Although the house is not furnished, its extensive woodwork is an exquisite display of Portsmouth craftsmen of the period. Fee charged.

Newington Historical Society, Nimble Hill Road, Newington 03801. Open Thursdays 2–4 in July and August. The Old Parsonage, built 1710, has local artifacts and a special children's room with antique toys. Across the street is the 1712 Old Meetinghouse, in continuous use since that time but structurally altered, and nearby is the Langdon Library with an extensive genealogical collection.

Also see To See and Do.

HISTORIC CEMETERIES   North Cemetery, Maplewood Avenue, Portsmouth. Dating from 1753, this cemetery holds the remains of prominent people from the Revolutionary War to the War of 1812. Diverse headstones reveal the skill of early stonecutters.

Point of Graves Cemetery, off Marcy Street, Portsmouth. Adjacent to Prescott Park, this old cemetery was established in 1671. Although most of the oldest stones have sunken from sight, many old and uniquely carved stones remain.

VILLAGES   Portsmouth is surrounded by four small towns: Newington, Greenland, Rye, and New Castle. **Newington**, upriver from Portsmouth, is the commercial and industrial center of the region. It has two major shopping malls, many other shops plus a large power plant, oil storage tanks, and other industries. Most of this commercial-industrial complex is located between the river and the Spaulding Turnpike (Routes 4/16). The residential area and village are south of the turnpike, by Pease Air Force Base, whose construction in the 1950s cut the town of Newington in half. **Greenland** is south of Newington, another residential town with a picturesque village green. East along the Piscataqua is the small island village of **New Castle**. Winding, narrow streets lined with eighteenth- and nineteenth-century homes combine to give New Castle the appearance of a town unchanged since the turn of the century. The historic Wentworth-by-the-Sea Hotel has been closed for a number of years, but the adjacent large marina keeps the town's tourist image alive even though New Castle no longer has lodging facilities. Next to New Castle is the largest of the four towns, **Rye**, once a popular summer retreat when it had several large hotels. Those old structures are gone now, and its summer residents live in ocean-front cottages. Several of the finest residential developments have been built in Rye, and it is a popular address for many seacoast executives. Route 1A along the coast of Rye is a fine bike route, passing several state parks, restaurants, and a few motels.

Also not to be missed is the **Isles of Shoals**, a historic nine-island group, about 10 miles off the coast and visible from Route 1A. Summer ferry service provides tours around the islands and a three-hour stopover on Star Island.

GREEN SPACE   Prescott Park, Marcy Street, Portsmouth. Open year-round. Marcy Street was once an area of bawdy houses, bars, and run-down businesses. The Prescott sisters, who were born in this section of the city, inherited millions of dollars and sought to clean up the waterfront by creating a park, which they gave to the city. Supported by a substantial trust fund, the park is famous for its beautiful gardens, but it also includes boat wharves, an amphitheater, picnic areas, sculpture, fountains, and the historic 1705 Sheafe Warehouse with exhibits. From July through mid-August it is the location of the daily Prescott Park Arts Festival (donation requested), offering outdoor summer theater, varied musical performances, an art exhibit, and children's theater and art programs. At the east end of the park, cross the bridge to adjacent Pierce Island, home of the state's commercial fishing pier, and walk out to Four Tree Island, a picnic ground, nearly in the middle of the river.

Urban Forestry Center (431-6774), Elwyn Road, off Route 1 south of Portsmouth. Open year-round; summer 8–8, winter 8–4, office hours Monday–Friday 8–4. This large site, bordering tidal Sagamore Creek, has nature trails, herb gardens, hiking, cross-country skiing, and snowshoeing, and offers environmental programs throughout the year. Free.

Fort Constitution, off Route 1A, New Castle. Open year-round 10–5. Turn in at the United States Coast Guard Station and park where indicated. This historic site was first used for fortifications in the early 1600s, but today it reflects the Revolutionary and Civil war periods. In December 1774, after being alerted by Paul Revere, local patriots raided the fort, overwhelmed its few defenders, and removed its powder and some weapons before British warships from Boston could reinforce the garrison. This is considered to be the first overt act against the king and predated the war's outbreak by some four months. The powder was used against the British at the battle of Bunker Hill. The last royal governor, John Wentworth, and his family fled their home in the city and remained in the fort before leaving the rebellious province for the last time. Restored and maintained by the state, the fort's entrance portcullis reflects the colonial period while the fortifications along the water date from the Civil War although there were no battles here. Adjacent to the fort is the picturesque and still important Fort Point lighthouse, and just off shore is the Whaleback lighthouse. Ten miles at sea the Isles of Shoals is visible. Free.

Fort Stark, Wild Rose Lane, off Route 1A, New Castle. Open weekends and holidays, May–October, 10–5. To protect the important Portsmouth Naval Shipyard during World War II, the military occupied several points at the mouth of the river. One was Fort Foster, across the river from Fort Constitution, and Fort Stark was another. Although used as a fort from 1746, the site today reflects its World War II service. Free.

New Castle Great Common, Route 1A, New Castle. Open year-round; a small fee is charged to nonresidents during the summer. Another World War II site, this was Camp Langdon, an army base. It was acquired by the town of New Castle as a recreation area and the site for a new office complex. There are rest rooms, picnic tables, a small beach, and a pier for fishing. Overlooking the mouth of the river and its two lighthouses, it is one of the scenic highlights along the coast.

Odiorne Point State Park, Route 1A, Rye. Open year-round; park fees charged in the main season, June–September. This 137-acre ocean-front park is the site of the first settlement in New Hampshire in 1623. Later fine mansions were built here; then the site was taken over during World War II and named Fort Dearborn with huge guns placed in concrete bunkers. As a park it has handicapped-accessible nature trails, a boat-launching ramp, picnic tables, and a fine nature center—open late June to late August—operated by the University of New Hampshire. The center has exhibits and offers varied daily nature programs using the park, its nearby marsh, and the ocean's intertidal zone. No swimming.

Rye Harbor State Park and Marina, Route 1A, Rye. Open year-round; fee charged in the summer season for the park and boat launching. The state's smallest state park, this jewel occupies an ocean point just south of Rye Harbor. It has picnic tables, a playground, a jetty for fishing, a view of the picturesque harbor, and cooling ocean breezes on hot summer days. Around the corner is the Rye Harbor State Marina with a launching ramp and wharves, where you can buy tickets for deep-sea fishing, whale watches, or sight-seeing boat rides.

SWIMMING BEACHES   **Wallis Sands State Park,** Route 1A, Rye. Open weekends mid-May–late June, then daily until Labor Day. A large sandy beach with lifeguards, rest rooms, parking, and a snack bar. Fee charged.

Jenness State Beach, Route 1A, Rye. Another large sandy beach with lifeguards, rest rooms, and parking meters. A snack bar is across the street.

OCEAN ADVENTURES AND BOAT RIDES   **Isles of Shoals Steamship Company** (431-5500, 800-441-4620), Barker Wharf, 315 Market Street, Box 311, Portsmouth 03802. Open daily mid-June–Labor Day and Memorial Day weekend; special fall schedule until September 28 and whale-watch cruises beginning in mid-April. This is the Isles of Shoals ferry, hauling passengers and freight to Star Island and providing one of New England's finest narrated tours. The 90-foot *Thomas Laighton* is a replica of a turn-of-the-century steamship, the type of vessel used when the islands were the leading New England summer colony, attracting the era's most famous artists, writers, poets, and musicians. The boat docks at Star Island, home of the Star Island Conference Center, a summer religious institution meeting here since the turn of the century. On the 11 AM ferry trip, a maximum of 100 visitors can leave the *Laighton* for a three-hour stopover, returning to the mainland on the 3 PM boat, which docks in Portsmouth at 4:30 PM. Buy tickets early for this cruise since it often sells out. Bring your picnic lunch and plenty of film for the camera. Since the *Laighton* is the supply line for the conference center, delivering food, drinking water, supplies, mail, and oil for the island's generators, it operates rain or shine. The trip to the islands takes about an hour, the round trip about three hours. In addition to the daily Isles of Shoals cruises, the *Laighton* is also used for dinner cruises, including clambakes and big-band dance cruises. The 71-foot *Oceanic* is used for whale watching (an all-day, offshore trip), special lighthouse cruises, the nightly sunset cruise to the islands, and weekend cocktail and dance cruises.

Portsmouth Harbor Cruises (436-8084, 800-776-0915) 64 Ceres Street, Oar House Dock, Portsmouth 03801. Open early June–Labor Day with a reduced schedule until late October. The 49-passenger *Heritage* offers a variety of daily, narrated cruises, which, depending on the tide, tour the harbor, down the Piscataqua, past the two lighthouses, around New Castle Island, through Little Harbor, and back to the dock. Several trips circle the Isles of Shoals, and fall foliage trips travel the winding rivers and expanse of Great Bay. Our favorite is the 5:30 sunset cruise, no narration, just a cool drink and a quiet ride after a hot summer day. Several trips regularly sell out, so buy tickets early. Also available is a large sailboat for single-day or overnight charters.

Schooner Appledore (534-0473), Box 6671, Portsmouth 03802. This 60-foot traditional, staysail, wooden schooner has sailed around the world. From Portsmouth Harbor *Appledore* is now available for groups of six people for two-hour, all-day, evening, or weekend cruises. Bring your own food and beverages. Reservations required. In September *Appledore* sails from Camden, Maine, for workshops on coastal cruising and photography.

New Hampshire Seacoast Cruises (964-5545, 382-6743), Rye Harbor State Marina, Route 1A, Box 232, Rye 03870. Open daily July–Labor Day; weekend whale watches May, June, September, and October. Ride the 150-capacity *Granite State* for a six-hour whale watch or a two-hour cruise around the Isles of Shoals.

Atlantic Fishing Fleet (964-5220), Rye Harbor Marina, Route 1A, Box 678, Rye 03870. Open Wednesdays and weekends in April for all-day fishing, two half-day trips daily Memorial Day–Labor Day and weekends through early October, and night fishing in season. The speedy 70-foot *Atlantic Queen II*, is designed for all-weather, ocean fishing. Offshore trips seek cod, cusk, pollock, and haddock. Rods for rent.

GOLF   **Portsmouth Country Club** (436-9719), Country Club Drive (off Route 101 south of Portsmouth), Greenland 03840. Open mid-April to mid-November. Designed by Robert Trent Jones, 18 holes, the longest course in New Hampshire with several picturesque holes on the shores of Great Bay. Cart rentals, full bar and food service, and pro shop. Call for starting times.

Wentworth-By-The-Sea (433-5010), Wentworth Road (Route 1B), Portsmouth 03801. Open April to mid-November. Designed by Donald Ross, a beautiful, challenging 18-hole course with several holes bordering picturesque Little Harbor. Pro shop, cart rentals, full service bar and restaurant. Open to the public weekdays and weekend afternoons, call for starting times.

LODGING   Portsmouth is well supplied with motels, most of which are located on Route 1 south of the city and at the traffic circle intersection of I-95, Route 1 bypass, and Routes 4/16 (Spaulding Turnpike). Among these motels are the **Anchorage Inn** (431-8111), **Comfort Inn** (433-3338), the **Meadowbrook Inn** (436-2700), **Howard Johnson Hotel** (436-7600), and **Holiday Inn** (431-8000). Downtown on Market Street (Exit 7 off I-95) is the new, full service **Sheraton Portsmouth** (431-2300) with 148 rooms, restaurant, lounge, and within walking distance to everything. The area's B&Bs are all attractive and well furnished.

BED & BREAKFASTS   **Sise Inn** (433-1200, outside NH 800-232-4667), 40 Court Street, Portsmouth 03801. Open year-round. The city's most luxurious accommodation, the Sise Inn is a beautifully restored, furnished, and decorated 1881 Queen Anne-style mansion with a new matching addition. The 34 rooms, including several suites, have private baths, mostly queen beds, TV, VCR (with free cassettes), telephones, alarm clocks, radios, tables, and comfortable chairs. Several rooms also have cassette tape players and whirlpool baths; one has a fireplace; and another, a skylight and a private staircase. With several meeting rooms, the inn was designed for the business traveler, but vacationers are welcome to share the Victorian luxury as well. A continental breakfast is served. Rates are $89–$175.

The Inn at Christian Shore (431-6770), 335 Maplewood Avenue, Portsmouth 03801. Open year-round. Antiques furnish this lovely in-town Federal house, restored and operated as a B&B since 1979 by Louis Socia, Thomas Towey, and Charles Litchfield. There are five rooms (one is for a single), two with private baths, all with air-conditioning and TV. Hearty gourmet breakfasts are served before a roaring fire under a candelabra with exposed old beams. Rates are $55–$75.

Martin Hill Inn (436-2287), 404 Islington Street, Portsmouth 03801. Open year-round. The city's first B&B, this classic inn is composed of adjacent 1820 and 1850 houses joined by a brick garden path overlooking an extensive garden. The main inn has three guest rooms with period furnishings and canopy or four-poster beds. The Guest House has four rooms, three of which are suites and one with an attached greenhouse. It has period furnishings and queen-size canopy, spindle, or iron and brass beds. All rooms have private baths, air-conditioning, writing tables, sofas, or separate sitting areas. A no-smoking inn. Full breakfast served in the elegant dining room. Jane and Paul Harnden, innkeepers. Rates are $70–$85.

Leighton Inn (433-2188), 69 Richards Avenue, Portsmouth 03801. Open year-round. This 1809 Federal in-town home has five rooms, some with private baths, all furnished with antique and period pieces. Two common rooms, one with a grand piano. Summer breakfasts are served on the screened porch; in winter the kitchen is a cozy spot for starting the day. A short walk to Portsmouth sights. Catherine Stone, innkeeper. Rates are $65–$75.

The Inn at Strawbery Banke (436-7242), 314 Court Street, Portsmouth 03801. The most in-town of Portsmouth's B&Bs, this circa 1800 house with a more recent addition, has seven individually furnished rooms, all with private baths, some with queen beds, others with a double and a single. Upstairs and down common rooms with TV, games, and books. Bright cheery breakfast room overlooks the gardens of the John Langdon mansion. A short walk to Strawbery Banke and Prescott Park. Full breakfast. Sarah Glover O'Donnell, proprietor. Rates are $60–$85.

The Captain Folsom Inn (436-2662), 480 Portsmouth Avenue, Greenland 03840. Open year-round. Built in 1758 and overlooking one of the state's prettiest village greens, this mansion has been lovingly restored and furnished with antiques by Faith and Bob McTigue. The six rooms, some with shared baths, have antique double beds (two rooms with twins), and handmade quilts. There are comfortable sitting rooms, a wraparound screened porch, and an outdoor pool. Afternoon tea and after dinner refreshments served. A full breakfast is served in an elegant dining room, where, by advance reservation, Faith also serves dinners she has cooked in her large colonial kitchen with its huge open hearth fireplace and beehive oven. Rates are $65–$85.

DINING OUT Portsmouth is famous for its numerous quality restaurants, the best collection of fine dining north of Boston. Several of the top restaurants are located in the Old Harbor area where Bow, Ceres, and Market streets intersect. Here six-story warehouses, the largest structures north of Boston when built in the early 1800s, have been remodeled as restaurants and shops. A treat for summer and early fall visitors are the five outdoor decks located here on the waterfront, open for lunch and late into the evening (until the legal closing for serving liquor). Everything from snacks to sandwiches and full dinners is available on the decks. View the tugboats and watch large oceangoing ships pass, seemingly within an arm's length.

Blue Strawbery (431-6420), 29 Ceres Street, Portsmouth. Open year-round, Tuesday–Thursday seating at 7:30 PM, Friday and Saturday at 6 and 9 PM, Sunday at 6 PM. Winter: same hours, but closed Tuesday and Wednesday. Confirmed reservations only. When this restaurant

Photo by Peter E. Randall

Relaxing on a Portsmouth deck beside the tugboats.

opened in 1970, even its three partners wondered if Portsmouth could support an expensive, gourmet restaurant seating only 40 diners, located in a warehouse on the city's rundown waterfront. Today the restaurant is nationally known; one of the original three partners is still there; and the place is justly recognized as one of the catalysts that began Portsmouth's cultural and fine dining renaissance in the 1970s. All diners are seated at the appointed hour and served a six-course, eight-item dinner. The rich American gourmet menu changes daily but always offers a choice of fish, meat, and fowl entrées. For a representative meal, begin with hot wine broth supreme soup and an appetizer of sea scallops wrapped in bacon with Benedictine and shallots served with toast rounds, then cleanse your pallet with a mixed salad and sage blue-cheese dressing. Your entrée might be half a roast duck with a green peppercorn honey lemon glaze; halibut, sea scallops, and shrimp baked in a duxelle Pernot lime butter; or beef Wellington with a lightly gingered Madeira wine and mushroom sauce. Vegetables are potatoes roasted in garlic and duck stock with zucchini and carrots sautéed in olive oil. Dessert is always the same: strawberries with sour cream and brown sugar. Fine wine and cocktails are also offered. $38 prix fixe; no credit cards.

Anthony's Al Dente (436-2527), 59 Penhallow Street, Portsmouth. Tuesday–Saturday 5:45–10 PM, Sunday 5–9 PM. Located in the cellar of the 1817 old Custom House, this fine Italian restaurant has a grotto atmosphere, enhanced by the brick walls and exposed beams. The northern and southern Italian menu is organized around appetizers, a fresh pasta first course, and meat entrée second course. Linguini with red or white clam sauce, baked pasta rolls with a meat filling or fettucini, all Alfredo, might be followed with veal scaloppine in lemon sauce, scampi, a daily squid entrée or chicken with Italian spiced ham and provolone cheese in white wine sauce. A relaxing spot for an evening of dining, the atmosphere is unhurried and keyed to cooking to order. Prices range from $9.95–$19.75.

The Dolphin Striker (431-5222), 25 Bow Street, Portsmouth. Lunch 11:30–2, Sunday brunch 11:30–3, dinner 5:30–9 and until 10 on Fridays and Saturdays. On the waterfront in a restored warehouse, this is an old favorite specializing in seafood pie with lobster, king crab, scallops, and shrimp seasoned with sherry and sour cream; stuffed haddock; shrimp scampi; and grilled salmon served on spinach with a fresh herb mayonnaise. Veal, rack of lamb, filet mignon, and breast of chicken sautéed with garlic topped with a wine glaze with tomatoes and green onions round out the menu. On the lower level is the Spring Hill Tavern, a lounge with entertainment and walls covered with photographs and other items celebrating the city's maritime heritage. Prices range from $11.95–$22.95.

L'Auberge (436-2377), 96 Bridge Street, Portsmouth. Lunch 11:30–1:30, dinner 5–9, Sunday brunch 12–4; closed Monday; reservations suggested. Intimate French continental dining by this husband-and-wife team who have been here since the late 1970s. Roast duck and beef Wellington are specialties, or try chateaubriand for two ($45), steak au poivre, sweetbreads, frogs' legs Provençal, or one of several veal or shrimp entrées. Lunch and brunch seem like bargains with some of the same dinner items offered from $6–$10. Dinner prices range from $12–$21.

Guido's Trattoria (431-2928), 67 Bow Street, Portsmouth. Open Tuesday–Saturday 6–9:30 PM; reservations appreciated. No smoking. This small, second-floor restaurant specializes in Italian Tuscan cuisine. The young owner/chef changes his menu regularly, gathering ideas from annual visits to Italy. Begin with a seafood antipasto of shrimp, calamari, mussels, and clams sauced with garlic, olive oil, white wine and a touch of tomato; then select from the first (perhaps your only) course: stuffed pasta of the day, quill-shaped pasta in a Gorgonzola cheese sauce, soup of the day, or perhaps just move on to the second-course entrées, such as scaloppine of veal with fresh sage and prosciutto, boneless duck roasted with figs and chestnuts, steak with garlic and red pepper, or rack of lamb. Price range from $16–$18.

Oar House (436-4025), 55 Ceres Street, Portsmouth. Lunch 12:30–2:30, Sunday brunch until 3:30 PM, dinner 5:30–9 PM and until 10 PM on Fridays and Saturdays, closed Monday except during the summer. Valet parking. Another longtime favorite on the waterfront in a remodeled warehouse and our choice for chowder. Seafood is featured and varies from bouillabaisse and baked stuffed lobster to broiled scallops and Oar House Delight, a sautéed combination of shrimp, scallops, and fresh fish topped with sour cream and crumbs baked in the oven. Sirloin with peppercorn sauce, rack of lamb, veal Barbara (medallions of veal dipped in egg wash, sautéed in butter, and topped with fresh crab, avocado, cheddar cheese, mushrooms, and green onions), and a daily varied chef's chicken are also offered. The Oar House deck, open Memorial Day–early autumn, is our favorite for picturesque riverside relaxing and dining. Prices range from $15.50–$18.95.

Sakura (431-2721), 40 Pleasant Street, Portsmouth. Lunch Monday–Friday 11:30–2:30, dinner 5–10. Fine Japanese dining with a long sushi bar where you can watch the chefs prepare creative and tasty portions of sushi and sashimi. We like the dinner box (the meal is actually served in a portioned box) with miso soup, rice, salad, and a choice of two portions of sushi, sashimi, tempora, teriyaki, and other specialties. Although fish is featured, there is beef and chicken teriyaki and sukiyaki (slices of beef and vegetables with soup and rice). For a special occasion, try "Heaven"—twelve pieces of sushi and two rolls with ten pieces of sashimi. Japanese beer, saki, and plum wine also served. Prices range from $8.50–$15.

State Street Saloon (431-4357), 268 State Street, Portsmouth. Open daily for lunch 11–3, dinner 5–9. Don't let the name or the less than fancy decor put you off, this is one of the city's best Italian restaurants and inexpensive, too. The locals would like to keep this place a secret because there is often a line at the door waiting for it to open, especially on weekends. Fettucini is offered with five sauces, spaghetti with six, tortellini with three, and manicotti with two; plus eggplant parmigiana with meat or tomato sauce, three varieties of veal scaloppine, six kinds of chicken, and a few seafood entrées provide a diverse Italian menu. Nightly specials, appetizers and salads, and a lively bar. Prices range from $6–$9, all a la carte.

Strawbery Court (431-7722), 20 Atkinson Street, Portsmouth. Open 6–9 PM, closed Monday and Tuesday. Just 11 tables in a restored Federal townhouse with a summer patio, provide for relaxed dining in what is perhaps the best of Portsmouth's best restaurants. The French cuisine menu changes several times a year to match the chef's whims and freshest ingredients. Try seafood Provençal with mussels, scallops, shrimp, clams, and squid in a sauce of lobster stock, fresh tomatoes, leeks, garlic, capers, black olives, anchovies, and pimentos served over pasta. Or roast rack of lamb or duck, marinated pork chops stuffed with apples, or marinated chicken breast grilled and stuffed with dates. Appetizers and desserts match the tasty entrées.

$38 prix fixe or a la carte entrées from $22–$25.

Seventy-Two (436-5666), 45 Pearl Street, Portsmouth. Open daily 5:30–10 PM. A remodeled Baptist church is the unique home of this "French with a New England flair" restaurant, that serves the city's most unusual offerings. Steak tartare mixed at your table; a nightly choice of duck, quail, rabbit, or venison; shrimp- or haddock-stuffed lobster; stuffed breast of pheasant; and seafood-stuffed ravioli are served with baked stuffed potato, fresh baked breads, and a medley of fresh vegetables. Swordfish, tuna, halibut, or salmon are also offered nightly with varying preparations and sauces. Appetizers range from frogs' legs and oysters to escargots and veal sausage with shallot cream sauce. Prices range from $18–$25.

The Carriage House (964-8251), 2263 Ocean Boulevard, Rye Beach. Open daily at 5 PM. Built as a restaurant in the 1920s, the Carriage House has been a favorite gourmet restaurant for two decades, offering quality continental cuisine at reasonable prices. Specialties are an Indian curry of the day, Sicilian conigilo (rabbit), and grilled rack of lamb. There are six pasta entrées, salmon poached with vermouth in parchment, sole Oscar, seafood-stuffed chicken, veal marsala, roast duckling, Szechwan-spiced chicken or beef, and several steaks. Appetizers, salads, and desserts to match. Prices range from $9.65–$16.25.

EATING OUT **Yoken's Thar She Blows Restaurant and Gift Shop** (436-8224), Route 1, Portsmouth. Open daily 1–8 PM, closed Mondays, except on holidays, and from Memorial Day to Columbus Day. The state's largest and best-known family restaurant, Yoken's, with its spouting whale neon sign, has become a landmark since it first opened with a 20-stool counter and 99-cent dinners in 1947. Today it seats 750 and serves more than two million meals a year. Reasonable price for a complete dinner has been the trademark here since it first opened. Lobster; fried, baked, and broiled seafood; entrée salads; and roast beef, roast turkey, liver and onions, and a few Italian dishes provide something for everyone. The 20-entrée luncheon menu, served until 4 PM, offers choice of appetizer, dinner, beverage, and dessert, all for under $6. The Spouter Gift Shop, open at 11 AM, with 20,000 square feet of space, is the largest in New England, selling everything from tourist mementos to fine china, collectible glass and figurines, handbags, cards, T-shirts, and more. Menu prices range from $4.95–$11.50.

Poco Diablo (431-5967), 37 Bow Street, Portsmouth. Open daily 11:30 AM–9 PM, Friday and Saturday until 11 PM. A popular Mexican restaurant with a dining room overlooking the tugboats and the river. Most any Mexican item you can imagine is here plus Mexican beer, sangria, and the best margaritas in the city. Their riverside deck opens as early as April and closes when it's too cool to use it. Prices range from $5.95–$11.25.

The Stockpot (431-1851), 53 Bow Street, Portsmouth. Open daily 11 AM–11:30 PM. This is a popular spot on the waterfront for lunch and light dinners. Homemade soups, a variety of salads and sandwiches, broiled scallops, and paella (a Spanish dish with chicken, mussels, crab, shrimp, chorizo, and veggies served over rice). A small deck, open whenever it is warm enough to use it, offers relaxing dining with views past the tugboats and up the river. Most dinners are under $10.

The Ferry Landing, Ceres Street, Portsmouth. Open April 15–September from 11:30 AM–9 PM, the bar until 11 PM. Light seafood dishes of many varieties, sandwiches, chowder, and burgers are served in this 100-year-old building which was the original ferry landing before the bridges were built. Hanging out over the river, right beside the tugboats, the place is mostly a deck. It is always busy (especially the bar on weekends) during its summer season. Prices range from $3.50–$12.50.

The Press Room (431-5186), 77 Daniel Street, Portsmouth. Open Tuesday–Saturday 11:30 AM–1 PM, Sunday 5–11 PM. Inexpensive, light meals, nachos, pizza, salads, soups, and sandwiches. The food is okay and served with draft beer, but the music is the best in the city. This Irish-style pub has live music most of the time. Acoustic guitar, folk, Irish, blues, and country sounds in an informal atmosphere make this a popular spot with the locals.

Celebrity Sandwich (433-7009; 433-2277 is the hotline for daily specials), 171 Islington Street, Portsmouth. Open 10:30 AM–6 PM Monday–Wednesday, Thursday and Friday until 8 PM, Saturday until 5 PM. One hundred sandwiches, each named for a different celebrity, served in a small art deco dining room. Box lunches, soups, salads, and desserts, too. Eat in or take out.

Little Harbor Grill, New Castle, adjacent to the Wentworth-by-the-Sea Marina. Open mid-June–Labor Day from 11:30 AM–8 PM, closed Mondays. On the shore of picturesque Little Harbor, where New Hampshire's first settlers arrived in 1623, is this relaxing, informal spot that serves outdoors or in the tent. Sandwiches, burgers, and chowder. Full bar service.

The Golden Egg (436-0519), 960 Sagamore Avenue, Portsmouth. Open daily 6 AM–2 PM. The seacoast's favorite breakfast spot, famous for its varied and unusual omelets, especially the changing daily specials written on the blackboard. Try one, and lunch will not be necessary. There is great granola, hot oatmeal, fresh-baked muffins, pancakes, French toast (with whipped cream and raspberry sauce) plus eggs any way you want them, including three variations of eggs Benedict. The trick on the weekends is to get there after the golfers and before the late sleepers! Homemade soups and sandwiches for lunch.

LOBSTER IN THE ROUGH   Lobsters are a seacoast specialty. The **Sanders**

family of Portsmouth is the largest local dealer. Their main lobster pound is at 54 Pray Street (436-3716), open Monday–Saturday 8 AM–6 PM, Sunday 10 AM–5 PM; and they own the **Old Mill Fish Market** (436-4568) nearby at 367 Marcy Street, open daily 9 AM–6 PM. The latter shop has all kinds of fresh fish in addition to live or cooked-to-order lobsters. Sanders can ship a mini-clambake anywhere in the country.

BAKERIES   **Ceres Street Bakery** (436-6518), 51 Penhallow Street, Portsmouth. Open 5 AM–5:30 PM, Saturday until 4 PM, closed Sunday. Our favorite bakery. Has the best bran muffins anywhere but also brioches, croissants, cookies, and a host of breads, cakes, and other diet busters. A few mostly vegetarian soups, quiches, and salads are served for lunch. Many local restaurants serve Ceres Bakery breads.

    Café Brioche (430-9225), 14 Market Square, Portsmouth. Open daily 7 AM–6 PM, Sundays until 5 PM. A French-style bakery with breads and sweets, serving homemade soups and a variety of sandwiches plus espresso and cappuccino. Especially popular in the warm weather when their outside tables give Market Square a European plaza atmosphere.

ICE CREAM   **Annabelle's** (431-1988), 49 Ceres Street, Portsmouth. Open for lunch until late in the evening, closed in the winter. Imaginative and tasty handmade ice cream comes from this popular local landmark. At the request of George Bush, they made and served red, white, and blueberry at the White House for the Fourth of July. Sandwiches and soups are secondary to the sundaes, sodas, banana splits, and hand-scooped cones.

    Lagos' Big Scoop, Route 1, Rye. Open from spring through early fall. They have a long list of flavors and also serve fried foods and sandwiches.

ENTERTAINMENT   Portsmouth's busiest performance season is September–May except for the Prescott Park Arts Festival, which has theater and music outdoors July through mid-August. The night scene is active all year with nearly a dozen restaurants and lounges offering live music weekends and several other nights: jazz, blues, big band, folk, and country music.

    Portsmouth Academy of Performing Arts (436-8084), 125 Bow Street, Portsmouth. Professional theater in the former Theatre-by-the-Sea building. Several different plays are performed September–early June.

    The Music Hall (436-2400), 28 Chestnut Street, Portsmouth. Built in 1878 as a stage theater and, more recently, revised as a movie theater, this restored hall has been acquired by a nonprofit group and offers a variety of dance, theater, and musical performances throughout the year. Tony Bennett, Pearl Bailey, international classical music, Sesame Street, magic shows, bluegrass, and jazz are among the recent offerings. Three to four events are held each month September–May.

Pontine Movement Theatre (436-6660), 135 McDonough Street, Portsmouth. This nationally known company with guest performers offers four productions between fall and spring but no summer performances.

The Press Room (431-5186), 77 Daniel Street, Portsmouth. Open Tuesday–Saturday 11:30–1, Sundays 5–11. This Irish-style pub has live music most of the time it is open. Acoustic guitar, folk, Irish, blues, and country sounds in an informal atmosphere make this a popular spot with the locals. Fridays 5–8 PM, is a country jam session, the only thing like it in the state when an ever-changing group of amateurs and professionals joins a group of regulars playing country tunes, sea chanties, and music from the British Isles. Sunday night is jazz with many nationally known performers sitting in with the best house combo in the region.

SELECTIVE SHOPPING   Portsmouth is filled with small shops, especially in the waterfront area bounded by Market, Bow, and Ceres streets. Here rows of mostly Federal-era brick buildings have been remodeled and restored and now offer the shopper everything from upscale clothing and antiques to natural foods, candles, secondhand clothing, jewelry, a fine children's shop, and even a Christmas shop. With several of the city's best restaurants and five waterfront decks, this is a busy and lively place until late in the evening since several shops are open until 11 PM.

Two great **Antiquarian Bookshops** are located in Portsmouth near Strawbery Banke. **The Book Guild of Portsmouth** (436-1758), 58 State Street, specializes in maritime and local books while the **Portsmouth Book Shop** (433-4406), 110 State Street, leans more to travel and literature.

SPECIAL EVENTS   Summer in the seacoast offers nearly an unlimited number of special events and activities for people of all ages. Check with local chambers of commerce, the Portsmouth Children's Museum, and Strawbery Banke for varied activities.

Late May: **Prescott Park Chowder Festival**. For a small donation, sample the city's best restaurant chowders.

Second Saturday in June: **Market Square Day** (436-5388). The center of Portsmouth is closed to traffic and the streets are lined with booths selling food, crafts, etc.; as many as four stages provide continuous entertainment. More than 30,000 people jam the city for this free event. A popular clambake is held the night before at the Port Authority; purchase tickets in advance.

Mid-June: **Blessing of the Fleet**, Prescott Park. The Piscataqua River's commercial fishing fleet, with all boats decorated, converge for a water parade and traditional blessing for safety at sea.

Late June: **Portsmouth Jazz Festival** (436-7678), Ceres Street. A fundraiser for local charities. The waterfront street is blocked off, and two stages offer continuous music from noon until 8 PM, showcasing New England's best performers.

Fourth of July–mid-August: **Prescott Park Arts Festival**, on the waterfront of Portsmouth. A daily variety of outdoor theater and musical events beginning late in the afternoon. Come early, bring a picnic basket, and spend a few enjoyable hours at one of New England's most popular summer festivals. Donation requested. There also are art shows and art classes for kids.

Mid-July: **Bow Street Fair** (433-7272). A colorful weekend street fair with music and booths selling food and crafts.

Mid-August: **Candlelight house tour** (436-1118). An evening tour of Portsmouth's historic houses, all lit by candles.

Columbus Day weekend: **Chili Cook-off**, Prescott Park. Sample the culinary skills of the city's best chili cooks.

Early December: **Candlelight Stroll** (433-1100), Strawbery Banke. See Strawbery Banke's historic houses by candlelight.

December 31: **First Night** (436-5388). A nonalcoholic, family-oriented, New Year's Eve celebration held annually in Portsmouth, late afternoon to midnight, with a wide variety of musical performances and other entertainment. Most events are held in downtown churches.

Hampton, Hampton Beach, Exeter, and vicinity

The two large towns of Hampton and Exeter were founded in 1638, but while Hampton has retained little of its architectural heritage, Exeter's streets are lined with old houses and buildings.

Hampton was mostly a farming town with a small beachside tourist community until the beginning of the twentieth century when trolley lines connected the town and its beach with the large cities of the Merrimack Valley and cities in Massachusetts and central New Hampshire. The low-cost trolley transportation made the beach an inexpensive and accessible place for the urban workers to bring their families for a day or a week. A large Casino was built to provide these visitors with games to play, lunches, and ballroom dancing, though not on Sunday. Hampton is now a fast-growing residential community. After World War II the population was about 2,300; now it is 12,000 people, and much of its open space has been developed except for large family holdings west of I-95. Hampton has a small shopping district, a movie complex, and several good restaurants.

While Hampton village was small, **Hampton Beach** boomed and became one of the leading family vacation centers in New England. Now, during peak summer weekends, more than 200,000 people jam the beach, nearly covering the long sandy oceanfront from one end to the other with blankets. Young people seem to predominate, but there are plenty of older folks who would not consider any other place to spend their summer free time. The center of the beach is still the 90-year-old Casino, complete with restaurants, shops, penny arcades, and a nightclub offering nationally known entertainment.

Often overlooked by residents and visitors alike is **Hampton River.** Here three family-owned fishing party businesses have been serving the public for more than 50 years, recently expanding to include whale watches and some sight-seeing cruises. Surrounding the harbor is the state's largest salt marsh, once thought of as a swamp and earmarked to be dredged and filled to create a lagoon-style seasonal home development. Although Hampton Beach development has pushed into the fringes of this 1,300-acre marsh, people now know the importance of the tidal wetlands as a source of nutrients for a wide variety of marine life, and the marshes are protected from filling by state and local laws. As a green space, the marsh is used by fishermen, boaters, and bird-watchers; and it is about the only piece of ground left on the seacoast that still looks today about the way it was when settlers arrived in the 1600s. South of the Hampton River bridge in Seabrook, bordering the marsh, is a recently protected sand dunes natural area.

West of Hampton is **Exeter** with a much larger commercial area, one of the country's premier prep schools, and a marvelous architectural diversity which reflects its past as a center of government and education as well as the economic success of its residents, especially when Exeter had a small industrial center. Exeter also has about 12,000 people, although its growth has been slower than Hampton's. During the revolution, Exeter was the center of government and many of its citizens were prominent participants in the rebellion. Several historic houses open to the public date from those times. The falls of the Squamscott River helped to power textile mills, giving the community an important economic base. Exeter is also the center of Rockingham County government with a courthouse and the offices of the registers of deeds and probate, two places well used by visitors seeking genealogical information.

Phillips Exeter Academy, one of America's leading preparatory schools, has a list of alumni whose members have achieved the highest levels of prominence in literature, business, and government service. Prominent visiting lecturers in all fields, who often speak or perform for the public, and a fine art gallery contribute to the cultural and educational atmosphere of the town and the area. Many students from surrounding towns attend the academy as day students. The academy's buildings reflect nearly three centuries of architectural design, contributing to the great diversity of Exeter's cityscape. The academy is in the center of the **Front Street Historic District**, where a wide variety of architectural styles ranges from colonial residences of the 1700s to twentieth-century institutional buildings. Notable are the First Parish Meetinghouse, a variety of Victorian buildings, and the contemporary Phillips Exeter Academy Library designed by Louis Kahn.

Historic Route 1 bisects the seacoast from south to north. On the Massachusetts border is **Seabrook**, home of the controversial nuclear power plant, a huge facility which pays most of the town's taxes, giving Seabrook one of the lowest property tax rates in the state. The low property tax, combined with the state's lack of a sales tax, has fueled commercial development in Seabrook; most of the retail shoppers come from heavily taxed Massachusetts. **Seabrook Beach** is a heavily developed residential area with little public access to the ocean since parking is limited, but many summer homes here are available for weekly rentals.

Seabrook's unplanned growth is in contrast to neighboring **Hampton Falls** with a strip development along the main highway, but elsewhere it is a residential community whose many farms are now being subdivided into exclusive home developments. North of Hampton along Route 1 is **North Hampton**, also primarily a residential community, but with a large colony of summer mansions along the coast in the section called Little Boar's Head.

Adjacent to Exeter, and extending west to the Merrimack Valley, are mostly small towns, once farming communities, now being heavily developed with residential subdivisions. Among these towns are **Stratham, Kensington, Epping, Newfields, Brentwood, Fremont, Danville, the Kingstons**, and **Nottingham**. Since New Hampshire has no sales or income taxes, and once had low property taxes, the seacoast area towns have been rapidly growing, popular bedroom communities for people who work in the Boston area, many of whom grew up in Massachusetts but moved north to escape the congestion of urban life for the peaceful countryside. The attractions of the seacoast and its proximity to metropolitan Boston are certain to make the area a magnet for new residents and for visiting tourists.

GUIDANCE   Hampton Beach Area Chamber of Commerce (926-8717, outside NH 800-GET A TAN), 180 Ocean Boulevard (winter and business office: 836 Lafayette Road, Box 790), Hampton 03842. A seasonal information center is open daily at the state park complex in the middle of Hampton Beach. The chamber runs daily summer events at the beach and seasonal programs in Hampton village and publishes a free accommodations and things-to-do guide.

Exeter Area Chamber of Commerce (772-2411), 120 Water Street, Exeter 03833.

GETTING AROUND   By car: Route 1 (Lafayette Road), between Seabrook and Portsmouth is lined with strip development and on summer weekends is especially snarled with traffic. If you want to go to Hampton Beach just to see the sights and the latest bathing suits, we do not recommend the weekends when traffic entering the beach from I-95 or Route 1A south may be backed up for several miles.

By taxi: Coastal Taxi (926-4334), serves Hampton and the adjacent towns. **Exeter Cab** (778-7778), serves Exeter and offers Logan Airport service.

By trolley: A seasonal trolley service serves Hampton Beach, running the length of Ocean Boulevard, with stops in Hampton village and the North Hampton Factory Outlet Center.

PARKING   Municipal and private parking lots behind the beach, just a short walk to the sand, are the best places to park if you are not staying at beach lodgings. The parking meters are part of the state park and are closely monitored, so keep them filled with quarters to avoid an expensive ticket.

Photo by Peter E. Randall

Hampton Beach.

MEDICAL EMERGENCY   **Exeter Hospital** (778-7311), 10 Buzzell Avenue, Exeter 03833. 24-hour emergency walk-in service. Exeter ambulance: 772 1212. Hampton ambulance: 926-3315.

TO SEE AND DO   **Hampton Beach** is an attraction by itself. The center of activity is the Casino, a historic rambling complex with arcades, gifts, specialty shops, and a nightclub. Adjacent is the Casino Cascade Water Slide. Nearby, along the half-mile business district, is the first seasonal McDonald's plus other fast-food takeouts, more arcades, shops, gift and clothing stores, miniature golf, and bike rentals. Across the street from the Casino is the ocean and the state park complex with the chamber of commerce information center, rest rooms, first-aid room, and the bandstand, which offers free concerts and talent shows throughout the summer. There are fireworks on the Fourth of July and every Wednesday night during July and August, the heart of the season; but many places are open weekends beginning in April, then open daily in June. A few of the newer, larger hotels are open year-round, and some have restaurants and lounges.

    Fuller Gardens (964-5414), 10 Willow Avenue, Little Boar's Head, North Hampton 03862. Open early May through mid-October, 10 AM–6 PM. One of the few remaining estate gardens of the early twentieth century, this beautiful spot was designed in the 1920s for Massachusetts Governor Alvin T. Fuller, whose family members still live in many of the surrounding mansions. There is an ever-changing display here as flowers bloom throughout the season. Among the highlights are 1,500 rose bushes, extensive annuals, a Japanese garden, and a conservatory of tropical and desert plants. Nominal fee charged.

The Science and Nature Center at New Hampshire Yankee (800-338-7482), Route 1, Box 300, Seabrook 03874. Open daily 10–4, Saturdays March–Thanksgiving. The Seabrook Nuclear Power Plant has been a continual controversy since it was proposed over 20 years ago. The best off-site view of the plant is from Route 1A at Hampton River where it rises above the marsh on the western shore of the estuary. After demonstrations, construction delays, lengthy and complex legal proceedings, and the bankruptcy of its prime owner, the plant finally began producing power in 1990. The center is its educational facility and has a variety of exhibits about electricity, nuclear power, and the environment, especially the nearby marsh habitat, which you can view on a mile-long nature trail. Free admission.

Tuck Memorial Museum, 40 Park Avenue, Hampton 03842. Open mid-June to mid-September, Tuesday–Friday 1–4 PM. The museum of the Hampton Historical Society has local memorabilia, especially related to early families, the trolley era, and Hampton Beach. Adjacent is the **Hampton Firefighter's Museum** with a hand engine, other equipment, and a district schoolhouse, all restored. Free admission.

Exeter Historical Society (778-2335), 47 Front Street, Exeter 03833. Open Tuesday, Thursday, and Saturday 2–5 PM. Located in the former 1894 town library, this society has research materials for local history and genealogy, artifacts, photographs, maps, and changing exhibits.

Atkinson Historical Society, 3 Academy Avenue, Atkinson 03811. Open Wednesdays 2–4 PM. The Kimball-Peabody Mansion houses a collection of local artifacts plus extensive genealogical materials.

Fremont Historical Society, Route 107, Fremont 03044. Open second and fourth Sundays, June–August. The museum was the town library, built 1894, and measuring only 20 feet by 14 feet. From 1965 until 1981 it was a first-aid society, lending its rural residents hospital equipment.

Sandown Historical Society and Museum (887-6100), Depot Road, Box 33, Sandown 03873. Open Sundays 1–5 PM, May 30–November 1. Local history and railroad artifacts; wheelchair access plus rest rooms, picnic tables, and a nearby public swimming beach.

Stratham Historical Society (778-0403), Portsmouth Avenue, Stratham 03885. Open 2–4 PM Thursdays and the first Sunday of each month. The former granite Wiggin Library has recently been acquired by the historical society. Local artifacts and some genealogical materials.

HISTORIC HOUSES   American Independence Museum (772-2622, 778-1805), One Governor's Lane, Exeter 03833. Open Tuesday-Sunday 10-4, May-

October 15; Tuesday and Saturday 12–4, November–April 15. Also known as Cincinnati Hall, and one of New Hampshire's most historic buildings, part of this place was constructed in 1721. It served as the state treasury from 1775 to 1789 and as governor's mansion during the 14-year term of John Taylor Gilman. The Gilman family members were political and military leaders during the Revolutionary War when Exeter served as the Revolutionary capital. The house has recently been restored, and its diverse exhibits revitalized. It is owned by the Society of the Cincinnati of New Hampshire, the state chapter of a national organization whose members are the eldest sons of direct descendents of officers of the Continental Line who originally formed the society.

Gilman Garrison House (436-3205) Water Street, Exeter 03833. Open June–October; Tuesday, Thursday, Saturday, and Sunday 12–5 PM. A portion of this house was built in 1660 as a garrison out of log construction, but most of the building reflects the eighteenth century with fine paneling, especially in the governor's council meeting room. Owned by the Society for the Preservation of New England Antiquities. Fee charged.

Moses-Kent House (772-2044), corner of Pine and Linden streets, Exeter 03833. Open Tuesdays 1–4 PM, June–September. Built in 1868, ' this is the finest of three mansard-style houses in the historic district. The continuous occupation by one family is responsible for the remarkable state of preservation in the house. In the museum rooms are original furnishings from 1903.

Fremont Meetinghouse and Hearse House, Route 107, Fremont. Open May 30 and third Sunday in August or by appointment; inquire locally. Built in 1800, this unique meetinghouse, unaltered since it was built, contains an early choir stall, slave pews, and twin porches. The Hearse house, built in 1849, has a hand engine built in that same year.

Sandown Meeting House, Fremont Road, Sandown. Owned by the Old Meeting House Association, this is the finest meetinghouse of its type in New Hampshire, unaltered since it was built in 1774. Its craftsmanship and architectural details are nationally recognized. One can easily imagine our colonial ancestors listening to a fire-and-brimstone sermon from the preacher standing in the wine-glass pulpit. Open on Old Home Day, the second Sunday in August, or by appointment. Inquire locally about a caretaker.

Old South Meetinghouse (Route 1) **and Boyd School** (Washington Street), Seabrook 03874. School open third Sunday in August. The old school has exhibits and local artifacts relating to salt hay farming, shoemaking, and decoys used for bird hunting. The church is open by appointment only; inquire locally. Built in 1758, it has been altered inside.

ORCHARDS, PICK YOUR OWN, FARMER'S MARKETS   Applecrest Farm Orchards (926-3721), Route 88, Hampton Falls 03844. Open year-round, but the best times to visit are in May when apple blossoms cover the hillsides and in late summer through fall when apples are harvested. Pick your own apples and enjoy weekend festivals in season. Also pick your own strawberries, raspberries, and blueberries. Cross-country ski in winter. The Apple Mart and gift shop are open year-round.

Raspberry Farm (926-6604), Route 84, Hampton Falls 03844. Open first week in July through October. The state's largest grower with 6.5 miles of rows to "pick your own" blackberries, black raspberries, and raspberries plus a farm stand with vegetables and baked goods.

Farmer's Markets are open Tuesday afternoons June–October at Sacred Heart School, Route 1, in Hampton and Thursday afternoons at Swasey Parkway in Exeter. Local homegrown vegetables, herbs, flowers, fruit, and plants plus baked goods and crafts.

OCEAN ADVENTURES AND BOAT RIDES   **Smith and Gilmore Fishing Parties** (926-3503), Route 1A, Hampton Harbor, Hampton 03842. All-day fishing, Wednesdays and weekends April–Columbus Day; daily half-day trips May–September; night fishing June–August, weekend evening whale watches July–August; fireworks cruises, Wednesdays July–August. Three, modern, speedy vessels provide a variety of fishing experiences for this longtime family-operated business. A specialty is a 24-hour overnight fishing trip, 50 to 90 miles offshore to New England's famed fishing banks; limited to 40 people. A great trip for seeing offshore birds. The business also has a bait-and-tackle shop, rowboats to rent for Hampton Harbor flounder fishing, and a restaurant.

Al Gauron Deep Sea Fishing (926-2469), State Pier, Hampton Harbor, Hampton 03842. All-day fishing, spring–Columbus Day; two half-day trips daily; bluefish trips; night fishing; fireworks cruises on Wednesday nights; evening whale watches. Four modern, speedy vessels including the 90-foot *Northern Star*. Family owned and operated for half a century.

Eastman's Fishing Parties (474-3461), Seabrook Harbor, Route 1A, Seabrook 03874. Open April–October. All-day fishing, half-day and evening fishing, morning and afternoon whale-watch trips. The oldest of the family-operated fishing business on the seacoast. The Lucky Lady fleet has three modern, speedy vessels. Tackle-and-bait shops plus a full restaurant and pub with patio dining overlooking the harbor.

GREEN SPACE   **North Hampton State Beach**, Route 1A, North Hampton. A long sandy beach with lifeguards, parking meters, and rest rooms. A small takeout food stand is across the street. For one of the area's most scenic walks, park here, then proceed north past the old fish houses, which are now summer cottages, and a beautiful garden maintained by the Little Boar's Head Garden Club. A sidewalk follows the coast for about two miles to the Rye Beach Club.

Hampton Central Beach, Route 1A, Hampton. From the intersection of High Street and Route 1A, south through the main section of Hampton Beach, is a state park with lifeguards, metered parking, and rest rooms. North of Hampton's Great Boar's Head the beach is much less crowded but at high tides has limited sand area. South of Great Boar's Head the beach is opposite the business and touristy area of the beach. At the main beach is an information center, first-aid room, and rest rooms. Opposite the Ashworth Hotel is the New Hampshire Marine Memorial, a large statue and plaque dedicated to state residents who were lost at sea during World War II.

Hampton Beach State Park and Harbor, Route 1A, Hampton. Fees charged for the beach and boat launching in season. At the mouth of Hampton River is this long sandy beach with some of the state's last oceanfront sand dunes. There is a bathhouse with dressing rooms, rest rooms, and snack bar. Across Route 1A is the harbor with a boat-launching ramp and the state pier.

Swasey Parkway, off Water Street, Exeter. A small park beside the Squamscott River in downtown Exeter. Picnic area and playground.

Kingston State Beach, off Route 125, Kingston. Open weekends beginning Memorial Day, daily late June–Labor Day. A small state facility on Great Pond, this park has a long sandy beach, picnic groves, and a bathhouse. Fee charged.

SCENIC DRIVES   Follow Route 1B through New Castle, then connect with Route 1A through Rye, North Hampton, and the north end of Hampton Beach. The ocean is in view most of the way, and there are several small restaurants and beaches. This route is also popular with bicyclists.

GOLF   **East Kingston Country Club** (642-4414), Route 107, East Kingston 03827. Open whenever weather conditions permit. 18 holes, cart rentals, snack bar.

Exeter Country Club (778-8080), Jady Hill Road (off Portsmouth Avenue), Exeter 03833. Open May–October. 18 holes, cart rentals, full bar, and food service.

Sagamore-Hampton Golf Course (964-5341), North Road (off Route 1), North Hampton 03862. Open mid-April to mid-December. 18 holes, no motorized carts allowed, pro shop, light food, and beverages. A busy recreational course, inexpensive.

RACING   **Seabrook Greyhound Park** (474-3065), Route 107, Seabrook. Open daily. Pick your racing greyhound and make a wager while watching this fast-paced sport. Lounge, snack bars, restaurant, and free parking.

LODGING   Hampton and Hampton Beach offer nearly an unlimited number of rooms for tourists, especially at the beach and along Route 1 between Hampton Falls and North Hampton. The **Hampton Beach Area Chamber of Commerce** (see Guidance) provides a guide to most of the motels, but we have listed a few lodgings below. Both Hampton and Seabrook beaches have numerous cottages to rent by the week, and Hampton also has many condo units. Seabrook Beach is just residential and thus quieter than Hampton, and its beach is uncrowded. For information try **Harris Real Estate** (926-3400), **Preston Real Estate** (474-3453 or 926-2604), or **Famous Door Real Estate** (926-4403).

HOTELS   **Ashworth By The Sea** (926-6762, outside NH 800-345-6736), 295 Ocean Boulevard, Hampton 03842. Open year-round. This full-service, oceanfront hotel has been a beach landmark and the finest beach lodging since the early 1900s. With the addition of a modern new wing and remodeling of the original hotel, it is now open year-round. Most of its 105 rooms have queen- or king-size beds; others have two doubles. There is a lounge with nightly entertainment, three restaurants, indoor and outdoor pools, and private sun decks overlooking the ocean. Six lobster entrées, baked and broiled seafood, and steaks are menu features (dinners range from $9.95–$16.95). An all-you-can-eat buffet ($11.95) is offered Tuesday–Saturday evenings in July and August, the peak beach season. Summer rates are $90–$155; off-season is $49–$78; discounts for multi-night stays.

Hampton House (926-1033, outside NH 800-458-7058), 333 Ocean Boulevard, Hampton 03842. Open year-round. Fifty-one spacious modern rooms, including several suites, in this new facility on the ocean. All rooms have two doubles or a king-size bed, air-conditioning, TV, private balcony, and refrigerator. Coffee shop. Summer rates are $105–$155, off-season is $50–$80.

Oceanside Hotel (926-3542), 365 Ocean Boulevard, Hampton 03842. Open mid-May to mid-October. This turn-of-the-century summer home, located across the street from the ocean, has undergone many changes, but its interior has been maintained and tastefully furnished to reflect its Victorian beginnings. This is not typical Hampton Beach lodging. There are 10 rooms; all with private baths; all distinctly decorated; many with antiques and period pieces, including two with canopy beds; a lovely Victorian common room; and two porches. Midsummer rates (late June–early August) are $90–$102; discounts for multi-night stays and before or after midsummer. Café serves breakfast July and August; complimentary continental breakfast at other times.

The Exeter Inn (772-5901, outside NH 800-782-8444), 90 Front Street, Exeter 03833-0508. Open year-round. In the middle of the Front Street Historic District, this comfortable brick Georgian-style inn and restaurant is owned by Phillips Exeter Academy. The 45 rooms include several family suites, all with TV, radio, and telephones, with new traditional reproduction furnishings replacing the older motel-type furniture. All size beds available. Afternoon tea served daily 3–5 PM. Lounge, living room fireplaces. Rates are $60–$100; suites from $125. Breakfast, lunch, and dinner served. The continental menu

($12.75–$17) ranges from fresh loin of venison and veal Roquefort to scampi Provençal and seafood primavera. Sunday brunch from 10–2 is a local favorite.

BED & BREAKFASTS   Inn at Elmwood Corners (929-0443), 252 Winnacunnet Road, Hampton 03842. Open year-round. Located 1.5 miles from the beach, this B&B was a boardinghouse at the turn of the century. Its energetic owners have renovated and remodeled the place into an attractive and comfortable village inn. All the rooms have queen-size beds and are furnished country-style with stencilling, handmade quilts, curtains, and braided rugs. Five rooms share three baths; two rooms are suites with full kitchens and private baths. Two sitting rooms with TVs and books; one has complimentary sherry. John and Mary Hornberger, innkeepers. Full breakfast. Rates are $50–$90, depending on season and accommodations.

The Victoria Inn (929-1437), 430 High Street, Hampton. Open year-round. This recently renovated former guest house has seven rooms, one with a private bath, most with double beds, and all with air-conditioning and overhead fans. Two sitting rooms, one with TV, and a screened porch. Off the beach. Continental breakfast. Bill Beynon, owner. Rates are $70–$85.

HOUSEKEEPING UNITS   Seaside Village (964-8204), One Ocean Boulevard, North Hampton. Open May–September, weather permitting. This is about the only place on the New Hampshire seacoast with lodging right on the sand, with no street to cross. There are 19 units, 13 of which are full housekeeping, and 6 motel units (for two to four people) with only refrigerators and hot plates. Housekeeping guests bring towels and linens and rent Saturday to Saturday. Except for eight new housekeeping units that have private master bedrooms and a loft for the kids, the other units are older and not fancy. Nevertheless, many of the units are rented by the end of one season for the next season to come. Marshall and Tammy Irving, hosts. Housekeeping units are $450–$750 per week; motel units are $60–$75 per night for two to three people, three-night minimum.

DINING OUT   Ashworth By The Sea (926-6762, outside NH 800-345-6736), 295 Ocean Boulevard, Hampton 03842. Open year-round. A full-service, oceanfront hotel The Ashworth been a beach landmark and and its restaurant is the best on the main beach. Six lobster entrées, baked and broiled seafood, and steaks are menu features (dinners range from $9.95–$16.95). An all-you-can-eat buffet ($11.95) is offered Tuesday–Saturday evenings in July and August, the peak beach season.

Ron's Beach House (926-1870), 965 Ocean Boulevard, Hampton. Open daily; lunch and Sunday brunch 11–3, dinner 5–10, lounge open until midnight; deck open Memorial Day weekend through at least Labor Day. Reservations recommended. Considered the best restaurant at this end of the seacoast, Ron's specializes in fish—as many as

14 different varieties are regularly offered, and each can be prepared baked, blackened Cajun-style, or charbroiled. A favorite entrée is cioppino, a Portuguese stew with lobster, clams, fish fillets, and shrimp; another is Norwegian pasta with salmon and fettucini of the day. Chicken, veal, and steaks complete the menu. For appetizers there is a raw bar, in-house smoked fish, several salads, and chowders. Sunday brunch ranges from eggs Benedict with lobster to Swedish fruit pancake. Located north of the main section of Hampton Beach, Ron's is on the trolley route. Prices range from $9.95–$17.95.

The Starving Chef (772-5590), 237 Water Street, Exeter. Open for lunch, dinner, and Sunday brunch. The chef certainly is not starving here, especially since the recent move from a storefront to the restored eighteenth-century Tilton-Tattersal House. Creative cuisine is the specialty, and it ranges from Greek and Italian to East Indian and Asian entrées with some traditional New England favorites such as broiled swordfish and baked scrod. We like chicken devannandah (Indian spiced chicken and mild sausage with Chinese cabbage, red pepper, onion, eggplant, pea pods, and bean sprouts seasoned with sherry, soy, and chili sauce and served with jasmine rice). There's also roast duck with raspberry sauce, three veal entrées, dinner crêpes, steaks, rich desserts, and a variety of special coffees. Changing art from local artists adorns the walls. Prices range from $10.95–$17.95.

The Half Barn (778-7898), Route 108, Newfields. Open Thursday–Saturday at 6 PM, Sundays at 4 PM. Built in 1793, this half barn (built shorter than it is wide) has been restored and turned into an intriguing, antiques-filled restaurant. The menu is not large, but there are nightly specials, including chef's choice chicken and veal dishes. Broiled haddock, roast duckling, rack of lamb, steaks, and broiled scallops en casserole are featured. Prices range from $11.95–$16.95; no credit cards.

EATING OUT   **Galley Hatch** (926-6152), Route 1, Hampton. Open daily 11 AM–10 PM, Friday and Saturday until 11 PM. A large and popular seacoast restaurant with a diverse and reasonably priced menu. Fish, chicken, steaks, pastas, and vegetarian entrées plus pizza, salads, and sandwiches. Many offerings are prepared to be heart healthy. Breads and pastries are made in their own bakery, which is open to the public. Two lounges; light meals served in the lounge until closing. Next door is the Hampton Cinema complex. Prices range under $10–$14.95.

Fried seafood, chowder, steamed clams, and lobster in the rough are seacoast specialties. Local favorites include the following places: **Little Jack's Seafood** (926-0444), 539 Ocean Boulevard, Hampton Beach, open late spring–Labor Day. **Brown's Seabrook Lobster Pound** (474-9858), Route 286, Seabrook Beach, open year-round. Its screened dining room is on the marsh beside the Blackwater River. **Newick's Fisherman's Landing** (926-7646), 845 Lafayette Road, Hampton. Open year-round Wednesday–Sunday 11:30 AM to 8 PM or 9 PM, open daily in the summer and early fall. Fish, clams, scallops, shrimp served deep fried, broiled, or baked plus lobsters cooked any way you want them. (Also see Newick's in Dover.) Fresh fish market and lobsters packed to travel.

LOBSTER   Lobsters are a seacoast trademark. For live or cooked lobsters, try the **New Hampshire Lobster Company** (926-3424), located at the Smith & Gilmore Pier at Hampton Harbor, open daily 9–5, summer until 6 PM; or **Al's Seafood** (946-9591), Route 1, Lafayette Road, North Hampton, open daily. Al's is a lobster pound and fish market with a small seafood restaurant, offering mainly fried seafood, but in warm weather, under a tent, they serve "lobster in the rough."

ENTERTAINMENT   **Hampton Playhouse** (926-3073), Winnacunnet Road, Hampton. Open July and August, Tuesday–Saturday at 8 PM, Sunday at 7 PM, Wednesday and Friday matinees at 2:30 PM, children's shows on Saturdays at 11 AM and 2 PM. For over 40 years this theater—in a remodeled, air-conditioned barn—has provided popular summer entertainment, often headlined with well-known stars. Most of the shows are musicals or comedies, with some version of burlesque, complete with risqué comics and dancing girls, a regular summer highlight.

SELECTIVE SHOPPING   **North Hampton Factory Outlet Center**, Route 1, North Hampton. More than 35 stores offer bargains in clothing, books, records, luggage, footwear, housewares, and gifts.

   League of New Hampshire Craftsmen (778-8282), 61 Water Street, Exeter 03833. Open Monday–Saturday 10–5. More than 200 craftsworkers are members of the league supplying a wide variety of distinctive handmade items.

   Exeter Handkerchief Fabrics and Custom Draperies Co. (778-8564), Lincoln Street, Exeter 03833. Open Monday–Saturday 9–5. A huge selection of yard goods and patterns make this place a "must stop" for the sewers in the family.

SPECIAL EVENTS   Summer in the seacoast offers nearly an unlimited number of special events and activities for people of all ages. Check with local chambers of commerce for varied activities.

   Mid-May: **New Hampshire Towing Association Wrecker Rodeo** (926-8717), Hampton Beach. Scores of wreckers parade and compete for prizes.

   Early summer: **Seacoast Seafood Festival** (436-7678), Hampton Beach State Park. Sample a variety of seafoods prepared by area restaurants.

   Early June: **Hobie Cat Regatta** (926-8717), Hampton Beach. A weekend of racing just off Hampton Beach makes a colorful spectacle.

   Late June: **Exeter Criterium** (778-0595), Exeter. Bicycle road race through the streets of Exeter.

Late June–early August: **Concerts in the Park** (778-0595), Swasey Park, Exeter, every Thursday.

July and August: **Hampton Beach Fireworks**, every Wednesday night. **Hampton Beach Concerts**, every Sunday evening at 7 PM.

Fourth of July: **Kingston Fair**, Route 125, Kingston. A Fourth-of-July weekend country fair.

Late July: **Stratham Fair**, Route 101, Stratham. A weekend, agricultural country fair with horse and cattle pulling, midway, children's events, fireworks, etc.

Mid-August: **Annual Children's Festival** (926-8717), Hampton Beach.

Late September: **Oktoberfest** (926-8717), Hampton.

Durham, Dover, and vicinity

Durham is the home of the University of New Hampshire, and its beautiful campus dominates the center of the town. Paul Creative Arts Center with its galleries, music, dance, and theater, and intercollegiate athletics has the most to offer visitors, though these activities tend to operate during the school year, September–May. **Dover**, long an important mill town, is not a tourist center, but it does have a summer arts festival, theater, and several fine restaurants and B&Bs.

GUIDANCE   **Greater Dover Chamber of Commerce** (742-2218), 299 Central Avenue, Dover 03820.

University of New Hampshire main switchboard (862-1234) can provide details of various events or direct your questions to the proper office.

GETTING THERE   By car: From Portsmouth, follow the Spaulding Turnpike (Routes 4/16) north, then Route 4 west for Durham, or remain on the turnpike and take one of the three Dover exits.

By bus: **C&J Trailways** (431-2424, 742-2990), provides many trips daily connecting Logan Airport and downtown Boston with Dover, Durham, and Portsmouth, New Hampshire; Newburyport, Massachusetts; and Portland, Maine.

GETTING AROUND   By bus: **COAST** (Cooperative Alliance for Seacoast Transportation) (862-1931), local bus transportation connects Portsmouth and major outlying shopping centers with Durham, Dover, Newmarket, Rochester, and Somersworth, New Hampshire, and Berwick, Maine.

MEDICAL EMERGENCY   **Wentworth-Douglas Hospital** (742-5252), 789 Central Avenue, Dover 03820. 24-hour emergency walk-in service. Dover ambulance: 911. Durham ambulance: 862-1212.

TO SEE AND DO   **Farmer's Market**, Welby Drug parking lot, Dover. Wednesday afternoons, June–October. Locally grown veggies and fruits, home-baked goods, and crafts.

Woodman Institute (742-1038), 182 Central Avenue, Dover. Open Tuesday–Saturday 2–5 PM. This three-building complex is Dover's historical museum. The Woodman House (1818) is a research library that has galleries and natural history and war-related museum rooms.

Thompson Hall, the administrative center of the University of New Hampshire.

Photo by Peter E. Randall

The 1813 Hale House is a historical museum with period furniture. The Damm Garrison, built in 1675, is an unique building that was used as a home and fortress by early settlers. Free.

Lee Historical Society, Mast Road, Lee. Open first Saturday after Labor Day. Local artifacts, including farm tools, household items, and antique photographs, are housed in an old railroad freight station, moved to this site between the town library and the police station.

New Market Historical Society (659-7420), Granite Street, Newmarket 03857. Open Thursdays 2–4 PM, Memorial Day–Labor Day. The old Granite School Museum has old tools and local artifacts plus photographs of Newmarket mills and shoe shops.

GREEN SPACE   **Hilton Park** is located on Dover Point, bisected by the Spaulding Turnpike. It has a boat launching ramp, picnic tables, outdoor grills, and play area.

GOLF   **Hickory Pond** (659-6565), Route 108, Durham. Open spring–early fall. This is a new 9-hole, par-3 course located at the Country House Inn. Pro shop and food served. Inexpensive.

Nippo Lake Golf Course (664-2030), Province Road (off Route 126), Barrington 03825. Open April–November. Nine holes, cart rentals, full bar and food service year-round; call for starting times on weekends.

Rochester Country Club (332-9892), Route 125, Gonic 03867. Open mid-April to mid-November. 18 holes, cart rentals, full bar and food service, and pro shop; call for starting times on weekends.

Rockingham Country Club (659-6379), Route 108, Newmarket 03857. Open mid-April to mid-November. Nine holes, cart rentals, pro shop, full bar and food service; call for starting times on weekends and holidays.

Sunningdale Golf Course (742-8056), Green Street, Somersworth 03878. Open mid-April to mid-November. Nine holes, cart rentals, full bar and light food.

LODGING   **The New England Center** (862-2800), 15 Strafford Avenue, Durham 03824. Located on the campus of the University of New Hampshire, this contemporary conference center (also open to the public) has 115 rooms, 61 of which are located in the newest of the two green ceramic brick towers that make up the complex. All rooms have wall-to-wall carpet, air-conditioning, TV, and phones, and the new wing has two queen-size beds in each room. All rooms have dramatic views across the campus or into the treetops of this heavily wooded site, and there is daily bus service to Logan Airport in Boston. Breakfast, lunch, and dinner available next door at the Woods Restaurant (see Dining Out). Rates are $75–$120 but vary by season and accommodations.

BED & BREAKFASTS   **Country House Inn** (659-6565), Route 108, RR 2, Durham 03824. Open year-round. Located south of Durham, nearly in Newmarket, this inn has 9 rooms with private baths, and 10 rooms that share three baths. The country-style furnished rooms have double or twin beds. All rooms have air-conditioning, and there is a common room with a TV and a kitchen for guests. Continental breakfast served; full breakfast may be available when their 9-hole golf course is open. Rick and Lisa Furnelli, proprietors. Rates from $48.

Pinky's Place (742-8789), 38 Rutland Street, Dover 03820. Open year-round. Two rooms in this restored Victorian share a bath. Located in a quiet residential neighborhood, it has a cozy living room and a tree-shaded porch. Full gourmet breakfast. Pinky and Bill Kram, hosts. Rates are $50 per room.

The Silver Street Inn (743-3000), 103 Silver Street, Dover 03820. Open year-round. This in-town Victorian B&B was built in the 1880s by a wealthy industrialist. It has been furnished to match the ornate architectural details, such as Spanish mahogany, Austrian crystal door-knobs, Italian slate, and French Caen stone for the fireplaces. Ten rooms (all but one with private bath) have air-conditioning, TV, and telephones. One downstairs room is handicapped-accessible and has two double beds. The dining and living rooms and the ornate library are comfortable and have fireplaces. Full breakfast; served in rooms by request. Cam Mirisola, innkeeper. Rates are $55–$85.

Highland House (743-3399), 148 County Farm Road, Dover 03820. Open year-round. This interesting brick Victorian country house is on the outskirts of the city; be sure to get directions. Four guest rooms share two baths. Beds include a queen-size with a canopy. Most rooms have a queen-size bed or a double and a single. Common rooms include a living room, library, and the dining room. Furnishings are antiques, enhanced by the unusual woodwork and architectural design of this house. Noreen and Andy Bowers, innkeepers. Some nights Andy entertains with his guitar, harmonica, or piano. Cross-country skiing from the house. Full breakfast. Rates are $60 per night.

DINING OUT   The Woods Restaurant and Wine Bar (862-2815), 15 Strafford Avenue, Durham. Open year-round for breakfast, lunch, and dinner. Dinner is 5:30–9 PM, Friday and Saturday until 10 PM. Sunday brunch from 11–2. Part of the New England Center, this is one of the popular restaurants in the region. It's as well known for its fine food as for its distinctive architecture, which features angled walls and huge win-dows that place diners seemingly in the midst of the surrounding for-est. Veal, roast stuffed leg of lamb, Norwegian salmon, and filet mignon are specialties, matched by varied appetizers, such as oysters on the half shell, and rich desserts. Sunday brunch has been called the best in New Hampshire by a statewide magazine. Prices range from $12.95–$18.95.

Firehouse 1 (742-2220), 1 Orchard Street (adjacent to the municipal parking off the lower square), Dover. Open daily 11:30 AM–9 PM, Friday and Saturday until 10 PM. Reservations recommended. Housed in a remodeled 1830s firehouse, this is Dover's best restaurant. The dinner menu is quite diverse, featuring veal, rainbow trout, fresh pasta dishes, Szechwan chicken, and seafood lo mein. Appetizers include seafood chowder, wonton ravioli, and baked stuffed mushroom caps. The bar is open until legal closing. Lunch ranges $5–$9, dinner $10–$15.

EATING OUT   **Newick's Lobster House and Restaurant** (742-3205), Dover Point Road, Dover. Open daily 11:30 AM–8 PM, Friday and Saturday until 9 PM, closed Mondays from after Columbus Day until Memorial Day weekend. Fresh fish and lobster right off the boat are the specialties here in this large, very popular restaurant overlooking Great Bay. Not fancy dining, but you can have deep-fried (in cholesterol-free vegetable oil) fish of all kinds with combinations of scallops, oysters, haddock, clams, or shrimp. Portions are huge. For those with lighter tastes, try boiled lobsters, steamers, or broiled, baked, or stuffed fish dinners. Also chicken, sandwiches, chowders, and lobster stew. Expect a wait at weekend dinner times. (Newick's Fisherman's Landing in Hampton is also operated by Jack Newick.) Prices range from $4.50–$16.95.

Work Day Café and Texican Grille (749-0483), Upper Square, Dover. Open daily from 11:30 AM. Cajun and southwestern- style cooking are featured with all items available mesquite-grilled, charbroiled, Cajun-style, or barbecued. Try jambalaya, shrimp and sausage gumbo, catfish and shrimp, seafood enchilada, or duck burrito. Crawfish tails for an appetizer and white chocolate mousse for dessert. Nightly entertainment downstairs in the small lounge.

ENTERTAINMENT   **Cochecho Arts Festival** (742-2218), Cochecho Falls Millworks Courtyard, Dover. Open June–early September. In the center of Dover beside the Cocheco River is a huge textile mill complex, recently remodeled into a business center. The courtyard is the location for Friday night, Wednesday noon, and occasional Sunday evening concerts featuring a variety of regional music groups. Children's concerts and programs are held Tuesdays at noon at nearby Henry Law Park.

Hackmatack Repertory Theatre (749-3996), 10 Franklin Plaza Cocheco Mills, Dover 03820. Open September–May. The professional cast produces nine varied shows including Shakespeare, musicals, drama, mysteries, and popular plays. A six-week summer children's workshop offers lessons and the chance for the young people to perform. The group runs a summer theater (207-698-1807) in nearby Berwick, Maine, during July and August.

SELECTIVE SHOPPING   **Calef's Country Store** (664-2231), Routes 9 and 125, Barrington. Open daily. Since 1869, five generations of Calefs have operated this old-fashioned country store. Penny candy, cheddar cheese, maple syrup, Barbados molasses, jams and jellies, pickles and crackers in the barrel, dried beans for baking, hand-dipped candles, pumpkins in the fall, gifts, etc.

Tuttle's Red Barn (742-4313), Dover Point Road, Dover. Open daily 10–6. Tuttles have lived on this site since 1632, making this the oldest continuously operating family farm in America. Once just a seasonal farm stand operating from the large, old red barn, it has been expanded as a market and garden center. In season much of the produce, especially sweet corn, comes from the surrounding fields, but they also have plenty of fresh vegetables and fruit, breads, and cheeses.

SPECIAL EVENTS   June: **Somersworth International Children's Day**, an all-day event with four entertainment stages including one for children, a crafts fair, food booths, hands-on crafts tent for children, and an activities section for children.

Late June to early September: **Cochecho Arts Festival** (742-2218), Dover. Music and children's programs, several times weekly.

September: **Lee Fair Day**, Mast Road, Lee. A community fair with exhibits, games, and food.

Mid-September: **Rochester Fair**, 72 Lafayette Street. A 10-day fair with a midway, agricultural exhibits, and pari-mutual harness racing.

Late September–early October: **Apple Harvest Day**, Dover.

II. The Merrimack Valley

- Pittsburg
- Colebrook

VII

- Stark
- Berlin

- Whitefield
- Littleton
- Franconia
VIc.
- Lincoln
- N. Woodstock

VIa.
Jackson

Woodsville

- N. Conway

VIb. • Waterville Valley

- Plymouth
Va.

Lake Winnipesauke

- Hanover
- Lebanon

IV   **Vb.**

- Wolfeboro
- Laconia

- New London
- Claremont

- Concord
II
- Manchester

- Dover   **I**

- Portsmouth
- Exeter
- Hampton   •: Isles of Shoals
- Hampton Beach

III
- Keene
- Peterborough

Introduction

The Merrimack, New England's second longest river, was an early New Hampshire highway, and today it's paralleled by I-93, New Hampshire's north/south transportation spine. One of the state's first settled corridors, the Merrimack Valley has recently been enjoying another migration rush from hundreds of companies and thousands of families moving north from Massachusetts to take advantage of New Hampshire's tax breaks (no sales or income tax).

Relatively few visitors, however, venture farther into this area than the fast-food chains just off I-93. The very way the highways slice through and around both Manchester and Concord does little to encourage exploration. Manchester's proud, old, brick shopping streets, its Currier Gallery of Art, and its Amoskeag Mills—once the world's largest textile "manufactury"—are rewarding stops. So are Concord's state capitol building, the neighboring New Hampshire Historical Society, and downtown shops. The headquarters for the New Hampshire Audubon Society (just off I-89) and the Society for the Protection of New Hampshire Forests (just off I-93) are also well worth the small detours they require.

Other genuine finds are salted around this little-touristed central New Hampshire corridor. Canterbury Shaker Village, just 15 miles north of Concord, remains a working Shaker community in addition to being one of New England's most interesting museums. "America's Stonehenge" is at Mystery Hill in North Salem. There are also numerous state parks with sandy beaches and a variety of outstanding shops, restaurants, and inns.

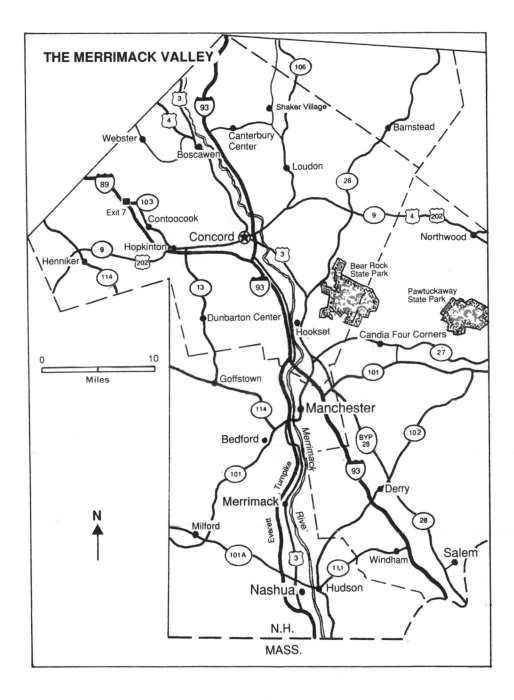

THE MERRIMACK VALLEY

Shaker Village

Barnstead

Webster

Canterbury Center

Boscawen

Loudon

Exit 7

Contoocook

Hopkinton

Concord

Northwood

Henniker

Bear Rock State Park

Pawtuckaway State Park

Dunbarton Center

Hookset

Candia Four Corners

Goffstown

Manchester

Miles

Bedford

Derry

Merrimack

Milford

Windham

Salem

Nashua

Hudson

Everett

Turnpike

Merrimack River

N

N.H.

MASS.

The Manchester Area

Manchester is by far New Hampshire's largest city (roughly 100,000 people). It's also arguably New England's most interesting "mill city," an image many current residents reject.

When white men first traveled up the Merrimack, they found a large Native American village at Amoskeag Falls. In 1650 the English missionary John Eliot set up one of his "Praying Indian" communities and called it Derryfield. The natives were later displaced by a white settlement early in the eighteenth century. By 1810 local Judge Samuel Blodgett foretold the community's future, suggesting that its name be changed from Derryfield to Manchester, the world's biggest manufacturing city (in England).

This early American Manchester population was just 615, but Judge Blodgett raised money to build a canal around Amoskeag Falls to enable flat-bottomed boats to glide downstream and onward, via the Middlesex Canal, into Boston. Both the canal and the town's first cotton mill opened in 1809.

It was a group of Boston entrepreneurs, however, who put Manchester on the map. By the 1830s these "Boston Associates" had purchased waterpower rights for the entire length of the Merrimack River and had begun developing a city full of mills in Lowell, Massachusetts, 32 miles downriver from Manchester. Incorporating themselves as the Amoskeag Manufacturing Company, they then bought 15,000 acres around Amoskeag Falls and drew up a master plan for the city of Manchester, complete with tree-lined streets, housing, churches, and parks.

Like Lowell, Manchester enjoyed an early utopian period during which "mill girls" lived in well-regulated boarding houses. It was followed by successive periods of expansion, fueled by waves of foreign immigration. With direct rail connections to Quebec, Manchester attracted predominantly French-Canadian workers but Polish, Greek, and Irish communities were (and are) also substantial.

At its height in the early twentieth century, the Amoskeag Manufacturing Company employed 17,000 workers, encompassed 64 mill buildings lining both sides of the Merrimack River for a mile and

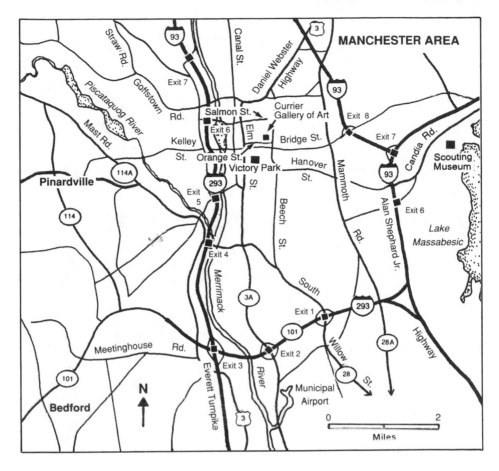

a half, and contained the world's largest single mill yard. The total mill space equaled that of the present World Trade Center in New York City. Imagine this space filled with the noise and movement of nearly 700,000 spindles and 23,000 looms!

Life for workers was unquestionably hard. The tower bells rang each morning at 4:30, and the first call for breakfast was 5:30; the workday began at 6:30, lasting until 7:30 in the evening. But it's a way of life that many workers remember fondly in the oral histories recorded in *Amoskeag: Life and Work in an American Factory-City* by anthropologist Tamara Hareven and photographer Randolph Langenbach. Based on interviews with thousands of former Amoskeag employees, this interesting book, published in 1978, vividly conveys what it was like to live within Manchester's tightly knit ethnic circles, reinforced by a sense of belonging to a full city of workers united like one family by a single boss.

The Amoskeag Canal and Mill Yard, 1943, by Charles Sheeler, from the collection of the Currier Gallery of Art, Manchester.

The Amoskeag Manufacturing Company went bankrupt in 1935, and the following year the mills were shut down. In desperation a group of local businessmen formed Amoskeag Industries, Inc., purchased all the mills for $5 million and managed to lease and sell mill space to diversified businesses.

"Diversify" has been the city's slogan ever since. Having once experienced complete dependency on one economic source, Manchester now prides itself on the number and variety of its industries and service businesses as well as on its current status as a financial and insurance center. New business and residential buildings rise high above the old mill towers.

Loosely circled by hills and with buildings that rise in tiers above the mills on the eastern bank of the Merrimack, Manchester is an attractive city with a Gothic Revival town hall, handsome nineteenth-century commercial blocks, and the gem-like Palace Theater. The Currier Gallery, one of the country's outstanding small art museums, is also located here.

Still, it's puzzling that while a half dozen other New England mill cities have opened visitors centers and museums, Manchester has done nothing to dramatize its story. Even as historic mill buildings in Lowell were being restored, the graceful curve of the Amoskeag's mile-long river wall was broken and the canals filled in. Check with the Manchester Historical Society and with the Currier Gallery of Art about both printed and walking mill-yard tours.

GUIDANCE   **Greater Manchester Chamber of Commerce** (666-6600), 889 Elm Street, Manchester 03101. Upstairs over Dunkin Donuts at the corner of Hanover and Elm, the chamber office stocks brochures and sells a city map for $2.

Greater Nashua Chamber of Commerce (891-2471), 1 Tara Boulevard, Suite 211, Nashua 03062.

GETTING THERE   By bus: From the **Manchester Transportation Center** (668-6133), Canal and Granite streets, you can get anywhere in the country; Concord Trailways, Vermont Transit Lines, and Peter Pan, all stop regularly.

By plane: The **Manchester Airport** (624-6539) is the largest airport in the state, served by United, USAir, Delta Connection, and Eastern Express, with nonstop flights to Washington, New York, Chicago, Philadelphia, Pittsburgh, and Boston. **Hertz, Budget, Avis,** and **Thrifty Car Rental** are all here and offer free airport transfers.

By car: The biggest problem with Manchester is finding your way in. It's moated by interstates 93 and 293 more effectively than it ever was by canals and mill walls. The simplest access to downtown is via the Amoskeag Bridge on I-293, Exit 6 to Elm Street. Approaching the city from the south, however, we actually prefer taking Exit 6 off I-93 and following Hanover Street across town. A handy map, available from the chamber of commerce (see Guidance), pinpoints parking garages, and there are reasonably priced (warning: and well-monitored) meters.

GETTING AROUND   **Hudson Bus Lines** (424-2446), 22 Pond Street, Nashua, offers limousine service between pick-up points in Concord, Manchester, Nashua, downtown Boston, and Logan International Airport.

MEDICAL EMERGENCY   **Elliot Hospital** (669-5300), 955 Auburn Street, Manchester.

TO SEE AND DO   *In Manchester:*   **Currier Gallery of Art** (669-6144), 192 Orange Street. Open Tuesday through Saturday 10–4, Thursday until 10 PM, Sunday 2–5. A fine landscape by Claude Monet; an 1850s painting of the spa at Clarendon Springs, VT, by James Hope; a spooky 1935 Edward Hopper Maine coastal scene titled *The*

Photo by Kristen Levesque

The Currier Gallery of Art offers programs for all ages.

Bootleggers; and a 1940s painting by Sheeler of the Amoskeag mills are a few of the unexpected treasures you might find displayed from the Currier's extensive collection of works—which ranges from a thirteenth-century Tuscan Madonna and Child to twentieth-century works by Rouault, Picasso, Wyeth, and Matisse. Silver, pewter, art, glass, furniture, and textiles are also displayed, and special exhibits are frequently outstanding. The Zimmerman House, designed in 1950 by Frank Lloyd Wright—his only house open to the public in New England—is also maintained by the Currier.

Guided tours are offered at the museum Thursday through Sunday, but they are by reservation through Ticketron. Concerts are also held in the museum's central courtyard once a month, October to April. The museum is free, and the Zimmerman House tours are $4 per adult; $2.50 per seniors and students. The museum is in a residential neighborhood on the site of the Victorian home of Moody and Hannah Currier, the couple who gave it and who specified in their will that their house be torn down to make way for the museum. The trick to finding it is beginning at either highway exit from which it's marked (the Amoskeag Bridge exit on Route 293 and the Wellington Street exit on I-93), following the Indian trail of signs. (Also see the map for Manchester in this chapter.)

Manchester Historic Association (622-7531), 129 Amherst Street. Open Tuesday through Friday 9–4, Saturday 10–4. Free. Special exhibits vary, and the permanent collection includes Indian artifacts, photographs, and furniture. The research library contains Amoskeag Manufacturing Company records, city records, and family papers.

Science Enrichment Encounters (669-0400), 324 Commercial Street. Open Saturday and Sunday afternoons 1–5. A hands-on science center geared to children of all ages. Experience weightlessness, experiment with a momentum machine, giant bubbles, gyrascopes, microwaves, and more.

The Amoskeag Mill Yard. Bounded by the Merrimack River and by Granite, Franklin, Market, Canal, and West Salmon streets, the buildings of the former Amoskeag Manufacturing Company still represent one of the country's leading examples of nineteenth- and early twentieth-century industrial architecture. The four- and five-story-high mills stand in two rows along the east bank of the river. Built variously from the 1830s to 1910, they look fairly uniform because as the older mills were expanded, their early distinctive features were blurred. The adjoining blocks lined with tidy, brick mill housing, however, reflect a progression of styles from the 1830s to 1920. The two large mills on the west side of the river were once connected to these by tunnels and bridges. Stand on Granite Street (by the Granite Street Bar & Grill) and look up the long brick column of buildings for a sense of nineteenth-century Manchester. Inquire at both the Currier Gallery of Art and the Manchester Historical Association (see above) about guided tours of the former mill yard.

Stark House (622-5719), 2000 Elm Street. Open May to October, Wednesday through Sunday 1:30–4:30. An eighteenth-century house built by Archibald Stark, a community leader and father of Major General John Stark, who commanded the Battle of Bennington.

The Lawrence L. Lee Scouting Museum (668-8919), Bodwell Road. Open daily July and August, 10–4; September to June, Saturdays 10–4. Exhibits include original drawings and letters of scouting founder Lord Robert Baden-Powell and exhibits about scouting throughout the world. The library of 3,000 books and bound periodicals also relate to scouting.

Manchester Institute of Arts and Sciences (623-0313), 148 Concord Street. Open Monday through Saturday 9–5. Just across Victory Park from the historical association, this arts center stages frequent gallery exhibits; also sponsors concerts, films, and lectures.

New Hampshire Art Association Gallery (622-0527), 26 Hanover Street. Open Monday through Friday 10–5. Displays of sculpture, watercolors, oils, acrylics, and photography—representing 400 juried artists statewide.

The Art Group Gallery (669-6081), 28 Hanover Street. Open daily except Sunday. A cooperative gallery representing New Hampshire artists.

In Nashua: New Hampshire's second largest city, Nashua has its share of monumental mill buildings along Water and Factory streets, built by the Nashua Manufacturing Company, which was chartered in 1823 to produce cotton fabric.

The Nashua Center for the Arts (883-1506), 14 Court Street, displays contemporary art, including photography and sculpture, in its gallery. It also sponsors a January to May "Downtown Live" performance series and a Saturday program of children's entertainment. In summer it sponsors outdoor performances in Holman Stadium.

The Nashua Historical Society (883-0015) exhibits its collections in the Florence Speare Memorial Building, 3 Abbott Street, and maintains the Abbott-Spalding House on Abbott Square. Open seasonally; call for hours.

For help with more Nashua area information contact the Greater Nashua Chamber of Commerce (see Guidance).

In surrounding villages: **Robert Frost Farm** (432-3091), 2 miles south of Derry on Route 28. Open June to October daily 10–6. An 1880s clapboard house, in which the poet lived between 1901 and 1909, is filled with original furnishings. An interpretive nature trail runs through surrounding fields and woods, past the "mending wall." Frost did the bulk of his writing here.

Taylor Up and Down Saw Mill, Island Pond Road, Derry. A water-powered up-and-down sawmill that processed logs into boards; open usually in spring when the water level is high enough to power it. Call the Department of Resources and Economic Development (271-3456) for details.

Old Sandown Railroad Museum (887-3259 or 887-4611), Route

121A, Sandown. Open June to October, Saturday and Sunday 1–5. Railroad memorabilia, telegraph equipment, old magazines, posters, photographs, and Civil War letters are among the exhibits.

America's Stonehenge, formerly "Mystery Hill" (893-8300; if no answer: 432-2530), off Route 111, North Salem. Take I-93 Exit 3 and follow Route 111 five miles east to Island Pond Road, then Haverhill Road to the entrance. Open daily June to Labor Day, 9–5; in May and September, 10–4; weekends in April and November. $5 per adult, $4 per senior, $3 per student, $1.50 per child. Billed as "one of the largest and possibly the oldest megalithic . . . sites in North America." The intriguing stone formations may or may not have been built by Celts 4,000 years ago, but it's a sight to see.

Anheuser-Busch Brewery (889-6631), Route 3, Merrimack (between Manchester and Nashua). At least two Clydesdales are always on view here; tours of the brewery are offered May to October daily 9:30–3:30; otherwise, Wednesday through Sunday 9:30–3:30.

Milford Historical Society (673-3385), 2 Union Street, Milford. The Carey House is open June to September, Saturdays 2–4. Milford is an old shopping and mill town with an ornate, Victorian-style town hall.

COVERED BRIDGE   Hopkinton-Rowell's Covered Bridge on Contoocook Road, north of Route 127, at West Hopkinton.

FOR FAMILIES   Canobie Lake (893-3506), I-93 Exit 2, Salem. Open daily Memorial Day to Labor Day, weekends mid-April to Memorial Day. One of New England's biggest amusement parks: more than 40 rides, including a big roller coaster, extensive Kiddieland, swimming pool, wild log flume ride, and excursion boat and mini-train ride around the park.

The Children's Metamorphosis (425-2560), 217 Rockingham Road. I-93 exit 5 then one mile north on Route 28. Open Tuesday–Saturday 9:30–5, Sundays 1–5 and Friday Evenings until 8. Geared to ages 2–8, 12 exhibit areas including a nature center, a construction site, grocery store, a hospital emergency, a "sticky" room, a world cultures room and a "climbing hall." Admission: $3.50 per person, $6.50 per family.

GREEN SPACE   Bear Brook State Park (485-9874), off Route 28 in Allenstown. Open mid-May to mid-October. Take the Hooksett exit off I-93. The park has 9,600 heavily forested acres with six lakes, swimming, rental boats, picnicking for up to 1,500 visitors under tall pines, a physical fitness course, nature trails, fishing (Archery Pond is reserved for fly-fishing), camping with 81 tent sites on Beaver Pond (where the swim beach is reserved for campers). The Bear Brook Nature Center also has programs, two nature trails, more than 30 miles of hiking trails in the park with separate marked routes for ski-tourers and snowmobilers in winter. Very crowded on summer weekends but not too bad midweek. Fee.

Pawtuckaway State Park (895-3031), off Route 156, Nottingham.

Open mid-May through mid-October. At Raymond, 3 1/2 miles north of the junction of routes 101 and 156. The attraction is a small beach on 803-acre Lake Pawtuckaway with good swimming, a bathhouse, a 25-acre picnic area, and hiking trails. Rental boats are available; outboard motors are permitted; and the lake is stocked for fishing. Horse Island and Big Island, both accessible to cars, have a total of 170 tent sites, many right on the water; campers have their own boat launch. Trails lead up into the Pawtuckaway Mountains. Both cross-country skiing and snowmobiling are popular here in winter. Camping: $14 for regular sites, $20 for waterfront sites. Day-use fee $2.50 per person.

Silver Lake State Park (465-2342), Route 122, Hollis. A great beach with a bathhouse, concession stand, picnic tables, and a diving raft. More than 100 picnic sites are scattered through the pine groves. Summer weekend crowds come from Nashua but midweek is pleasant. Fee.

Clough State Park (529-7112), Weare. Between Routes 114 and 13 about 5 miles east of Weare. Open daily late June to Labor Day. The focus here is 150-acre Everett Lake, created by the United States Corps of Engineers as a flood-control project. The 50-acre park includes a sandy beach and bathhouses, a picnic grove, and playground. Motorized boats are not permitted, but there is a boat launch and rental boats are available. Fee.

SCENIC DRIVE   Goffstown to New Boston. Both Goffstown and New Boston are unusually handsome towns and the ride between is one of the most pleasant around. The road follows the winding Piscataquog River, a good stream for fishing and canoeing. Take Route 114 west from Manchester and Route 13 to New Boston.

CANOEING   Detailed boating maps ($2.95) and guides ($1.95) of the Merrimack River are available from the **Merrimack River Watershed Council**, 694 Main Street, West Newbury, MA 01985. For information about local rentals and events try 224-8522 or the council's headquarters at 508-363-3777.

GOLF   Candia Woods Golf Club (483-2307), High Street, Candia. Eighteen holes, open to the public.

Valley View Golf Club (774-5031), Dunbarton. Nine holes.

HORSE RACING   Rockingham Park (898-2311), Routes 28 and I-93, Salem. Major league thoroughbred racing.

LODGING   Bedford Village Inn (472-2001), 2 Old Bedford Road, Bedford 03102. Just 12 rooms carved out of an old barn, all with four-poster beds, large screen TVs, Jacuzzi baths, and all rooms opening onto a central meeting space. Rates are $93–$165.

Highlander Inn and Tavern (625-6426), 2 Highland Way, Manchester 03101. Near the airport, an attractive motel with a good restaurant and outdoor pool, rates are $80–$90.

All the chain motels are represented including: **Super 8 Motel** (623-0883), 2301 Brown Avenue, Manchester 03103; rates from $38.

Sheraton Tara Wayfarer Inn (622-3766) at the Bedford Interchange, Route 3 in Bedford 03102. Attractive and handy to the shopping mall; rates are $79–$107.

Nashua also has its representatives from every major chain ranging from **Suisse Chalet** to **Hilton**. **The Fairfield Inn** (424-7500), Route 3, Exit 11, Nashua 03054, is an opulent 114-room motel which has had a name change and rate reduction in the past year. Despite the reproduction antiques, designer wallpapers, and pool, it's $39.95 per room at this writing.

DINING OUT **Café Pavone** (622-5488), 75 Arms Park Drive, Manchester. Open Monday through Saturday for dinner, weekdays for lunch. A trendy trattoria down below Canal Street in the mill complex, featuring seminola pasta made fresh daily. Specialties include homemade fettucini served in a light cream and cheese sauce with shrimp, lobster, and scallops ($14.95) and pasta primavera with fresh sautéed vegetables in a light tomato cream. All pastas come with a cup of minestrone soup or an Italian green salad. All heavier entrées—which range from eggplant parmigiana ($7.59) to veal saltimbocca ($14.95)—come with a pasta marinara. The children's menu includes pizza, pasta, and chicken parmigiana for $4.95; a cup of soup and soft drink included.

Bedford Village Inn (472-2001), 1 Old Bedford Road, Bedford. Open for lunch and dinner daily, Sunday from 3 PM. This beautifully restored (some say over-restored), eighteenth-century house has been the talk of Manchester since its owners went broke investing millions renovating it. The dining rooms are elegant (request one of the smaller rooms in the house itself), and there's also a cheery tavern with its own less-expensive menu. Fare is traditional New England. "Chicken New Hampshire" is a specialty. Entrées range from $12–$20.

Levi Lowells (429-0885), 585 Webster Highway, Merrimack. Three attractive dining rooms with fireplaces and a large menu that ranges from French Nouvelle to "Upbeat New England." Entrées range from braised chicken ($13.50) to roast lamb noisettes ($20.95), and include beef Wellington, a carefully cooked and garnished roast duck, and haddock poached in wine and butter that is finished with smoked Maine shrimp in cream sauce. For appetizers try New England crab cakes or mushroom strudel. Generally ranked among the best places to eat in southern New Hampshire.

Ya Mama's (883-2264), 41 Canal Street, Nashua. Open for lunch Thursday and Friday, for dinner Tuesday through Saturday. Word is getting out about this small, superb Italian restaurant owned and run by Michael and Michelle Ferrazzini. Just 40 people can be seated in the cheery, informal dining room where both northern and southern Italian dishes are lovingly prepared. Entrées run from $6 for pasta to $14.95 for veal Michael; there are usually seafood specials.

High Five Restaurant & Night Club (626-0555), 555 Canal Street, Manchester. Open for lunch Monday through Friday, for dinner nightly, Sunday brunch. On the seventeenth floor of the Wall Street Towers with a spectacular view of Manchester. Traditional menu: veal parmigiana and pasta, surf and turf. Entrées range from $11–$17.

Travers Tavern (497-3978), 7 High Street, Goffstown. Open for dinner Tuesday through Saturday. Fine dining in this gracious old town in a choice of dining rooms. Entrées range from $13–$17.

Lord Jeffrey's (673-7540), The Meeting Place, Route 101, Amherst. A classic, cozy dining room with romantic atmosphere. Specialties include lobster bisque and lobster Savannah, chateaubriand served tableside, and flaming desserts. Entrées range from $11–$20.

EATING OUT   Shorty's Mexican Roadhouse (424-0010), 450 Charles Bancroft Highway (Route 3A), Litchfield. Open daily from 11:30 AM, Sunday from 1 PM. This is a local favorite: a '40s roadhouse atmosphere with Mexican reliables like tacos, fajitas, and enchiladas; also dinner specials like chicken mole and grilled fish with salsa. Entrées from $5; same menu all day.

Café at the Atrium (623-7878), 1001 Elm Street in Manchester's big downtown office complex. Open Monday through Saturday for lunch, Thursday through Saturday for dinner. Tables are small but well spaced in this spacious, bright restaurant. The favored downtown lunch spot specializing in seafood and steak with pastas and interesting sauces. Entrées range from $3.95–$9.95.

Granite Street Bar & Grill (622-0900), 50 Phillipee Cote Street, Manchester. A pleasant, pubby atmosphere and standard menu.

Tiya's Restaurant (669-4365), 8 Hanover Street, Manchester. A clean, attractive Thai eatery well-sited right downtown near the corner of Elm and Hanover. You can get a tuna salad or Reuben, but stir-fry dishes like shrimp, scallops, sea legs, broccoli, pepper, and mushrooms are just $4.95. The house specialty is Pad Thai: stir-fried egg, chicken, bean sprouts, and spicy sauces garnished with crushed peanuts.

The Black Forest (672-0500), Salzburg Square, Route 101, Amherst. Open 9–5 daily. One in a lineup of Austrian-style facades in this shopping mall; known for its pastries, which you can buy to go; also good for omelets, quiche, soups, good shopping-out fare.

ENTERTAINMENT   The Palace Theater (668-5588), 80 Hanover Street (PO Box 3006), Manchester 03105. Opened in 1915, reopened and restored in 1974, this 883-seat theater is a beauty—with small, glittering chandeliers, bright local art, and an intimate feel. Its own resident company mounts six productions a year, and during the summer Stage One Productions (see below) uses the facility to stage musicals. Magic shows, children's theater, ballet, and opera are also frequently performed. Phone for the current program.

Stage One Productions (669-5511), at the Palace Theater, performs dinner theater during winter months and musicals during the summer.

American Stage Festival Theater (673-7515), Milford, stages a series of summer productions, mid-July to early August.

Currier Gallery of Art (669-6144), 192 Orange Street. Concerts are held in the museum's central courtyard once a month, October to April.

The Nashua Center for the Arts (883-1506), 14 Court Street, Nashua. The center sponsors a January to May "Downtown Live" performance series and a Saturday program of children's entertainment. In summer it sponsors outdoor performances in Holman Stadium.

SELECTIVE SHOPPING   *Along "The Strip":*   **The Mall of New Hampshire**, 1500 South Willow Street, has 88 stores including Lechmere, Filene's, and Sears.

K-Mart Plaza, 1535 South Willow Street, has a Filene's Basement Store.

Willow Tree Mall, 575 Willow Street, and **TJ Maxx Plaza**, 933 South Willow Street, are also large.

The Bedford Mall, South River Road, Bedford, has 27 stores including Anderson-Little, Montgomery Ward, Jordan Marsh, and Marshall's.

In Downtown Manchester: **McQuades** (625-5451), 844 Elm Street. Open 9:30–5:30 Monday through Saturday, 12–5 Sunday, and until 9 PM Thursday and Friday. The nicest kind of family-owned clothing store. Coffee is always hot for shoppers and caged birds are chirping. The bargains in the basement range from coats to comforters with plenty for both adults and children. In this the largest of the three McQuades (there's one on Concord's Main Street, another in Nashua's Simoneau Plaza), cash and checks are still shunted from cash registers through tubes.

Anyone expecting to find mill buildings filled with outlets will be disappointed. This is a far cry from Fall River. Most outlets are clumped in a small warehouse complex on Canal Street across from the mills. The only outlets large enough to note are:

Pandora Factory Store (668-4802). Open daily 9–5, Thursday until 9 PM. Sweaters, women's clothing.

Burlington Coat Factory (622-3718). Open daily 9–5; Monday, Thursday, Friday until 9 PM. A large warehouse filled with racks of coats, parkas, and bargain-priced skiwear.

SPECIAL EVENTS   May: **Hillsborough County Annual Sheep and Wool Festival** (763-5859), New Boston. **Little Nature Museum Open House** (529-7180), Weare. Nature activities, guided walks, museum tours.

July: **Family Outdoor Discovery Day,** Bear Brook State Park Campground (see Green Space).

August: **Annual Antique Dealers Show** (286-4908), Manchester.

September: **Riverfest,** Manchester. Three days with fireworks, live entertainment, canoe competitions, country fair exhibits. **Hillsborough County Agricultural Fair** (674-2510), New Boston. **Hanover Street Fine Arts Fair**, Manchester. **Deerfield Fair** (463-7421), Deerfield.

October: **Annual Weare Craft Bazaar**, Weare. **Head Of The Merrimack Regatta** (888-2875), Nashua.

The Concord Area

The golden dome of the state capitol building still towers above downtown Concord. Since 1819, when it was built out of local granite by convict labor, this building has been the forum for the state's legislature—now numbering 400 members—said to be the fourth largest deliberative body in the world.

The Indians called this site Penacook, or "crooked place," for the snake-like turns the Merrimack makes here. Concord's compact downtown clusters along the western bank of the river, and it's encircled by the concrete wall of I-93 along the opposite bank.

Concord owes its prominence to two forgotten phenomena: the Middlesex Canal—opened in 1815 to connect it with Boston—and the steam railroad from Boston, completed in 1842. Today Concord remains an important transportation hub—the point at which I-89 forks off from I-93 to head northwest across New Hampshire and Vermont, ultimately linking Boston with Montreal.

Concord is really just a medium-sized town of 34,500 residents, and you are quickly out of it and in the countryside of East Concord at the Society for the Protection of New Hampshire Forests headquarters or in the western countryside at Silk Farm, New Hampshire's Audubon House.

While still very much in the Merrimack Valley, Concord—in contrast to Manchester—is just beyond southern New Hampshire's old industrial belt with its ethnic mix. Some of Concord's surrounding towns are as Yankee—and as picturesque—as any in New England.

Canterbury Shaker Village, a striking old hilltop community, is a gathering of white wooden buildings surrounded by spreading fields. Hopkinton, a proud early nineteenth-century town, offers a different kind of serenity and some good antiquing. And Henniker is a mill town turned college town, with more to offer visitors than most resorts.

GUIDANCE   The Greater Concord Chamber of Commerce (224-2508), 244 North Main Street (just off I-93, Exit 15), Concord 03301. Open June to Labor Day, Monday through Friday 8:30–5. Easy to miss and with lim-

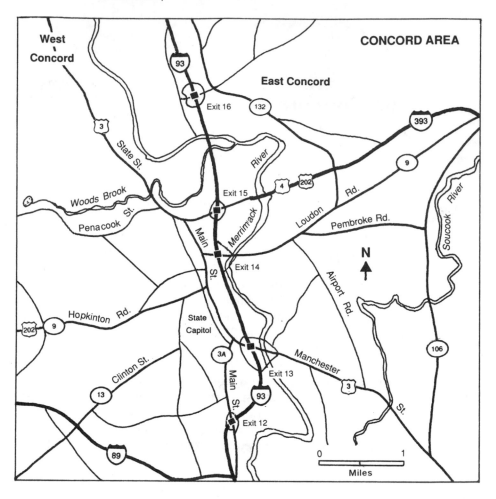

ited parking, but friendly and helpful once you get inside. The chamber also maintains an information kiosk downtown near the state house, open June to Labor Day, dependent on the availability of volunteers.

GETTING THERE   By bus: **The Concord Bus Terminal** (228-3300), Depot Street, is served by Concord Trailways, Peter Pan Bus Lines, and Vermont Transit.

GETTING AROUND   By taxi: **AA Taxi** (225-7433), **A&P Taxi** (224-6573), **Central Taxi** (224-4077). **Hudson Bus Lines** (424-2446), based at 22 Pond Street, Nashua, offers limousine service between pick-up points in Concord, Manchester, downtown Boston, and Logan International Airport.

PARKING   Not a problem downtown.

MEDICAL EMERGENCY   **Concord Hospital** (225-2711), 250 Pleasant Street.

TO SEE AND DO   **Canterbury Shaker Village** (783-9511), Shaker Road, Canterbury 03224. Open early May to late October daily, Monday through Saturday 10–5, Sunday 12–5. The 90-minute guided tours leave on the hour 10–4, and on the half hour during July, August, and October. Open late October to December, Fridays and Saturdays 10–5, Sundays 12–5; in April by special arrangement.

The single most rewarding sight to see in central New Hampshire, this complex of 22 buildings set in 600 acres conjures up a unique, almost vanished way of life that produced many inventions and distinctive art, food, and music. Between the 1780s and 1990 some 2,300 Shaker men, women, and children lived in this rural community, putting their "hands to work and hearts to God." In the 1850s, when this Shaker village owned 4,000 acres with 100 buildings, it was one of 18 such American communes extending from Kentucky to Maine to Ohio. Today just six communities survive in shape enough to tell their story, and Canterbury is one of the few settlements that has never been out of Shaker hands. At this writing Sister Ethel, age 94, continues to follow the way of life she once shared with dozens of "sisters" and "brethren" here. In 1969 Eldress Bertha (who died in 1990) had the foresight to incorporate the present buildings and property as a nonprofit museum.

Nine buildings are presently open, and five are included on the tour—which includes many stories of life as it was lived here, demonstrations of Shaker crafts, and frequently Shaker music in the chapel. (Note the many special happenings listed at the end of this chapter under Special Events.) Special evening dinners and candlelight tours of the village are also offered by reservation ($32 per person) Thursday through Saturday. The village's Creamery Restaurant, generally rated one of the best places to lunch in New Hampshire, is also open daily when the museum is open. $6.75 per adult, $3.50 per child 6–12, $17 per family. Southbound on I-93 the village is marked from Exit 18. Northbound use Exit 15E and follow I-393 east for 5 miles; then Route 106 north for 7 miles and turn at the sign for Shaker Road.

New Hampshire International Speedway (783-4744), Route 106, Loudon. Billed as "the country's newest auto racing facility," it offers a 55,000-seat grandstand, stockcar racing.

Christa McAuliffe Planetarium (271-STAR), 3 Institute Drive, Concord. Take I-93 Exit 15, then east on I-393 to Exit 1 and follow signs. Open Tuesday - Sunday. Christa was a teacher at Concord High School when she was chosen from among 11,000 to be the first teacher-in-space. Dedicated to her memory, this facility, with its dramatic rendition of the universe, has the most sophisticated electronics system of any planetarium. Although geared primarily to schoolchildren, it has a variety of programs. There are several shows daily, but the gen-

Photo courtesy of New Hampshire Historical Society

Historic Concord Coach is on display at the New Hampshire
Historical Society, Concord.

eral public must reserve in advance since seating is limited to 92 persons. $5 per adult, $3 for children, college students, and seniors.

In Concord: A self-guided walking tour of Concord leaflet, "The Coach and Eagle Trail," is available from the chamber of commerce booth. It includes the following:

New Hampshire Historical Society Museum and Library (225-3381), 30 Park Street. Open year-round Monday through Friday 9–4:30, Saturday and Sunday 12–4:30. Closed holidays; library closed Sundays. Free. A classic little museum building with a Concord Coach occupying center stage in the marble rotunda. Here you quickly learn that the Concord Coach, first manufactured in 1827 by wheelwright Lewis Downing and coach builder Stephen Abbot, was soon available in 14 styles. Over the next century more than 3,000 were made in town, each weighing some 2,400 pounds, costing between $775 and $1,250. A painting by John Burgum depicts "an express freight shipment of 30 coaches April 15, 1868, by Abbot, Downing & Co., Concord, NH, to Wells Fargo Co., Omaha, Neb." The picture vividly supports Concord's claim to having helped open up the West.

New Hampshire's only statewide historical society, this is a combination research library/museum, with limited exhibit space and changing exhibits. Fundraising is currently underway to fund "The Museum of New Hampshire History" to be located in a stone warehouse behind the Eagle Hotel. The library will always remain in this classic 1911 building.

New Hampshire State House and The State House Plaza (271-2154), 107 North Main Street. Open year-round, weekdays 8–4:30. A handsome 1819 building, this is the oldest state capitol in which a legislature still meets in its original chambers. A visitors center contains dioramas and changing exhibits. More than 150 portraits of past political figures are displayed.

The Eagle Hotel, North Main Street. For over 135 years the Eagle Hotel was the center of Concord's social and political happenings. Andrew Jackson, Benjamin Harrison, Jefferson Davis, Charles Lindbergh, and Eleanor Roosevelt were all guests. The hotel is now the **Eagle Square Marketplace**, mostly offices with a few shops and a restaurant.

HISTORIC HOUSES   **The Pierce Manse** (224-9620), 14 Penacook Street, Concord. Open mid-June to mid-September, Monday through Friday 11–3, or by advance appointment. Closed holidays. Built in 1838 and moved to its present site in 1971, this Greek Revival structure was home for Franklin and Jane Pierce from 1842–1848, between the time Franklin served in the United States Senate and was elected fourteenth president of the United States. Exhibits include many items owned by the Pierce family prior to 1869.

Kimball-Jenkins Estate (225-3932), 276 North Main Street, Concord. Open for "tea and tours" May to October and for special monthly events throughout the year. Built in 1882, a high Victorian brick and granite mansion with hand-carved oak woodwork, frescoed ceilings, oriental rugs, and many original furnishings. Special events include an October Mystery Night, a December Victorian Christmas, and a March Gilbert and Sullivan dinner theater night. Staff are all in Victorian dress, and any food served is from Victorian recipes.

VILLAGES   *Henniker.*   West of Concord at the junction of routes 9/202 and 114 (take Exit 5 off I-89), the "only Henniker in the world" is a delightful little college town with an outstanding small ski area, cross-country ski center, and a number of interesting shops and restaurants.

When Walter and Hazel Patenaude arrived in Henniker in 1917, it was a bustling crossroads town with a thriving inn, a number of farms, and three mills on the Contoocook River—one mill making bicycle rims; another, handles; and the third, leatherboard for shoes. "The mills went out with the '36 flood," recalls Merle Patenaude. "Then the college came in." An engineer, Patenaude built the covered bridge that's now part of New England College, an institution that arrived in the 1940s and now forms the heart of the town. The former Henniker Inn now houses the college's administration office, and the art gallery next door showcases New England art. The combined student and faculty is roughly 1,000. The college and its graduates have helped revitalize the town, creating a green strip along the Contoocook River that's a pleasant place in summer.

Hopkinton.   Just west of Concord off I-89 with a Main Street that's lined with early white-clapboard mansions, Hopkinton is known for the quality and quantity of its antiques shops and for its old-fashioned State Fair, held Labor Day weekend. **The New Hampshire Antiquarian Society** (746-3825) on Main Street is open year-round, Mondays 1–5 PM and 6:30–8:30 PM and Wednesdays 9–11 AM and 1–5 PM. The collection includes genealogical materials, paintings, and changing exhibits.

COVERED BRIDGES   Hopkinton-Rowell, West Hopkinton. Built in 1853 across the Contoocook River; rebuilt in 1965.

Henniker-New England College. A single-span, 150-foot bridge across the Contoocook River on the New England College campus.

FOR FAMILIES   White's Farm (435-8258), marked from Route 28 (off Routes 4/202) in Pittsfield. Open May to September, daily 10–5. Mike White breeds miniature horses; the petting farm is a sideline. Visitors are welcome to pet the horses, miniature donkeys, goats, and pigs. You won't find any food or soft drink machines, just friendly animals and an atmosphere that will make you want to linger. $3 per adult, $2 per child ages 2–12.

GREEN SPACE   **Audubon Society of New Hampshire Headquarters** (224-9909), 3 Silk Farm Road (follow Audubon signs from I-89 Exit 2), Concord. Open year-round, Monday through Saturday. Exhibits, overview of Audubon centers and programs in the state, Discovery Room with a "touch table," research library, Eyrie for spotting passing birds, and resident barred owls. The adjacent Silk Farm Wildlife Sanctuary offers two trails, one to Great Turkey Pond.

Society for the Protection of New Hampshire Forests Headquarters (224-9945), 54 Portsmouth Street (take I-93 Exit 15 east), East Concord. Open year-round, Monday through Friday 8:30–4:30. The passive solar building has exhibits and a gift shop; sits above its 95-acre spread of pine which stretches down to the river with views of the capitol beyond. A 2-mile nature trails leads down to the Merrimack.

Elm Brook Park and Wildlife Management Area, off Route 127, West Hopkinton. Swimming and picnic areas; built and managed by the United States Army Corps of Engineers.

Hannah Duston Memorial, west of I-93, Exit 17 (4 miles north of Concord), Boscawen. The monument is on an island at the confluence of the Contoocook and Merrimack rivers. It commemorates the courage of Hannah Duston, a woman taken prisoner from Haverhill, Massachusetts, during a 1696 Indian raid. She later made her escape, killing and scalping 10 of her captors (including women and children), at this spot on the river. The 35-foot-high monument, erected in 1874, depicts a busty lady with a tomahawk in one hand and what looks like scalps in the other. Open all winter, but the trail from the parking lot is unplowed in winter.

BICYCLING   **The Biking Expedition** (428-7500), 10 Maple Street, Box 547, Henniker 03242. The specialty is organized long-distance tours for children, but customized tours with a support van, camping, or inn-to-inn tours can be arranged in this area.

CANOEING   See Manchester (Canoeing) for the Merrimack River Watershed Council.

Canterbury Canoes (783-4479), West Road, Canterbury 03224. Rentals.

Hannah's Paddles (753-6695), I-93 Exit 17, Route 4 West, Penacook. Offers rentals and a livery service for the Merrimack and Contoocook rivers.

Note that the Contoocook between West Hopkinton and Henniker is a favored white-water canoeing and kayaking stretch in spring.

FISHING   The **New Hampshire Fish & Game Department** (271-3211 or 271-3421), 2 Hazen Drive, Concord, is a source of information about where to fish as well as how to obtain licenses. Trout fishing is particularly good in this area.

GOLF   **Beaver Meadow Golf Course** (228-8954), Concord. Eighteen holes. **Dustin Country Club** (746-4234), Hopkinton. Nine holes. **Plausawa Valley Country Club** (224-6267), Pembroke. Nine holes.

HORSEBACK RIDING   **Morning Mist Farm** (428-3889), 15 College Hill Road, Henniker. Trail rides by reservation for all levels of riders; also English riding lessons.

DOWNHILL SKIING   **Pat's Peak Ski Area** (428-3245), Route 114, Henniker. The mountain rises steeply right behind the base lodge. It's an isolated 1,400-foot-high hump, its face streaked with expert trails and a choice of intermediate and beginner runs meandering down one shoulder; a half dozen more beginner runs—served by their own lifts—down the other. In all, 14 top-to-bottom trails are served by seven lifts, including a double and triple to the summit. All but a few peripheral trails are covered by snowmaking. Big, old fir trees are salted around the base area, and the summit and some of the intermediate trails—certainly Zephyr, the quarter-mile-long beginner's trail off the top—convey the sense of skimming through the woods. When it comes to expert runs Tornado and Hurricane are wide and straight, but Twister is an old-timer—narrow, twisty, and wooded. Lift tickets are $28 on weekends, $20 midweek, $16 for juniors at all times. A friendly, family-owned and -run area, this is a good place to take lessons.

LODGING   Wyman Farm (783-4467), RFD 13, Box 163, Concord 03301. Despite its urban address this is actually one of the most rural and remote-feeling hideaways around—and one of the most beautiful. This eighteenth-century "extended" cape rambles along the very top of a hill with lawns and fields that seem to roll away indefinitely. The hilltop farm is actually in Loudon, a 10-minute drive from Canterbury Shaker Village. The living room retains its small paned windows and original woodwork, giving a sense of age and comfort. The farm has been in Judith Merrow's family for many generations, and accommodating guests has been a tradition since 1902 when this was "Sunset Lodge" and the going rate for room and board was $5 a week. Today Wyman Farm remains a bargain for the genuine luxury it offers. All three bedrooms have private baths and sitting areas. Breakfast is cooked to order from the menu guests receive when they check in, and it is served in a cheery dining area with a soapstone stove and grandfather clock. Rates are $40–$60 per room.

The Meeting House Inn and Restaurant (428-3228), Flanders Road, Henniker 03242. Up a hill road, right across from the entrance to Pat's Peak, this is a 200-year-old farmhouse with six country-elegant rooms, to which breakfast is delivered in a basket because there is no dining room (instead the barn has been turned into one of the area's most popular dining spots; see Dining Out). Because the restaurant is in an adjoining but separate building, inn guests have their privacy and a common room with a TV and VCR; with the public they share access to the inn's tub and sauna (it's between the inn and restaurant). Rates are $65–$73 double and $93 for the two-room efficiency suites.

Colby Hill Inn (428-3281), just west of the village center, PO Box 778, Henniker 03242. An attractive 200-year-old homestead that's been upscaled as an inn by a series of owners. The 15 guest rooms all have private baths and antiques; $85 double plus 10 percent gratuity.

Lake Shore Farm (942-5521), 25 Jenness Pond Road, Northwood 03261. An informal resort catering to snowmobilers, square dancers, and seniors.

Hitching Post B&B (798-4951), Routes 4 and 202, Chichester 03301. An eighteenth-century farmhouse featuring fabulous breakfasts.

DINING OUT   Crystal Quail Restaurant (269-4151), Pitman Road, Center Barnstead. Dinner by reservation, Wednesday through Sunday. BYOB. You may luck out and find a free table tonight, but this unusual restaurant—limited to just a dozen patrons per night who dine on five courses in the dining room of an eighteenth-century house—is frequently booked at least a week in advance. Three entrées are always offered, and one is always a game dish, not necessarily but frequently quail. Organically raised veal is another specialty, and there is often a vegetarian (organic) dish. Needless to say, everything is made from scratch, and the desserts are exquisite. Be sure to ask for directions—there is no sign outside, and Barnstead is one of those towns webbed with back roads; even chef/owner Harold Huckaby admits to not knowing them all. $40 prix fixe.

The Horseshoe Tavern (746-4501), Route 103, Hopkinton. Open for lunch Tuesday through Friday, dinner Tuesday through Sunday, and Sunday brunch. Chef-owned with a reputation for consistent high quality. The setting is an old house with one large and three smaller dining rooms—an elegant, intimate atmosphere. The emphasis is on fresh ingredients, and the soups, salad dressings, and baking, as well as the sauces, are all made from scratch. Specialties include seafood and veal, prepared a variety of ways. Dinner entrées are $12.95–$18.95 and include salad and vegetables.

Candlelight Evening at the Creamery (783-9511), 288 Shaker Road, Canterbury. Chef Jeffrey Paige has an excellent reputation for dishes like sherried pumpkin apple soup, corn and blueberry salad, and baked sole with salmon stuffing. The candlelight evening meals are by reservation only, Thursday through Saturday at 7 PM. $32 prix fixe includes a guided, candlelit tour of Canterbury Shaker Village. (Also see Eating Out.)

Eagle Court (228-1982), 1 Eagle Square, Concord. Open for lunch, dinner, Sunday brunch. This large space is broken into a number of pleasant areas, and the fare has earned an excellent reputation. The menu is traditional: veal Oscar, baked native haddock, duckling with apricot plum glaze. Prices range from $9.95–$14.95. "You can spend a lot of money here, and you can also dine very reasonably," observes Gregory Makris, co-owner with his brother James.

Vercelli's (228-3313), 11 Depot Street, Concord. Open Monday through Friday for lunch and dinner; also Saturday dinner. This gets top votes from many Concordians as the best place in town—spacious and fashionably pink, black, and green, with traditional Italian specialties and decadent desserts. Prices range from $11–$15.

Thursday's (224-2626), 6–8 Pleasant Street, Concord. Open Monday through Saturday for lunch; also Sunday brunch. An informal, friendly dining room with excellent soups and stews, quiches, and crêpes. Light and reasonably priced dinner specialties include chicken mandalay and vegetable and cheese strudel. Entrées range from $6–$13.

The Meeting House Inn and Restaurant (428-3228), 35 Flanders Road (off Route 114, across from Pat's Peak), Henniker. Open for dinner Wednesday through Saturday 5–9:30 PM, Sunday 4–8 PM. You enter through an inviting, solar-sided pub—its walls hung with dozens of baggies filled with sand that patrons have sent from all corners of the world. The attractive dining area fills this 200-year-old barn. Specialties range from breast of chicken basque with sweet Italian sausage and pimentos in chicken stock and white wine ($12.50) to beef Wellington ($17.95). Lunch can be a char-broiled Angus burger or ribs. The favorite dessert at all meals is mud pie.

Daniel's (428-7621), Main Street, Henniker. Open for lunch Monday through Saturday, dinner nightly, Sunday brunch. An unusually attractive dining space that overlooks the Contoocook River; there's also a brick-walled lounge. Lunch can be a Mediterranean salad (fresh greens, roast turkey, smoked ham, and imported cheeses garnished with marinated vegetables for $5.25) or simply a Cajun burger. For dinner you might try chicken Contoocook, a breast of chicken baked with an apple, walnut, sausage stuffing and glazed with a maple cider sauce ($11.95).

Colby Hill Inn (428-3281), off Western Avenue, Henniker. Open Tuesday through Saturday 5:30–8:30 PM, Sunday in-season. Candlelight makes the paneling and furniture glow, and the view of fields adds to the romantic old-country-tavern feel of this dining room. You can dine on lobster and crabmeat pie ($18.95) or veal Oscar ($21.95).

Country Spirit (428-7007), junction of routes 202/9, and 114, Henniker. Open daily 11–9, Friday and Saturday until 10 PM; closed Christmas and Thanksgiving. Walls are festooned with memorabilia from "the only Henniker on earth": old tools, signs, and photos. The ceiling of the tavern is literally wadded with dollar bills (all donated by patrons) which the restaurant passes on to charity at regular intervals. Specialties include the restaurant's own smoked meats, aged Angus sirloin, and fresh fish. Dinner menu ranges from $9.95 for fresh Boston scrod to $15.75 for steak.

EATING OUT   The Creamery (783-9511), 277 Shaker Road, Canterbury. Lunch Monday through Saturday. The soups and breads are outstanding, and all the Shaker-inspired dishes are imaginative and nicely herbed and spiced.

Tio Juan's (224-2821), 1 Bicentennial Square, Concord. Open nightly from 4 PM. This former police station is now the downtown singles bar. A great place to dine in the old jail cells (very private) on Mexican fare: burritos, quesadillas, tacos, and enchiladas.

Hermanos Cocina Mexicana (224-5669), 6 Pleasant Street Extension, Concord. Open for lunch and dinner except Sundays. Yet another Mexican restaurant, and this one gets high ratings for authenticity and incredible margaritas.

Capitol City Diner, just off I-93 Exit 13, Concord. Open daily 6 AM–9 PM. A great highway stop; '50s diner atmosphere under the same ownership as The Common Man (see the Lake Winnipesaukee Region [Dining Out]). Specials like 99-cent hamburger nights and Saturdays when you dine half-price if you come in a '50s or '60s car.

The Grist Mill Restaurant and Bow Mills Pub (226-1922), just off I-89 in Bow. This is a large, attractive new place built on an old mill site; a good way stop with an immense all-day menu, everything from a tuna salad sandwich to a Cajun blackened 10-oz. sirloin ($11.95).

SELECTIVE SHOPPING   *Antiques:*   Route 4 between the Epson Circle and the Lee Rotary is widely known as "Antique Alley." The more than two dozen shops here represent up to 400 dealers; the primary customers are antiques store owners and other dealers from throughout the country. This area is just far enough off the beaten tourist path to make for exceptional pickings. For a flyer listing and mapping most of the shops, contact Town Pump Antiques, Route 4, Box 288, Northwood 03261.

Hopkinton represents another cluster of antiques shops.

Crafts: **Canterbury Shaker Village** (783-9511), Shaker Road, Canterbury. The museum shop features Shaker crafts (see To See and Do).

Shaker Pine Crafts Center (783-4403), 418 Shaker Road, Canterbury. Shaker reproductions, crafts, toys, wrought iron.

North Woods Chair Shop (783-4595), 237 Tilton Road, Canterbury. Open Monday through Friday 12:30–4:30 PM, Saturday 9–1. Fine Shaker-style furniture and furnishings.

The League of New Hampshire Craftsmen (224-1471) is headquartered at 205 North Main Street (a red colonial across from the chamber of commerce office just off I-93 Exit 15) in Concord. The gallery here is open weekdays and has changing shows. The league's downtown shop in Phenix Hall, 36 North Main Street (228-8171), is open Monday through Saturday and has juried crafts in a range of media and prices.

Mark Knipe Goldsmiths (224-2920), 13 South State Street, Concord. Custom-made jewelry studio and gallery.

The Fiber Studio (428-7830), Foster Hill Road, Henniker. Open year-round Tuesday through Saturday 10–4. Wide selection of natural knitting/weaving yarns and spinning fibers; looms, spinning wheels, knitting machines, handwoven and knit items, workshops.

Country Quilter (746-5521), Hatfield Road (follow signs from routes 202/9), Hopkinton. Open May to December, Tuesday through Sunday 10–5:30; closed Sundays rest of the year. Ready-made and made-to-order quilts, pillows, wall hangings, and handcrafts in a 200-year-old barn.

The Fragrance Shop (746-4431), College Hill Road, Hopkinton. Open May to Christmas, Tuesday through Saturday 10–5. An eighteenth-century barn filled with potpourri, herb wreaths, crafts, and a display garden. Follow signs from Hatfield Road (see Country Quilter above).

Special shops: **Granite State Candy Shoppe** (225-2591), 13 Warren Street, Concord. A great old-fashioned candy shop that's been in business since 1927, making its own mints and butter chocolate creams among a wide assortment of chocolates, all made on the premises. A number of customers are also hooked on the freshly roasted cashews.

Caring Gifts (228-8496), 11 Hills Avenue, Concord. Specializes in baskets filled with everything from toys to gourmet foods, depending on the need.

Britches of Concord (255-4184), One Eagle Square, Suite 105, Concord. The city's number one tweedy and traditional clothing source.

Rare Essentials (226-2407), 97 North Main Street, Concord. Housed in a former bank building, a boutique with imaginative and expensive women's clothing and accessories.

McQuade's (228-5451), 45 North Main Street, Concord. Like the Manchester store, this family-run Merrimack Valley chain features caged birds and basement bargains.

The New Hampshire Winery (428-WINE), 38 Flanders Road (the access road to Pats Peak Ski Area—2 miles south of the village off Route 114), Henniker. Founded in 1964 near Lake Winnipesaukee and moved to Henniker in 1990, this remains the only grape winery in northern New England. Open daily 10 AM–9 PM, closed certain holidays so please call ahead. At present the vineyard is producing a wide variety of white and red wines ranging in price from $5–$12.

The Golden Pineapple, off routes 202/9, Henniker. A trove of unusual gifts.

SPECIAL EVENTS   May: **Annual Herb Day,** Shaker Village, Canterbury. Plants, herbal crafts, garden tours, demos.

June: **Annual Farm Day,** Shaker Village, Canterbury. Plowing contest, working sheep dogs, horse-shoeing, butter churning, hayrides. **New Hampshire Concord Coach & Carriage Festival,** early June at New Hampshire Technical Institute, Concord. Horse-drawn parade, rides, competitions.

July Fourth Fireworks, Memorial Field, Concord. **Strawberry Festival,** Contoocook. 5-kilometer road race, 5-mile canoe race, parade, strawberries.

Early July: **statewide fireman's muster,** Pembroke.

Mid-July: **Old Fashion Bargain Days,** downtown Concord. Main Street closes to traffic for three days; entertainment.

End of July: **Canterbury Fair,** Canterbury. Chicken BBQ, auction, antiques, juried crafts, Morris Dancers. **Annual Bean Hole Bash Weekend,** Northwood. Food, games, raffle, auction, flea market.

August: **Annual Hot Air Balloon Rally,** Drake Field, Pittsfield. Twenty balloons usually come; arts, crafts, entertainment. **Annual Northwood Community Craftsmen's Fair,** Northwood. Country fair, more than 60 craftsmen, music, food, folk dancers, flower show.

September: **Annual Kiwanis Antique & Classic Car Show,** New Hampshire Technical Institute, Concord. **Annual Wool Day at Canterbury Shaker Village,** Canterbury. Natural dyeing, rag-rug weaving, fleece-to-shawl.

October: **Annual Harvest Day at Canterbury Shaker Village,** Canterbury. Ox-cart rides, apple head dolls, pumpkin paintings.

December 31: **First Night New Hampshire,** Concord. New Year's Eve, some 130 performances in 30 locations around the city.

III. The Monadnock Region

Pittsburg

Colebrook

VII

Stark

Berlin

Whitefield
Littleton
Franconia
VIc.
Woodsville
Lincoln
N. Woodstock
VIb.

VIa.
Jackson

N. Conway

Waterville Valley

Plymouth
Va.
Lake Winnipesauke
Hanover
Lebanon
IV
Vb.
Wolfeboro
Laconia
New London
Claremont

Concord
Dover
I
II
Portsmouth
Manchester
Exeter
Hampton
Isles of Shoals
III
Hampton
Beach
Keene
Peterborough

Peterborough, Keene, and surrounding villages

Mt. Monadnock towers a dramatic 2,000 feet above the surrounding roll of southwestern New Hampshire. Not only is the mountain visible from up to 50 miles in every direction, it's as much a part of the dozens of surrounding towns as the steeple on their meetinghouses.

Uplands around the mountain, in turn, rise like a granite island a thousand feet above the rest of southern New Hampshire. Hardy spruce, fir, and birch are the dominant trees, and the rugged terrain has deflected both developers and interstate highways.

Depending on where you draw the line, the Monadnock Region as a whole encompasses some 40 towns, all characterized by narrow roads, quintessential New England villages, and mountain vistas.

A region of rushing streams, this entire area was once spotted with small nineteenth-century mills, and many of these buildings survive. Harrisville, with its two cupola-topped mills graceful as churches, is said to be the country's most perfectly preserved early nineteenth-century mill village. Larger brick mill buildings in South Peterborough and in Keene now house shops and restaurants, and a half dozen old mills are still producing a wide variety of products: paper, light bulbs, and matchbooks for starters.

Mt. Monadnock itself spawned the region's tourism industry early in the nineteenth century. Early settlers had trimmed its lower beard of hardwood and spruce, planting orchards and pasturing sheep between tidy stone walls, right up its rocky shoulders. Then they took to burning the summit. The idea was to kill off the wolves, but the effect was to expose the mountain's bald pate. Once this bare spot was created, alpine flora (usually found only on mountains twice as high) took root, and hikers could enjoy not only the high altitude landscape but also the spectacular view.

"Grand Monadnock" quickly became a famous freak. By 1823 a shed, the "Grand Monadnock Hotel," was selling refreshments just below the summit, and a rival, "Dinsmore's comfortable shantee," opened high on the mountain a few years later. By the '50s local farmers and innkeepers had blazed trails up every side of the Monadnock, and from 100 to 400 people could be found hiking them on any good day.

In the 1850s the mountain had inspired works by Henry David Thoreau and Ralph Waldo Emerson; and around the turn of the century, Dublin became known as a literary and art colony—writers included Samuel Clemens and Willa Cather, artists included Abbot Thayer, Frank Benson, and Rockwell Kent. In 1908 the MacDowell Colony in Peterborough became one of the country's first formal retreats for musicians, artists, and writers. The region's cultural climate remains rich, expressed through the unusual number of art galleries and musical and theatrical productions.

Most of the nineteenth-century summer hotels around Mt. Monadnock are long gone, but a half dozen of the region's earlier stagecoach taverns survive, and over the past few years a couple dozen attractive bed & breakfasts have opened.

So the Monadnock Region is once more a destination area. But even innkeepers will tell you that a resort area it isn't. Residents take pride in the fact that Mt. Monadnock is the world's second most heavily hiked mountain (after Mt. Fuji in Japan), but everyone wants to keep the region's roads as delightfully little-trafficked as they are.

While Mt. Monadnock itself is unquestionably the region's spiritual and physical hub, there's some rivalry between Keene and Peterborough for recognition as its commercial center. In fact they are twin centers: Keene for the western region, Connecticut River Valley towns and Peterborough for the hillier eastern side of the region.

Keene (population 22,351) is the shire town of Cheshire County, home of Keene State College and the place most residents of southwestern New Hampshire come to go to the movies and the hospital or to seriously shop. Peterborough (population 5,162) prides itself on having "the first tax-supported Free Public Library in the world," on having inspired Thornton Wilder to write "Our Town," and on serving as home for one of New England's oldest summer theaters. It also offers some unexpectedly fine shopping and dining.

The Monadnock Region remains pristine in part because of its location: too near Boston to be viewed as a place to spend the night, too far from New York to draw the crowds that tend to get no farther east than Vermont. So it happens that despite its beauty; its ski areas and cross-country ski centers; its hiking trails, biking routes, and wealth of antiques shops; and the quality of lodging and dining, prices are relatively and refreshingly low.

GUIDANCE   **The Monadnock Travel Council,** composed of the area's four chambers of commerce, publishes a useful brochure/guide to the region, available at all local chambers.

Greater Keene Chamber of Commerce (352-1303), 8 Central Square, Keene 03431. The Keene chamber's easy-to-find, walk-in office is also a source of brochures and detailed information about the western and Connecticut River Valley sides of the region.

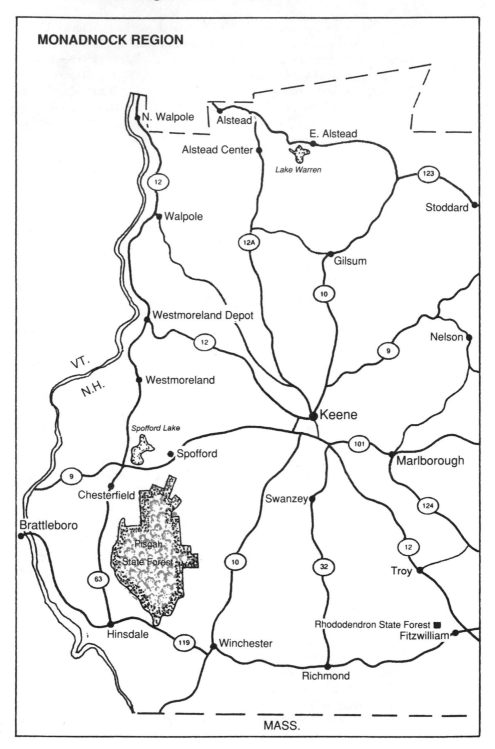

MONADNOCK REGION

N. Walpole

Alstead

E. Alstead

Alstead Center

Lake Warren

123

Stoddard

12

Walpole

12A

Gilsum

10

Westmoreland Depot

Nelson

12

9

VT.

N.H.

Westmoreland

Spofford Lake

Keene

Spofford

101

Marlborough

9

Chesterfield

Swanzey

124

Brattleboro

Pisgah
State Forest

12

10

32

Troy

63

Rhododendron State Forest

Hinsdale

119

Winchester

Fitzwilliam

Richmond

MASS.

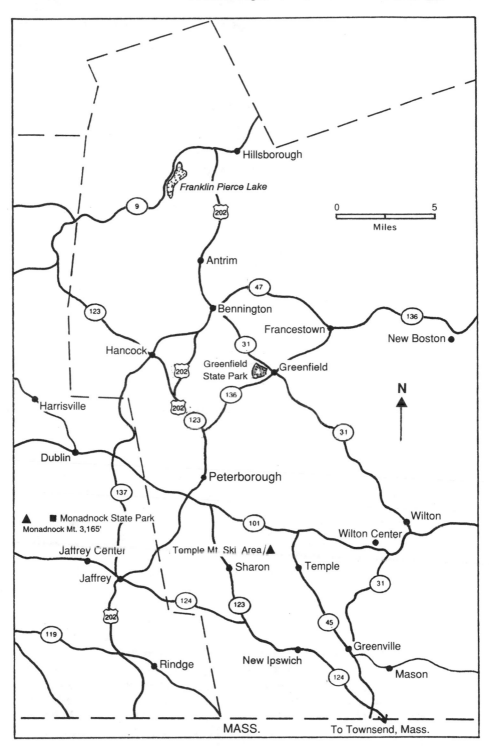

Hillsborough

Franklin Pierce Lake

9

202

0   5
Miles

Antrim

47

123

Bennington

Francestown

136

New Boston

31

Hancock

202

Greenfield
State Park

Greenfield

Harrisville

202

136

N

123

31

Dublin

Peterborough

137

Wilton

Monadnock State Park
Monadnock Mt. 3,165'

101

Wilton Center

31

Jaffrey Center

Temple Mt. Ski Area/▲

Temple

Sharon

Jaffrey

124

123

31

202

45

119

Greenville

Rindge

New Ipswich

Mason

124

MASS.

To Townsend, Mass.

Peterborough Chamber of Commerce (924-7234), PO Box 401, Peterborough 03458, publishes a booklet guide to the 20 central and eastern towns in the region, and the walk-in information center (with a rest room) at the junction of routes 101 and 202 is unusually friendly and helpful.

Jaffrey Chamber of Commerce, PO Box 2, Jaffrey 03452, publishes its own helpful brochure.

GETTING THERE   By air: **Jaffrey Municipal Airport** (532-7763) and **Dillant & Hopkins Airport** in Keene (357-9835) are both private.

By bus: **Vermont Transit Lines** (800-451-3292; in Keene 352-1331) stops a half-dozen times a day in Keene (Gilbo Avenue), Troy, Fitzwilliam, and West Rindge, en route from Boston to Montreal. The Fitzwilliam stop is right at the Fitzwilliam Inn, putting this exceptional town within reach of car-free urbanites.

GETTING AROUND   Taxi: **Countryside Limo Service** (924-7229).

MEDICAL EMERGENCY   **Cheshire Hospital** (352-4111), 580 Courts Street, Keene.

Monadnock Community Hospital (924-7191), Old Street Road, Peterborough. 24-hour emergency department.

TO SEE AND DO   **Cathedral of the Pines** (899-3300), marked from Route 119, a few miles east of Route 202, Rindge. Open May to October, 9 AM–dusk. Tall pine trees shelter the simple wooden benches, and the backdrop of the ridge-top stone altar is Mt. Monadnock, rising grandly beyond intervening, heavily wooded hills. The roadside farmhouse and its 400 acres had been the summer home for Douglas and Sibyl Sloane for quite some time before the 1938 hurricane exposed this magnificent view, and their son Sandy picked the site for his future home. When Sandy was shot down over Germany in 1944, his parents dedicated the hilltop "Cathedral" to his memory. In 1956 the United States Congress recognized it as a national memorial to all American war dead. It's used for frequent nondenominational services and for weddings (performed in the nearby stone Hilltop House in case of rain). On the stone Memorial Bell Tower at the entrance to the pine grove, four bronze bas-reliefs, designed by Norman Rockwell, honor American Women. A museum in the basement of the Hilltop House is a mix of religious and military pictures and artifacts, thousands of items donated by visitors from throughout the country. Visitors are welcome to stroll the extensive grounds. Please: no dogs, no smoking, no picnicking (the Annett Wayside Area is a mile up the road).

HISTORIC HOUSES AND MUSEUMS   **The Barrett Mansion** (878-3283), Main Street, New Ipswich. Open June to October, Tuesday, Thursday, Saturday, and Sunday noon–5 PM; admission $2. One of New England's finest Federal-style rural mansions, built in 1800 as a wedding gift. The bride's father is said to have boasted he would furnish as large a house as the groom's father could build. Both fathers outdid themselves, and it remained in the family until 1948. The rich furnishings are mainly Empire and Victorian, and they offer a sense of the surprisingly early sophistication of this area.

Franklin Pierce Homestead (478-3165 or 464-5858), 3 miles west of town near the junction of routes 9 and 31, Hillsborough. Open Friday through Sunday and Monday holidays; only weekends in May, June, and September. This is the restored, vintage 1804 home of the fourteenth president of the United States, the only one from New Hampshire. The hip-roofed, twin-chimney colonial house is beautifully restored to illustrate the gracious home Pierce lived in during his boyhood.

Jaffrey Civic Center (532-6527), just west of the junction of routes 202 and 137, Jaffrey. Open year-round, Monday through Saturday 1:30–5 PM. A historical society collection with information about past Jaffrey personalities like Willa Cather, Amos Fortune, and Hannah Davis (see Jaffrey Center under Villages) and changing exhibits by local artists. Films are also occasionally shown. Note the "Buddies" World War I monument outside carved from one block of granite.

Peterborough Historical Society (924-3235), Grove Street, Peterborough. Open Monday through Wednesday 10–4; 2–4 for guided tours in July and August; admission $1. An unusually large and handsome facility with an intriguing upstairs exhibit of the town's past products—from thermometers to soapstone stoves. Even a quick visit will help fill in the obviously missing buildings along Grove and Main streets. Note the photos of the big old Tavern Hotel that stood at the head of Grove Street and in the middle of Main Street until 1965; of the Depot; and of the Phoenix Cotton Mill that used to stand near the middle of town. Two of the old mill houses have been preserved behind the museum, one depicting a mill girl's boarding house and the other, a family home. An early general store and kitchen can be seen in the museum's basement. There is also an extensive research library.

Swanzey Historical Museum, Swanzey. Open daily summer through foliage season, Monday through Friday 1–5 PM, Saturday and Sunday 10–6. Exhibits include a steam fire pumper made in Manchester and an authentic stagecoach.

In Keene: **Horatio Colony House Museum** (352-0460), 199 Main Street. Open mid-May to mid-October, Tuesday through Saturday 11–4; free on Saturdays. A Federal-era home filled with elegant family furnishings and souvenirs collected by Horatio and Mary Colony from their extensive travels throughout the world. Special collections include cribbage boards, walking sticks, Buddhas, beer steins, paperweights, and thousands of books.

The Colony House Museum (357-0889), 104 West Street. Open June to Labor Day, Tuesday through Saturday 11–4; Labor Day to

Columbus Day, Saturday 11–4; admission $1. An outstanding Federal-style house with a fine collection of early glass and Hampshire Pottery produced in Keene between 1871 and 1923. Revolutionary-era silver and documents, antique dolls, Civil War relics, and fine china are also displayed.

The Wyman Tavern (352-1895), 39 Main Street. Open June to Labor Day, 11–4. This was the scene of the first meeting of the trustees of Dartmouth College under President Eleazar Wheelock in 1770, and it was from this site that 29 of Keene's Minute Men set out for Lexington in April of 1775.

Historical Society of Cheshire County (352-1895), 246 Main Street. Open weekdays 9–5. Primarily an archival library, the building also contains a "Monadnock Room" hung with paintings by members of the Dublin art colony (see Introduction) and another room with works by muralist Barry Faulkner.

Thorne-Sagendorph Gallery at Keene State College (358-2719). At this writing the gallery is in the Mason Library Building, but it is due to move to the Arts Center on Brickyard Pond sometime in 1991. An extensive permanent collection of nineteenth-century landscapes and changing exhibits.

COVERED BRIDGES   **The Swanzey area,** just south of Keene, boasts one of the densest concentrations of covered bridges in the country. My favorite is the white, red-roofed **Winchester-Ashuelot** built in 1864 across the Ashuelot River just off Route 119 in Ashuelot.

The 1830s **Winchester-Coombs bridge** across the Ashuelot is west of Route 10, one-half mile southwest of Westport.

The 1860s **Swanzey-Slate bridge** across the Ashuelot is east of Route 10 at Westport.

The 1830s, 155-foot **Swanzey-West Swanzey bridge** across the Ashuelot is east of Route 10 at West Swanzey.

Swanzey-Sawyer's Crossing, rebuilt in 1859, bridges the Ashuelot 1 mile north of Route 32 at Swanzey Village.

The Swanzey-Carlton bridge across the South Branch of the Ashuelot River is east of Route 32, 1/2 mile south of Swanzey Village.

Off by itself 1 mile east of Route 202 or 3 1/2 miles west of Greenfield is the **Hancock-Greenfield bridge,** built in 1937, which spans the Contoocook.

VILLAGES   Each of these small centers fits everyone's vision of what a New England village should look like. Each has a town clerk, listed with directory assistance, who can furnish further information.

Alstead.   There are actually three Alsteads (pronounced "Aalsted"), a grouping of quiet hill towns in the northwestern corner of the region, not far from the Connecticut River. From the handsome old white houses and the Congregational Church in East Alstead, Route 123 dips down by Lake Warren—into Mill Hollow, by eighteenth-century waterpowered

Chase's Mill, and by Vilas Pool, an unusual dammed swimming area with an elaborate island picnic spot, complete with carillon. The center of Alstead includes a general store and the Shedd-Porter Memorial Library, a domed neoclassic revival building given by native-son John Shedd. Shedd was an associate of Marshall Field, who gave an almost identical library to his home town of Conway. Turn left at the library and follow Hill Road up into Alstead Center, another hilltop cluster of old homes. It's a quick ride back to Keene via Route 12A.

Dublin.   The flagpole in the middle of the village sits 1,493 feet above sea level, making it New Hampshire's highest village center. But the best views (a mile or so west on Route 101) are of Mt. Monadnock rising above Dublin Lake. Large old summer homes are sequestered in the greenery around the lake and on wooded heights which enjoy this view. The original offices of *Yankee Magazine* and *The Old Farmer's Almanac* are in the middle of the village, as is the "oldest public library in the United States supported by private funds."

Fitzwilliam.   The buildings gathered around this handsome green include an elegantly steepled town hall, an inviting double-porched inn, and a number of pillared and Federal-style homes, one now a library and another a friendly historical society called the **Amos J. Blake House.** The Amos J. Blake House, open Memorial Day to Labor Day on Saturdays 10–4 and Sundays noon–4, has a small country store selling local food and crafts. Its 13 rooms include a law office, old-time schoolroom, military room, and a vintage 1779 fire engine.

The town hall was first built as a Congregational Church in 1816 and then totally rebuilt after lightning struck it the following year. The spire is four-tiered: a belfry above the clock tower, then two octagonal lanterns topped by a steeple and a weathervane. The facade below is graced by a Palladian window and slender Ionic pillars set in granite blocks quarried right in town. Of course, the bell was cast by Paul Revere.

Laurel Lake on the western fringe of town is a favorite local swimming hole, and Pinnacle Mountain, just down the street from the Fitzwilliam Inn, offers inviting walks in summer and cross-country skiing in winter. For a description of Rhododendron State Park on the edge of town, see Green Space. Also see Antiques under Selective Shopping.

Francestown.   Named for Governor Wentworth's wife, Francestown has an almost feminine grace. The white-pillared, 1801 meetinghouse (site of monthly contra dances) stands across from the old meetinghouse at the head of a street lined on both sides by graceful Federal-era houses. One of these is now the George Homens Bixby Memorial Library with wing chairs, rag rugs, and a children's story corner that many a passing adult would like an excuse to curl up in. Pick up a guide to local antiques shops in the Francestown General Store. Crotched Mountain is just up the road (see Hiking).

Greenfield.   Greenfield is best known for its state park, with Otter Lake as its centerpiece, and for the Crotched Mountain Rehabilitation Center, which sits high on the shoulder of the mountain and has spectacular views. The village itself is appealing. The vintage 1795 Congregational Church is the oldest meetinghouse in New Hampshire, serving both as a church and a town hall. It stands tall with maples in front and a graveyard curving up the hill behind. It was built from local timber by Hugh Gregg and his descendant, Governor Judd Gregg, who lives here in town. The heart of the village is Greenfield Industries, a mansard-roofed complex across from the church and a source of penny candy, locally made quilts, and Swedish oatmeal cookies.

Harrisville.   What excites historians about this pioneer mill village is the uncanny way in which it echoes New England's earliest villages. Here life revolved around the mills instead of the meetinghouse: the mill owner's mansion supplanted the parsonage and the millpond was the common. What excites most other people about Harrisville is its beauty. This little community of brick and granite and white-trimmed buildings clusters around a millpond and along the steep Goose Creek Ravine below. The two mills have cupolas, and the string of wooden workers' houses, "Peanut Row," is tidy. Two decades ago when the looms ceased weaving, townspeople worried that the village would become an industrial version of Old Sturbridge Village. Instead new commercial uses have been found for the old buildings, a few of them appropriately filled by Harrisville Designs (see Special Programs and Selective Shopping), founded by John Colony III the year after his family's mill closed. "Wool has been spun here every year since 1790," he notes.

Hancock.   The John Hancock Inn, one of the oldest, continuously operating inns in New England, forms the centerpiece of this village, and Norway Pond shimmers on the edge. There's also a green with a bandstand. A number of the aristocratic old homes have been occupied by "summer people" since the mid-nineteenth century. The Harris Center for Conservation Education (see Hiking) offers guided and unguided walks and workshops.

Jaffrey Center.   Jaffrey itself is a workaday town, but Jaffrey Center, west on Route 124 just east of Mt. Monadnock, is a gem. Its centerpiece is a white, steepled meetinghouse built in 1773, the site of the summer lecture series known as the Amos Fortune Forum (see Entertainment). Willa Cather, who spent many summers in attic rooms at the Shattuck Inn writing two of her best known books, *My Antonia* and *Death Comes to the Archbishop*, is buried in the cemetery here. So are Amos Fortune (1710–1801), an African-born slave who bought his freedom, established a tannery, and left funds for the Jaffrey church and schools; and "Aunt" Hannah Davis (1748–1863), a beloved spinster who made, trademarked, and sold this country's first wooden bandboxes. The

Photo by W. A. Russell

The Old Meetinghouse at Jaffrey Center, with Mt. Monadnock in the background.

Monadnock Inn, in the middle of the village, welcomes visitors year-round.

Mason.   Another picture-perfect cluster of Georgian- and Federal-style homes around a classic Congregational Church, complete with horse sheds and linked by stone walls. A historic marker outside one modest old house explains that this was the boyhood home of Samuel Wilson (1766–1844), generally known as "Uncle Sam" because the beef that he supplied to the army during the War of 1812 was branded "U.S."

Nelson.   This quiet gathering of buildings includes an 1841 Greek Revival and Gothic Revival church and an early, plain-faced but acoustically fine, town hall that's the site of contra dancing every Monday night and the third Thursday of every month, sponsored by the Monadnock Folklore Society (see Entertainment).

Stoddard.   Sited on a height-of-land that's said to divide the Connecticut and Merrimack rivers watersheds, Stoddard is known for the fine glass pro-

duced in three (long-gone) nineteenth-century factories. The Stoddard
Historical Society is open Sundays 2–4 PM in July and August.

Temple.   The common, framed by handsome old homes and a tavern, is classic. Known for its glass works in the eighteenth century, Temple is
now known chiefly for its band, founded in 1799 (see Entertainment).

Walpole.   A particularly handsome grouping of houses around a common
with a fine Unitarian Church. Summer band concerts are staged on the
common, and the historical museum (displaying costumes, dolls,
paintings, and tools), is open Sundays 2–5 PM in July and August.

Wilton Center.   Just off Route 101, but seemingly many miles away, is a ridge
line of grand old houses ranging from eighteenth-century to late nineteenth-century summer homes. Continue through the center of town,
and follow signs to the Frye's Measure Mill (654-6581; open May to
December 15, Tuesday through Saturday 10–4), a red clapboard and
shingled nineteenth-century mill, its works still waterpowered, turning out Shaker-style boxes.

FOR FAMILIES   Friendly Farm (563-8444), Route 101, Dublin. Open daily 10–5
(weather permitting), late April to Labor Day, then weekends through
mid-October. $3.50 per adult, $2.50 per child. Operated since 1965 by
Allan and Bruce Fox, this 7-acre preserve is filled with barnyard animals: cows, horses, pigs, goats, sheep, donkeys, chickens, geese,
turkeys, rabbits, and a working beehive. Feeding and cuddling welcome. Don't forget your camera. (Honest, we usually don't go for
these things but the photo of Chris's presently 165-pound son feeding
a Friendly Farm goat when he was a cute little thing is one of her most
prized possessions.)

Monadnock Children's Museum (357-5161), 147 Washington
Street, Keene. Open 10–4 daily. The museum, a vintage 1840s house
with translucent minerals lit up in its stairs, has a real tree house to
climb into and a variety of engaging and changing exhibits.

GREEN SPACE   Pack Monadnock Mountain in **Miller State Park** (924-7433),
Route 101, 3 miles east of Peterborough. For those who don't feel up
to climbing Mt. Monadnock, this 2,300-foot-high summit is a must. A
1 1/2-mile winding, steep but paved road leads to the top where there
are walking trails, picnic sites, and views of Vermont to the west and
(on a good day) Boston skyscrapers to the south. Opened in 1891, this
was New Hampshire's first state park.

Chesterfield Gorge, Route 9, Chesterfield. Open weekends from
Memorial Day, daily from late June to mid-October. Footpaths along
the gorge were carved by a stream that cut deep into ledges. The half-
mile trail crosses the stream several times, and there are plenty of picnic tables within sound and sight of the rushing water. Nominal fee
on weekends and holidays.

Rhododendron State Forest, Route 119 west of the village,
Fitzwilliam. The wild rhododendron grow up to 30 feet high and are

salted along paths above wildflowers and ferns and under pine trees. It is one of those deeply still and beautiful places. These *Rhododendron maximum* bloom in mid-July. A great place for a picnic.

The Heald Tract, off Route 31 near Greenville. A new Society for the Protection of New Hampshire Forests (SPNHF) preserve with fairly flat trails, pond views.

Shieling Forest, off Old Street Road, Peterborough (marked from Route 202 north of town). This is one place you can walk your dog. There are 45 acres of tree-covered ridges and valleys.

Fox State Forest (464-3453), Center Road, Hillsboro. Twenty miles of trails within 1,445 acres of woodland. A detailed booklet guide is available from the state's Division of Forests Office in Concord.

MacDowell Reservoir (924-3431), Peterborough. Good for picnicking, boating, fishing. Maintained by the United States Army Corps of Engineers.

In Keene: **Drummer Hill Preserve**, off Elm Street. Logging roads wind through 140 acres of public and private conservation land.

Horatio Colony Trust, off Daniels Road (take a left, 1/2 mile west of the blinking light on Route 9). A 450-acre bird and animal preserve with marked trails through the woods.

Bear Den Geological Park, Route 10, Gilsum. Look for a large pull-off area on the right (heading north). This is a geologically fascinating area with glacial potholes and caves.

Pisgah Natural Area, off Route 63, 2 miles east of Chesterfield. Other than a parking lot and pit toilets, the park has no facilities. It does offer old logging trails (good for hiking and cross-country skiing) and ponds to satisfy the adventurous fisherman. In all, this is a 13,000-acre wooded wilderness.

Society for the Protection of New Hampshire Forests (SPNHF) Properties. New Hampshire's oldest and largest conservation organization (the one for actually preserving Mt. Monadnock itself), SPNHF owns and manages 16 properties in the region, among them:

Charles L. Peirce Wildlife and Forest Reservation, Stoddard. From Route 9 in Stoddard, follow Route 123 north approximately 2 miles; turn right at fire station; cross bridge. At junction go straight on dirt road approximately 1 mile; park on lot 300 feet beyond woods road on left. The 5-mile Trout-n-Bacon Trail, beginning at a small brook to the left of the road, offers outstanding views from Bacon Ledge and leads to Trout Pond. This is a 3,461-acre preserve with over 10 miles of hiking trails and woods roads that wind over ridges, through deep forest, and around beaver dams. SPNHF also owns the 379-acre Thurston V. Williams Forest and the 157-acre Daniel Upton Forest in Stoddard.

Gap Mountain Reservation, Jaffrey. From Troy, follow Route 12 south 0.4 mile; turn left on Quarry Road; continue past transmission lines. At a sharp left in road, a woods road continues straight uphill. Park and hike up the hill. Near the top, trail markers bear left through the woods. Gap Mountain is a favorite with berriers and picnickers. The 1,107-acre preserve includes three peaks, two bays, and a rich variety of plants and wildlife.

McCabe Forest, Antrim. Route 202 north from Antrim 0.2 mile; right on Elm Street Extension; right to the parking area. This former 192-acre farm has 2 miles of trails, including a fine self-guided interpretive trail, and a variety of wildlife.

AIR RIDES   Year-round Harvey Sawyer (532-8870) offers scenic plane rides in a four-person Cessna plane. From $10 per person for 10 minutes. Also inquire about ultra-light flights.

BICYCLING   The Monadnock Region's many miles of back roads and widely scattered lodging places endear it to bicyclists of all abilities. *Peterborough Bike Tours* by Ann Harrison describes 10 one-day tours ranging from 14 to 50 miles; it's available, along with reasonably priced lodging ($13 with full kitchen privileges, $2 extra for sheets), from the **Peterborough A.Y.H.** (924-9832), 52 Summer Street, Peterborough. Eight Monadnock Region tours are also described in *30 Bicycle Tours in New Hampshire* by Tom and Susan Heavey ($9.95; Backcountry Publications).

Spokes & Slopes (924-9961), 50 Depot Square, Peterborough. Rental bicycles, both mountain and touring bikes.

Monadnock Bicycle Touring (827-3925), Keene Road, Harrisville. Based at the Harrisville Squires' Inn (see Lodging), they offer self-guiding on- and off-road tours or jaunts from 10 to 20 miles plus (from Harrisville). Inn-to-inn tours to New Ipswich, Greenfield, Marlborough, and Antrim are also offered.

BOATING   Boat rentals are available at **Greenfield State Park** (547-3497), which also offers a boat launch on Otter Lake.

Public Boat Landings can also be found (ask locally to find them) in Antrim on Franklin Pierce Lake, Gregg Lake, and Willard Pond; in Bennington on Whittemore Lake; in Dublin on Dublin Lake; in Francestown on Pleasant Pond and Scobie Lake; in Hancock on Norway Pond; in Jaffrey on Frost Pond; and in Rindge on the Contoocook River, Emerson Pond, Grassy Pond, and Pool Pond. A popular canoe route begins in Peterborough, where the Contoocook River crosses under Route 202, with a take-out at Powder Mill Pond in Bennington. The Audubon Society of New Hampshire's Willard Pond is rich in water wildlife.

CAMPING   **Greenfield State Forest** (547-3497) offers 252 tent sites, handy to a public beach and nature trails.

Monadnock State Park (532-8862) offers 21 sites; $14 fee. Private campgrounds are listed in the regional brochure (see Guidance).

GOLF   **Angus Lea** (464-5405), routes 9 and 202, Hillsboro.

Mt. Monadnock, viewed from Dublin Lake.

Bretwood Golf Course (352-7626), East Surry Road, Keene. Twenty-seven holes, par 72; driving range, pro shop, golf carts, snack bar.

Keene Country Club (352-0135). Eighteen holes, par 72.

Monadnock Country Club (924-7769), Peterborough. A 9-hole course with back tees for the second nine.

Shattuck Inn Golf Course (532-4300), Jaffrey Center. Eighteen holes, public welcome.

Tory Pines Resort (588-2000), Francestown.

Hooper Golf Club (756-4020), Prospect Hill, Walpole. Nine holes.

Woodbound Inn Golf Club (532-8341), Woodbound Road, Jaffrey. Nine holes, rental clubs, par 3 course.

GREYHOUND RACING   Hinsdale Greyhound Park (336-5382 or 800-NH-TRACK), Route 119, Hinsdale. Year-round racing, dining room, club room.

HIKING   Mt. Monadnock (532-8862), Monadnock State Park. Marked from Route 124, just west of Jaffrey Center. "Monadnock" is said to be Algonquin for "mountain that stands alone," and in the early nineteenth century the name spread from this mountain to designate every solitary prominence in the world that rises above its surroundings. To distinguish it from all others, purists now call this mountain "Grand" Monadnock. It acquired its bald summit in the 1820s (see Introduction) and has been one of the country's most popular hiking mountains ever since. In 1885 the town of Jaffrey managed to acquire 200 summit acres, and, with the help of SPNHF (which still owns 3,672 acres), much of the rest of the mountain was gradually acquired. The state park on the western side of the mountain is 900 acres. There are 40 miles of trails and a half dozen varied routes up to its 3,165-foot summit. First-timers, however, are advised to follow either the White Dot or White Cross trails from the state park in Jaffrey. Detailed information about the mountain is available at a small museum, the **Ecocenter**. There are also rest rooms, a snack bar, and picnic grounds. The park and its 21-tent campground ($12 weekends, $10 weekdays) is open year-round, and 12 miles of marked cross-country trails are maintained. Admission is $2.50 for visitors over age 11 on weekends, $2 on weekdays. Dogs are not permitted on the trails.

We strongly recommend buying a copy of the fourth edition of *Monadnock Guide* by Henry I. Baldwin (revised and edited by Martha Carolson, published by SPNHF), an excellent detailed guide to the mountain's history, flora and fauna, as well as trails. *Grand Monadnock* by Julia Older and Steve Sherman (Appledore Books) is also a must for the mountain habitués.

Harris Conservation Center (525-3394), follow signs from Hancock Village. A nonprofit land trust with 7 miles of hiking trails, including two mountains with summit views; guided hikes and snowshoeing treks offered on weekends.

Crotched Mountain. Three trails lead to this 2,055-foot summit. The start of the Bennington Trail is marked 3 miles north of Greenfield on Route 31. The Greenfield Trail starts just beyond the entrance to Crotched Mountain Rehabilitation Center (also Route 31). The Francestown Trail starts beyond the entrance to the Crotched Mountain Ski Area on Route 47 and follows the easiest ski trail.

Long-distance trails: Hikers are advised to pick up trail maps to the following trails from the Mt. Monadnock State Park Ecocenter (see Mt. Monadnock under Hiking).

Metacomet Trail. The northernmost 14 miles of a trail that theoretically leads to Meriden, CT. The two most popular sections are **Little Monadnock**, accessible from the parking lot at Rhododendron State Park in Fitzwilliam, and **Gap Mountain**, accessible from trailheads on Route 124 west of Jaffrey Center from a spot just east of the Troy town dump. The trail is marked with white rectangles and famed for its abundance of wild blueberries in July.

Monadnock–Sunapee Trail. The 47-mile northern continuation of the Metacomet Trail, originally blazed in the 1920s by the Society for the Protection of New Hampshire Forests (SPNHF), was reblazed in the early 1970s by Appalachian Mountain Club volunteers. It descends Mt. Monadnock on the Dublin Trail, then cuts across Harrisville, through Nelson Village, up and down Dakin and Hodgeman hills in Stoddard, up Pitcher Mountain (a rewarding stretch to do from Route 123 in Stoddard), up Hubbard Hill (prime blueberry picking), then up 2,061-foot Jackson Hill, through Washington, and then up through successive, high ridges in Pillsbury State Park to Sunapee. Sounds great to me, but since I've never done it, be sure to pick up a detailed trail map from the Ecocenter, which displays a bas-relief of the entire trail, or from SPNHF.

Wapack Trail. A 21-mile ridge line trail with many spectacular views from North Pack Monadnock in Greenfield to Mt. Watatic in Massachusetts. The trail crosses roads about every 4 miles. Just west of Miller State Park on Route 101 turn right on Mountain Road, continue until "Ts," then turn right. After the road turns to gravel, look for a trail to the right. You will see a parking area. A 45-minute climb here yields great views.

HORSEBACK RIDING   **Honey Lane Farm** (563-8078), Box 353, Dublin. Offers "riding holidays," including food and lodging as well as instruction and trail riding for all abilities (see also Lodging).

Morning Mist Farm (428-3889), 15 College Hill Road, Henniker. Just north of Hillsboro, offers guided trail rides for all levels of riders. (See the Merrimack Valley [Concord Area].)

SPECIAL PROGRAMS   **Harrisville Designs** (827-3996), Harrisville 03450. Weekend weaving workshops are held throughout the year; some are simply introductions to weaving, others are specialized and advanced courses. The workshops are held in the Weaving Center overlooking the millpond. Current tuition for two days, including equipment and yarns, is $60. Nominally priced housing is available down the hill in the Cheshire Mills Boardinghouse, built in 1850 for transient weavers. Day-long workshops are also offered; request a schedule.

Sargent Camp (525-3311), Windy Row, Peterborough 03458. A variety of outdoor skills and environmental programs are offered. Housing is in heated cabins and in dorms; family-style meals are served. (Also see Cross-country Skiing.)

SUGARHOUSES   Maple Sugaring season in the Monadnock Region is March to mid-April, but farmers may not be "boiling" (40 gallons of sap boils down to 1 gallon of syrup) every day so be sure to phone ahead to make sure there's something to see—and something to eat. Most maple producers offer "sugar parties": sugar on snow (usually crushed ice these days) and maybe the traditional accompaniment (a pickle). Most sell a variety of maple products.

Bascom's Sugar House (835-2230 or 835-6361), between Alstead and Acworth off Route 123A. One of the largest maple producers in

New England, a huge sugarhouse and warehouse set high on Mt. Kingsbury. Visitors are welcome to tour the plant with its unusual reverse osmosis evaporators. Sugar parties on weekends.

Chadwick Farm (532-8811), south of Route 202 (Gilmore Pond Road to Peabody Hill Road to Chadwick Road), Jaffrey.

Dan's Sugar House (532-7379), Jaffrey. See above. Follow signs at Gilmore Pond Road.

Bacon's Sugar House (532-8836), Dublin Road, just south of Monadnock State Park entrance, Jaffrey Center. The familiar plastic jug now used by 75 percent of the country's maple producers was invented in 1973 by Charles Bacon, who welcomes visitors on weekends. Flanked by two cross-country networks, this vintage 1910 sugarhouse stands on a farm that's been in the family since 1780.

Barrett's Sugar House (352-6812), Route 12 northwest to Wyman Road, Keene. Old brick schoolhouse converted into a sugarhouse.

Parker's Maple Farm (878-2308), Mason (signs from Route 13 in Brookline). Big dining barn. (See Eating Out.)

Fisk's Little Sugar House (654-9784), Dale Street just off Route 31, Wilton. Specializing in maple candy.

Stuart & John's Sugar House and Pancake Restaurant (399-4486), junction of routes 12 and 63, Westmoreland. Open weekends in spring and fall; syrup available year-round.

SWIMMING   While the region is spotted with clear lakes and ponds, public beaches are jealously town-held; understandably, given their proximity to Boston. Guests at local inns and B&Bs, of course, have access to local sand and water.

Greenfield State Park (547-3479), off Route 136 in Greenfield, offers the only truly public beach, and it's mobbed on summer Sundays. $2.50 per person.

Manahan Park, Hillsboro. A town beach that offers swimming on Pierce Lake, just off Route 9 across from the Franklin Pierce Homestead.

Contoocook Lake, Jaffrey. A small but lovely strip of soft sand along Squantum Road, east of the junction of routes 124 and 202; take Stratton Road to Squantum.

Surry Mountain Dam and Lake, Route 12A in Surry. Also offers picnicking and a sand beach. Free.

Otter Brook Dam and Lake, Route 9 in Roxbury. A man-made lake with lawns and sandy beach.

Vilas Pool, just off Route 123 in Alstead. Open in summer Wednesday through Sunday. A dammed pool in the Cold River with bathhouse and picnic area.

At **Warren Lake** in Alstead you can also swim from the public landing.

Spofford Lake, Route 9 in Spofford. Town-run beach.

Franklin Pierce Lake, Antrim, has a public beach.

CROSS-COUNTRY SKIING   Windblown (878-2869), Route 124 west of the village, New Ipswich. Since 1972 Al Jenks has been constantly expanding and improving his high, wooded spread that straddles the Wapack Trail. Thanks to the elevation and northerly exposure, this 35-km network frequently has snow when the ground is bare just 10 miles away. There's an unusual variety to the trails: easy loops from the ski shop and around Wildlife Pond; wooded, more difficult trails up on the Wapack; backcountry trails, including a climb to Mt. Watatic (1,800 feet high); and a long, 75-foot-wide open slope for practicing telemarking. Hot soups, sandwiches, and home-baked munchies are served at the shop; warming hut and a couple of cabins. Open daily, weather permitting. Rentals, instruction. $8 trail fee.

Temple Mountain (924-9376), Route 101 east of Peterborough. A well-maintained network: 20 km of groomed trails that tie into the Wapack Trail's 20 more miles. Snowmaking and lighting on a 1.5-km loop. The trail fee also includes one ride to the top on an alpine lift, but you have to come down the ski trail. Rentals, instruction, telemarking, and guided tours. Food available in the base lodge (see Downhill Skiing). Skiers can also use Temple Mountain's nursery. $9 trail fee.

Road's End Farm (363-4703), Jackson Hill Road, Chesterfield. Phone ahead for conditions and directions. Open weekends, holidays; also weekdays by reservation. This 600-acre farm has been in the Woodman family since 1945 and since 1958 has served as a summer riding camp. In winter 32 km of bridle paths are groomed and track-set. Views are off across the neighboring Pisgah Wilderness Park to Mt. Monadnock on the east, across Lake Spofford to Mt. Ascutney on the southwest. Rentals and lessons are offered. Soups and sandwiches are served in the 1820 guest house, and "simple" accommodations (bring your towel and sleeping bag) are available at the farm where, according to proprietor Tom Woodman, "reservations are a must and privacy a pipe dream." Trail fee: $7 adult, $4 juniors and seniors.

Boston University Sargent Camp (525-3311), west on Peterborough's Union Street to Windy Row. An 850-acre wooded preserve webbed with 20 miles of touring trails. Rental equipment, lessons, and snacks available. (Also see Special Programs.)

Shattuck Inn (532-6619), Dublin Road (off Route 124 en route to Monadnock State Park), Jaffrey Center. The new 18-hole golf course was designed with cross-country skiing in mind. Ten km of trails are along the cart path which curves up and down and dips in and out of woods. Another 6 km are in the woods and through Bacon's sugarbush (see Sugar Houses), connecting with state park trails. Rentals and trail fee on weekends and holidays.

The Inn at East Hill Farm (242-6495), Jaffrey Road, Troy. Some 13 miles of trails meander gently around this property with its great view of Mt. Monadnock. Rentals and instruction are offered, and informal meals are available at the inn. A warming hut on the trail, with fireplace and woodstove, serves hot drinks on weekends.

Woodbound Inn (532-8341), Jaffrey. Fourteen km of wooded trails, rental equipment. $8 trail fee.

Mt. Monadnock State Park (532-8862), Dublin Road from Route 124, Jaffrey Center. A 12-mile, well-marked but ungroomed, system of trails web the base of the mountain. Loops from 1 mile to more than 7 miles. Winter camping is also available. The entrance fee is $2.50 per visitor over age 11; $2 weekdays. No dogs allowed.

DOWNHILL SKIING   Temple Mountain Ski Area (924-6949), Temple Mountain, Route 101, Peterborough. One of New England's oldest ski areas, Temple has been in business every winter since 1937. Thanks to its elevation (1,460 feet at the base), exposure, and a natural snow pocket, the skiing is frequently better here than farther north. A quad chair services the summit, accessing all 17 trails. A T-bar also runs almost to the top, and another serves the three trails on the western side of the mountain. Another T-bar and rope tow serve beginners. Snowmaking covers 90 percent of the terrain, and night skiing is offered Monday through Saturday. The base lodge is new but still small and friendly, and the West Lodge warming hut is still vintage '30s. This is a true family area, owned and managed by Peterborough native Sandy Eneguess. Lift tickets are $25 for adults, $20 for juniors (age 14 and under) and seniors on weekends; $14 and $12 midweek.

SLEIGH RIDES   Silver Ranch (532-7363) has a variety of sleighs: large pungs for groups, classic small sleighs for couples and families. A 45-minute ride through the woods. Warm drinks and square dancing can be arranged for larger parties.

Inn at East Hill Farm (242-6495), Jaffrey Road, Troy. Sleigh rides offered along with cross-country skiing to nonguests (see also Lodging).

Stonewall Farm (357-7278), Chesterfield. Mike Kidder offers sleigh rides.

RESORTS   Inn at East Hill Farm (242-6495), Troy 03465. The setting is spectacular, on a back road between Troy Village and Route 124 with Mt. Monadnock rising above the pond out back. This isn't a fancy place. Over the years (since 1973) David and Sally Adams have created a lively, friendly family resort. The core of the complex is an 1830s inn with a fireplace in its attractive living room and six guest rooms including "Grandmother's Attic," a suite with TV. The old-style cottages, all nicely furnished and spanking clean, each have two or three bedrooms, a living room, and one or two baths; Trailsend, a lodge with large, motel-style rooms, overlooks the pond and mountain. Amenities include a basic indoor and two outdoor pools, a lake beach, tennis, shuffleboard, boats, and water skiing, plus the barn full of animals. The large dining room is usually open to the public for lunch and dinner, but call ahead to make sure it hasn't been reserved by a bus group. Off-season the inn is also frequently filled with square dancing groups. Summer rates: $357 per adult, $122.50–$245 per child (depending on age) weekly, including all meals. Daily rates are also available when possible and holiday weekend packages; B&B rates in spring and fall.

Woodbound Inn (532-8341 or 800-688-7770), Woodbound Road, Jaffrey 03452. A rambling, old, 40-room, family-geared inn on a small lake with its own 9-hole golf course, presently owned by New Hampshire Savings Bank but open for business as usual. $95–$135 double includes two meals.

INNS   **Antrim Inn** (588-8000), Main Street, Antrim 03440. This rambling, old village inn has been thoroughly, tastefully restored in recent years and each of the 14 guest rooms now has a bath and is furnished in reproduction and real antiques. One front room has a canopy bed and working fireplace, but we would pick a rear room to be away from Route 202 (Main Street). Common rooms are attractive and the dining room is "country elegant"; a bar menu is served in the comfortable pub (see Dining Out). Wayne and Laura Lesperance charge $70–$90 per room.

The Birchwood Inn (878-3285), Route 45, Temple 03084. Henry Thoreau is counted among past guests at this small brick inn, built around 1800 in the center of a tiny backroad village. Since 1980 Bill and Judy Wolfe have taken personal pride in both the kitchen and seven guest rooms (five with private bath), each decorated around a theme and each very different; the one ground-floor room is wheelchair accessible. There's a cheerful BYOB bar and a fine little dining room with 1820s murals by Rufus Porter (see Dining Out). Temple Mountain, good for both alpine and nordic skiing, is just 3 miles away. $60–$70 double, breakfast included.

Chesterfield Inn (256-3211), Route 9, West Chesterfield 03466. The original house served as a tavern from 1798 to 1811, but the present inn is pure 1980s. Vermont architect Rodney Williams has created many windowed spaces and the nine guest rooms all have phones, controlled heat or air-conditioning, optional TVs and wet bars; some have working fireplaces, others have Jacuzzis. Innkeepers Phil and Judy Hueber have created a popular dining room (see Dining Out) in an entirely separate wing that guests access through the kitchen. The inn is set back from busy Route 9, the main road between Keene and Brattleboro, VT. $99–$149 double includes a full breakfast.

The Fitzwilliam Inn (585-9000), Fitzwilliam 03447. The three-story, double-porched, Greek Revival inn serves as a centerpiece for one of New England's most handsome towns, and it's the kind of place anyone feels comfortable walking into. We must admit to using this route, as Vermont Transit does, between Boston and Vermont; and we know that we can always duck into the rest room right next to the front desk or use the phone without anyone asking questions. Everyone does. Built in 1830, the inn has been in the Wallace family for 18 years and involves three generations of the family (at age 90 plus Grannie Wallace still keeps the ledgers and shucks all the beans). It offers 28 guest rooms, simply but nicely furnished, some with stenciling and matching stenciled curtains; some with, others without bath. But Yuppies beware. If elegantly furnished rooms are more your style, you can find them around the corner (see Bed & Breakfasts). Families, on the other hand, may want to note the large third-floor rooms with shared bath ($40 double, $10 per extra person, cribs $3 extra). Three meals a day are served (see Dining Out) and the pub is inviting. Amenities include a summer pool, winter ski-touring, and Sunday afternoon chamber concerts. Since Vermont Transit stops several times per day en route from Boston to Montreal, this is one country inn accessible to car-free urbanites. From $35 single to $55 double.

The John Hancock Inn (525-3318), Main Street, Hancock 03449. Built in 1789, this pillared inn is said to be the state's oldest, but its look is nineteenth century, thanks to two-story pillars and a mansard roof. It sits in the center of a picture-perfect village with Norway Pond shimmering at one end of the street. The Carriage Room Lounge, with its shiny tables made from old bellows and seats from early buggies, and a dining room fill much of the first floor. The 10 upstairs guest rooms (all with private baths) are furnished with canopied and four-poster beds, braided and hooked rugs, rockers and wing-backs. You might want to request the Mural Room with its walls painted by nineteenth-century artist Rufus Porter. Glynn and Pat Wells have presided over the inn since 1972. Children and pets are welcome ($5 per day charge for pets). $62.50 single, $72.50 double, $10 extra for a port-a-crib.

The Inn at Crotched Mountain (588-6840), Mountain Road, off Route 47, Francestown 03043. The 1820s brick inn is now a centerpiece for wooden wings, but it still contains a gracious parlor and two dining rooms. The Pine Room also serves as a small gathering space for guests, away from dinner patrons (see Dining Out). The real beauty of this place, aside from its food and the warmth of its longtime innkeepers John and Rose Perry, is its setting at 1,300 feet, high on a ridge with sweeping views. Four of the 14 rooms have working fireplaces and all have private baths. Amenities include a pool, tennis courts, and cross-country skiing. Alpine skiing at Crotched Mountain is minutes away. $100–$120 double, MAP; B&B and midweek rates also available; add 15 percent for service.

The Monadnock Inn (532-7001), Box B, Jaffrey Center 03454. Sally Roberts has kept the hearths burning, pub humming, and dining room popular for 16 years in this landmark, the last survivor among

Mail boxes, East Alstead.

many right around Mt. Monadnock itself (see Dining Out). This white, wooden landmark sits in the middle of one of the region's most beautiful villages, giving it a friendly heart. The 15 rooms are homey, nothing fancy, and some bathrooms are shared. $35–$40 single, $50–$60 double.

Jaffrey Manor Restaurant & Inn (532-8069), 13 Stratton Road, Jaffrey 03452. In the middle of busy Jaffrey this roadside inn is a 1980s rehab of an older home. The eight guest rooms are nicely furnished as is the sitting room with piano and TV. From $35 single (shared bath) to $50 double (private bath); continental breakfast included.

BED & BREAKFASTS   **The Monadnock Region Bed & Breakfast Association** (PO Box 236, Jaffrey 03452) publishes a brochure describing more than two dozen members. For quick access to the list phone the Peterborough Chamber of Commerce (924-7234). They are listed here, as in their brochure, by town.

Alstead 03602:   **Darby Brook Farm** (835-6624). Open May through October. Alstead is in the little-touristed northwestern corner of the region, handy to canoeing on the Connecticut River; there's also a choice of swimming holes in town. Howard Weeks has summered all his life in this Federal-style house that's been changed little by the three families who have owned it since the 1790s. Weeks has devoted his retirement to maintaining the house and its 10-acre hay field, the apple orchard up above the field, and the berry bushes and sizable vegetable garden just behind the house; also the animals: five sheep, some chickens and turkeys. The two large front rooms share a bath but have working fireplaces, set in their original paneling, and the $44 double ($22 single) rate includes tax as well as a full breakfast, served in the elegant old dining room.

Antrim 03440:   **Uplands Inn** (588-2407), off Route 31. An 1830s cape set in 32 acres, a lodging place for more than 100 years. Six rooms are usually available. $50 double, $35 single, $15 per extra person in room.

Fitzwilliam 03447:   **The Amos A. Parker House** (585-6540) is a standout. It sits right on Route 119 (little trafficked after dark), but the back deck overlooks a deep, formal, and flowery garden with woods and mountains extending the view. Some of the rooms have working fireplaces and private baths and all are furnished with carefully chosen antiques. A downstairs suite, great for honeymooners, has its own fireplace, bath, and kitchenette. Guests can relax in the formal front parlor, with its original hearth and wainscotting, or in the informal den, filled with books and magazines. Memorable breakfasts, featuring delicacies like stuffed French bread and soufflés, are served on fine china in the dining room. An enthusiastic transplant from the midwest, innkeeper Freda Houpt is unusually knowledgeable about the area and an outstanding hostess. Even pets are welcome by advance approval. $65–$80 double. No credit cards please.

   Hannah Davis House (585-344), 186 Depot Road. A few doors up from the Amos Parker House, Kaye and Mike Terpstra have turned an 1820s Federal-style house into another outstanding bed & breakfast. Guests enter through a cheery country kitchen and gather in the sunny sitting and breakfast rooms. All three of the upstairs bedrooms have been nicely furnished. My favorite is Chauncey's Room with the queen-size antique iron bed and working fireplace. The loft room above the garage is a find for families: a queen-size bed, a sleeper sofa, cathedral ceiling, and view out over the back garden and woods. $65–$75 per room includes a full breakfast.

Greenfield 03047:   **The Greenfield Inn** (547-6327). Vic and Barbara Mangini have turned this expansive village mansion into an appealing bed & breakfast. Each of the nine rooms has its own name and lacy decor, but all are furnished with antiques and 1890s touches. A two-level hayloft apartment with kitchenette is available by the week, and a glass-walled deckhouse lends itself to meetings and wedding receptions. Rates are $45–$70 with a full breakfast. Ask about weekend packages with dinner out, conceived as getaways for working couples.

Hancock 03449:   **Westwinds** (525-6600), Route 137. A fine old house with mountain views, set in 19 acres with a pond; five gracious guest rooms furnished with antiques and Brenda's handmade quilts. Chris and Brenda Prahl serve a hearty breakfast. $35–$55 double, including breakfast.

Harrisville 03450:   **Harrisville Squires' Inn** (827-3925), Keene Road, Box 19. A roadside mid-1800s house on the outskirts of a gem of a village. Innkeepers Pat and Doug McCarthy go all out for bicyclists, offering a series of self-guided tours—on- and off-road, some loops, some to other inns. The inn is on the Monadnock-Sunapee Trail (see Hiking), and Doug will happily provide shuttle service. The comfortable living room with fireplace and five guest rooms are all furnished thoughtfully. Breakfast and dinner (by special arrangement) is served in an attractive, wicker-filled dining room. In winter Doug regularly grooms the cross-country ski trails that web the 30 acres out back. Pat, a justice of the peace, both performs and caters weddings. $45 for a room with private bath, $55 with shared bath.

Hillsborough 03244: **Stone Bridge Inn** (464-3155), Route 9. Clara and George Adamy maintain four rooms in this handsome, old roadside house as a retirement hobby of sorts. They used to own the far larger New London Inn. From $45 for a single, $55 double; continental breakfast included.

Stonewalls Farm (478-5424), Hillsborough Upper Village. Two rooms with private bath, $70 with breakfast.

Jaffrey 03452: **The Benjamin Prescott Inn** (532-6637), Route 124, East Jaffrey. This stately 1850s farmhouse has been meticulously restored. Each of the 10 guest rooms has a private bath and charm of its own, and a few of the rooms, especially the upstairs back suite with views out across the fields, are ideal for honeymooners. Another downstairs suite is ideal for families. A full breakfast is served in the attractive lemon-colored dining room and sitting rooms. Hosts Barry and Janice Miller are adept at helping guests find their way around on two or four wheels. $50–$75 single, $60–$120 double.

The Galway House (532-8083), Old Peterborough Road. The first bed & breakfast to open in the region, Joe and Marie Manning's hospitable home offers two large rooms, ideal for families since one has both a double bed and twin beds, and the other has a double, single, and crib. $50 double, $40 single, includes a full breakfast. The Mannings are longtime residents and are delighted to point guests in rewarding directions.

Lilac Hill Acres Inn (532-7278), 5 Ingalls Road. Overlooking Gilmore Pond, Ellen and her daughter Jacqulyn McNeill offer six guest rooms. $70 with private bath, $60 with shared bath; includes a full breakfast. No smoking or children under age 14.

The Gould Farm (532-6996), PO Box 27, Prescott Road. Two rooms with a third available for families. $50 per night includes breakfast; children welcome.

Keene 03431: **Carriage Barn Guest House** (357-3812), 358 Main Street. Hidden away behind an imposing house, within walking distance of the college, downtown shops, movies, and restaurants; a Civil War era barn now holds four attractive guest rooms and a cheerful breakfast room.

$40 single and $50 double, includes tax as well as breakfast.

289 Court (357-3195), 289 Court Street. Zoning precludes a B&B sign in this posh neighborhood, and the house itself is so imposing that you tend to check the address twice. Your welcome is unfailingly warm. Laverne and Bill Horne have raised six children in this comfortable 1870s mansion, and they now offer three large guest rooms, each with private bath and an adjoining smaller room if needed. A continental breakfast is served on the large enclosed porch or in the living room, depending on the weather. From $39 single to $57 double, includes both breakfast and tax.

Goose Pond Guest House, East Surry Road (a right off Court Street, 2 miles north of Central Square). Zoning precludes a sign out front, but it's hard to miss this big, vintage 1790, white home (on a knoll on the left) with the Sise family name on the mailbox. Just one room (really a suite) is available, $50 single, $55 double, includes a private breakfast. The Bretwood Golf Course (27 holes) is just up the road.

Marlborough 03455:   **Thatcher Hill Inn** (876-3361), Thatcher Hill Road, off Route 124. The original parsonage part of the house dates from 1794, and the solid addition which includes a tin-ceilinged dining room is vintage 1910. The imposing barn housed Guernsey cows until the 1960s when the dairy farm became too much for two elderly spinster sisters, relatives of Marge and Cal Gage, who took the 60-acre property on as a retirement project. Marge Gage spent two years creating the quilts on the brass and wooden beds in the seven guest rooms. All have private baths with old claw-foot tubs and heated towel bars. A full, buffet-style breakfast is served in the Victorian-style dining room. Be sure to ask Cal to show off his collection of antique music boxes in the living room. In winter cross-country skiing is possible in the surrounding fields, and year-round Mt. Monadnock's hiking trails are just up Route 124. $55–$75 including breakfast; $140 for the two-bedroom suite, sleeping six. Special weekend winter rates: $88–$130 double covers two nights, plus Friday dinner and a late Sunday checkout.

Munsonville 03457:   **Old Mill House** (847-3224). The old cotton mill across the road is gone, but this early nineteenth-century mill boardinghouse continues to welcome guests. Susan and Walter Lawton offer seven rooms sharing two baths. Granite Lake, good for boating in summer and ice skating in winter, is just across the road. $45 double, $35 single; extra person in the room, $12. A full country breakfast is included.

Nelson 03455:   **Tolman Pond** is a special place, home to seven generations of Tolmans, noted musicians and writers among them. The house overlooks a 40-acre pond, good for swimming and canoeing, and guests have their own kitchen. Just one room in winter but three in summer, children welcome. $35–$55.

New Ipswich 03071:   **The Inn at New Ipswich** (878-3711), PO Box 208, Porter

Hill Road. A handsome 1790s farm, just far enough away on Route 124. Two of the six guest rooms have fireplaces, and breakfast is served by the hearth in the old keeping room. Innkeepers Ginny and Steve Bankutt are recent and enthusiastic Monadnock Region converts, happy to steer guests to local sites. Windblown, the area's outstanding cross-country ski center, is a few minutes drive. $40 single, $50 double; includes a full breakfast. No smoking and no children under age 8 please.

Peterborough 03458:   **Apple Gate B&B** (924-6543), 199 Upland Road. A nicely sited country house not far from the Sharon Arts Center with three guest rooms. $70 including breakfast.

Walpole 03608:   **The Josiah Bellows House** (756-4250), PO Box 818, North Main Street. Built in 1813 this is one of the grander, more historic houses in the region. Set in 6 acres, it is within walking distance of a beautiful village and sweeping views off across the Connecticut River to Vermont. Two of the four rooms have private baths. A full breakfast is included in $70 double, $60 single. No smoking and no children please.

Wilton 03086:   **Auk's Nest**, East Road in Temple (mailing address is RFD #1, Wilton). Anne Lunt's 1770s cape sits at the edge of an apple orchard. It's filled with books and antiques, offers a low-beamed living room, a stenciled dining room, and two homey guest rooms. Both pets and children are welcome by prior arrangement. From $35 single to $60 double, full breakfast included.

Stepping Stones Bed & Breakfast (654-9048), Bennington Battle Trail, Wilton Center. This remarkable house, at once unusually cozy and airy, is hidden away in a bend off a back road to a picture-perfect old village. There are three guest rooms with handwoven rugs and throws and down comforters, two with shared bath. A full breakfast is served in the solar garden room, filled with sun and flowers. There's also a friendly living room with books, pillows, a stereo, and woodstove; a weaving room; and a small dining room. The gardens are inviting and extensive, reflecting Ann Carlsmith's skill as a landscape designer. $35 single, $40–$45 double; full, imaginative breakfast included.

Gray's Corner (654-6773), RR 2, Box 208. This proud eighteenth-century farmhouse set in 4 acres of rolling fields offers four double-bedded guest rooms, each with a shared, adjoining bath. Guests can relax in the library/game room or in the parlor around the Rumford fireplace. No pets or children please.

MOTELS   **Salzburg Inn and Motel** (924-3803), off Union Street on Steele Road. Rooms in the inn tend to be rented on a weekly or long-term basis. Motel rooms are $56 plus tax.

Jack Daniel's Motor Inn (924-7548), Route 202 north. A standard, comfortable motel with two double beds and cable TV. $78 double.

OTHER LODGING   American Youth Hostel (924-9832), 52 Summer Street, Peterborough 03458. Ann and Peter Harrison have built a new wing onto the back of their old house. Downstairs is a comfortable living room and communal kitchen and dining space; upstairs the rooms are both dorm-style and double, all bunk beds equipped simply with pillows or blankets. You can bring your own sleeping bag or rent linen. Nominal rates.

Equestrian Center at Honey Lane Farm (563-8078), Box 353, Dublin 03444. This unusual complex doesn't fit in any other category but it's a real find for horse lovers, even those who don't know how to ride. In summer the Coutu family have run a riding camp, but in spring and fall they offer riding weekends and five- and seven-day riding packages. Guests can choose from the new lodge with its fireplaced living room and private baths or the no-frills old bunkhouse. Weekends include all meals, instruction, and trail riding (these are real horses, not hacks). $290–$370 per couple per weekend to $450–$550 for a family of four; $650–$798 per couple for five days, $899–$1,148 for seven days.

DINING OUT   *In and around Keene:*   Henry David's (352-0608), 81 Main Street. Open daily 11:30 AM–11 PM. Somehow it's difficult to imagine its namesake—Henry David Throeau—eating amidst this downtown restaurant's glitz and greenery, but Henry's maternal grandmother did build a part of the 1770s house that's now a part of this 1980s complex with its central atrium and skylights. Good for over-sized sandwiches at lunchtime and a varied dinner menu ranging from prime rib to Mexican and oriental dishes ($10–$18).

One Seventy-Six Main (357-3100), 176 Main Street. Open 11:30 AM–11 PM daily; until midnight Saturday, 10 PM Sunday. Brunch Saturday and Sunday 11–4. "Casual gourmet dining," featuring Mexican food on Monday and Tuesday, Italian on Wednesday, seafood on Thursday and Friday.

The Chesterfield Inn (256-3211), Route 9, Chesterfield. Open for dinner Tuesday through Saturday 5:30–9, nightly in foliage season. Chef Carl Warner has an enviable reputation for imaginative dishes and the setting is an eighteenth-century tavern. The menu changes every two months. Prices from $17–$22.

The Fitzwilliam Inn (585-9000), Fitzwilliam. Open daily for all three meals. Baskets dangle from the low beams in the old dining room. The dinner menu is traditional: chicken marsala ($12.50), scallops baked with stuffing ($13.75), roast duck ($14.95), Boston scrod ($12.95); meal includes juice, soup or appetizer of the day (e.g., marinated mushrooms), salad, starch, vegetable, beverage, and homemade dessert. At lunch you can choose from crabmeat with melted Swiss cheese on a toasted muffin, a variety of sandwiches, or reasonably priced entrées like southern fried chicken ($6.50).

Major Leonard Keep Restaurant (399-4474), Route 12, Westmoreland. Open for lunch and dinner; closed Tuesdays and February. A traditional go-out-to-eat place for locals, an oldie country atmosphere with an all American menu ($15–$20): baked stuffed shrimp, Yankee pot roast, fresh fish.

In and around Peterborough: **Latacarta** (924-6878), 6 School Street, Peterborough. Open for lunch Tuesday through Friday 11–5, Saturday 12–5; and for dinner Tuesday through Thursday 5–9, Friday and Saturday 5–9:30, Sunday 5–7. Sunday brunch is 11-5. Hiroshi Hayashi is a master chef who has turned an old movie theater into a restaurant. Fans of Hayashi's "nouvelle naturale" cuisine drive up for dinner from Boston (his previous restaurant was on Newbury Street). Fresh, natural ingredients are stressed, and there's little salt or sugar in eclectic dishes like fresh salmon lightly baked with herbs, served with sautéed snow peas, mushrooms, and tomatoes in a fresh dill sauce, and served with salad, fresh vegetables, and rice ($14.75); teriyaki beef, served in traditional teriyaki sauce with sake and soy sauce; or a vegetarian dish of vegetables and tortellini with olive oil, parsley, and pine nuts. Pastas and Mexican dishes are also featured and both soups and salads are specialties. The wine list is respectable. Dinner entrées run $9.50–$14.75, lunch entrées $4.75–$6; a pub menu ($6.25–$7.70) is served all evening in the small lounge.

The Folkway (924-7484), 85 Grove Street, Peterborough. Open Tuesday through Saturday 11:30–midnight, and for special Sunday concerts. A restaurant and gathering place to hear folk music and jazz during the late '70s and '80s, this landmark closed in 1988 when its founder, Widdie Fall, died of cancer. In the summer of '90 it was reopened as a nonprofit foundation with the aim of perpetuating the tradition of fine music and food. Right on the main street with parking in the rear, the restaurant is in a Victorian house with garden dining in warm weather—an attractive place to lunch on vegetarian chili ($3.25 a bowl) with house salad ($2.95), a chicken teriyaki sandwich ($4.95), or a Brie turnover followed by fettucini with shrimp and scallops ($8.95) or vegetable pot pie ($7.95). Call to inquire about live entertainment and the cover charge. Sunday jazz brunches are an institution.

The Boiler House at Noone Falls (924-9486), Route 202 south of Peterborough. Open for lunch Tuesday through Friday 11:30–2, dinner Tuesday through Saturday 5:30–9, and Sunday brunch. Overlooking the waterfall beside the former textile mill in which it is housed, a fairly formal dining room with iffy service but a locally respected chef. Venison, lamb, duck, and sautéed fresh fish are staples. Rack of lamb ($15.95) is a specialty. Dinner entrées range from $10–$20 and the wine list is both extensive and expensive. Lunch is also served on an outside terrace in summer.

The Birchwood Inn (878-3285), Route 45, Temple. Open for breakfast every day but Monday and for dinner every night but Sunday. BYOB. Innkeeper Bill Wolfe is the chef and with the help of his wife Judy makes everything from scratch on the premises—the reason for the low prices and strong local following. The dining room is small (so be sure to reserve ahead), candlelit, and decorated with murals painted in the 1820s by itinerant artist Rufus Porter. The four-course dinner is a reasonably priced $15–$18. The blackboard menu always lists a choice of chicken, duckling (a specialty) or veal, red meat, and fish. Homemade breads, soups, and delectable desserts like chocolate hazelnut torte and Temple trifle are all made daily from scratch. The inn's reasonably priced, multi-course breakfasts are also worth noting for those Mt. Monadnock-bound hikers who like getting up and out, eating an hour or so later.

The Monadnock Inn (532-7001), Route 124, Jaffrey Center. Rated a shade higher than other local inn dining rooms (in our unscientific, local opinion poll), this homey dining room offers a large selection—from pasta (different each day) for $13.50 to chicken mandalay (dredged in curried flour, then sautéed with ginger, apricot and orange marmalade, white wine and butter) for $13.95 to filet mignon for $16.75. Entrées include soup or salad, vegetable, starch, and breads. Lunch choices average $6.

Del Rossi's Trattoria (563-7195), Route 137, Dublin. Open Tuesday through Saturday for lunch and dinner. A real find. David and Elaina Del Rossi have created a genuine Italian trattoria in a pleasant old house just north of Route 101. The lunch menu changes daily, always includes a choice of salads, a quiche, and homemade pasta. Dinner might be veal marsala ($14.95), spicy shrimp marinara ($11.95), or haddock Parmesan ($10.95). Live folk music is featured Friday and Saturday nights. Wine and beer are reasonably priced.

The John Hancock Inn (525-3318), Main Street, Hancock Village. Open for all three meals daily. An eighteenth-century inn with three dining rooms. You can actually dine lightly, if you are in a hurry, on appetizers like fettucini with shrimp and mushrooms, herring marinated in wine, or smoked trout. Entrée staples include chicken popovers, medallions of pork dijonaise, prime rib, duckling with black currant sauce, baked scrod, and fettucini primavera. Desserts are all house made: cream puffs and pecan pie are the standbys. Entrées range from $9.96–$16.95, including the house cheese spread, salad, and homemade breads. A bar menu covers the hours between meals.

Crotched Mountain area (northeastern part of region):   **Maitre Jacq** (588-6655), Route 47 and Mountain Road, Francestown. Open Tuesday through Sunday 5–9:30, closed Sundays in winter. Chef/owner Robert Jacq comes from Brittany and his cuisine is French Provençal—bouillabaisse Provençal (scallops, shrimp, clams, mussels, and fresh fish in a white wine broth with saffron) for $19.50, medallions of pork loin with artichoke hearts and béarnaise sauce for $16.50, chicken chasseur (with mushrooms, tomatoes, shallots, and wine sauce) for $13.75. The price includes an appetizer and desserts like chocolate mousse with curacao (although selected appetizers like escargots and desserts like baked Alaska, are extra). Herbs and vegetables are from the garden out back. The two dining rooms are simple and dimly lit, tables draped in white linen.

The Inn at Crotched Mountain (588-6840), Mountain Road, Francestown. Open for dinner Wednesday through Saturday 6–8:30, weekends only off-season. Reserve. Rose Perry hails from Indonesia, and her native specialties add an exotic touch to the otherwise traditional menu: New York sirloin ($16.95) and eggplant Parmigiana ($10.95). The liver, onion, and bacon ($13.95) gets rave reviews from liver lovers. Nightly specials may include stuffed sole in puffed pastry; swordfish sautéed oriental-style with tomatoes, pepper, and onion; and celephane noodle soup. The entrée price includes a soup, salad, breads, and vegetable.

Powder Mill Pond Restaurant (588-2127), Route 202 south of Bennington. Open for lunch Tuesday through Friday; dinner Tuesday through Saturday; all-you-can-eat, Sunday-brunch buffet from 11–1:30. In warm weather you can dine on the screened porch overlooking the pond, and the two dining rooms also have a light and airy feel. Chef/owner Jerry Willis offers a large menu, a cheerful mix of oriental, Mexican, and traditional dishes. Some regulars just come for the sticky buns. The watercolors and pastels on the walls (for sale) are by Jerry's parents, well-known local artists.

The Antrim Inn (588-8000), Main Street, Antrim. Dinner every night but Tuesday 6–9; Sunday brunch 10–2, dinner 1–7. The most elegant of the region's dining rooms, recently redecorated with rose-colored balloon curtains to match the table linens. You might start with baked stuffed mushrooms ($41.25), followed either by baked Boston scrod ($10.75), Antrim Inn Chicken (a boneless breast of chicken, stuffed with herbal Borsin cheese and rolled in seasoned cracker crumbs for $11.75), or filet mignon ($17.50). Entrées include a seasonal salad, starch, and vegetable.

Rynborn (588-6162), Main Street, Antrim. Open daily for lunch 11:30–3, dinner 5–10; Sunday brunch 11–2, dinner 4–8. Just across the street from the Antrim Inn, an informal, chef-owned restaurant with a large, varied menu. Appetizers include a heaping bowl of mussels poached in white wine and garlic, and the two dozen entrées include steak au poivre ($14.95), veal marsala ($10.95), Cornish game hens citron (two plump hens baked with a lemon and garlic glaze for $10.95) and baked stuffed shrimp ($11.95). The children's menu includes batter-fried chicken ($3.25).

Southeastern corner of the region: **Ram in the Thicket** (654-6440), Maple Street, Wilton. Open Friday and Saturday 5:30–9:30; otherwise 5:30–8:30, but always call ahead. A Victorian mansion complete with a crystal chandelier and oriental rugs is the relaxed setting for unusual, memorable meals mixing Greek, Indonesian, Mexican, and continental dishes, combining ingredients in salads and entrées that may never have been combined before. What's more they work. The owner/chefs are Rev. Dr. Andrew and Priscilla Tempelman.

    Pickity Place (878-1151), Nutting Hill Road (2 1/2 miles off Route 31), Mason. Open year-round, daily for three lunch sittings: 11:30, 12:45, and 2:00. Reserve ahead because there are just 12 tables in this 200-year old-house. Home-grown herbs are the draw here and you come for "herbal lunches." The set menu changes each month. At this writing it happens to be a bell pepper soup followed by a choice of glazed baked ham or walnut/broccoli crêpe, with a carrot/sprout salad and summer squash, all garnished with edible flowers, washed down with herbal tea. The $10.95 prix fixe includes homemade breads and dessert. Children can have a Little Red Riding Hood basket of sandwiches and fruit for $4.95; the reason they come is to see "Grandmother's bed" in the Red Riding Hood Museum.

EATING OUT   *In and around Keene:*   **Lindy's Diner** (352-4273), Gilbo Avenue just off Main Street across from the bus station. Open daily 6 AM–9 PM, until 10 PM on Saturdays. Arietta Rigopoulos takes particular pride in their chowders and chicken pies.

    The Bench Cafe (357-4353), Colony Mill Marketplace. Open daily for lunch and dinner. The only real restaurant in the marketplace, it's now a cousin to a trendy Manchester, VT place by the same name. It's attractive, predictable, fairly fast service and just what you may want if you're shopping or passing through. Entrées include Mexican and Cajun dishes and grilled specialties like baby back ribs ($5.50–$14.95).

    The Stage Restaurant (352-9626), 30 Central Square, Keene. Open Monday through Saturday 7–9:30, Sunday 8–3. A trendy cafe across from the County Courthouse.

    Libby's Family Restaurant (352-4727), Route 12 east of Keene. Coffee shop open 6 AM–9 PM except Sundays when it's 7 AM–8 PM; Fireside Room open Wednesday through Saturday 11:30–9 and Sunday 10–8. This is one of those great roadside food places we depend on when cutting up Route 12 from Boston to Vermont. There's always a feeling of comradery around the formica counter where the soups and sandwiches are fine; the Fireside Room offers a full menu.

    Monadnock Mountain View Restaurant (242-3300), Gathering Mall, Route 12, Troy. Open daily, Sunday brunch a specialty. A dependable lunch or dinner stop with the best Mt. Monadnock view of any area restaurant. A large bar and lounge. Good sandwiches; dinner entrées like veal marsala, Cajun fried shrimp, tortellini. Bargain-priced Sunday brunch.

In and around Peterborough: **Twelve Pine Street** (924-7941), 12 Pine Street, Peterborough. Open Monday through Friday 11–6, Saturday 11–3. The aroma is a mix of coffee, spices, and baking which, combined with the array of salads, quiche, calzone, and soups, is something to savor before deciding on any one thing. This tiny house expands the definition of a takeout place, and Daniel and Jan Thibeault have a strong local following. Ideally this is the source of a classy picnic to be consumed in one of the settings we've listed under Green Space; practically, it's a source of outstanding chicken burritos ($3.75) or egg rolls ($1.50) to be consumed on the steps of the neighboring Unitarian Church, by the neighboring Contoocook River, or maybe in the small riverside park behind the library.

The Café at Noone Falls (924-6818), Route 202 south of Peterborough in the renovated Noone Falls mill. Open Monday through Friday 7 AM–8 PM, Saturday 9-4. Quick, delicious, and fun, one of the most popular eating spots around. One whiff of the stuffed croissants and you know this is no ordinary fast-food place; soups, breads, pastries are all made from scratch and the salads are good, too. There's usually plenty of seating space at the garden café-style tables.

The Peterborough Diner (924-6202), Depot Street. Open Monday through Saturday 6 AM–9 PM, Sunday 6 AM–1 PM. A 1950s green-and-yellow diner featuring homemade soups, pies, daily and nightly specials. Choose from the counter or wooden booths.

Jaffrey Manor Restaurant & Inn (532-8069), 23 Stratton Road (right at the junction with Route 124 in the middle of town), Jaffrey. A family find, nicely decorated dining rooms serving hearty hot and cold sandwiches (the grilled Reuben comes with Swiss cheese and sauerkraut for $3.75) plus a vegetarian plate for lunch. At dinner entrées include baked haddock ($8.95), chicken almondine ($7.95), and a deluxe burger ($6.25); wine and beer are served.

Noni's Bakery (924-3451), Grove Street. Open from early morning to 2 PM. Doughnuts made daily, full breakfasts, soups, sandwiches, local gossip.

Crotched Mountain area (northeastern part of region):   **The Lobster Man's Family Restaurant** (588-3000), junction of routes 31, 47, and 202 in Bennington. Open Tuesday through Saturday 4–9, Sunday 4–8. Housed in the snug little old house that was Petit Maison, this friendly wayside stop specializes in fried (in vegetable oil) fish, seafood, and chicken; steaks; chicken (grilled and fried); and, of course, lobster. Most dinners are under $10 and a hot dog is $1.75; beer by the glass and pitcher, wine by the glass.

Alberto's (588-6512), near junction of routes 202, 47, and 31 (next to the old mill dam), Bennington. It advertises "Best food by a dam site." A local favorite, Italian menu, reasonably priced.

Southeastern corner of the region: **Parker's Maple Barn and Sugar House** (878-2308), Brookline Road, Mason. Tuesday through Friday 8–9, Saturday 7–9, Sunday 7–8. Dinner reservations recommended. Best known for its breakfast featuring Parker's own maple syrup. The dinner menu is "home cooked meat and potato."

Wilton Diner (654-6567), Main Street, Route 31 (next to the fire station), Wilton Village. A classic diner but with window boxes and curtains suggesting a female touch. Specialties include an authentic, bargain-priced Wednesday night smorgasbord, Friday chowder, and superlative pies (we recommend the walnut).

ENTERTAINMENT   *Music:*   **Monadnock Music** (924-7610), Box 255, Peterborough. This is a prestigious series of some two dozen concerts, operas, and orchestra performances staged by highly professional artists in town halls, churches, and schools; also under a tent high on Crotched Mountain. Some are free, others range in price from $8–$21.50; all are in July and August. The three major locations are the Jaffrey Center Meeting House, the Pine Hill School in Wilton, and under a tent at the Crotched Mountain Foundation in Greenfield, site of most larger orchestral and opera performances (the audience is invited to bring a picnic to enjoy the spectacular view). Call or send for the current calendar, or check local listings.

Apple Hill Chamber Players (847-3371), Apple Hill Center for Chamber Music, Apple Hill Road, Nelson 03455. Tuesdays evenings 8 PM. In June, July, and August faculty concerts are free. This noted group also performs throughout the country and world.

Temple Band (878-2829). Said to be the oldest town band in the country, performs at the Sharon Art Center, the Jaffrey Bandstand and a number of scheduled festivities throughout the summer. Past masters of oompahpah.

Jaffrey Bandstand. Performances Wednesday evenings in the summer. (Also see The Folkway and Del Rossi's Trattoria under Dining Out.)

Theater: **Peterborough Players** (924-7585), Peterborough. Since 1933 this group has performed everything from Will Shakespeare to Tom Stoppard. One of New England's better known summer theaters.

American Stage Festival (673-7515), Milford. Summer productions usually include a classic, like Shakespeare or Moliero, and new plays. The Young Company stages children's matinees. Tickets $16–$20.

Actors Theater Playhouse (256-8727), Brook and Main streets, West Chesterfield. Serious productions and children's theater in summer months.

Andy's Summer Playhouse (654-2613), Wilton Center. Summer theater for "children of all ages," with classics like "Wind in the Willows." Tickets are reasonably priced.

The Arts Center on Brickyard Pond at Keene State College in Keene and Franklin Pierce College in Rindge. Both stage musical, theatrical, and dance performances. Check local listings.

The Colonial Theater (352-2033), 95 Main Street, Keene. A majestic, magical old theater featuring both current and classic films and live performances.

Dance: **Monadnock Folklore Society** (847-9974), Nelson. Call for the current calendar of events. It always includes Monday night contra dancing in the Nelson Town Hall; also other events in this elegantly simple old building and similar settings throughout the region.

Inn at East Hill Farm is the scene of frequent square dancing (see Lodging).

Lecture and performance series: **Amos Fortune Forum Series**. Ongoing since 1947, Friday evenings in July and August at the Jaffrey Center Meeting House.

Monadnock Summer Lyceum (924-6245), Unitarian Church, Main Street, Peterborough. Every Sunday in July and August at 11 AM.

SELECTIVE SHOPPING   *Antiques:*   Listing every antiques store in the Monadnock Region would fill the rest of this book. Be it said that antiquing is BIG but composed of many small shops, thickest in the **Francestown** and **Fitzwilliam** areas. Free, frequently updated flyers describing these shops and their whereabouts are available locally. **Fitzwilliam Antiques** at the junction of routes 12 and 19, houses the merchandise of 43 dealers. **Noah's Ark Antiques Center** (654-2595), in Wilton, showcases more than 150 dealers. **The Granite State Antique Dealers & Appraisers Association** pamphlet, available from the Peterborough Chamber of Commerce (see Guidance), lists some 20 more dealers beyond the towns covered by the other two free guides.

Galleries: **The Sharon Arts Center** ((924-7256), Route 123, Sharon. Open Tuesday through Saturday 10–5, Sunday 1–5, Mondays seasonally. The three parts to the center are: the Killian Gallery, showcasing quality painting, sculpture, and furniture, most of it for sale; the Handcraft Shop, one of the most extensive crafts shops in the state; and studio space, the scene of classes and workshops in a variety of arts. The museum-like complex is the setting for frequent lectures and concerts.

Monadnock Studios (876-4355 or 876-4779), Fisk Mill, Water Street, Marlborough (turn at the blue house in the middle of the village). A combination work space and gallery for a number of prominent artists—notably Robert Collier, Sandy Sherman, and Nicholas Schrenk, who have gathered here to work with nationally known portrait and landscape artist Richard Whitney. Fine-art photographer Neal Landy and designer Doreen Buffington are also part of the complex. Art lovers will be pleasantly surprised both by the quality and prices. A call ahead is appreciated.

The English Gallery (924-9044), 6 Old Street Road (junction of routes 101 and 123), Peterborough. An extensive gallery with changing exhibits, dependably interesting and quality work.

The North Gallery at Tewksbury's (924-3224), across Route 101 from the English Gallery, Peterborough. A trove of quality crafts: jewelry, hand-blown glass and crystal, lamps, toys, handwoven clothing, blankets, rugs as well as paintings, watercolors and prints.

Unicorn Gallery (357-4567), 13 Roxbury Street, Keene. Open Tuesday through Saturday 11–4. This is a serious gallery featuring "contemporary realism," well-established artists.

Peter Granucci (352-6828), Hammon Hollow, Riverrun Farm, Gilsum. Nationally recognized for his portraits and landscapes, Granucci welcomes visitors to his studio. Just call ahead, please.

Crafts: **Granite Lake Pottery** (847-9908), route 9, Munsonville. Open year-round, daily except Sunday. Handthrown dinnerware and accessories from mugs to lamps to bathrooms sink (the sinks are a specialty).

Five Wings Studio (585-6682), East Lake Road, Fitzwilliam. Susan Link makes and sells her attractive dinnerware—porcelain with an oriental look—and two stoneware lines; also table lamps.

Harrisville Designs (827-3993), Harrisville. Tuesday through Saturday 10–5. Hand-weaving looms are designed and made here, priced from $400 to $3,000. A variety of yarns and weaving accessories are also sold in **The Weaving Center,** housed in an 1850 brick storehouse by the millpond.

Frye's Measure Mill (654-6581), Wilton Center. Open May through December 15, Tuesday through Saturday 10–4. Mill tours are conducted on Saturdays at 2 PM, June 15 to October 15. Housed in part of a nineteenth-century mill that retains its original machinery, some still water-powered to make woodenware. Quilts and coverlets, salt glaze pottery, and other country folk art are also sold.

Peterborough's Mega-stores: Hidden away north of town on Route 202 are two unusual stores which draw their patrons from a hundred miles around.

Brookstone Co. (924-7181), Vose Farm Road. The exterior is a warehouse-like corporate headquarters but step into the retail store and you might well be on Fifth Avenue. The array of clever labor-saving devices is dazzling—tools and homewares you can easily spend hours examining. It's impossible to get away without something wonderfully basic—a $15 desktop device to keep your coffee cup perpetually hot, another $15 device to light your charcoal grill without fluid, etc., etc. Sure you can get the catalog but seeing and fiddling is much more fun.

Eastern Mountain Sports (924-9572), Vose Farm Road. Open Monday through Wednesday 9–6, Thursday 9–9, Saturday 9–6, Sunday noon–6. Founded in Wellesley, MA in 1967, specializing in hard-to-find equipment and clothing for backpacking and climbing enthusiasts, EMS now has 43 stores across the country. This is corporate headquarters and one of the largest stores, the only one with a discount corner.

Marketplaces: **Colony Mill Marketplace** (357-1240), 222 West Street, Keene. Open daily 10–9, Sunday 11–6. This nineteenth-century brick woolen mill now houses 33 shops and a food court. The anchor store is Cherry, Webb & Touraine and the most interesting is **Country Artisans**, a large, handsome crafts gallery displaying batik, kites, quilts, pottery, weaving, ironwork, lamps and shades, toys, etc., etc. **Toadstool Bookstore** is also here.

    Keene Mill Outlet, 149 Emerald Street (just down from the Colony Mill Marketplace), Keene. Houses 23 outlet stores; brand names include Aileen sportswear, Gitano, Dunham, Mighty-Mac, Crazy Horse, Bass and Van Heusen. **Toy Liquidators** also features thousands of brand name items at big savings and **The Book Warehouse** promises 50 to 90 percent discounts.

Special Shops: **Ashwood Basket Corp.**(924-0000), 350 Union Street, Peterborough. Classic picnic baskets, hampers, even bassinets; a variety of sturdy products made on the premises, sold throughout the country.

    Joseph's Coat (924-6683), 26 Main Street, Peterborough. Quilting is what this place is about, but there are a variety of sewing workshops; handmade clothes.

    The Toadstool Bookstore (924-3543), 3 Main Street, Peterborough. Much bigger than it looks from the outside, a book lovers' bookstore with two floors crammed full of a wide assortment of titles, including regional and art books.

    Keene Mill End Store (352-8683), 55 Ralston Street, Keene. A great source of curtains and custom blinds as well as a vast array of fabrics and trims.

    Eagle's Loft Ltd. (352-4046), 87 Main Street, Keene. Gifts with a capital G and displayed so glitzily that it's well worth an ogle.

    The Oasis (352-5355), 45 Central Square, Keene.. An appealing New Age store selling crystals, clothing, candles, cards, jewelry, a large selection of self-help books, notions of all kinds.

    Thistledown (588-3192), Mountain Road, Francestown. Open Wednesday through Sunday 10–5. Handmade baskets, salt-glazed pottery, reproduction furniture, dried flowers, herbs all make for a worthwhile stop.

    Herb Barn (357-4479), Sawyer's Crossing Road, Swanzey Center. Open weekends 10–4. Extensive gardens and selection of herb products. Guided garden viewing with plant identification and folklore followed by a "Garden Tea" is available by reservation.

    Pickity Place (878-1151), Nutting Hill Road, Mason. A large herb garden and gift shop, catalog (also see Dining Out).

Antiquarian bookshops: **Eagle Books** (357-8721), 19 West Street, just off Central Square, Keene. Open daily except Sunday and holidays. 12,000 volumes specializing in WPA writers' project books.

Homestead Bookshop (786-4213), Route 101 just east of Marlborough Village next to Wilber Brothers Supermarket, Marlborough. Open daily. 45,000 volumes specializing in juvenile series, town histories, older fiction.

Hurley Books (399-4342), east side of Route 12 (just north of Route 63), Westmoreland. Open by appointment or chance. 35,000 volumes specializing in religious, farming, and gardening.

Rainy Day Books (585-3443), Fitzwilliam. Open May to mid-November, Thursday through Monday 11–5:30. Specialties include mountaineering, fiber arts, cooking.

SPECIAL EVENTS   May: **Spring Concert,** Monadnock Chorus and Orchestra.

Late June: **The Annual Rock Swap in Gilsum** (behind the elementary school on route 10) attracts 8,000–10,000 mineral buffs.

July: (See Entertainment for music, theater, and lecture series in July and August.) **July 4th celebrations,** fireworks in Peterborough. **Fourth of July Summer Festival,** sponsored by Monadnock Community Day Care.

August: **Peterborough Days.** Two-day sales, family entertainment, fireworks. **Festival of Fireworks,** Jaffrey Airport. **Oak Park Festival,** Greenfield. At Full Moon the **Old Homestead** is performed in the Potash Bowl, a natural amphitheater in Swanzey. **Medal Day,** MacDowell Colony. **Old Home Days,** Hancock.

September: **Annual Arts & Crafts Fair,** Crotched Mountain Ski Area. **Labor Day Festival,** Francestown. **Annual Benefit Auction,** Peterborough Players. **Annual Balloon Festival,** Monadnock Travel Council.

October: **Annual Wool Arts Tour.** Sheep farms in Francestown, Antrim, and Hillsborough invite visitors in for a weekend to see spinning, dyeing, knitting, and weaving. Check with the Hillsboro Chamber of Commerce (see Guidance). **Foliage Festivals** in Francestown, Greenfield. **Antique Auto Show and Octoberfest,** at Crotched Mountain Foundation. German music, food, and classic cars. **Annual Quilt Show,** Monadnock Quilters Guild. **Annual Book Fair,** MacDowell Colony.

November: **Monadnock Music Christmas Fair,** Peterborough Elementary School.

December: **Christmas Teas** at the Sharon Arts Center. **Messiah Festival** at Franklin Pierce College. **Monadnock Chorus & Orchestra Christmas Concert** at Peterborough Town Hall.

Ongoing art exhibits at Sharon & Eng Art gallery. Crimson-Grey cultural series at Franklin Pierce College during school year.

IV. The Upper Connecticut River Valley

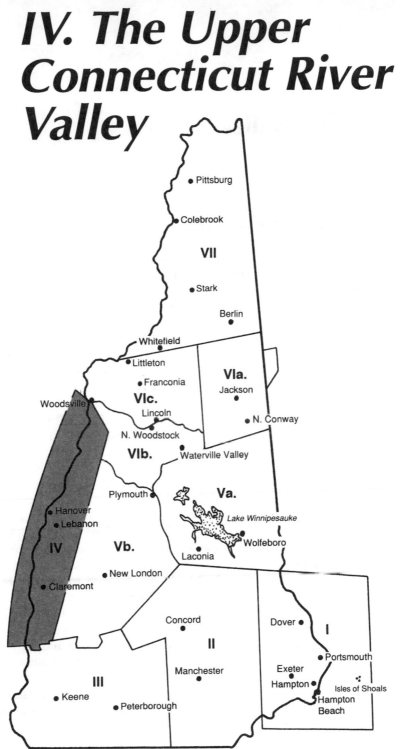

Pittsburg

Colebrook

VII

Stark

Berlin

Whitefield

Littleton

Franconia

VIc.

Lincoln

N. Woodstock

VIb.

Woodsville

Hanover

Lebanon

IV

VIa.

Jackson

N. Conway

Waterville Valley

Va.

Plymouth

Lake Winnipesauke

Wolfeboro

Vb.

Laconia

New London

Claremont

Concord

Dover

I

II

Portsmouth

Manchester

Exeter

Hampton

Isles of Shoals

III

Keene

Peterborough

Hampton
Beach

Upper Valley Towns

The Upper Valley ignores state lines to form one of New England's most beautiful and distinctive regions. Its two dozen towns are scattered along both the Vermont and New Hampshire banks of the Connecticut River for some 20 miles north and south of Dartmouth College.

"Upper Valley" is a name coined in the 1950s by a local daily, *The Valley News,* to define its two-state circulation area. The label has stuck, interestingly enough, to the same group of towns that, back in the 1770s, tried to form the state of "New Connecticut." The Dartmouth-based, pro-New Connecticut party was thwarted, however, by larger powers (namely New York and New Hampshire) along with the strident Vermont independence faction—the Green Mountain Boys.

The valley itself has prospered, as evidenced by the exquisite Federal-era meetinghouses and mansions still salted throughout this area. The river remained the area's only highway into the 1820s when steamboats traveled upriver to Woodsville and Wells River.

Of the dozens of bridges that once linked towns on either side of the river only 10 survive, but they include the longest covered bridge in the United States (connecting Windsor and Cornish). The Upper Valley phone book, moreover, includes towns on both sides of the river, and Hanover's Dresden School District reaches into Vermont. Several Independence Day parades start in one state and finish across the bridge in the other. The Montshire Museum, founded in Hanover but now in Norwich, combines both states in its very name.

The cultural center of the Upper Valley remains Dartmouth Green in Hanover. With the nearby medical complex and West Lebanon shopping strip, this area forms the region's hub, handy to the highways radiating, the way rail lines once did, from White River Junction.

North and south of the Hanover area, old river towns drowse and the river roads are well worth finding. On the river itself canoes remain the prime mode of transportation; campsites and inns are spaced along the shore.

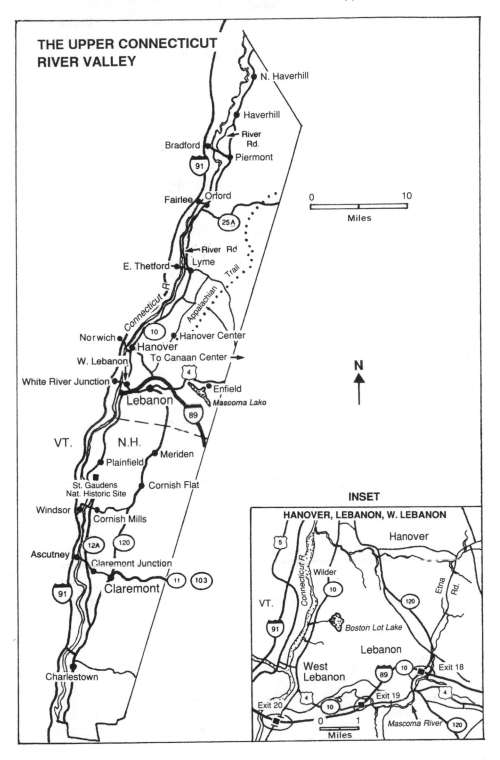

THE UPPER CONNECTICUT
RIVER VALLEY

N. Haverhill

Haverhill

River
Rd.

Bradford

91

Piermont

Fairlee   Orford

25 A

0   10
Miles

River Rd

E. Thetford   Lyme

Appalachian   Trail

Connecticut R.

10

Norwich   Hanover Center

Hanover

W. Lebanon

To Canaan Center →

White River Junction

4

Enfield

Lebanon

Mascoma Lake

89

N

VT.   N.H.

Meriden

Plainfield

St. Gaudens
Nat. Historic Site

Cornish Flat

Windsor

Cornish Mills

12A   120

Ascutney

Claremont Junction

91

Claremont

11   103

Charlestown

INSET

HANOVER, LEBANON, W. LEBANON

Hanover

5

Wilder

Connecticut R.

10

Etna Rd.

120

VT.

91

Boston Lot Lake

Lebanon

West
Lebanon

10

Exit 18

89

4

Exit 19

4

Exit 20

10

Mascoma River   120

0   1
Miles

GETTING THERE   By car: Interstates 91 and 89 converge in the White River Junction (VT)/Lebanon (NH) area, where they also meet Route 5 north and south on the Vermont side; Route 4, the main east-west highway through central Vermont; and Route 10, the river road on the New Hampshire side.

By bus: White River Junction, VT is a hub for **Greyhound/Vermont Transit** (800-321-0707 or 802-293-3011) with express service to Boston. This is one of New England's few pleasant bus stations with clean, friendly dining and snack rooms.

By air: The **Lebanon Municipal Airport** (298-8878), West Lebanon, has service to and from Boston's Logan Airport, New York's LaGuardia Airport, and the Newark Airport via Business Express and Northwest Airlines.

National, Avis, Hertz, Alamo, and American International are all available for **car rentals**.

By train: **AMTRAK** (802-295-7160 or 800-872-7245) stops in White River Junction en route to and from New York's Penn Station—7:55 AM and 10:40 AM southbound; 12:10 PM and 8:15 PM northbound.

GUIDANCE   The **Upper Valley Convention and Visitors Bureau** (800-370-6488). Weekdays 9–5. Offers advice on local lodging as well as attractions; keeps a log on local vacancies during crunch times like big football game weekends and foliage season.

The **Hanover Chamber of Commerce** (643-3115), 37 South Main Street, Hanover. Open 9–noon weekdays. The chamber dispenses flyers and brochures year-round and, in conjunction with Dartmouth College, maintains a kiosk on Dartmouth Green during summer months—a source of even more brochures, maps, advice on where to eat, what to see, and the starting point for regularly scheduled tours of the campus.

The **Greater Lebanon Chamber of Commerce** (448-1203), PO Box 97, On The Mall, Lebanon 03766. Weekdays 9–5. The Upper Valley information line actually rings in this office just off Coburn Park—a source of brochures and advice.

Greater Claremont Chamber of Commerce (543-1296), 52 Tremont Square, Claremont 03743.

Charlestown Town Office (826-4400), Charlestown 03603.

MEDICAL EMERGENCY   **Dartmouth-Hitchcock Medical Center** (646-5000), 2 Maynard Street, Hanover. Generally considered the best hospital in northern New England. As of September 1991, the complex is scheduled to move to Route 120.

TO SEE AND DO   Unless otherwise indicated, all telephone numbers are New Hampshire (area code 603).

In Charlestown (from south to north):   **Fort at Number 4** (826-5700), Route 11, 1 mile north of the village. Open Memorial Day to Columbus Day 10–4 (closed Tuesdays and weekdays during the first two weeks in

September). A reconstruction of this stockaded village as it looked in the two decades after 1743. A full 50 miles north of any other town on the Connecticut, it fell once but then withstood repeated Indian attacks. The complex includes a Great Hall, cow barns, and furnished living quarters, an audiovisual program and crafts. Admission: $4.75 adults, $3.25 children 6–11.

Charlestown Main Street was laid out in 1763, 200 feet wide and a mile long, with more than five dozen structures that now comprise a National Historic District; ten buildings predate 1800. Outstanding buildings include the 1840s Congregational Church; the former Charleston Inn (1817), now a commercial building; the Stephen Hassam House (1800); and the Foundation for Biblical Research, housed in a 1770s mansion that's open to the public. Historic Charlestown Walkabout, a walking guide, is available in most town stores.

In Claremont: Traffic from all directions funnels through this city-sized town's **Tremont Square** with its ornate brick buildings, including the massive Italian Renaissance Revival-style **City Hall** with its recently restored Opera House (see Entertainment); the mammoth brick **Monadnock Mills** on Water Street (off Broad and Main) on the Sugar River, generally considered the best preserved nineteenth-century small urban mills in New Hampshire; the gambrel-roofed brick **Sunappee Mill** (1842-22) across the river; and the small brick overseers' cottages (1840s) on Crescent Street. A walking tour is available from the chamber of commerce (see Guidance). Architecture buffs may also want to seek out old **St. Mary's** (Jarvis Hill Road, Route 12A), completed in 1824, and New Hampshire's oldest Catholic church—its lines are unusual, to say the least.

In Cornish: **The Saint-Gaudens National Historic Site** (675-2175), Route 12A. Open 8:30–4:30 daily, late May through October; nominal admission. Along with Dartmouth Green (see Hanover), this is THE sight to see in the Upper Valley. The sculptor's summer home, Aspet, is furnished as it was when he lived here between 1885 and his death in 1907. Saint-Gaudens is remembered for such public pieces as the Shaw memorial on Boston Common, the statue of Admiral Farragut in New York's Madison Square, and the equestrian statue of General William T. Sherman on New York's Fifth Avenue near Central Park. The estate includes a barn/studio, a sculpture court, and an art gallery, set in formal gardens with Mt. Ascutney across the river as a backdrop. Saint-Gaudens loved the Ravine Trail, a quarter-mile cart path now marked for visitors, and other walks laid out through the woodlands and wetlands to the Blow-me-Down Natural Area. Visitors are invited to bring picnics before the Sunday concerts (2 PM) in July and August; also to view the changing art exhibits in the art gallery. The site is maintained by the National Park Service.

The Cornish-Windsor Covered Bridge, Route 12A, is the country's longest covered bridge. It was built by James Tasher in 1866, rebuilt in 1989.

Trinity Church, Route 12A. Completed in 1808, a classic old meetinghouse in a timeless setting.

Blow-Me-Down Mill, Route 12A, just beyond the entrance to Aspet. Designed by Standford White. Saint-Gaudens and White worked on a number of projects together, like New York's old Madison Square Garden—designed by White with a statue of Diana by Saint-Gaudens on its tower.

The Cornish Colony. Continuing up Route 12A from Aspet (see above) you notice a number of fine old mansions, many of which served as turn-of-the-century summer homes for artists and writers. This "Cornish Colony" included actress Ethel Barrymore; artists Charles Dana Gibson, Maxfield Parrish, and George de Forest Brush; and the American novelist Winston Churchill (a historic marker about 200 yards south of the Plainfield-Cornish line marks his estate which was used as a summer White House by President Woodrow Wilson in 1914 and 1915).

Two More Covered Bridges. Two bridges, both designed by James Tasker in 1882, span the Mill Brook—one in Cornish "city" and the other in Cornish "Mills" between routes 12A and 120.

In Enfield: **Museum at Lower Shaker Village** (632-4346), Route 4A. Open June to October 15, Monday through Saturday 10–5 and Sunday noon–5 ; October 15 to June 1 closing at 4. Admission: $3 per adult, $1 age 10–18; guided tours extra. The Shaker community, founded in 1793, prospered here through the nineteenth century, but the complex was sold to the Catholic order of La Salette in 1924. The Great Stone House, said to be the largest Shaker dwelling anywhere, is now a combination restaurant and conference center, and surrounding buildings—the former Catholic chapel and school buildings and a developer's new condos—create a hodgepodge effect. The small museum is the scene of frequent workshops in Shaker crafts: woodworking, chair-taping, natural dyeing,herbal wreath-making. Winter and spring lectures are also offered.

La Salette Shrine and Center (632-4301), Route 4A. In 1985 the La Salette brothers sold most of their complex—including most of the Shaker buildings on Lake Mascoma—to developers. They still maintain the shrine, founded in 1951, on a hill behind their shop. Inquire for Mass and devotional schedule.

In Hanover: **Dartmouth College.** Chartered in 1769, Dartmouth is the ninth oldest and one of the most prestigious colleges in the country with 4,000 undergraduate men and women and 1,000 graduate students. Dartmouth's handsome buildings frame three sides of its elm-shaded green, and the fourth side includes a large inn, an arts center, and an outstanding art museum. The information kiosk on the Green is

The Hood Museum of Art and the Hopkins Center, on the campus of
Dartmouth College.

Photo by Stuart Bratesman

staffed by knowledgeable Dartmouth alumni during summer months
and is the starting point for historical and architectural tours of the
campus. For information about other year-round tours phone the
admissions office: 646-2875.

Baker Memorial Library (for tour hours phone 646-2560). A 1920s
version of Philadelphia's Independence Hall dominates the north side
of the Green. Visitors are welcome to see the set of murals, "The Epic
of American Civilization" by Jose Orozco, painted between 1932 and
1934 while he was teaching at Dartmouth. (Some alumni once
demanded these be removed or covered because of the Mexican
artist's left-wing politics.) In the Treasure Room (near the west stair
hall on the main floor) Daniel Webster's copies of the double elephant
folio first edition of John Audubon's *Birds of America* are permanently
displayed.

Hood Museum of Art (646-2808), Dartmouth Green. Open Tuesday
through Sunday 11–5; Saturday until 8. Free. Housed in a 1980s building designed by Charles W. Moore, the collection is billed as the coun-

try's oldest, begun in 1773 when the colonial governor of New Hampshire presented Dartmouth President Wheelock with a silver monteith. It now ranges eclectically from Assyrian bas-reliefs, donated by missionary graduates in the 1850s, to Italian masters, American eighteenth-century portraits, and nineteenth-century landscapes to a huge abstract piece by Dartmouth graduate Frank Stella. Treasures include an 1840s polychrome baseball player donated by Abby Aldrich Rockefeller in 1935. Special exhibits change frequently and informal chamber music concerts are held regularly in the museum.

Hopkins Center for the Arts (646-2422) was designed by Wallace Harrison a few years before he designed Lincoln Center in New York (which it resembles). It contains two theaters, a recital hall, and art galleries for permanent and year-round programs of plays, concerts, and films. It's also home base for the Dartmouth Symphony Orchestra.

Dartmouth Row. These striking white Greek Revival buildings on the rise along the east side of the Green represent all there was to Dartmouth College until 1845. Three of the buildings were designed in the 1820s by Lebanon architect Ammi Young.

Webster Cottage (643-2326), North Main Street (two blocks north of the Green). Memorial Day to Columbus Day, Wednesday, Saturday, and Sunday 2:30–4:30 and by appointment. Built in 1780 as the home of Abigail Wheelock (daughter of Dartmouth founder Eleazar Wheelock), it was also the senior-year (1801) residence of Daniel Webster and birthplace in 1822 of Henry Fowle Durant, founder of Wellesley College. Maintained as a museum by the Hanover Historical Society.

Shattuck Observatory (phone the Physics Department, 646-2034). Weekdays 8:30–4:40. Open Tuesday and Thursday evenings year-round by reservation. No charge. Designed by Ammi Young, built in 1843. Senior students use the 9.4-inch refractor telescope or the 10-inch Celestion telescope for an introduction to astronomy and a view of the northern sky.

In Haverhill: The town of Haverhill is immense, composed of seven very distinct villages, including classic examples of both Federal-era and railroad villages. Thanks to a fertile floodplain, this is an old and prosperous farming community and even with agricultural land now under 9,000 acres, it still boasts more than 20 farms. It has also been the county seat of Grafton County since 1773.

The Village of Haverhill Corner on Route 10/11 is a gem. It is a grouping of Federal-era and Greek Revival homes and public buildings around a double, white-fenced common (the site of all-day flea markets on the last Sunday of summer months). Just north of the village (but south of the junction of Route 10 with 25) a sign points the way, down through a cornfield and along the river, to the site of the **Bedell Bridge**. Built in 1866 it was one of the largest surviving exam-

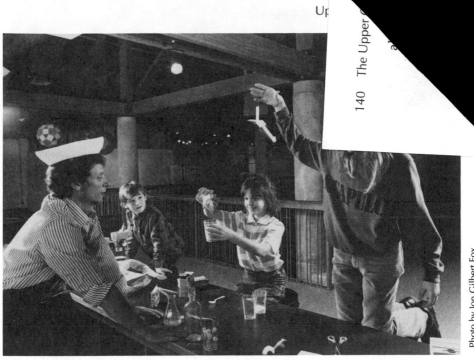

The soda fountain is a new hands-on activity at the Montshire Museum, in Norwich, Vermont, just across the Connecticut River from Hanover.

ples of a two-span covered bridge until it was destroyed by a violent September windstorm in 1979 (it had just been completely restored). The site is still worth finding because it's a peaceful riverside spot, ideal for a picnic. North of North Haverhill you come unexpectedly to a lineup of modern county buildings—the courthouse, a county home, and a jail—and then you are in **Woodsville** with its ornate 1890s brick Opera Block and three-story, mustard-colored railroad station. The **Haverhill/Bath covered bridge**, built in 1829 and billed as the oldest covered bridge in New England, is just beyond the railroad underpass (Route 135 north).

In Lyme: **The Congregational Church**, completed in 1812, is a splendid, Federal-style meetinghouse complete with Palladian window, an unusual tower (three cubical stages and an octagonal dome), and no less than 27 numbered horse stalls. The gathering of buildings, including the inn, fine old houses, and general stores, is one of New Hampshire's most stately. Take the **River Road** north by old farms and cemeteries, through an 1880s covered bridge.

In Norwich, VT: **The Montshire Museum of Science** (649-2200), the first left after the bridge from Hanover (before the I-91 off-ramp). Open daily 10–5, until 8 PM Tuesdays. Admission: $4 per adult, $2 per child. An offshoot of a fusty old Dartmouth College museum filled with stuffed birds, now a nationally recognized science education center geared to all ages. It includes a microscopium, a theater of video microscopy, and exhibits ranging from leaf-cutter ants (more than 25,000 of them) to a Physics Playground. The 100-acre site includes two nature trails, a short walk along the Connecticut River, and a longer hike through woods and meadows.

In Orford: **The Ridge Houses,** Route 10. A lineup of seven houses so strikingly handsome that Charles Bulfinch has been (erroneously) credited as their architect. They were built instead by skilled local craftsmen using designs from Connecticut Valley architect Asher Benjamin's do-it-your-self guide to Federal styles, *The Country Builder's Assistant*. These houses testify to the prosperity of this valley in the post-Revolutionary War era. Each of these exquisite houses was built by an Orford resi-dent—with money earned in Orford—between 1773 and 1839. The best remembered of the residents was Samuel Morey. While all his neigh-bors were in church one Sunday morning in 1793, Morey gave the country's first little steam-powered paddlewheeler a successful test run on the river. Sam kept tinkering with the boat and in 1797 came up with a sidewheeler, but at this point Robert Fulton, who had encour-aged him to freely discuss and demonstrate his invention with him, turned around and went into the steamboating business, using a boat clearly patterned after Morey's. It's said that an embittered Morey sank his boat in the Vermont lake across the river which now bears his name. He also heated and lighted his house with water gas, and in 1826 patented a gas-powered internal combustion engine. The Samuel Morey House is the oldest of the seven, a centerpiece for the others; it's open by appointment from June through Columbus Day with tours by its owner, local historian Alice Doan Hodgson (353-4815).

In Piermont: **Polygonal Barn,** built in 1906, is a 16-sided barn north of Piermont Village on Route 10.

In Wilder, VT: **Wilder Dam Visitors' House and Fish Ladder** (295-3191), Route 5. Open daily 9–5, Memorial Day to Columbus Day; free. Displays about salmon, the fish ladder, and energy. In June and part of July fish, sometimes salmon, can occasionally be seen using the ladders.

In Windsor, VT: **The American Precision Museum** (802-674-5781), South Main Street. Open May 30 to November 1, 9–5; nominal admission. An important, expanding collection of hand and machine tools assembled in the 1846 Robbins, Kendall & Lawrence Armory, itself a National Historic Landmark. The firm became world famous in 1851 because of its displays of "the American system" of manufacturing inter-changeable parts, especially for what became the renowned Enfield rifle.

Old Constitution House (802-674-6628), North Main Street. Open daily, mid-May to mid-October. This is Elijah West's tavern (but not in its original location) where delegates gathered July 2, 1777, to adopt Vermont's constitution. It now holds an intriguing collection of antiques, prints, documents, tools and cooking utensils, tableware, toys, and early fabrics.

(For **Bath** and **Lisbon** see Franconia and North of the Notches.)

WALKS   **Pine Park,** just north of the Dartmouth campus between the Hanover Country Club and the Connecticut River, Hanover. Take North Main Street to Rope Ferry Road and park at the trail sign above the clubhouse. These tall pines along the river are one of the beauty spots of the valley. The 125-year-old trees were saved from the Diamond Match Company in 1900 by a group of local citizens to whom anyone who walks through them is deeply grateful. The walk is 1.5 miles.

Rinker Tract, Route 10, 2.5 miles north of Hanover. This is an 18-acre knoll with a pond, at the bottom of the hill below the Chieftan Motel. The loop trail is marked by blue blazes.

More than three dozen more easily negotiable walks are described in *Walks & Rambles in the Upper Connecticut River Valley* by Mary Kibling (Backcountry Publications).

AIR RIDES   **Ladco** (298-8728), Lebanon Airport. Offers scenic tours of the Upper Valley. $46 per hour for one person, $57 for three.

Boland Balloon (802-333-9254), at Post Mills Airport, West Fairlee, VT. Offers year-round morning and sunset balloon rides. On the summer evening we tried it, the balloon hovered above hidden pockets in the hills, and we saw a herd of what looked like brown and white goats that, on closer inspection, proved to be deer (yes, some were white!). After an hour or so we settled down gently in a farmyard and broke out the champagne. Flights are $150 per person, less when combined with packages at nearby Silver Maple Lodge (see Bed & Breakfasts). Scenic plane rides and flight instruction also offered.

BICYCLING   Given its unusually flat and scenic roads and well-spaced inns, this area is beloved by bicyclists. Search out the river roads (for some reason they're not marked on the official New Hampshire highway map): from Route 12A (just north of the Saint-Gaudens site) on through Plainfield until it rejoins Route 12A; from Route 10 north of Hanover (just north of the Chieftan Motel) through Lyme, rejoining Route 10 in Orford. A classic, 36 mile loop is Hanover to Orford on Route 10 and back on the river road. The loop to Lyme and back is 22 miles. A variety of rides, including some for mountain bikers, are described in the *Hanover Area Recreation Guide* by Carol Selikowitz (see Dartmouth Bookstore under Selective Shopping).

Wilderness Trails (802-295-7620), at the Quechee Inn, Quechee, VT. Rents 18- and 21-speed mountain bikes, $13 a day (that includes the option of canoeing on the adjacent pond).

The Ascutney Resort Activities Center (484-7711), Brownsville, VT. Also rents mountain bikes, $18 per day.

BOAT CRUISES   **Connecticut River Party Boat** (649-3860). Inquire about cruises from Ledyard Bridge to Wilson's Landing.

CANOEING   With its usually placid water and scenery, the Connecticut River through much of the Upper Valley is ideal for easy-going canoeists.

Connecticut River Watershed Council (675-2518), Box 189, Plainfield 03781, with offices on Route 12A in Cornish. *The Complete Boating Guide to the Connecticut River* ($11.95), the bible to the river, is available from the council or in local bookstores; essential for nonguided trips. Inquire about educational day and camping trips.

"Canoeing on the Connecticut River," a free, detailed pamphlet guide to this particular stretch of the river, is available from the Vermont Division of Recreation and Department of Water Resources Agency of Environmental Conservation, Montpelier VT 05602.

Most of the outfitters listed below provide their own basic maps.

The Ledyard Canoe Club (646-2753), in Hanover, is billed as the oldest canoe club in America. It's part of Dartmouth but open to the public 9–8 daily in summer, shorter hours in spring and fall. Canoes and kayaks are rented, and instruction is available.

North Star Canoes (542-5802), Route 12A in Cornish. This riverside red barn is well stocked with canoes and free maps; also the source of a reasonably priced shuttle service to the particularly scenic stretch of the Connecticut between Charlestown on the south and Hartland Rapids on the north. Camping available at Wilgus State Park (802-674-5422) in Windsor.

Wilderness Trails (802-295-7620), at the Quechee Inn, Quechee, VT. Martin Banak will shuttle canoes and patrons—putting in at the White River, taking out at North Hartland. $40 per canoe (two people).

Inn-to-Inn Tours (802-333-9124), or write Arthur Sharkey, Stone House Inn, North Thetford, VT 05054. The oldest inn-to-inn canoeing program in New England, this is a self-guided, three-day package put together by two New Hampshire and one Vermont inn. Participants rendezvous on Monday afternoons at the Ledyard Canoe Club (see above) and are shuttled to the Haverhill Inn. Tuesday they canoe downriver to the Stone House and Wednesday to Hanover for a final night high on a ridge at Moose Mountain Lodge. The $250 fee includes all meals, shuttles, and taxes; rental canoes are $45 for the three days.

Canoe USA (802-496-3127) also offers guided inn-to-inn tours to segments of the river.

FISHING   You can eat the fish you catch in the Connecticut River—it yields brown and rainbow trout above Orford. There's a boat launch at the Wilder Dam.

Lake Mascoma is a popular angling spot. Boat launches are found along Route 4A in Lebanon and Enfield.

Wilderness Trails (802-295-7620), at the Quechee Inn, Quechee, VT. Runs a Vermont Fly-Fishing School geared to all levels of experience; also "fishing for the whole family," expeditions to Dewey's

Mills Waterfowl Sanctuary where 6-pound largemouth bass are not uncommon.

GOLF   **Hanover Country Club** (646-2000), Hanover. Open May to October. Founded in 1899, an 18-hole facility with four practice holes, pro shop, PGA instructors.

Carter Golf Club (448-4488), Lebanon. Nine holes, par 36.

Lake Morey Country Club (802-333-4800 or 800-423-1211). Eighteen holes, site of the Vermont Open for the past 40 years (third Sunday of June).

Windsor Country Club (802-674-6491), Windsor, VT. Nine holes, par 34, no lessons.

Fore-U Driving Range (298-9702), Route 12A, West Lebanon. Buckets of balls to hit off mats or grass.

MAPLE SYRUPING   **Brokenridge Farm** (542-8781), Route 120, Cornish. Sap is gathered with horses on weekends; sugar-on-snow, tours.

Orford has the biggest local concentration of maple syruping operations, including:

Mount Cube Farm (353-4709), Route 25A. Owned by former New Hampshire Governor Meldrim Thompson. The Sugar House Lodge here serves pancake breakfasts on weekends all winter.

Gerald and Toni Pease (353-9070), Pease's Scenic Highway, off Route 25A. Draft horse with wagon or sleigh.

Sugar House at Indian Pond (272-4950), Indian Pond Road.

Sunday Mountain Maple Products (353-4883), Route 25A. Sugar House open year-round, tours.

STOCK CAR RACING   **Claremont Speedway** (543-3160), Bowker Street, 4 miles east of I-91, Claremont. April to September, racing Saturdays 7:30 PM.

SWIMMING   **Storrs Pond Recreation Area** (643-2134), off Route 10 north of Hanover (Reservoir Road then left). Open June through Labor Day, 10–8. Bathhouse with showers and lockers, lifeguards at both the (unheated), olympic-size pool and 15-acre pond. Fee for nonmembers.

Treasure Island (802-333-9615), on Lake Fairlee, Thetford, VT. This fabulous town swimming area is on Route 244 (follow Route 113 north of town). Open late June to Labor Day, 10–8 weekends, 12–8 weekdays. Sand beach, picnic tables, playground, tennis. Nominal admission.

Union Village Dam Area (802-649-1606), Thetford, VT. Open from Memorial Day to mid-September: five swimming areas along the Ompompanoosuc River.

CROSS-COUNTRY SKIING   **Occum Touring Center** (646-2440), Rope Ferry Road (off Route 10 just before the country club), Hanover. Closed Mondays. Thirty-five km of trails through Storrs Pond and Oak Hill areas; rentals, lessons, waxing clinics. The center is on the lower level of the Outing Club House.

Mt. Cube (353-4709), Route 12A in Orford. Rentals, equipment, pancakes at Sugar House Lodge, 20 km of trails, rentals.

Ascutney Mountain Resort (802-484-7771), Ascutney, VT. A touring center with instruction, rentals, 32 km of trails.

Lake Morey Inn Resort (802-333-4800 or 800-423-1211). Turns the golf course into a touring center; rentals, instruction.

Wilderness Trails (802-295-7620), at the Quechee Inn, Quechee, VT. Twelve miles of touring trails through woods and meadows, one trail to Quechee Gorge.

DOWNHILL SKIING   Ascutney Mountain Resort (802-484-7771), Route 44, Brownsville, VT. A family-geared, self-contained resort with 31 trails and slopes, three triple and one double chairlifts, 1,530-foot vertical drop, 70 percent snowmaking, SKIwee program. $30 per adult weekends, $15 midweek; $18 per junior weekends, $15 midweek.

Dartmouth Skiway (795-2143), Lyme Center. Sixteen trails, two chairlifts, a beginners' J-bar, 900-foot vertical drop, ski rentals, instruction, 54 acres covered by snowmaking. $26 per adult weekends, $21 weekdays; $21 per junior weekends, $19 weekdays.

Storrs Hill (448-4409), Lebanon. Open Tuesday, Wednesday, Friday 6–9; Saturday noon–5. Managed by the Lebanon Outing Club, run by volunteers: one poma lift, two trails. Single ride: 25 cents. Evenings: $3 per adult, $2 per child (to age 16); Saturdays: $4 per adult, $3 per child.

ICE SKATING   Occum Pond, next to the country club, Hanover. Kept plowed and planed, lit evenings until 10 unless unsafe for skating; warming hut.

Ascutney Mountain Resort (802-484-7771), Brownsville, VT. Lighted skating rink with rental skates.

SLEIGH RIDES   North Star Canoe (542-5802), Route 12A, Cornish. Rides offered along the Connecticut River and up through a hidden valley; hot cider included in price of the ride. $8 per person but $50 minimum to go out.

HOTELS   The Hanover Inn (643-4300 or 800-443-7024), Hanover 03755. This is the Ritz of the north country. Like the Boston Ritz it overlooks THE cultural common (the Dartmouth Green) of New Hampshire and exudes a distinctly tweedy elegance. Guest rooms are each individually and deftly decorated and the junior suites—with canopy beds, eiderdown quilts, armchairs, a silent valet, couch, and vanity—are pamperingly luxurious. A four-story, 92-room, neo-Georgian building owned and operated by Dartmouth College, the "inn" traces itself back to 1780 when the college's steward, General Ebenezer Brewster, turned his home into a tavern. Brewster's son parleyed this enterprise into the Dartmouth Hotel, which continued to thrive until 1887 when it burned to the ground. The present building dates in part from this era but has lost its Victorian lines through successive renovations and expansions. It remains, however, the heart of Hanover. In summer the front terrace is crowded with faculty, visitors, and residents enjoying a light lunch or beer. Year-round the lobby, the porch rocking chairs, and the Hayward Room (a comfortable sitting room with claw-foot sofas and flowery armchairs, dignified portraits, and a frequently lit hearth) are popular spots for friends to meet. Roughly half the inn's guests are Dartmouth-related. Both the Ivy Grill and more formal Daniel Webster Room draw patrons from throughout the Upper Valley (see Dining Out). Rates are $144–$267, no charge for children under age 12; senior citizens' discount; honeymoon, ski, golf, and seasonal packages.

In Vermont: **The Hotel Coolidge** (802-295-3118 or 800-622-1124), 17 South Main Street, White River Junction. A "find" for the enterprising, economy-minded traveler. Built in 1925 and recently renovated, this 53-room hotel is across from the AMTRAK station, one of the last of New England's old railroad hotels. Rooms are brightly papered, furnished in solid old pieces, all with phones and TVs; some adjoining, good for families. Local buses to Hanover and Lebanon stop at the door and rental cars can be arranged. The hotel's informal restaurant, Cashie's, is well loved locally (see Eating Out). Owner/manager David Briggs, a seventh-generation Vermonter, takes his role as innkeeper seriously and will arrange for special needs. $45–$55 double; many packages including murder mystery weekends.

RESORTS   **Loch Lyme Lodge and Cottages** (795-2141 or 800-423-2141), Route 10, RFD 278, Lyme 03768. Main lodge open year-round; cabins, Memorial Day to Labor Day. There are four rooms in the inn, 26 brown-shingle cabins are spread along a wooded hillside; some are housekeeping with up to four bedrooms. The big attraction here is a private lakefront beach with a float and fleet of rowboats and canoes; also a windsurfer. Two tennis courts, croquet, a baseball field, a basketball court, a volleyball net, and a recreation cabin are there for the using, and babysitting is available for parents who want time off. Lunch and dinner are served; picnic lunches available in summer when there's also a snack bar. Paul and Judy Barker are your hosts; the lodge has been in their family since the '40s. No credit cards. Pets permitted in cabins. From $24 per person off-season (when there's cross-country skiing on the property and the Dartmouth Skiway is just up the road) to $37 per person per night in summer. Housekeeping cabins are $315–$500 per week; weekly MAP and children's rates also available.

Kluge's (632-4335), Sunset Hill, Enfield 03748. A private beach on Mascoma Lake, all rooms with private bath, a swimming pool, and 300 acres of private woodland and meadow are the draws here. Seasonal. $75 double per day, $300 per person per week; includes three meals.

In Vermont: **Rutledge Inn & Cottages** (802-333-9722), Fairlee 05045. Open May through Labor Day on Lake Morey with a private beach, rowboats, canoes, sailboats, and an old-fashioned "casino" rec hall. Three bountiful meals are served in the cheerful dining room of the central lodge, a building that also includes a lounge and library. From $51 per day in the lodge to $63 in the best cottages, less for children; by the week and in May before the dining room opens.

COUNTRY INNS   **Moose Mountain Lodge** (643-3529), PO Box 272, Moose Mountain Highway, Etna 03750. Closed November to December 25 and late March through May. Just 7 miles from Dartmouth Green, the feel is remote and the view, spectacular. The design is "classic lodge," built from stones and logs cleared from these hills, walled in pine. The roomy back porch (flower-filled in summer) is like a balcony seat above the valley, commanding a view of Vermont mountains from Ascutney to Sugarbush, with Killington off across lower hills, stage center. This is also the view from the sitting room with its window seats and massive stone fireplace. Upstairs the rooms are small but inviting (with spruce log bedsteads made by Kay Shumway herself) and shared baths, which are immaculate. Kay is justly famed as a cook, one adept at preparing nightly feasts for the groups of hikers (the inn is just off the Appalachian Trail), bikers, and cross-country skiers (there's a long ride trail) who frequent the place. Kay and Peter Shumway have been innkeepers here since 1975 and still welcome each new guest with enthusiasm and interest. $74 per person MAP in summer and fall, $80 per person AP (all meals) in winter. No smoking.

The Lyme Inn (795-2222 or 795-4404), On the Common, Lyme 03768. Closed late November through most of December and two weeks in late spring. This distinctive-looking, vintage 1809 inn across from a picture-perfect church (see To See and Do [Lyme]), fits many people's idea of what a country inn should look like: flowery wallpaper, stencils, hand-stitched quilts, antiques, hooked rugs, low-beamed dining rooms, collectibles everywhere. The front lobby with its many things for sale actually looks like a general store. The hearth in the comfortable side parlor is frequently lit, and the adjoining tavern room is inviting. Each of the 12 guest rooms and 2 suites is distinctly decorated; 12 have private baths. Breakfast and dinner are served. $48–$75 per person MAP, depending on room and season.

Dowd's Country Inn (795-4712), On the Common, Lyme 03768. Tami and Mickey Dowd are an enterprising young couple who have turned a 1780s house into an attractive, informal 21-room inn. The old barn now harbors a large living room, a meeting space, a small dining room, and a row of upstairs rooms overlooking the spacious backyard. But I still prefer the rooms in the old house. The Presidential Suite, with its sitting room, can comfortably accommodate a family of five. The cheery breakfast room is also in the old house. $55–$110 per room (depending on room and season), includes breakfast and afternoon tea. The spaces lend themselves to weddings and meetings and group rates are offered.

Home Hill Inn (675-6165), RR 2, Box 235, Cornish 03745. "Ninety-five percent of my business is dining and five percent is sleeping," admits Roger Nicolas, owner of one of the valley's four-square 1820s river mansions. Rooms are predictable: brass beds, country wallpaper, maybe a handmade quilt. There are also a two-room suite and a three-room cottage by the pool. The setting is beautiful: 25 acres by the river, good for walking and cross-country skiing. But dining is what this place is about (see Dining Out). $85–$120 depending on the room and season.

The Shaker Inn (682-7800), at Lower Shaker Village, Route 4A, Enfield 03748. Unfortunately the day I stopped by all the rooms were occupied by an Elderhostel group, so I still can't conscientiously recommend them. This Great Stone Dwelling House, the largest Shaker dwelling ever built, was used as dormitory space for retreats by the La Salette brothers from 1922 until 1985, and 26 rooms ($28–$34) are now available as part of the Shaker Inn and Conference Center. Other more elaborate rooms in the Mary Keane House are $64–$95. Meals are served.

BED & BREAKFASTS   **Haverhill Inn** (989-5961), Route 10, Haverhill 03765. A classic 1810 Federal-style house with canopied beds and working fireplaces in its big, square guest rooms (private baths). My favorite is the "blue room" with its graceful old vanity, cane-backed rocking chair, and Victorian couch. Downstairs walls are decorated with old Grafton County maps, and comfortable chairs and sofas in the sitting room are within reach of plenty to read. Innkeeper Stephen Campbell keeps local menus and is delighted to orient guests. Breakfast is served in front of the mammoth old hearth. $65 per couple (less for a single) includes a full breakfast, midweek.

The Chase House (675-5391), Route 12A, Cornish 03745. Another classic Federal-style mansion, this one begun around 1775 and moved back from the river in the mid-1840s to make way for the Sullivan County Railroad. Salmon Portland Chase, born here in 1808, is remembered as Lincoln's Secretary of the Treasury, a founder of the Republican Party, namesake of the Chase Manhattan Bank, and the man on the $10,000 bill. The house has been carefully restored, its six guest rooms exquisitely decorated in period wallpapers and reproduction antiques, fitted with private baths; windows richly draped with swags. You can walk along the riverbank across the road, and there are trails for skiing and hiking. $75–$95 includes a full breakfast, $15 more in foliage season.

Maple Hedge (826-5237), Box 638, Route 12, Charlestown 03603. Open June through October. Dick and Joan DeBrine have come from

California to fulfill Joan's longtime dream of running a New England B&B. This is a beauty, a big, handsome 1790s Main Street house with elegant spaces—five guest rooms with private baths, each decorated around a theme (the twin-bedded "Cobalt Room" is very red). $75–$85 per couple.

Goddard Mansion (543-0603), 25 Hillstead Road, Claremont 03743. A grand, turn-of-the-century mansion set on a knoll overlooking Mt. Ascutney and tiers of smaller hills. Built in 1905 as a summer home by the president of International Shoe, it has an airy, easy elegance. Frank and Debbie Albee spent two years restoring the house and decorating the eight guest rooms. The living room has a 4 1/2-foot fireplace and a baby grand piano, and there's also a sitting room, a library, and a dining room with a tiffany lamp. The rates are $65–$95 depending on the room and includes a "natural breakfast" of homemade muffins served with preserves made from home-grown fruit; also fresh fruit and whole-grain cereals.

The Occum Inn (646-7053), North Main Street, Hanover 03755. An informal, reasonably priced find, a longtime guest house now owned by Hitchcock Clinic with 10 rooms, 6 with private bath. $46–$60.

Trumbull House (643-1400), Box C-29, Hanover 03755. A handsome old home 3 miles from the Dartmouth campus on the Etna Road. Five elegantly decorated guest rooms with private baths and 16 acres of land with a brook and cross-country ski trails. $85–$130 (for the suite), including a full breakfast.

Piermont Inn (272-4820), 1 Old Church Street, Piermont 03779. A 1790s stagecoach stop with six rooms, four in the adjacent carriage house (only the two in the inn are open year-round), all with private baths. Breakfast and dinner (served Friday and Saturday evenings and by prior arrangement). Your host is Charlie Brown, an enthusiast on canoeing this stretch of the Connecticut.

White Goose Inn (353-4812), Route 10, Orford 03777. An 1830s brick house with an 1850s porch that encircles an old elm tree. The 15 rooms testify to Karen Wolf's stenciling skills; the bicycle groups who frequent the inn have their own space. From $75 with shared bath to $135 for the suite with French doors overlooking the pond and Strawberry Hill; all rates include a full breakfast.

In Vermont: **The Stone House Inn** (802-333-9124), North Thetford 05054. Built in 1835 from schist quarried across the river in Lyme, this year-round inn has an unusually comfortable feel. There are a piano and fireplace in the living room and rockers on the wide, screened porch. The six guest rooms share baths; our favorite room is in the back with windows on the river. There are 12 acres in all, stretching flat and green to the river. Innkeepers Art and Diane Sharkey cater to canoeists (see Canoeing), but they make all guests feel welcome. $48 double includes breakfast.

Juniper Hill Inn (802-674-5273), RR 1, Box 79 (off Route 5 on Juniper Hill Road), Windsor 05069. This is a 28-room, turn-of-the-century mansion, with a view of Mt. Ascutney and the valley. Nine guest rooms have fireplaces. Inn guests gather for meals around the immense table in the pink dining room. Innkeepers Jim and Krishna Pennino encourage guests to canoe (North Star Canoe Livery is just across the covered bridge; see Canoeing). $65–$100 per room, full breakfast included.

Silver Maple Lodge & Cottages (802-333-4326), RR 1, Box 8, Fairlee 05045. Scott and Sharon Wright offer nine modestly priced, nicely appointed guest rooms in the old farmhouse and five pine-paneled, shaded cabins. The $38–$58 per couple rates include continental breakfast; special hot air balloon, bicycling, canoeing, and walking packages available.

MOTELS   **The Chieftan Motor Inn** (643-2550), Route 10 (north of Hanover), Hanover 03755. The 22 units are pine-paneled with heat control, air-conditioning, cable color TV, and phones, and a number have views of the river. There's also a pool, and a continental breakfast is included. $57 double ($49 single) plus tax.

The Sunset (298-8721), Route 10 in West Lebanon, 4 miles south of Hanover. A tidy, family-run place bordering the Connecticut River; 12 of the 18 units have river views. Rooms are cheery with matching wallpaper and curtains; a continental breakfast is included in the $50–$70 per couple rates; less November to April.

DINING OUT   **D'Artagnan** (795-2137), in the Ambrose Publick House, 7 miles north of Hanover on Route 10 in Lyme. Open for dinner Wednesday through Sunday, lunch Sunday only. Generally considered the best (and most expensive) restaurant in the Upper Valley, and the place we plan to celebrate if this book takes off. The setting is a low-beamed, brick-walled room in a reconstructed eighteenth-century tavern near the river, overlooking a brook. The $33 prix fixe, four-course menu changes nightly but typically includes a choice of 10 appetizers—maybe mussel soup with saffron and cream or pâté of fresh pheasant perfumed with green peppercorns and thyme. The half dozen entrées might include sautéed escalope of salmon with leeks, smoked trout sauce, and veal loin with artichokes, mushrooms, and port wine; for dessert, perhaps white chocolate mousse with almond-hazelnut praline and orange creme caramel with orange zeste, Grand Marnier. Needless to say the wine list is extensive. The French-trained chef/owners are Peter Gaylor and his wife, Rebecca Cunningham.

The Hanover Inn (643-4300 or 800-443-7024), corner of Main and Wheelock streets, Hanover. Michael Gray has put the inn's Ivy Grill and the Daniel Webster Room on the culinary map with his variations on traditional New England fare. **The Ivy Grill** is an attractive, informal setting for daily lunch and dinner (serving until 10 PM); the menu includes pizza and burgers but runs to grilled halibut steak with lime, ciantro, and coriander oil ($16.50) and linguini with tomato, mahogany clams, scallops, and mussels ($11.95). In the large, formal **Daniel Webster Room** (open daily for all three meals), with its windows overlooking Dartmouth Green, you might begin with escargot sautéed with cob-smoked ham, shallots, and thyme ($6.25) or a salad of seared quail with apricot, arugula, and bay lettuce, then proceed to grilled marlin with a basil-tomato beurre blanc ($17.50) or poached veal steak and crispy sweetbreads with caramelized shallots, jerez vinegar, and savory ($18.95). A set "tasting menu" is $24.

Café la Fraise (643-8588), 8 Wheelock Street, Hanover. Open for dinner, Monday through Saturday. A yellow 1820s house with geraniums in its window boxes and small, candlelit dining rooms is the setting for continental dining. The constantly changing entrées might include roast duckling with black currant and orange Grand Marnier sauce ($20) and sautéed breast of fresh Vermont pheasant served with a tart green apple sauce ($18).

The Lyme Inn (795-2222), On the Common, Lyme. Open for breakfast and dinner nightly. The atmosphere is traditional New England country inn: three low-beamed, candlelit dining rooms decorated with myriad nineteenth-century baskets, pictures, samples, maps. Specialties include French onion soup and hasenpfeffer ($13.95) and the night's special might be roast leg of lamb ($17.95).

Café Buon Gustaio (643-5711), 72 South Main Street, Hanover. Dining nightly from 5:30–9:30, café bar from 4:30. A cheery, attractive, small café with folk music Tuesdays and Thursdays and a daily changing menu posted outside. Entrées usually include homemade pastas (around $12), maybe veal medallions at $16, steak at $17, calzones at $8.

Home Hill Country Inn (675-6165), River Road, Plainfield. Open for dinner Tuesday through Saturday. A four-square 1820s mansion with a long, formal blue canopy proclaiming its formal dining status. The series of low-ceilinged dining rooms are dressed in white napery. A prix fixe of $28 might include a soufflé of sole and crab with lobster sauce, chateaubriand of New Zealand venison, and white and dark chocolate mousse with raspberry sauce.

Deckelbaum's (643-4075), 11 South Main Street, Hanover. Open for lunch and dinner daily. A brother (definitely not a sister) to the Woodstock restaurant by the same name, a distinctly men's club atmosphere: dark and pubby, with tile floors, a glassed-partitioned area around a long bar with a campy, vaguely Joan of Ark statue as its focal point, walls hung with old photos. The equally eclectic menu runs from tostadas ($5.25), salads, sandwiches and burgers to shrimp santorini.

The Shaker Inn (632-7800), at Lower Shaker Village, Route 4A, Enfield. Closed for dinner Tuesdays, otherwise open daily for breakfast and lunch, Sunday brunch. This is the original Shaker dining hall in the Great Stone Dwelling, and the furnishings are Shaker-style chairs and simple tables; the menu includes Shaker touches. But this is a far cry from the quality of the Creamery at Canterbury Shaker Village (see the Merrimack Valley [Concord Area]). Its reviews are mixed. A typical dinner menu might include baked scrod with cucumber sauce, "duck of the day," chicken New England, and pasta primavera; entrées range from $11–$18 and a multi-course prix fixe dinner is $28.

Indian Shutters Restaurant (826-4366), Route 12, North Charlestown. Open for lunch and dinner Tuesday through Saturday; Sunday brunch and dinner. Probably the oldest tavern in the valley, first licensed in 1799. Named for its original inside sliding shutters, both the atmosphere and menu are traditional American: open-faced sandwiches, burgers, and salad plates for lunch; shrimp cocktail ($6.95), surf and turf ($14.95), baked stuffed chicken breast ($9.95), or prime rib ($14.95) for dinner.

Jesse's (643-4111), Route 120, Hanover. Open daily for dinner. A glitzy high-Victorian atmosphere with greenhouse, featuring salad bar, steak, and seafood. Entrées range from $9.75–$15.

In Vermont: **La Poule a Dents at Carpenter Street** (802-649-2922), Main Street, Norwich. Open for lunch Monday through Friday, for dinner Monday through Saturday. Prix fixe lunch and a la carte dinner menu, after-dinner menu with late night jazz until midnight. A meal in this 1820s house with a cheerful bar and beamed café might begin with broth of wild mushrooms and include chartreuse of pheasant with braised savoy cabbage and poached figs with homemade cookies.

Windsor Station Restaurant (802-674-2675), Depot Avenue, Windsor. Open daily for lunch and dinner. Windsor's original railroad station is more plush than ever with gleaming woods and brass, velvet, and railroadania. Lunch can be a burger but the large dinner menu includes veal Oscar ($13.95), roast duckling with apricot sauce ($13.50), and scallops Mornay ($13.75); a children's menu is offered.

EATING OUT   *South to north:*   **R. J. Panhandler's** (826-5951), Main Street, Charlestown. Housed in a fine old building. Good for grinders, baked and fried fish, also T-bone steak.

Claremont Railroad Junction Restaurant (543-0017), Plains Road, Claremont Junction. Open except Sunday for lunch and dinner. The menu includes seafood nachos, an interesting assortment of sandwiches—including BBQ swordfish—also shrimp tempura and veal Oscar.

Pleasant Restaurant (542-6515), Tremont Square, Claremont. Open except Sunday for lunch and dinner. Under same ownership as the

Junction (above). Known for Cajun chicken, but their large menu also has predictables like steak and shrimp. Nice atmosphere, reasonable prices.

West Lebanon Fast Food Strip. Route 12A just south of I-89 Exit 20 is lined with representatives of every major fast-food chain in New England—a godsend to families with cars full of kids. Over the years our own carfull has come to favor this Burger King, simply for its size and efficiency but you may prefer McDonalds, Pizza Hut, Wendy's, Ponderosa, or the **Weathervane** (specializing in reasonably priced seafood).

China Lite (298-8222), West Lebanon. Open for lunch and dinner daily. Reliable, reasonably priced Cantonese and Szechwan dishes.

Cashie's (802-295-3118), Hotel Coolidge, South Main Street, White River Junction, VT. Cheerful pub and eatery, open daily for all three meals. Entertainment Thursday through Saturday evenings. A large menu, from taco salads to vegetarian stir-fries to prime rib.

In Hanover: **Lou's** (643-3321), 30 South Main Street. Open for breakfast weekdays from 6 AM, Saturdays from 7, and Sundays from 8. Lunch Monday through Saturday until 3 PM; "Mexican Suppers," Wednesday through Sunday 5–9. Since 1947 this has been a student and local hangout and it's great: a long formica counter, tables and booths, irresistible peanut butter cookies at the register—crowded all day and the Mexican fare is fine.

Peter Christian's Tavern (643-2345), 39 South Main Street. Daily from 11:30 AM–12:30 AM. Dark, pubby, smoky, and known for good soups and great sandwiches—like turkey boursin—at noon; reasonably priced dinner entrées, blackboard specials, a wide selection of ales and beers.

Everything but Anchovies (643-6135), 5 Allen Street (behind the Dartmouth Bookstore). Open daily from 11 AM–2 AM. Toppings include broccoli, fresh garlic, artichoke, and spinach; also subs, sandwiches, a pasta of the day, and bargain-priced dinners like chicken breast with "super spuds" and garlic bread for $5.75. Known affectionately as the EBA, this is THE local pizza place.

Molly's Balloon (643-2570), 43 Main Street. Open daily for lunch and dinner. This is a fun, extremely popular place. The greenhouse up front shelters the big, inviting bar that encourages single dining. Youngsters receive helium-filled balloons. The menu is immense and reasonably priced: big salads, enchiladas, elaborate burgers at lunch, pasta to steak for dinner. The adjunct deli is also worth checking out.

North of Hanover: **The Village Pancake House and Bakery**, Route 10, North Haverhill. Open for lunch except Tuesday, Friday night seafood special. Bishops ice cream. An 1820s house but very simple—good for lunch, home-baked breads, good sandwiches.

Barge Inn Restaurant (747-2551), junction of routes 10 and 302. Open from 6 AM–10 PM, across from a lumber mill. A place that's

The Connecticut River Valley has the largest concentration of farms in New Hampshire. This spread is near Haverhill.

Photo by Ann Kennard

expanded over the years, with basics and specials like linguini and meat sauce ($4.95) and a big salad bar.

Chalet Schaefer (747-2071), Woodsville on Route 10 just south of the Opera Bock. A well-established, local German restaurant with a reasonably priced menu featuring hassenpfeffer, sauerbraten, etc.

Colatina Exit (802-222-9008), Main Street, Bradford, VT. Open daily for dinner. Casual but candlelit atmosphere (checked tablecloths, pictures of Italy), affordable wines, a great antipasto, homemade pastas, fresh seafood, poultry, and vegetarian dishes. Most entrées under $10.

ENTERTAINMENT   Hopkins Center (box office: 646-2422), Dartmouth Green, Hanover. Sponsors some 150 musical and 20 theater productions plus 200 films per year, all open to the public.

White River Theater Festival (802-296-2505), Briggs Opera House, White River Junction, VT. A wide variety of professional productions.

The Parish Players (802-785-4344), based in the Eclipse Grange Hall, Thetford Hill, VT. Year-round community players.

Lebanon Opera House (448-2498), in Town Hall, Coburn Park. An 800-seat, turn-of-the-century theater hosts frequent concerts, lectures, and summer performances by the North Country Community Players.

Upper Valley Community Band

Claremont Opera House (542-4433), Tremont Square, in the City

Hall, Claremont. Recently restored gilded-era theater, the scene of frequent concerts, plays, live performances of all kinds.

SELECTIVE SHOPPING   The Upper Valley has a wide range of unusual shopping centers.

Powerhouse Shopping Mall, Route 10, West Lebanon. Open Monday through Friday 10–9; Saturday 10–6; Sunday noon–5. A total of 40 stores are in this unusual complex which combines an old brick electric power house, a large new but mill-style two-story arcade, and several older buildings moved from other places. There is no big anchor store, just a genuine variety of small specialty stores: clothing, toys, furnishings, antiques, food, etc.

Hanover Park, 40 South Main Street, Hanover. The anchor store here is **Kaleidoscope** (643-4327 or 800-333-3448), a widely respected source of fine crafted furniture and furnishings from throughout the world which moved here from smaller quarters across the street when its owners developed this small but handsome complex. Includes toy, chocolate, and jewelry shops, a deli, a florist and a showroom for Pompanoosuc Mills.

Galleries and crafts centers: **AVA Gallery** (448-3117), 11 Bank Street (Route 4 just west of Coburn Park), Lebanon. Open Monday through Saturday 11–5. From its Hanover beginnings the "Alliance for the Visual Arts" has grown to fill a sun-filled former mill building. The Soho-style (and quality) gallery mounts frequent exhibits.

Hanover League of New Hampshire Craftsmen (643-5050), 13 Lebanon Street, Hanover. Closed Sundays. Behind Hopkins Center, a wide selection of local and regional crafts pieces.

Vermont State Craft Center (802-674-6729), Windsor House, Route 5, Windsor, VT. Open year-round, Monday through Saturday 9–5; also Sundays, June to January. Housed in a brick, mid-nineteenth-century hotel, showcasing outstanding work by local craftspeople, most of whom live within an easy drive and welcome visitors.

Antiques: Pick up a copy of the leaflet map/guide "Antiquing in the North Country," available at most inns and information booths. It lists a dozen dealers between West Lebanon and Haverhill.

William Smith (675-1549) holds antique auctions year-round.

Bookstores: **Dartmouth Bookstore** (in NH: 800-462-9009; outside NH: 800-624-8800), 33 South Main Street, Hanover. One of the largest bookstores in northern New England, in owner Phoebe Storrs Stebbins' family since 1884 and currently managed by her son-in-law, David Cioffi. Supplier of textbooks to the college and its graduate schools; also to local community colleges. The store stocks 130,000 different titles including medical, technical, literary criticism, and history; also general interest titles. It also publishes the *Hanover Area Recreation Guide* by Carol Selikowitz and *The Dartmouth Story, a narrative history of its Buildings, People and Legends* by Robert Graham. Open Monday through Thursday 8:30–5,

Wednesday through Friday 8:30–9, Saturday 9–5.

Dartmouth Bookstore-After Hours, Buskey Alley (off Allen Street), Hanover. Video sales and rentals, comics, books, tapes, magazines. Open 9 AM–9 PM Monday through Saturday, 12–5 Sunday (except in summer when Friday and Saturday are the only after-5 days and it's closed on Sunday).

Best Sellers (298-7980), Power House Mall, West Lebanon. Full-service bookstore, mall hours.

Lilac Hedge Bookstore (802-649-2921), Main Street (just past Dan and Whit's general store, also worth a stop), Norwich, VT. Open Thursday through Sunday 10–5, or by appointment or chance. Large stock of not-so-new fiction, art, history, and regional titles; well arranged.

Special shops: **Dana Robes—Wood Craftsmen, Inc.** (632-5385), Lower Shaker Village, Route 4A, Enfield. Showroom open weekdays 9–5; Sundays 10–5. Meticulously crafted, traditional Shaker-design furniture, each piece signed by the craftsmen who created it. Products, made on the premises, range from cherry oval boxes, trays, and towel racks to custom-designed cupboards, tables, armoires, and beds.

Pompanoosuc Mills (802-785-4851), Route 5, East Thetford, VT. Dartmouth graduate Dwight Sargeant began building furniture in this riverside house, a cottage industry that has evolved into a riverside factory with showrooms throughout New England. Some seconds. Open daily until 6, Sunday 12–5.

Vermont Salvage Exchange (802-295-7616) Railroad Row, White River Junction, VT. Doors, chandeliers, moldings, mantels, old bricks, and other architectural relics.

Dartmouth College Co-op, Main Street, Hanover. A large men's department, sports clothes, an extensive line of Dartmouthania: T-shirts, sweats, boxes, mugs, cushions, etc.

James Campion (643-4220), Main Street, Hanover. Traditional, tweedy clothing and footwear for both men and women.

Mia (643-5398), 37 South Main Street, Hanover. Trendy women's clothing, accessories, and shoes.

Powers Country Store & Family Outfitters (542-7703), Route 120, Cornish. Specializing in sensible, quality country clothing: robes, jeans, mittens, sweaters, boots, jackets.

Fat Hat Factory (802-296-6646), Tucker Mountain, Quechee, VT. Unusual and comfortable women's clothing made on the spot.

The Mouse Menagerie of Fine Crafts (542-9691), Route 120, Cornish. Admittedly you have to be into mice, but if you are, they have dozens of stuffed mice in a range of costumes; also mice puppets and dolls.

Gould's Country Smokehouse (272-5856), Stop & Save Building, Piermont, down by the Connecticut River bridge. Since 1921 ham, bacon, turkey, and chicken are smoked in a local smokehouse; available through a catalog and the retail store, open usual business hours.

Heather Hill Farm (543-0137), Route 12A, North Charlestown. Calre Murray designs hooked rugs, made from home-spun yarns and hooked in China. A line of handmade wooden toys is also carried.

Catamount Brewing Company (802-296-2248), 58 South Main Street, White River Junction, VT. Vermont's first brewery in a century. Store hours Monday through Saturday 9–5; seasonal tours.

SPECIAL EVENTS   For details about any of these events, phone the town clerk, listed with information.

Mid-February: **Dartmouth Winter Carnival,** Hanover. Thursday through Sunday. Ice sculptures, sports events, ski jumping.

Early March: **Meriden Wild Game Dinner,** Kimball Union Academy's Miller Student Center. Usually a Saturday: to benefit the Meriden Volunteer Fire Department. Bear, raccoon, and boar are usually on the menu.

Mid-May: **Dartmouth Pow-Wow,** Hanover. A gathering of native American craftspeople and dancers on the second Saturday of May; sponsored by Native Americans at Dartmouth (646-2110) and the Native American Studies Program (646-3530).

Late May: **Muster Day,** Hanover Center. Memorial Day. Recitation of the Gettysburg Address and Dr. Seuss prayer by children of the third grade on the site of Hanover's pre-revolutionary musters.

Mid-June: **Bradford-Thetford Lions Club Fair,** Route 5, one mile north of Orford-Fairlee bridge. Carnival rides, ox-pulling, demolition derby, fiddlers' contest. **Muskeg Music Festival,** Norwich. Contra dancing, juried crafts fair, concerts, dance workshop.

Late June: **Quechee Balloon Festival and Crafts Fair** (802-295-7900), Quechee, VT. Some 20 hot air balloons gather; rides, dawn and dusk, barbecue, sky diving, crafts, food booths. **Summer Strawberry Festival,** Plainfield Historical Society Clubhouse, Route 12A, Plainfield. **Lyme Summer Suppers and Horse Shed Crafts Festivals,** Lyme Congregational Church horse sheds, Lyme. Begin the last Wednesday in June, then every other week for four Wednesdays. The crafts festivals begin at 1 PM and the suppers, also at the church, begin at 6 PM.

July Fourth: **Independence Day Open Fields Circus,** Thetford, VT. A take-off on a real circus by the Paris Players. **Plainfield Fourth of July Celebration,** Plainfield. Community breakfast, foot races, parade, Firemen's Roast Beef Dinner.

Mid-July: **Hanover Street Fest** (643-3115), Hanover. Street bazaar, hay wagon rides, entertainment.

Late July: **Hanover Center Fair,** Hanover. Friday night games, dancing, food; Saturday starts with a children's costume parade, ox-pulling, food, games. **Connecticut Valley Fair,** Bradford, VT. Ox- and horse-pulling, sheep show, midway, demolition derby. **La Salette Fair** (632-4301), at the La Salette Shrine, Route 4A, Enfield. Usually a midway with rides, flea market, crafts booths. **Cracker-Barrel Bazaar,** Newbury. Big old-time fiddlers' contest, antiques show, quilt show, sheep-dog trials, church suppers.

Early August: **Canaan Old Home Day,** Canaan. Dances, parade, booths, suppers. **North Haverhill Fair,** Horse show and pulling, evening live entertainment, midway. **Thetford Hill Fair.** Small but special: a rummage sale, food and plant booths, barbecue.

Mid-August: **The Country Revels,** Singing, dancing; bring picnics to Lyme. **The Shrine Parade and Maple Sugar Bowl,** in the Dartmouth Memorial Stadium, Hanover. Noontime pre-game parade features a dozen Shrine temples. The game pits Vermont and New Hampshire high school all-stars. **Cornish Fair.** Horse- and ox-pulling, agricultural exhibits, ham and bean suppers, a Saturday woodsman's field day.

Late August: **Quechee Scottish Festival,** Quechee, VT. Sheep dog trials, highland dancing, piping, highland "games," ladies rolling-yin toss, more.

Mid-October: **Horse Sheds Crafts Fair,** at the Lyme Congregational Church, Lyme. Saturday of Columbus Day weekend 10–4; also a Fall Festival lunch at the church.

Late November: **Bradford United Church of Christ Wild Game Supper,** Bradford. The Saturday before Thanksgiving this Vermont town nearly doubles its population as hungry visitors pour into the church to feast on 2,800 pounds of buffalo, venison, moose, pheasant, coon, rabbit, wild boar, and bear. But getting in the door isn't easy. Write to Mrs. Raymond Green (802-222-4670), Box 356, Bradford, VT 05033, before the middle of September to request to be put on the mailing list for ticket information.

Early December: **Dickens of a Christmas** (643-3115), Hanover. Begins with Friday evening tree lighting on the green; Charles Dickens himself reads "A Christmas Carol"; Dickensian-style feasting in local restaurants, caroling, street concerts, and dancing; Victorian dress. **Christmas Pageant,** Norwich, VT. Traditional pageant with Mary on a donkey to the Norwich Inn, on to a stable. **Christmas Mystery,** Revels North in Hopkins Center. Song and dance. **Christmas Illuminations,** at the La Salette Shrine, Route 4A, Enfield. Weekends in early December.

V. Central New Hampshire Lakes

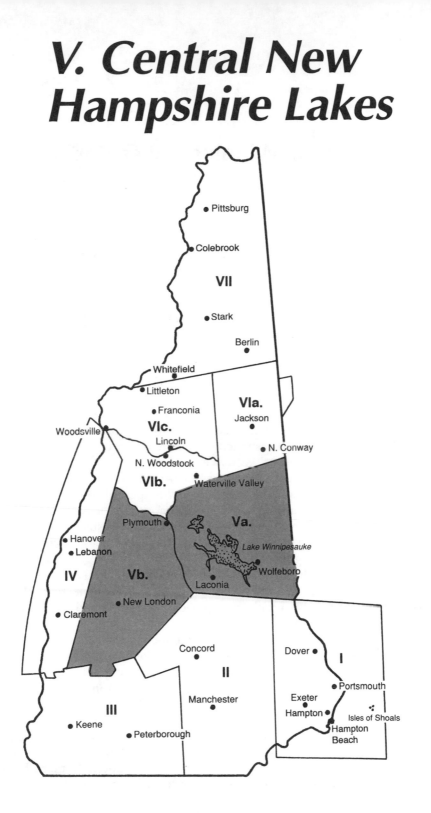

- Pittsburg
- Colebrook

VII

- Stark
- Berlin
- Whitefield
- Littleton
- Franconia

VIa.

Jackson

VIc.

Lincoln

Woodsville

- N. Conway
- N. Woodstook

VIb.

Waterville Valley

Plymouth

Va.

Lake Winnipesauke

- Hanover
- Lebanon

IV

Vb.

Wolfeboro

Laconia

- New London
- Claremont

- Concord
- Dover

I

II

- Portsmouth
- Manchester
- Exeter
- Hampton

Isles of Shoals

III

Hampton
Beach

- Keene
- Peterborough

The Lake Winnipesaukee Region

The Lake Winnipesaukee Region, that section of New Hampshire that surrounds Lake Winnipesaukee, is often described as a single place, but it has several different environments for visitors. East and north of the lake are mostly small towns where New Hampshire's rural character offers a quiet, pastoral landscape with fewer services for vacationers, except for Wolfeboro, which boasts that it was America's first summer resort.

Ironically, views of, and access to, the lake are limited unless one is a property owner or guest at a motel, cabin colony, exclusive club, or condominium development. Squam Lake, made famous to nonresidents by the movie *On Golden Pond*, is a pristine jewel that is relatively undeveloped and has only limited public access. Even some public beaches are restricted to town residents or property owners. In sharp contrast is the western side of Winnipesaukee from Alton Bay to Meredith. Although many sections are heavily developed, there are numerous broad lake views and Winnipesaukee's only waterfront state park. From the honky-tonk atmosphere of Weirs Beach to the more upscale environment of Meredith, the western side of the lake is a busy place in the summer with enough activities to keep any vacationer on the go.

Between these two extremes are such smaller lakes as Wentworth, Ossipee, Crystal, Chocorua, Province, or Merrymeeting. Here are found less commercial development, more parks, and some of the better inns and restaurants.

There is a unique character to summers in the Lakes Region. Unlike North Conway or Hampton Beach, where hotels and motels host the majority of visitors, the Lakes Region's summer population leans more to property owners who have their own lakefront cottages (or mansions, in some cases) or to week-long renters of housekeeping cottages. Many families have owned their summer places for generations, and many renters-by-the-week have similarly returned to the same cottages for the same week year after year. Indeed, while there are numerous housekeeping colonies, we have not listed many because few of them have any weeks open for new vacationers.

Although winter brings skiing, snowmobiling, and ice fishing, the Lakes Region is primarily a summer recreation area. Motels and some of the inns are closed between the end of foliage season and ice-out, but the off-season traveler will find ample accommodations and discover that the Lakes Region is a quiet alternative to the more developed winter vacation areas of the state.

Historically, the summer residential pattern in this part of New Hampshire precedes the coming of Europeans to America. For centuries, Native Americans camped on lake shores to fish. Although they may have remained in the region during the winter, they moved away from the shores to avoid cold winds that still blow across ice-covered waters. Their old camping areas have become the sites of archaeological digs, and their Indian geographical names remain. Winnipesaukee, for example, means variously, "Smile of the Great Spirit" or "Beautiful water in a high place." One of their most popular locations was on the western side of the lake where they set their weirs (today's Weirs Beach) to catch fish and eventually made a permanent settlement.

Although land grants were made in this region as early as 1748, it was not until the 1760s, and the end of the dangers caused by the French and Indian wars, that widespread settlement began in the Lakes Region. Royal Governor Benning Wentworth became a millionaire by granting new townships and retaining a portion of each grant for himself. It was his nephew John Wentworth, however, who deserves the credit for much of the early settlement in central New Hampshire and for beginning the summer vacation business there. In 1763 Wentworth began building a summer estate on his huge holding in today's Wolfeboro, and in 1769 he completed a road from Portsmouth to that farm, eventually extending it to Hanover, home of the then new Dartmouth College. The so-called Governor's Road encouraged other wealthy seacoast families to build summer homes in the region. Thus the concept of a summer vacation place was born. The road also helped other settlers to move to the area. Wentworth and his family were forced to flee the colony in 1775 as the Revolutionary War was beginning, abandoning his mansion which later burned in 1820. It is now a historic archaeological site.

Although Wolfeboro remained a vacation area, the western side of Winnipesaukee developed more quickly since it was on the main stagecoach route from the south and eventually was served by railroads pushing north toward the White Mountains. From those years until the early twentieth century brought the development of automobiles, the railroad-steamboat combination serviced lake visitors and residents alike. Various types of vessels have hauled freight and passengers around the lake since settlers first arrived here over 250 years ago. Steamboats at one time dominated the traffic. Train passengers

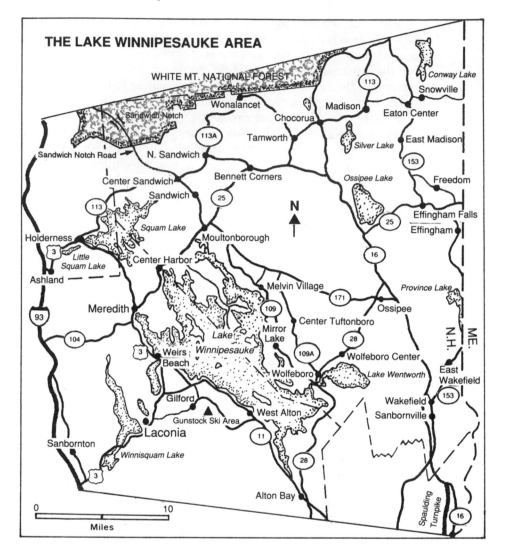

THE LAKE WINNIPESAUKE AREA

stopping at the Weirs, Alton Bay, or Wolfeboro could transfer to boats bound for other land ports and islands all around the lake. Some boats offered direct service to various hotels or connected with smaller vessels sent to major ports from villages or hotels in some of the bays. This convenient transportation system led to the rapid residential development of the lake so that by the late 1800s Winnipesaukee was a full-fledged recreation area. A section of the main street at Weirs Beach retains this turn-of-the-century Victorian atmosphere.

One of the more famous of the steamboats was the *Mount Washington*, a wooden side-wheeler in service from 1872 until it was destroyed by an off-season fire in December 1939. She was replaced by the present steel-hulled *Mount Washington II* a year later but remained in port for most of World War II when her engines were commandeered for the war effort. In 1946 she returned to service as the *M/V Mount Washington*. Lengthened in 1983 and changed to M/S (motor ship status), she continues today as the queen of the lake and a New Hampshire landmark.

The relative lack of commercial development on the eastern side of Lake Winnipesaukee dates back to the days when the railroads originally serviced only the western side of the lake, and much of the eastern shoreline was contained within large estates. Except for Wolfeboro, other eastern shore towns remained small, mostly farming communities with a few guest houses, even as the large estates were eventually sold and subdivided for summer cottage lots. By 1895 a single railroad spur line reached Wolfeboro from a junction in Sanbornville, a stop on the Boston & Maine Railroad route between the seacoast and North Conway. This line insured Wolfeboro's importance to the vacation business, but it did little to boost the fortunes of the surrounding towns, many of which still appear as they did at the turn of the century.

Just as it has been for nearly two and a half centuries since European settlement, Lake Winnipesaukee remains the centerpiece of the Lakes Region. The sixth largest natural lake completely inside United States borders, Winnipesaukee covers some 72 square miles, is 28 miles long and 13 miles wide. It has 274 habitable islands, ranging in size from mere piles of rocks to 1,000 acres, and contains 283 miles of shoreline; it is ringed by mountains—even Mt. Washington can be seen. This is one of the most beautiful lakes in the world, and it is obviously a boat lover's paradise. On its shores are uncounted numbers of camps, cottages, year-round homes, condominiums, and mansions, and it appears that every one has at least one boat. With thousands of boats docked at marinas, there is an opportunity for anyone to launch a vessel at the many public and private launching sites. On major holiday weekends the lake often appears to be wall-to-wall boats. Everything from sailboards to schooners, from jet skis to high-speed runabouts, from canoes to luxury cabin cruisers can be seen among the more than 20,000 registered vessels using the lake. With all of this activity, there are marine patrol officers, speed limits at certain congested areas, and a goodly number of accidents each summer. No driver's license is required to operate a boat, but one must be 16 years old to operate one with more than 25 horsepower. This is not to suggest that boaters avoid the lake, only to use caution and constant vigilance. Also, keep an eye on the weather because high winds, sudden squalls, and thunderstorms can quickly whip the lake surface into waves as rough as the ocean, an especially dangerous situation for those in small boats who have no experience in such conditions.

There are more than two dozen other lakes of 100 or more acres (273 lakes and ponds of all sizes) in this region so there are plenty of alternatives to boating, fishing, and other water sports. There are also mountains to climb, summer theater to attend, amusement parks and rides to enjoy, covered bridges to find, fruit to pick, horses to ride, slopes to ski, and racing sled dogs to watch. It is New Hampshire's most diverse recreational area, stretching from the foothills of the White Mountains nearly to the ocean. For family fun and recreation, it is a tough place to beat.

GUIDANCE   **Lakes Region Association** (569-1117), Box 300, Wolfeboro 03894. The year 1991 marks the 55th edition of this association's popular *Where to in the Lakes Region*, a handy guide to towns, accommodations, and attractions. Write for a copy or look for the guide throughout the region at rest areas and information centers.

Alton-Alton Bay Chamber of Commerce, Box 550 (summer office in the old railroad station, Route 11), Alton 03809.

Centre Harbor-Moultonborough Chamber of Commerce, Box 824, Centre Harbor 03226.

Greater Laconia Chamber of Commerce (524-5531 or 800-531-2347), 9 Veterans Square, Laconia 03246. A summer information booth is maintained on Route 3, just south of Weirs Beach.

Meredith Chamber of Commerce (279-6121), Box 732 (office across from the town dock on Route 3), Meredith 03253-0732.

Greater Ossipee Chamber of Commerce (539-6201), RD 1, Box 137, Center Ossipee 03814.

Squam Lakes Area Chamber of Commerce (968-4494), Box 498, Holderness 03245.

Squam Lakes Association (968-7336), Box 204, Holderness 03245. Contact this nonprofit association for hiking, boating, and wilderness information and maps.

Wolfeboro Chamber of Commerce (569-2200), Box 547 (in the old railroad station), Wolfeboro 03894.

GETTING THERE   By air: **Skymaster** (524-7784), Route 11, Laconia Airport, offers daily flights between Laconia and Boston's Logan Airport. There is no other scheduled airline service to the Lakes Region although there is regular service to airports in Manchester (see Merrimack Valley) and Lebanon (see Upper Valley), both of which are just a short drive via rental car from the Winnipesaukee Region.

By bus: **Concord Trailways** (800-852-3317), provides scheduled service from Boston's Logan Airport to central and northern New Hampshire via Londonderry, Manchester, Concord, Tilton, Laconia, New Hampton, Meredith, and Plymouth. Daily service varies.

MEDICAL EMERGENCY   **Lakes Regional General Hospital** (524-3211 or 800-852-3311), Highland Street, Laconia 03246. Walk-in care 9–9, 24-hour emergency service.

Photo by Peter E. Randall

New Hampshire Farm Museum, Milton.

Franklin Regional Hospital (934-2060), Aiken Avenue, Franklin 03235.

Huggins Memorial Hospital (569-2150), South Main Street, Wolfeboro 03894.

Moultonborough Medical Center (253-7721), Route 25, Moultonborough 03254.

TO SEE AND DO   **New Hampshire Farm Museum** (652-7840), Box 644, Plumer's Ridge, Route 16 (Exit 18 off Spaulding Turnpike), Milton 03851. Open Tuesday through Saturday 10–4, mid-June to Labor Day, then weekends until mid-October. Museum office open weekdays 9–2, all year. Also inquire about special "Beat-the-Winter Doldrums" scheduled for alternate Saturdays in winter. New Hampshire's rural agricultural heritage is maintained in this unusual collection of buildings, situated about midway between the Lakes Region and the seacoast. The huge barn is filled with wagons and a host of other farm artifacts, plus there are blacksmith and cobbler shops, a country store, and a furnished farmhouse, once the home of the Jones family. The best part of this museum occurs on most Saturdays and Sundays when there are special events. In 1990, 33 different programs featured workshops and demonstrations of weaving, blacksmithing, beekeeping, ice-cream making, herbs, stonewall repairing, chair-seating, rug-braiding, butter-making, fiber to fabric, and reed basket-making.

Special days are devoted to pigs, sheep, dairy animals, goats, and even llamas. The second Saturday in August is annual old-time farm day with 60 farmers, artists, and craftspeople gathered to demonstrate their skills. A chicken barbecue is served. Fee charged. Detailed program of events available. The facility is also the museum of the Milton Historical Society.

Winnipesaukee Railroad (528-2330), South Main Street, RFD 4, Box 317, Meredith 03253. Open weekends (except Father's Day) from Memorial Day to late June, then daily until mid-October. Board from Meredith or Weirs Beach. Ride beside the lake on historic coaches of the '20s and '30s or connect with the *M/S Mount Washington* for a boat ride (see Boat Excursions). Fall foliage trips go north to Plymouth.

Science Center of New Hampshire at Squam Lakes (968-7194), Box 173, junction of routes 25 and 113, Holderness 03245. Open May through October 9:30–4:30, except 1–4 on Sundays in spring and fall. More than 50,000 children and adults each year benefit from programs operated by this nonprofit organization. While most of their activities are aimed at school groups, the center offers plenty to do and see in July and August. A 3/4-mile walking trail displays live bear, deer, bobcat, fox, bald eagle (and other birds of prey), and many other creatures. Hike through 200 acres of meadow and forest, past streams and brooks. A pontoon boat is used for exploring Squam Lake. Inquire about special summer family activities, which include two live animal programs daily. Gift shop. Fee charged.

Castle in the Clouds (476-2352), Route 171, Moultonborough 03254. Open weekends May to early June; then daily mid-June to mid-October. Built in the early 1900s at a cost of $7 million, this stone mansion is high on the side of the Ossipee mountains, overlooking Lake Winnipesaukee. Part of a 6,000-acre estate constructed by an eccentric multi-millionaire, the castle has become a family recreation area. Tour the mansion, ride a paddleboat, take a hayride, picnic, or take a guided horseback trip on part of the 85 miles of graded carriage trails. Fee charged.

HISTORIC SITES   Governor Wentworth Historic Site, Route 109, Wolfeboro. Open in the summer months. This was the location of Royal Governor John Wentworth's summer estate, now owned by the state of New Hampshire, and the site of much archaeological work conducted under the auspices of the state Historic Preservation Office. Visitors are welcome. No facilities. (See the introduction to this chapter for background.)

Libby Museum, Route 109, 4 miles north of Wolfeboro Village. Open daily, except Monday, Memorial Day through Labor Day, 10–4. This natural history museum was built by a native in 1912 and is now operated by the town. It has a varied collection of mounted bird, fish, and animal specimens; Indian relics, including a dugout canoe; old maps and photographs; and eighteenth- and nineteenth-century country-living artifacts. Programs include nature walks, lectures, musical presentations, and art exhibits. Small fee.

Endicott Rock Historical Site, Route 3, Weirs Beach. A large boulder has been preserved here that dates to 1652, when a surveying party claimed this region for the Massachusetts Bay Colony. The second oldest historic landmark in the country, the site is named for Governor John Endicott, who ordered the survey. Adjacent is a city-maintained beach on Lake Winnipesaukee.

Ashland Historical Society, Whipple House Museum, 4 Pleasant Street, Ashland 03217. Open Wednesdays and Saturdays 1–4, July through Labor Day. Owned by the town of Ashland, the house was the home of a Nobel Prize winner for medicine, Dr. George Hoyt Whipple, and features exhibits related to his life plus local artifacts. Next door is the Pauline Glidden Toy Museum.

Centre Harbor Historical Society, Plymouth Street (Route 25B), Centre Harbor 03226. An 1886 schoolhouse, open Saturday afternoons in July and August.

Harold Gilman Museum, routes 11 and 140, Alton. Open Wednesday and Saturday, July through September, and the first Sunday of each month. An eclectic collection of country antiques including furniture, dolls, guns, china, glass, pewter, toys, clocks, and a working Regina floor model music box.

Meredith Historical Society, Winona Road, Meredith 03253. Open Saturdays 1–4 in July and August, meetings first Tuesday of each month, April to December. Formerly the Oak Hill church, the museum has tools, costumes, photographs, "made-in-Meredith" items, and local historical information.

Ossipee Historical Society, Old Route 16, Center Ossipee 03814. The society opens Grant Hall, Tuesday and Thursday 1–4, in July and August.

Sanbornton Historical Society (286-7227), Sanbornton Square, Route 132, Box 2, Sanbornton 03269. The old Lane Tavern is open Sundays in July and August, 2–4.

Sandwich Historical Society (284-6269), Maple Street, Center Sandwich 03227. The Elisha Marston House is open June through September, Tuesday to Saturday (June and September, 1–5; July and August, 11–5), and the first Sunday of each month. On display are portraits by native Albert Gallatin Hoit, and there are special annual exhibits.

Tamworth Historical Society, Tamworth Village 03886. Meetings (held every third Wednesday April to October) of local, state, and, occasionally, national interest.

Tuftonboro Historical Society, Main Street (Route 109), Melvin Village 03850. Open July and August daily, except Sunday, 2–4.

Photographs and literature relating to Lake Winnipesaukee and reference material on local families.

Thompson-Ames Historical Society, 24 Belknap Mountain Road, Gilford (mailing: Box 2532, Laconia 03247). Former church, now a museum open first Monday of each month, except in winter. Recently acquired an old Grange hall.

Wolfeboro Historical Society (569-4997), South Main Street, Wolfeboro 03894. Open July to August daily, except Sunday, 10–4:30. This is a three-building complex including the restored and furnished 1778 Clark House, an 1820 one-room school, and the replica 1862 Monitor Engine Company, complete with a restored 1872 horse-drawn, Amoskeag steam-pumper fire engine and an 1842 Monitor hand engine. When completed in 1983, this complex received a national award for historical excellence.

COVERED BRIDGES   *In Ashland:*   A new Graton covered bridge just off Route 3 was built for the town by resident Milton Graton, a renowned builder and restorer of covered bridges throughout the northeast.

In Ossipee: The Whittier bridge crosses the Bearcamp River, just off Route 16 and north of Route 25, in West Ossipee.

In Sandwich: The Cold River bridge is a little difficult to find but well worth the effort. It is located off Route 113A just north of North Sandwich.

VILLAGES   **Alton.** One of the lake's early tourist centers, Alton Bay's waterfront area appears little changed from the turn of the century when train passengers transferred to steamboats. Concerts are held in the bandstand, and the old railroad station is the information center. Cottages around the bay shore evoke memories of the days when summer places were small houses, not condos. The chamber of commerce issues a detailed schedule of numerous summer events (see Guidance).

Tamworth. Centered around the old Tamworth Inn and the Barnstormers is a fine collection of private and public buildings. Combined with a fast-running brook for swimming and a neat general store, the town has an "I'd like to live here" feeling about it. It is easy to see why Grover Cleveland, the two-term president, summered here; why his son Francis moved here to stay; and why Francis founded the Barnstormers some 60 years ago. A village of Tamworth, **Chocorua** sits astride busy Route 16. The view across the waterfall and its mill pond may look familiar; it has appeared in several national advertising campaigns. Have a tasty treat at the Dam Ice Cream Shop in the lee of the waterfall.

Melvin Village. Seemingly the antiques center of the eastern Winnipesaukee region, this little town still looks like the nineteenth century when many of the houses lining the main street were built. Some of these homes now have antiques shops, and one business repairs antique motor-boats.

Centre Harbor. At the head of Winnipesaukee is the winter home of the *M/S Mount Washington*—Centre Harbor. This town is bisected by Route 25, but it still retains its nineteenth-century character. The town was named for the Senter family, but the *S* became a *C*, and *Center* became *Centre*. There is similar spelling confusion with the names of many New Hampshire towns that end with "borough," often spelled "boro." Just one of the many little details which makes New England so interesting!

Center Sandwich. In all of New England there is not another village with such a distinguished reputation and tradition as a center for craftsworkers. Who would not want to live and work here among the picturesque white eighteenth- and nineteenth-century buildings in the village center—even the old gas station has been recycled as a frame shop. Just driving to the village is a relaxing experience with its location off the main roads. Follow Route 113 east from Route 3 in Holderness or Route 109 north from Route 25 in Moultonborough. Or take one of the most scenic and rural drives in the state by joining Route 113 at Route 16 in Chocorua Village, then motor to Tamworth; follow 113A to Wonalancet and North Sandwich, and rejoin 113 to Center Sandwich. After following the country roads past old farms and mountain and lake views, the village is like a civilized oasis in the near-wilderness countryside. Shop for handmade crafts and lunch at the Corner House Inn. The Sandwich Fair, held on Columbus Day weekend, is the last one of the year. While the fair retains an old-fashioned feeling, the traffic clogging the winding roads to the fairgrounds is more like a city rush hour.

Tilton. This community west of I-93 is not exactly a quaint village, but it does boast that no other American town of its size has so many statues. From the interstate, one first notices the 55-foot high granite Tilton (actually in Northfield) arch, an exact copy of a Roman memorial built in 79 A.D. Beneath it is a Numidian lion carved from Scottish granite, a tribute to Charles E. Tilton, the town's wealthiest mid-nineteenth-century citizen and a descendant of the first settler. He persuaded the town of Sanbornton Bridge to change its name to Tilton in 1869, a decision no doubt made easier by his gift of statuary. Such allegorical figures as America, Asia, and Europe can still be found around town along with Tilton's mansion, now the library of the private preparatory Tilton School, founded in 1845.

FOR FAMILIES   Centre Harbor Children's Museum and Shop (253-TOYS), Route 25, Centre Harbor 03226. Open daily July through Labor Day, 9–8; Monday through Saturday the rest of the year, 9–5; Sunday 10–5. An interactive children's museum with a music room, a lake boat wheelhouse, country store, dress-up acting room, and similar things for kids. The toy shop has wooden toys, educational games, puzzles, and activity books. Fee charged.

The *Sophie C.* unloads at Weirs Beach.

Weirs Beach, at the junction of routes 3 and 11B, is the attractions center of the region, THE place to go for many folks, and THE place to avoid for others. It is difficult to be ambivalent about two water slides, miniature golf, a go-cart track, the country's largest arcade, and a strip of pizza parlors, fast-food spots, gift shops, and penny arcades. Right beside all of this activity is a summer religious conference center dating back to the turn of the century, a fine beach, one of the oldest historical markers in New Hampshire, the wharf for the *M/S Mount Washington* (see Boat Excursions), and the Winnipesaukee Railroad. Whatever you think about Weirs Beach, it is difficult to avoid passing through a section of it on the west side of the lake, so maybe you can stop for a while, have a pizza, let the kids take a few rides, and remember that you, too, were young once.

Surf Coaster (366-4991), Route 3, Weirs Beach. Open weekends Memorial Day to mid-June, then daily until Labor Day. The largest water slide complex in the region with seven slides, changing rooms, and lifeguards. Pay once and slide all day. Also, two 18-hole miniature golf courses (additional fee).

Weirs Beach Water Slide (366-5161), Route 11B, Weirs Beach. Open weekends Memorial Day to mid-June, then daily until Labor Day. This complex includes a variety of slides for beginners through experts. The Super Slide for experts is the longest in New England.

Funspot (366-4377), Route 3, one mile north of Weirs Beach. Open all year, 24 hours a day, July through Labor Day. If you like games, there are 550 here, the largest complex of its type in the country. From pinball to video and driving games, this has something for people of all ages, including both candlepin (a mostly New England game) and 10-pin bowling, driving range, and miniature golf.

GREEN SPACE   **Gunstock Recreation Area** (293-4341), Route 11A, Gilford. Operated by Belknap County, this 2,000-acre facility includes the Gunstock Ski Area and a large campground with related facilities. The 420-site campground has swimming, fishing, horseback riding, store, and playground. Extensive hiking trails lead to the summits of the Belknap Mountains, one of which is Gunstock. Trail maps are available. Warm-weather events include dances, crafts and woodsmen's festivals, and Oktoberfest. The ski area has twenty slopes and trails, six double chairlifts, and two ski jumps plus snowmaking and a cross-country center. The annual winter carnival is held in February.

Cate Park, Wolfeboro, on the waterfront by the town wharf. Occasional concerts and art exhibits in the summer, a delightful place to sit and relax any time.

Hemenway State Forest, Route 113A, Tamworth. Two trails here, one a short, self-guided nature trail, the other longer with a spur to the Great Hill fire tower offering views of the southern White Mountains.

Brochures for both trails usually can be found in the summer in a box a few yards up each trail.

White Lake State Park, Route 16, Tamworth. Open late May through mid-October. Here is a picturesque sandy beach and a 173-site campground, one of the most popular in the state. Great trout fishing and rental boats available. Hike the 1.5-mile trail around the lake or climb nearby Mt. Chocorua. The park's large stand of tall pitch pines is a national natural landmark. Fee charged; no reservations.

Chocorua Lake, Route 16, Tamworth. Just north of Chocorua Village, this location offers perhaps the most photographed scene in the country: rugged Mt. Chocorua viewed across its namesake lake. This area gets its name from an old legend about an Indian who, after an altercation with early settlers, climbed the mountain, then leaped to his death to avoid capture. Most of the lake shore has been preserved for its scenic beauty, and nary a summer cottage disturbs the pristine character of the place. At the north end of the lake, adjacent to the highway, is a popular swimming area and a place to launch a canoe or sailboard, but there are no public facilities, save a disgusting, smelly outhouse.

Sandwich Notch Road, from Center Sandwich to Route 49 in Campton. Sandwich Notch was once a farming region, but it has reverted to virtual wilderness and is now part of the White Mountain National Forest. The 11-mile road is sound but steep, rough, and slow-going; it is maintained that way to keep it from becoming too popular as a shortcut between the south and Waterville Valley. It is not winter-maintained. About 3.5 miles from Center Sandwich is Beede Falls in a town park. Several hiking trails lead from the road, including several for Sandwich Dome and Mt. Israel.

Chamberlain-Reynolds Forest, College Road, off Route 3, two miles north of Meredith Village. Owned by the New England Forestry Foundation, this is a 150-acre managed woodland on the shore of Squam Lake. With beaches, trails, and picnic tables, it is a quiet spot to enjoy the country.

Stonedam Island Wildlife Preserve (279-3246), operated by the Lakes Region Conservation Trust, Box 1097, Meredith 03253. Open weekends from July 4 through Labor Day, Saturday and holidays 10–5; Sunday noon–5. Stonedam Island is an undeveloped 112-acre preserve in Lake Winnipesaukee. A variety of family-oriented nature programs are offered to the public on weekends, but visitors are also welcome to walk the trails, relax under a tree on the shoreline, or pursue their own nature study. Transportation to the island is provided on weekends by Weirs Beach Boat Tours ($2 per person, call the preserve for departure schedules). Private boats may dock at the 60-foot pier on the northeast side of the island. Bring water as none is available on the island; no pets, audio equipment, smoking, fires, or glass containers. Programs are free.

SCENIC DRIVES   The northern and eastern sides of the lake abound with country routes. Our favorite is Route 153 (see A Country Road Alternative). **Routes 113** and **113A** from Tamworth to Holderness, **Route 109** from Wolfeboro to Sandwich, **Route 171** from Center Ossipee to Moultonborough, **Route 11** from Alton Bay to Glendale, and **Route 140** from Alton to Gilmanton are also favorite scenic drives.

BEACHES   **Ellacoya State Beach**, Route 11, Gilford. Open weekends from Memorial Day, daily mid-June to Labor Day. The only state beach on Lake Winnipesaukee. A 600-foot beach with refreshment stand and changing rooms; handicapped accessible. The view across the lake to the Ossipee Mountains is one of the best in the region. Fee charged.

    Wentworth State Beach, Route 109, Wolfeboro. Open weekends from Memorial Day, daily mid-June to Labor Day. This small park on Lake Wentworth has a bathing beach, play field, changing rooms, and shaded picnic area. Fee charged. Nearby is the Governor John Wentworth Historic site.

AIR RIDES   **Laconia Airport** (524-5003), Route 11, Laconia 03246, is an all-weather, paved runway facility with several air-taxi operators available for charter.

    Lakes Region Airport (569-1310), off Route 109, Wolfeboro, is a community facility, with a paved runway, operated since 1939 by Ralph Horn. Adjacent is a seaplane base offering sightseeing rides. **Moultonboro Airport** (476-8801), Route 25, Moultonborough 03254. Sightseeing rides.

    Seaplane Services (524-0446), Route 3, Weirs Beach 03246. Daily seaplane, sightseeing rides from the shores of Paugus Bay.

BOAT EXCURSIONS   *Winnipesaukee: M/S Mount Washington* (366-5531), Lakeside Avenue, Weirs Beach 03246. Open late May through June 30 for two cruises daily, July 1 to Labor Day three cruises daily, then one cruise daily until late October. Special theme cruises and dinner and moonlight dancing cruises (two floors and two bands). For a first-time Lakes Region visitor, a ride on this famous vessel is a great introduction to Lake Winnipesaukee. Some 230 feet long with space for 1,250 passengers, the Mount cruises at 14 knots on a 3 1/4-hour, 50-mile route beginning at the Weirs, with stops at Wolfeboro and, on alternate days, Centre Harbor and Alton Bay. Round trips are available from all four ports. Depending on the schedule, dinner cruises depart from and return to Weirs Beach, Wolfeboro, or Alton Bay. Breakfast, luncheon buffet, snacks, and cocktails are served. Adult fares $12, children 5–12 $6, under 5 free. Reduced fares and special family package fares on new 2 1/4-hour cruises from Wolfeboro and Weirs. Dinner dance and theme cruises $25–$32, reservations required, under age 21 not admitted unless with parent, guardian, or spouse over 21.

    M/V Sophie C (366-5531), Lakeside Avenue, Weirs Beach 03246. Departs Weirs Beach. Open weekends only early May to early June, daily mid-June to the week after Labor Day, then weekends until Columbus Day. This is the floating U.S. Post Office and its cruises wind around the islands, into coves and channels, delivering mail to island dwellers, many of whom meet the boat at their wharfs. Depending on the day, there are two- or three-hour cruises, some with mail stops, some without. Also nightly sunset cruises (BYOB, complimentary snacks). Light refreshments are available. Adult fares $8, children 5–12 $4, under 5 free.

Queen of Winnipesaukee (366-5531), Lakeside Avenue, Weirs Beach 03246. Departs Weirs Beach. Open weekends (weather permitting) for two sailings mid-May through June and after Labor Day through mid-October; daily for three cruises July through Labor Day; also special BYOB evening cruises with complimentary snacks. This 46-foot sloop offers a wind-powered alternative to the motorboats plying the lake. Adult fares $9.50, children 5–12 $6, under 5 free, sunset $13.

M/V Doris E (366-5531), Lakeside Avenue, Weirs Beach 03246. Departs Meredith and Wolfeboro. Open July through Labor Day for three daytime and one sunset cruises (BYOB, complimentary snacks). Discover Meredith Bay and many islands on these 1 3/4-hour trips. On weekends the *Doris E* departs from Wolfeboro, and the *Sophic C* runs from Meredith. Light refreshments available. Adult fares $8, children 5–12 $4, under 5 free.

M/V Judge David Sewall (569-3016) departs from the Wolfeboro town dock, but reservations are made through the Wolfeboro Inn. Open for luncheon cruises Monday, Wednesday, and Friday, June through mid-September. A summer buffet is served on this 60-foot replica of an old steamboat which makes a 1 1/2-hour cruise. Available for charters.

Squam Lake: **Squam Lakes Tours** (968-7577), Route 3, PO Box 185, Holderness 03245. Open May through October, two two-hour cruises daily, reservations suggested. See this pristine lake, the second largest in New Hampshire, aboard Capt. Joe Nasser's 28-foot, canopy-top pontoon boat. He'll show you loons, Church Island, and the spot where *On Golden Pond* was filmed. Available for charters. Joe also runs a fishing-guide service.

Golden Pond Tour (968-3348) departs from the Manor on Golden Pond, daily 10–4, Memorial Day through foliage season. Two-hour cruise in an all-weather boat to see loons, the islands, and the movie-filming location. Reservations suggested.

BOAT RENTALS   While many visitors are content to go swimming or take a cruise, other people bring their own boats or rent from a local marina. Listed are some of the businesses that provide motorboat rentals by the day or week and launching. Note that many motels and cottage colonies on the water also offer launching areas and limited dock space to their guests. Most towns provide public launching sites; inquire locally. Boat rentals usually require reservations.

Wolfeboro and east side of the lake: **Goodhue and Hawkins Navy Yard** (569-2371), Sewell Road, Wolfeboro.

> **Wolfeboro Marina** (569-3200), Bay Street, Wolfeboro.
>
> **KRB Marine** (544-3231), Melvin Village. Rentals only.
>
> **Melvin Village Marina** (544-3583), Melvin Village. Launching only.
>
> **Wentworth State Beach** and **White Lake State Park** (see Green Space).

West and north sides of the lake: **Castle Marine** (875-2777), Echo Lake Shores, Minge Cove, Alton Bay. Launching only.

> **Fay's Boat Yard** (293-8000), 71 Varney Road, Smith Cove, Gilford. Also canoes.
>
> **Smith Cove Marina** (293-2007), 17 Dock Road, Gilford.
>
> **Anchor Marine** (366-4311 or 524-3724), Winnipesaukee Pier, Weirs Beach. Rentals and tours.
>
> **Thurston Enterprises** (366-4811), Route 3, on the bridge, Weirs Beach.
>
> **Meredith Marina** (279-7921), Bay Shore Drive, Meredith Bay, Meredith. Also canoes.
>
> **The Sailing Center on Squam Lake** (968-3654), PO Drawer R, Route 3, Holderness 03245. Sailboat, sailboard, motorboat, and canoe rentals by the half-day, day, or week. Also sailing instruction.

GOLF   Most courses in this region operate from mid-April through October, weather permitting, and all offer cart rentals.

> **Den Brae Golf Course** (934-9818), Prescott Road, off Route 127, Sanbornton. Nine holes, driving range, full bar and light food.
>
> **Indian Mound Golf Course** (539-7733), off Route 16, Center Ossipee. Nine holes, full bar and food service.
>
> **Kingswood Golf Course** (569-3569), Route 28, Wolfeboro. Eighteen holes, full bar and food service. This is a busy summer place, so call for tee times.
>
> **Laconia Country Club** (524-1273), off Elm Street, Laconia. Eighteen holes, full bar and food service. Call for tee times, none available to the public on weekend mornings.
>
> **Lakeview Golf Course** (524-2220), Ladd Hill Road, opposite Belknap Mall, Belmont. Nine holes, sandwiches and bar service. Great views of the lake from this hilltop course.
>
> **Mojalaki Country Club** (934-3033), Prospect Street, off Route 3, Franklin. Challenging nine-hole course, food and bar service; tee times needed, especially on weekends.
>
> **Oak Hill Golf Course** (279-4438), Pease Road, off Route 104, Meredith. Nine holes, full bar and food service. No tee times.
>
> **Pheasant Ridge Country Club** (524-7808), Route 11 A, Gilford. Nine holes, light food and bar service, tennis.

Province Lake Country Club (207-793-9577), Route 153, East Wakefield. Eighteen holes, full bar and food service; tee time reservations available seven days in advance. The Maine-New Hampshire state line cuts through the course, and several holes line picturesque Province Lake.

Waukewan Golf Course (279-6661), off routes 3/25, Centre Harbor. Eighteen holes, full bar and food service. No tee times, so plan ahead for busy weekend play.

White Mountain Country Club (536-2227), off Route 3, Ashland. Eighteen holes, full bar and food service, tee times suggested on weekends.

HIKING   Most people head for the White Mountains to hike, but the Winnipesaukee region offers a variety of trails with fewer hikers and splendid mountaintop lake views (although the peaks are not so high as those farther north). The ambitious hiker could follow connecting trails from Mt. Chocorua to Waterville Valley. The standard reference is the *AMC White Mountain Guide*, although the Squam Lakes Association, which maintains many trails in this region, also has a guidebook (see Guidance). We have listed only a few of the many possible trails in the region. We do recommend one of these guidebooks because many of these trails are used less and marked less than the more famous trails farther north. All times shown are for the ascent only. Although brooks abound in the mountains, hikers should carry their own water.

Chocorua Region. Mt. Chocorua is only 3,475 feet high, but its rugged, treeless summit makes it a popular destination; and it has many trails to the summit from a variety of points. The **Piper Trail** begins on Route 16 at a restaurant-campground-parking lot (fee charged for parking) a few miles north of Chocorua Lake. The well-trod trail is 4.5 miles long and requires about 3.5 hours hiking time. The **Liberty Trail** begins on Paugus Mill Road which is off Route 113A, southwest of the mountain. Some 3.9 miles long, requiring about 3 hours, 20 minutes, this oldest trail on the mountain passes the Jim Liberty cabin, a mountainside cabin with bunks. The **Champney Falls Trail** ascends the mountain from the Kancamagus Highway on the north and is described in the Mount Washington Valley chapter. West of Chocorua are mounts Paugus, Passaconaway, and Whiteface, all of which can be climbed from a parking lot off Ferncroft Road, at Wonalancet on Route 113A.

Sandwich Notch Region. Sandwich Notch Road connects Center Sandwich with Route 49, the main road to Waterville Valley. Mt. Israel (elevation 2,620 feet) offers fine views of the Lakes Region for only modest effort. On Sandwich Notch Road, about 2.6 miles from Center Sandwich, watch for signs to Mead Base, a Boy Scout camp. The **Wentworth Trail** is 1.6 miles long, and estimated hiking time is 2 hours. Park in the field below the camp buildings and enter the woods at a sign at the left rear of the main building. The **Algonquin Trail** ascends Sandwich Dome (elevation 3,993 feet), also from Sandwich Notch Road, about 3.7 miles south of the junction with Route 49. The 4.5-mile-long trail is rough but offers fine views from its rocky ledges. Hiking time is 3.5 hours.

Red Hill. A fine view of Lake Winnipesaukee is the prize at the end of the **Red Hill Trail.** In Centre Harbor, at the junction of routes 25 and 25A, take Bean Road for 1.4 miles, then follow Sibley Road (look for the fire tower sign) to a parking lot with a gate. Past the gate is a jeep road changing to the trail. The hike is 1.7 miles and requires just over an hour. A famous Bartlett lithograph, often found in local antiques shops, shows a gathering of Indians on Red Hill.

Belknap Range. On the west side of the lake is a low ridge of mountains with many trails. A good starting point is the Gunstock Recreation Area on Route 11A in Gilford (see Green Space). Several trails ascend beside the ski slopes. Ask for a map at the camping area office.

Mount Major. Located just north of Alton on Route 11, this is everybody's popular climb. **Mount Major Trail** is only 1.5 miles long and requires about 1 hour, 20 minutes; views across the lake are impressive. Hike on the right day and watch the *M/V Mount Washington* as she cuts through the waters of Alton Bay.

SAILING   **Winni Sailboard's School** (528-4110), 687 Union Avenue, Lake Opechee, Laconia. Rentals of sailboards, rowboats, canoes, and paddleboats.

WATER SPORTS   **North Country Scuba and Sports** (569-2120, Wolfeboro; 524-8606, Laconia), Main Street Wolfeboro, 334 Union Avenue, Laconia. Open all year. Scuba instruction, rentals, air, and guided scuba dives on old wrecks. Also water-ski and sailboard instruction and canoe rentals.

CROSS-COUNTRY SKIING   **Deer Cap Ski Touring** (539-6030), Route 16, Center Ossipee.

Gunstock (293-4341), Route 11A, Gilford. This country-operated area has both downhill and cross-country facilities plus ski jumping.

The Nordic Skier (569-3151), North Main Street, Box 269, Wolfeboro. Open daily 9–5:30. Sales, rentals, and instruction for cross-country and telemark skiing, also sales and rentals of toboggans, ski skates, and snowshoes. They also schedule moonlight tours and races and maintain a 20-km trail network. Visit the shop for maps or suggestions for backcountry skiing.

Perry Hollow Cross Country Ski Area (569-3151 or 569-3055, ext. X-C), 2.5 miles south of Wolfeboro on Middleton Road. A country club with 20 km of trails and services maintained by the Nordic Skier.

LODGING   *Wolfeboro and vicinity:*   **Lakeview Inn** (569-1335), 120 North
Main Street, Box 713, Wolfeboro 03894. Open all year. Situated on a hill
just a short distance north of the village, this is a combination restored
old inn and adjacent two-level motel. All rooms have private baths,
TV, and phones; and a few have kitchenettes. Beds are doubles and
queens (two beds in motel units). The inn features one of the area's
best dining rooms (see Dining Out). $55–$85 for two depending on the
season.

    The Wolfeboro Inn (569-3016), 44 North Main Street, Wolfeboro
03894. Open all year. This inn dates back to 1812; but thanks to its 1988
expansion, it offers the region's finest accommodations and one of its
better restaurants. Nine guest rooms are in the old front portion of the
inn while the modern addition, built with a contemporary design to
resemble an old barn, has 32 more rooms, including some suites with
four-poster beds. The country-style rooms have private baths and
king, queen, double, or twin beds, with phones, TV, and individually
controlled heat and air-conditioning. The deluxe water-view rooms in
the addition have decks where one can watch lake activities or catch
cooling breezes. The center sections of the three-story addition have
open areas with chairs and reading nooks. The inn has a private beach
on the lake; and, with its village location, guests can leave their cars
behind as they take a short walk to shopping or to the dock of the *M/S
Mount Washington.* In season, guests are invited on a free morning lake
cruise aboard the *M/V Judge David Sewall,* a 70-passenger reproduction
of an old lake boat. It is also used for luncheon buffets (see Boat
Excursions). The inn also has conference facilities, a large dining room
(see Dining Out), and Wolfe's Tavern, which is located in the old portion of the inn. $89–$185 for two includes continental breakfast; MAP
package plans available and discounts for weekday and three-day or
longer stays.

    Tuc' Me Inn (569-5702), 68 North Main Street, Wolfeboro 03894.
Open all year. This nineteenth-century inn, with screened porches and
a cozy common room, is just two blocks from the downtown area.
Seven rooms, three with private baths (the others share two full baths).
Rooms have queen, double, and twin beds. Full country breakfast. $73
for two for private bath room, $60 for shared bath room.

    The Hardie House (569-5714), Route 109, Box 344, Mirror Lake
03853. Open all year. This 1850s guest house has been a B&B, operated
by Cheryl Marsh and Harmon Hudson, since 1984. The six rooms are
furnished with family antiques, double and twin beds (two rooms
have one of each, just right for a family). A country location and one
of the very few off-season places to stay on this side of the lake
between Wolfeboro and Moultonborough. No pets or children under
8. $65 for two.

    Pick Point Lodges (569-1338), off Route 109, Mirror Lake 03853.

Open early May to late October. If a week on the lake is your idea of a perfect summer vacation, it is difficult to find a better place than this collection of cottages in a 113-acre pine forest with a half-mile of shoreline. Other people apparently agree since the place is 60-percent booked by Labor Day for the following summer, and many guests come back for the same week every summer. A perfect family spot—the kids can wander the woods on trails, use the playground, or swim in the lake. The ten housekeeping cottages, seven on the water, have one to four bedrooms each, with a fully equipped kitchen, one to two baths, cable TV, telephones, and all linens, towels, and blankets. Two cottages have fireplaces, and all have king beds in the master bedrooms, with double and twin beds in other rooms. There is daily maid service and no tipping. Just bring your vacation clothes and wash them in the guest laundromat. The cottages rent weekly only in the summer when guests arrive on Saturday. Guests are welcome at complimentary breakfast on Sunday morning and the get-acquainted cookout on Monday night. Two rooms in the lodge (daily or weekly rates offered) have king beds and include daily breakfasts. In addition to indoor and outdoor tennis courts, the main lodge has four fireplaces, a large common room, books, and a game room for kids and adults. Weekly rates, early July to Labor Day, $1,100 (one to two persons) to $1,900 (four to eight persons); before and after Labor Day, rates range from $700 up. Daily rates available only in spring and fall.

North and east of the lake (see "A Country Road Alternative" for Eaton, Madison, Freedom, Effingham, and Wakefield): **Staffords-in-the Field** (323-7766), off Route 113, Chocorua 03817. Open all year. Some 25 years ago Fred and Ramona Stafford bought an abandoned house in the countryside, where, with hard work and imagination, they have created one of New Hampshire's classic inns. They have 17 rooms, 6 with private baths, 1 with a fireplace, and 3 rooms in separate cabins. The eclectic furnishings are mostly cozy, older pieces, adding to the country character of the setting. Two common rooms have books and games; there is a short walk to Chocorua Lake for swimming and miles of trails for walking or cross-country skiing. Plan on some exercise to have plenty of room for Ramona's "on-the-gourmet-side" cooking, the inn's trademark (see Dining Out). MAP $120 (higher in foliage season) plus tax and 15 percent service charge.

The Tamworth Inn (323-7721), Main Street, Tamworth 03886. Open all year. Built in 1833, this village inn retains its nineteenth-century charm. There are 14 individually decorated rooms, including 4 suites, all with private baths. Beds range from kings to twins. There is a comfy pub, and the library has books, videos, and a fireplace. Summer guests enjoy the outdoor pool and strolling (or trout fishing) beside the river. Just across the street is the Barnstormers summer theater.

Rates include a country continental breakfast. The inn is popular locally for lunch and dinner (see Dining Out). Phil and Kathy Bender, innkeepers. $80–$130 for two (higher during foliage season or holiday-skiing weeks) plus tax and 15 percent service charge.

Corner House Inn (284-6219), Center Sandwich 03227. Open all year. Another New Hampshire favorite located in a special town, this popular place fills up quickly since it has only four rooms. It has been an inn for over 100 years but has been owned for a decade by Don and Jane Brown, who have turned it into the kind of comfortable inn one dreams about. The four rooms, one with a private bath, are furnished with antiques and older pieces. You will find plenty to do in the shops of Center Sandwich. Nearby is Squam Lake for hiking and swimming. Full breakfast to guests; lunch and dinner also served in this popular restaurant. $60–$70 for two.

Kona Mansion (253-4900), off Moultonborough Neck Road (turn at the blinker on Route 25 and follow the signs; mail: Box 458, Centre Harbor 03226). Open daily Memorial Day to Columbus Day and weekends earlier and later. Over 100 years ago, 16-year-old Herbert Dumaresq began working as an office boy for the Jordan Marsh Company, a large Boston department store. Thirty-three years later, he married the boss's daughter and became a partner in the business, which had become a leading New England retailer. Dumaresq used his fortune to buy up a large number of farms on Moultonborough Neck, creating a large summer estate where he built this mansion in 1900. The Crowley family bought the mansion and 130 acres of hilltop and lakefront in 1971, operating an inn since then. Drive up the hill to the mansion and enter a private country-club-like atmosphere, complete with a 9-hole, par-3 golf course, tennis courts, and lake boat dock. The inn has 10 rooms with twin or one or two double beds and private baths. On the lakefront are four housekeeping cottages with one to four bedrooms and two two- to three-bedroom chalets. Some of the inn rooms are small, but all are well decorated and comfortable. Relax in the lounge with a view across the lake to the Belknap Mountains. Breakfast and dinner served to the guests and the public (see Dining Out). EP $55–$150; MAP for two (weekly only), $880–$1,200; inquire about B&B rates. Cottages by the week, $400–$675.

The Gilman Tavern (323-8940), Main Street, Tamworth 03886. Open all year. This eighteenth-century village tavern has been beautifully restored and furnished with antiques by Bill and Sue McCarthy. There are four rooms, one with a private bath. We loved the Village Center room with its stencilled floors and 1830s country furnishings including a canopy bed. Full breakfast served on the patio in warm weather. Afternoon refreshments are served to guests at 4. $60–$85 for two.

West Ossipee House (539-2874), Covered Bridge Road, Box 420, West Ossipee 03890. Open all year. An inn 80 years ago, then a ski club, this old building was remodeled in 1986 as a B&B. There are seven nicely furnished rooms, three with private baths. Most beds are doubles, and some rooms have a double and a twin. Full country breakfast. Diane and Drew Scamman also plan to offer gourmet dining ($8.95–$14.95, choice of four entrées) three nights a week. Rooms for two are $65 with private bath, $55 for shared bath.

The Farmhouse (323-8707), just off Route 16, Chocorua Village 03817. Open May through October. After 13 years of being open all year, innkeeper Katherine Dryenforth has decided to close for the winter. There are four rooms sharing two baths, three rooms with double beds, one with twins. Just a short walk to the tasty treats of the Dam Ice Cream Shop beside the cooling waterfall. Full breakfast, featuring their own eggs and maple syrup. Bus service almost to the door. $60 for two.

Chocorua View House (323-8350), Route 16, Box 348, Chocorua 03817. Open all year, winter by reservation only. Seven rooms share two baths, full breakfast. $55 for two.

Strathaven (284-7785), Route 113, North Sandwich 03259. Open all year. This is a special little B&B with a rural location and beautiful grounds that include extensive gardens, a pond for swimming or skating, and an English croquet court. There are four lovely rooms, two large rooms each have two double beds and a private bath, and two rooms share a bath. Many rooms feature antiques as well as Betsey Leiper's embroidery, a craft she teaches occasionally in week-long workshops at the inn. $55–$60 for two with full breakfast.

Long Island Inn (253-4478), Old Long Island Road (off Route 25, turn at the blinker), Moultonborough (mail: Box 378, Star Route 62, Centre Harbor 03226). Open June through September, depending on the weather. It is not the fanciest place in the region (it needs a good exterior coat of paint), it is not easy to find, and it is not for everyone; but it is a special place at a bargain price for guests who want to relax and entertain themselves. Three generations of Barbara Austin's family have operated this inn, which began in 1874 when guests arrived only by steamboat from Weirs Beach, just across the lake, and the inn served three full meals daily. On the exterior, the inn looks unchanged from its early days when it accommodated large numbers of guests who came for a least a week or, more likely, for the whole summer. The towns around the lake were once dotted with houses like this one, but hardly any remain. Now the inn has just five rooms (four doubles and a single), each freshly decorated and antiques-furnished, with two shared baths. Just a short walk is the beach where the steamboats used to dock; but the sun still sets, and you will probably encounter wild deer that wander this island in great numbers. Full breakfast. $45 for a double, $35 for the single room.

West and northwest of the lake: If it's a motel you are after, Weirs Beach has a
wide choice, especially along Route 3 (Weirs Boulevard), between the
beach and Laconia. Some places are on Paugus Bay; others are across
the street. The most luxurious is the **Margate** (524-5210, outside NH
1-800-MARGATE), a full resort with indoor pool, lake swimming,
health club, tennis, and a restaurant ($55–$164). Nearby are **The
Naswa Lakeside Resort** (366-4341) and **Christmas Island Motel and
Steak House** (366-4378). You'll also find many lovely inns, B&Bs, and
cottages.

   Red Hill Inn (279-7001), Route 25B and College Road (RFD 1, Box
99M), Centre Harbor 03226. Open all year. In just five years this inn
has become another of New Hampshire's classics; but when Rick
Miller and Don Leavitt bought the place in 1985, it was totally derelict,
and friends suggested tearing it down. Built as a mansion in 1904 as
part of a several-hundred-acre estate, the inn most recently was the
administration building of the now-defunct Belknap College. When
the school closed in 1974, the building was abandoned and eventually
vandalized. The current owners immediately began transforming it
into an inn and restaurant, a process which continues. Currently there
are ten rooms in the main inn, all have private baths, three have fireplaces, four have Jacuzzis, and several have separate sitting rooms. A
separate stone cottage has three rooms (all with fireplaces, two with
Jacuzzis), and the recently completed farmhouse has eight rooms (six
rooms with Franklin fireplaces, two with Jacuzzis). Three rooms have
twin beds, all the rest have doubles, and all have antique furniture and
easy chairs. To feed these fireplaces (and another large one in the living room), the innkeepers annually cut some 35 cords of wood on the
surrounding 50 acres. The hilltop location offers sweeping views of
Squam Lake and the mountains, a panorama that improves in the
winter when the Red Hill Cross-country Ski center opens (groomed
trails and rentals). Dining is a highlight here as well, and the inn
serves three meals daily, with menu items enhanced by more than 30
herbs gathered in the unique garden lining the path to the dining
room patio. The lounge, with a 1940 Chris Craft runabout as the bar,
offers guitar music on Saturday nights (see Dining Out). B&B
$65–$125 for two. MAP five-day mid-week packages begin at $450 for
two; also three-day packages (three breakfasts, dinner one night)
beginning at $185 for two.

   The Manor on Golden Pond (968-3348 or 800-545-2141), Shepard
Hill Road and Route 3 (Box T), Holderness 03245. Built in 1903–07, this
inn is another of the region's many mansions built as summer estates
by millionaires. It has survived a checkered past of auctions and various inn operations and names; and, since 1983, has been the Manor
of Golden Pond, managed for the past six years by Andre Lemourex.
It is now part of a small chain of country inns that include the New

England Inn at Intervale, New Hampshire. Begin outside where the 13-acre hilltop location provides a 65-mile panorama across Squam Lake and surrounding mountains. Inside, leaded glass windows, ornate woodwork, and detailed architectural elements remain from the past. No two of the inn's seventeen rooms are alike, but all are furnished mostly with antiques (four-poster beds), have private baths, and some have fireplaces. Most rooms are large, especially the deluxe rooms which have king, queen, or two double beds, ceiling fans, air-conditioning, and lake views; some have balconies. Two large common rooms have fireplaces and plenty of books and games, and a second-floor sitting room has a TV. Three detached housekeeping cottages are suitable for four, and another on the lakeshore has a fireplace and sleeps up to six. All have porches, living rooms, and kitchens. There are tennis courts and the manor's private 300-foot beach with a boat dock. Guests can enjoy special Squam Lake cruises. Breakfast and dinner served daily. Rates for two are: EP, mid-May through foliage season and winter holiday weeks, $88–155; the rest of the year $59–$125. MAP, mid-May through foliage season and winter holiday weeks, $142–$208, the rest of the year $128–$178. Cottages, mid-May through foliage season only, $400–$600 per week.

Inn at Mills Falls (279-7006), Route 3, Meredith 03253. Open all year. Built around a tumbling waterfall adjacent to an old mill, this large, 54-room complex is perhaps the most upscale place to stay in the region. Each decorator-designed room has New Hampshire-made maple or Shaker pine furnishings with easy chairs and desks, air-conditioning, TV, and telephone. Beds are queens, twins, or a queen and a twin, and half the rooms have views out to Meredith Bay. There is an indoor pool, spa, and sauna plus two restaurants and 20 shops, galleries, and boutiques. EP, lake view, summer and fall, $125–$160; off-season $98–$125. Less for limited-view rooms, two- or three-night minimum for peak weekends. Packages for two nights $99–$135 per person, including two breakfasts and one dinner.

The Nutmeg Inn (279-8811 or 800-642-9229), Pease Road, RFD 2 (off Route 104), Meredith 03253. Open all year. Part of this building was built over 200 years ago as a stagecoach tavern, and it has been an inn since the 1940s; but Daryl and Cheri Lawrence completely restored and renovated the place in 1988, creating a comfortable country oasis, complete with a top restaurant. The inn has eight guest rooms, six with a private bath, two with fireplaces, and one with a king bed and a separate sitting area. Two rooms have twin beds; the rest are doubles. Curl up in a cozy corner, or swim in the outdoor pool. No smoking, TV, or telephones. A full breakfast is served to guests only. $60–$85 for two.

Hedgecroft Inn (253-6328), Route 25B in the village (RFD 1, Box 547), Centre Harbor 03226. Open all year. Patte and Frank Fancher turned an 1820 village home into a three-room B&B. The rooms, which share a bath, have double, queen, and king beds. You can walk to the lakefront where the *M/S Mount Washington* docks (see Boat Excursions), shop in the new mall, or just relax on the inn's front porch hammock. $60 for two.

Watch Hill B&B (253-4334), Old Meredith Road, in the village (Box 1605), Centre Harbor 03226. Open all year. A professionally trained cook and former kennel owner, Barbara Lauterbach, bought one of the oldest houses (1772) in Centre Harbor and turned it into a comfortable B&B. Four rooms—two with twins, two with queens—share two baths. Antiques furnish the house, and there is a cozy woodstove in the breakfast room, where Barbara applies her cooking talents. She also offers special cooking class weekends where guests can help plan and prepare the meals. $55 for two, discount for three nights or more.

Country Options (968-7958), 27–29 North Main Street, Ashland 03217. Open all year. Five rooms with two shared baths, furnished with antiques. Innkeepers Sandy Ray and Nancy Puglisi also operate a special-order bakery so one can imagine the treats offered for breakfast. For dinner, just walk across the street to the Common Man, a leading regional restaurant (see Dining Out). $45–$50 for two.

The Glynn House Inn (968-3775), 43 Highland Street, Ashland 03217. Karol and Betsy Paterman have transformed this ornate, in-town, 1890 Queen Anne-style Victorian into an impressive B&B. The house retains all of its handsome, original woodwork and ornate oriental wallpaper. There are four rooms, each with a private bath, one with a fireplace, and each furnished to the period. Beds are queens; one room has a queen and a single. Karol is a professional chef, having recently sold a local, popular restaurant, and his breakfast talents include eggs Benedict, apple strudel, and fresh popovers. $75, weeknights $65 for two.

The Inn on Golden Pond (968-7269), Route 3 (Box 126), Holderness 03245. Open all year, except December. Bill and Bonnie Webb left other careers to open this large B&B in 1984. It is located right on Route 3, although well back from the road. Most of the nine rooms have queen beds, and seven have private baths. All the rooms are furnished differently and have one or two easy chairs, a nice touch since so many places lack this amenity. You may wander the inn's 55 wooded acres or test your skills in table tennis or darts in the separate sports shed. The living room has a fireplace, and a second common room has cable TV. $75–$85 for two.

Tuckernuck Inn (279-5521), Red Gate Lane (RFD 4, Box 88), Meredith 03253. Open all year. This is a five-room village inn, within walking distance to the shops and Lake Winnipesaukee. Each room is individual, but early American decor is featured with stencilled walls and floors, quilts, and other antique touches. Two rooms have private baths, some have two double beds. There is a large fireplace in the living room along with a huge shelf of books and games to play. Breakfast is continental, but the selection of teas, coffee, hot muffins, fresh fruit, and cereals is more than filling. $55–$65 for two. Innkeeper Ernie Taddei also operates New Hampshire Bed and Breakfast, a reservation service with some 60 locations throughout the state, from oceanfront to mountains, private homes to large inns.

Parade Rest B&B (524-3152), Parade Road, Laconia 03246. Open all year. Just two rooms with private baths, one with a kitchen, in a 1766 farmhouse out in the country. Watch for their sign; it's tiny. $65 for two with full breakfast, three-day package available.

Hickory Stick Farm (524-3333), Laconia 03246. Call for reservations and directions. Open Memorial Day to Columbus Day. Two rooms (one with a double, one with twin beds) furnished with antiques. The breakfast is served in a country kitchen. These two rooms are part of the region's best known restaurant (see Dining Out). $60 for two.

Ferry Point House (524-0087), off Route 3 in Winnisquam (mail: R1, Box 335, Laconia 03246). Open Memorial Day through Labor Day, weekends through October. We found this place by accident, even though they have been open for five years and deserve to be better known. Make sure to get directions to their country location. They are situated on Lake Winnisquam and offer wide views from their 60-foot veranda and a waterfront gazebo. Guests may use the horseshoes, raft, paddleboat, or rowboat. The five rooms, all with private baths, have a lacy Victorian decor highlighted by old high-back beds and claw-foot tubs. Since the Damato family has published its own breakfast cookbook, be prepared for a gourmet start to your day. Try stuffed French toast, crêpes, cheese-baked apples, stuffed pears, and fresh breads and muffins. $65–$75 for two.

Black Swan (286-4524), Main Street, Tilton 03276. Open all year. An 1880s millowner's mansion with seven guest rooms. Stained glass and ornate woodwork in the parlors and a spacious feeling to the bedrooms makes this a comfortable, interesting place to stay. No children under 12. Full breakfast. Bob and Janet Foster, innkeepers. $55–$65 for two.

The Anchorage (524-3248), Route 3, Winnisquam (mail: RFD 1, Box 90, Laconia 03246). Open mid-May to mid-October. While this place is not fancy, it attracts a worldwide clientele, and cottages are booked early, often by folks who return year after year. With 35 acres and nearly a mile of shore on Lake Winnisquam, the Anchorage has 30 fully equipped (just bring groceries and a beach towel) housekeeping cabins that sleep from 2 to 8 people, plus two houses that accommodate 18. On the lakefront are three beaches, several boat docks, and rafts. Rent canoes, motorboats, or paddleboats, or fish from the shore for salmon and trout. Cook your catch on the charcoal grills while you watch the kids play lawn sports, use the playground and the ball fields, or run about with new friends through the fields, orchard, or woods. With no roads to cross, children can play safely all day. There are play areas for kids and adults and occasional organized cookouts and campfire sing-a-longs. Rates by the week, beginning on Saturday, late June through Labor Day, $390–$1,050. Houses $1,800–$2,300; off-season $240–$540. Minimum three-day stays also available off-season.

Ames Farm Inn (293-4321, 742-3962), 2800 Lake Shore Road (Route 11), Gilford 03246. Open late April (for fishermen) to first weekend in October. Tradition! This 300-acre inn and cottage community just celebrated its 100th anniversary in 1990, having been operated by five generations of the Ames family. One guest, who has come to this inn for 64 years, probably knew them all. Another family of guests has stayed regularly for four generations. Needless to say, book early for the short peak season of July and August. Seventeen fully equipped housekeeping cottages are spread out on the lakefront. Each has one or two bedrooms, kitchenette, living room, and screened porch. The view across Lake Winnipesaukee stretches across the Broads for miles to the Ossipee Mountains and Mt. Washington. Away from the shore are buildings with housekeeping apartments and fifteen modern guest rooms with private baths. No charge to launch and dock a boat, and some rental boats are available. The inn restaurant is open daily 8–2, from late June to Labor Day. Weekly rates; apartments and small cabin, $310; housekeeping cottages, $595 peak season, $325 off-season. B&B for the private rooms, weekly, $295 per person; three days-two nights, $100.

DINING OUT *Wolfeboro and vicinity:* **The Lakeview Inn** (569-1335), 120 North Main Street, Wolfeboro. Open all year, nightly 5:30–10. Dining is in the restored rooms of this old inn. Highly regarded locally, this restaurant has a diverse menu of American and continental entrées. Filet boursin Wellington ($16.95), scampi a la Carbonarra ($17.95), roast duckling ($14.95), and shrimp fantasia (17.95) highlight the menu. Fresh baked breads and pastries, homemade soups. The adjacent lounge serves sandwiches, soups, salads, and lighter fare. Reservations suggested.

The Wolfeboro Inn (569-3016), 44 North Main Street, Wolfeboro. Open all year, Wolfe's Tavern from 11:30, the dining room 5–9:30. Located in the old section of the inn, the tavern serves a huge (70 items) variety of lighter fare, from hot and cold sandwiches and salads to soups, pizza, munchies, and dinners. More than 40 brands of beer, too. The dining room features new American cuisine with prices ranging from $11.95–$14.95. Sample lobster, seafood fettucini, double-thick lamb chops, veal medallions, or farm-raised venison.

The Cider Press (569-2028), Middleton Road, South Wolfeboro. Nightly, except Monday, 5:30–9; Sunday until 8. A popular rustic spot with barnboard walls, candlelight dining, and varied menu. Baby-back ribs, chicken Parmesan, lamb chops, fried shrimp, and roast duck are featured. Prices $7.95–$15.95.

East of Suez (569-1648), Route 28, South Wolfeboro. Open daily June through early September (closed Mondays) 6–9:30. Asian food of all descriptions is prepared by the Powell family. Japanese, Chinese, Philippine, and Korean specialities, huge portions, and moderate prices ($10–$13) make this place a dining adventure, one which many people bypass because the old building looks as if it could use some work. They have been here for 20 years, yet remain a secret, even for many locals.

The Bittersweet Restaurant (569-3636), Route 28 (north) and Allen Road, Wolfeboro. Open daily all year, Monday to Friday noon–8:30; Saturday 5–9; Sunday brunch 11–2, dinner 5–8. Here's another old barn, furnished with antiques, recycled as a fine restaurant. The international cuisine ($9.50–$16.50) ranges from grouper and Norwegian salmon with seafood mousse to stir-fry seafood and liver and onions. The lounge has lighter, less expensive fare.

The Foxy Johnnie Restaurant and Firehouse Lounge (859-3381), off Route 11, New Durham. Open daily 5–9, Friday and Saturday until 10; Sunday 12–9. Part of this popular rambling place was built in 1764, and many old elements remain, including the massive fireplace, hand-hewn beams, and wide floorboards. Roast beef and steaks broiled over live coals are the specialty. Several entrées including tenderloin and baked seafood such as haddock, shrimp, scallops, or mixed casserole. All steaks are served with sautéed mushrooms or pan-fried onions. Other entrées include sautéed lobster, fried seafoods, and veal parmigiana ($10.95–$21.50).

Bailey's Dockside, on the water off Main Street in the center of town, Wolfeboro. Open mid-May to mid-October for lunch and dinner. An old favorite located on the wharf where the *M/S Mount Washington* docks. Known for their ice cream. Also see Bailey's on South Main Street. Open all year for breakfast, lunch, and dinner—a tradition for over 50 years.

North and east of the lake (see also "A Country Road Alternative"): **Ramona's** (323-7766), off Route 113, Chocorua. Three entrées are offered nightly in the summer, one entrée the rest of the year. Lamb with prunes, pork tenderloin, or sole Florentine might be offered along with homemade tasty soups, distinctively prepared vegetables, and scrumptious desserts. Fred is the bartender and dines with the guests.

The Tamworth Inn (323-7721), Main Street, Tamworth. Open all year for dinner, 6–8, Sunday brunch 11–2. This old inn's attractive dining room has a diverse, changing menu ($9.50–$17.25). Sample curried lamb, beef Stroganoff, baked cod, or chicken ricotta. Appetizers include smoked trout, tortellini with pesto, or baked brie for two.

Fresh-made soups and homemade pies and cakes complete the menu offerings. Lighter fare is served in the pub. Summer theater packages include room, dinner, and tickets to the Barnstormers.

The Greenhouse (323-8688), Route 16, Tamworth. Monday through Friday 5–9, Sunday noon–8. Situated in the woods near White Lake State Park, this newly built restaurant specializes in European cuisine. Featured are schnitzel, sauerbraten, and rolladen (a traditional German beef roll stuffed with bacon, pickles and onions), plus prime rib and steak au poivre. Chicken, seafood, and roast duck also offered along with homemade desserts. Two greenhouse dining rooms give the place its name ($7.75–$16.95).

Corner House Inn (284-6219), Center Sandwich. Open all year, June through October, lunch (11:30–2:30) and dinner (5:30–9:30) daily (except no Sunday lunch), November through May, lunch and dinner Wednesday to Sunday (except no Sunday lunch). Reservations suggested. Candlelight dining, antiques, and local art, some of which are for sale, serve to accent the delicious dining found here ($10.95–$17.95). Fresh-made breads and ever-changing soups and desserts complement such menu highlights as chicken Oscar, veal piccata, tournedos Normandy, double-thick lamb chops, shellfish sauté, and lobster and scallop pie. Lunch ($1.95–$8.95) is not to be missed either if one cares for fresh breads with large hearty sandwiches such as the black angus: carved steak topped with onions, tomatoes, and buttermilk dressing on French baquette. Salads, quiche, crêpes, and soups, plus delicacies such as broiled scallops and Maine crab cakes with Cajun sauce, round out the menu.

Christopher's Restaurant (475-2300), junction old Route 109 and Route 25, Box 669, Moultonborough. Open all year, dinner only. Once an inn, this place has been transformed into an interesting restaurant by owner/chef David McDonald, who prepares what he calls New American Cuisine. The comprehensive menu ($9–$17.50) features vegetarian dishes, chicken, seafood, beef, veal, and pork. Begin with broiled shrimp and scallops on a bed of poached spinach with lobster sauce, or choose grilled steak salad with tomato cucumber and cheddar cheese. For an entrée select baked stuffed chicken breast, king salmon arbonara, veal Christopher (medallions coated with herbs, finished with a lemon veal demi-glacé), or grilled pork loin Dijon. There are desserts to match.

The Woodshed (476-2311), Lee's Mill Road, off Route 109, Moultonborough. Open all year for dinner. To operate a successful restaurant in the countryside, on a side road, off a less-than-major route, in a small spread-out town, you must have atmosphere and good food. This place has both in abundance ($10.95–$18.95). What began as a small restaurant in an old farmhouse a decade or so ago, has grown into a large operation using the barn, its loft, and even a screened-in patio. The barn is exquisite, retaining its old hand-hewn features and decorated with antiques and collectibles. An evening could begin at the "raw" bar for clams and oysters or peel-and-eat shrimp and escargot. Prime rib is the specialty, but how about a combination with king crab or lobster? After sole in parchment, shrimp kabob, steak teriyaki, or chicken gourmet, no wonder the dessert menu begins with "We dare you?" Cheesecake, a one-scoop hot chocolate sundae, or Indian pudding can complete the repast.

The Sweetwater Inn (476-5079), Route 25, Moultonborough. Open all year for dinner. Despite the name this is a restaurant only, specializing in Italian dishes with pasta made fresh daily. Generally prices range from $10.95–$17.95 but this menu includes 15 items priced between $4.95 and $9.95. One could order pizza or something traditional like chicken Parmesan, pasta with clam sauce, or Alfredo. Or you have other choices: fettucini jambalaya with sautéed chicken, scallops, and Andouille sausage with garlic, sherry, onions, peppers, tomato, and Cajun spices; lobster ravioli; medallions of veal with shallots and fancy mushrooms; seafood paella; or chicken Veronique. Favorites like steak au poivre, baked haddock, and oriental stir-fry round out the menu. The Belgium chocolate dessert specialty changes daily, and there are many delectables from the dessert tray.

Kona Mansion (253-4900), off Moultonborough Neck Road (turn at the blinker on Route 25 and follow the signs; mail: Box 458, Centre Harbor 03226). Open daily Memorial Day to Columbus Day, and weekends earlier and later. Salads, veal du jour, Delmonico steak, shrimp, and chicken Kona (breast stuffed with spinach and cheese, topped with white wine sauce) are featured in this mansion overlooking the lake on Moultonborough Neck. Dine in the ornate Victorian spaces once used as the mansion's library, living, and dining rooms.

Northwest and west of the lake: **Red Hill Inn** (279-7001), Route 25B and College Road (RFD 1, Box 99M), Centre Harbor. Open all year, lunch 12–2 summer and fall, Sunday buffet brunch 11–2, dinner 5–10. Gourmet dining with candlelight and fresh flowers. Everything is made fresh from scratch with noncholesterol butter seasoning for sautés. Try oven-fried rabbit, roast pheasant, broiled lamb chops, baked stuffed chicken breast, shrimp with lobster stuffing, or lemon pepper scallops plus steaks, king crab legs, haddock, veal, and a variety of vegetarian dishes ($7.95–$25.95). Homemade dessert offerings change daily, and we haven't mentioned the appetizers, salads (12 dressings), and homemade soups and desserts, especially the berry pies.

The Manor on Golden Pond (968-3348 or 800-545-2141), Shepard Hill Road and Route 3 (Box T), Holderness. Open daily for breakfast and dinner (5:30-9, weekends until 9:30, off-season until 8:30); Sunday brunch (11–2). Feel like a Victorian millionaire in the manor's ornate dining room while sampling roast duckling, pork tenderloin sautéed with ginger and tarragon, rack of lamb, veal with king crab and scallops in champagne basil cream, or sautéed chicken topped with spinach boursin and dill havarti cheeses ($11.50–$20). Their apple pie has been judged the best in New England.

The Common Man (536-4536), North Main Street, Ashland. Open daily for lunch and dinner, except no lunch Sunday and Monday. Opened in 1971, this is the original, and still popular, restaurant in a group which has grown to include the Capital City Diner in Concord (see Merrimack Valley), and Glove Hollow in Plymouth (see Western Whites). The country decor features old posters, books, tools, and art, a comfortable feeling for relaxed dining. The varied menu (dinner $9.95–$26.95) ranges from pasta primavera and veal or chicken Oscar, to chicken Kiev and crab and scallop pie. The "Grate Steak," a large planked with a medley of vegetables served family-style can feed up to three people for $26.95. All the swordfish is served fresh, never from frozen, and the beef ages in their own walk-ins for three to five weeks. White chocolate mousse or brownie sundae, mudpie, or chocolate decadence cake.

Hickory Stick Farm (524-3333), Laconia. Open Memorial Day through Columbus Day daily at 5, except Monday; Sunday at noon. Also open Thursday, Friday, and Saturday nights in winter. Reservations are required, so ask for directions. Charlie and Dee, the first generation of Roeders, started this unique restaurant in 1950 and must have had plenty of courage since it is well off the beaten path. Success solved the location problem, however, as this place has a national reputation, especially for their specialty, roast duckling. Scott Roeder and his wife Mary ran the business for many years and now son Greg is in charge. The main dining room has early American decor, but the large screened gazebo overlooking the gardens is our favorite spot. For an appetizer, among other items, try duck-liver pâté, fried duck livers, or duck soup. Roast duck is prepared for one, or a whole duck for parties of two, three, or four ($27.50–$43.80). Slow roasted to remove the fatty layer under the skin, these 4–5 lb. Wisconsin-bred ducks have crisp skin with moist, fork-tender meat beneath. Frozen, cooked duck with a packet of orange sherry sauce is available in their gift shop or by mail. Casseroles of seafood, scallops, or vegetables, baked chicken, filet Wellington, and rack of lamb are among other menu specialities. Dinners ($9.95–$16.95) include orange curl rolls, a molded pineapple salad, or country green salad. Desserts are made from scratch.

Mame's (279-4631), Plymouth Street, adjacent to the Mill Falls Marketplace, Meredith. Open daily for lunch (11:30–3), dinner (5:30–9), and Sunday brunch (11:30–2). An 1825 brick house with barn, now with six dining rooms, Mame's offers varied and reasonably priced dining ($8.95–$18.95). Chicken baked in white wine with lemon and mushrooms, vegetable Alfredo, lobster-scallop divan, baked haddock, or roast prime rib are offered, along with the evening dinner special (soup to white chocolate for $9.95) and surf and turf for two at $19.95. Mud pie, liqueur parfaits, cheesecake, and more for dessert.

The Nutmeg Inn (279-8811 or 800-642-9229), Pease Road, RFD 2 (off Route 104), Meredith. Dining room open April through October, Wednesday to Sunday 5:30–9. Three fireplaces accent the early-American decor in this restored old tavern. The specialty is chicken New Hampshire (breast of chicken with ham, mushrooms, and cheese with a walnut coating, served with country gravy), but other items include tournedos Campignon, blackened swordfish, shrimp, and scallop fettucini, and beef Wellington ($10.95–$15.95). Have stuffed clams or seafood crepes for an appetizer and top off the meal with apple dumplings or strawberry torte. A no-smoking restaurant and inn.

The William Tell Inn (293-8803), Route 11, West Alton. ($11.95–$15.95) Open for dinner daily, except Monday, spring to fall; Thursday to Sunday in winter. With a name from Switzerland and housed in a chalet, expect Swiss cuisine. One of the region's better restaurants with a variety of continental favorites, served by owner/chef Peter Bossart and his wife Susan. Weiner or Holstein schnitzel, roast duck, filet mignons of beef, veal, and pork charbroiled and served with various sauces, or boiled meats with sauerkraut and parslied potatoes provide hearty dining. The desserts feature dark Tobler chocolate imported from Switzerland.

Hart's Turkey Farm Restaurant (279-6212), Route 3, Meredith. Open all year at 11:15 AM for lunch and dinner. Turkey is the specialty but there are also steaks, seafood, and sandwiches in this large, popular restaurant, family-owned since 1954.

Pauli's Bakery (286-7081), 170 Main Street, Tilton. Open 6:30 AM–3 PM, Monday through Saturday; also Thursday and Friday nights and Sunday brunch. Step into this perfectly ordinary-looking eatery and enjoy everything homemade from breads and quiches to soups and pies. Try strawberry waffles or crab and cheese omelets for breakfast; buffalo or venison stew or a smoked fish for dinner in this small oasis. A lunch special is chicken and crab (boneless breast of chicken sautéed and topped with sliced tomatoes, broccoli, crabmeat, and melted cheese).

ENTERTAINMENT **The Barnstormers** (323-8500), Tamworth 03886. Open July and August. New Hampshire's oldest professional theater celebrated its 60th anniversary in 1990. Director-founder Francis G. Cleveland stages outstanding plays with an equity cast. Musicals, some popular plays, and other lesser known offerings. Dinner-theater packages available with the Tamworth Inn.

The Arts Council of Tamworth (323-8693), presents monthly (except summer) performances in the Tamworth-Sandwich area. Included are classical pianists, string quartets, and vaudeville.

New Hampshire Music Festival (253-4331). This regional music institution begins in early July for six weeks; all performances held at 8. Chamber music on Tuesdays at Boyd Hall, Plymouth State College; orchestral symphony Thursdays at Newfound Regional High School, Bristol, and (repeat of Thursday) Fridays at Gilford Middle-High School.

Belknap Mill Society (524-8813), Mill Plaza, Laconia 03246. Open all year, weekdays 9–5, Saturdays 9–1. Built in 1823, this is the oldest unaltered textile mill in the country. There are tours of the building, but this mill, which was saved from demolition, is also the headquarters of the only year-round arts center in the region. Art exhibits and displays, music, lectures, and children's programs are among the many events open to all.

SELECTIVE SHOPPING　Annalee Dolls (279-6542), off Route 3 or Route 104, Meredith 03253. Open all year (except two weeks in January), hours vary by the season. Dolls are for kids, of course, but these dolls are also among the more collectible items one can purchase today, so probably more golden-agers stop here than children. Annalee Thorndike began making her felt dolls in 1934, and now she runs a major local industry employing more than 450 people; and her dolls are sold and collected nationally. For collectors, the best inventory is maintained here, including more that 1,000 different early dolls. You can see the finished pieces in the gift shop, the doll museum, and the Annalee Doll Antique and Collectible Doll Shoppe. Join the Annalee Doll Society and receive a free doll, membership pin, newsletter, and an invitation to the annual barbecue and doll auction held on the last Sunday of June. Small fee for the museum, dolls for sale; also a catalog.

Ayottes' Designery (284-6915), Center Sandwich. Open year-round, Thursday to Saturday 10–5, or by appointment. This is the home-studio-shop of renowned handweavers, Robert and Roberta Ayotte. They weave apparel, wall hangings, rugs, pillows, and placemats; they sell looms, accessories, and weaving supplies; and they display handmade crafts by others.

Basket World (366-5585), Route 3, Weirs Beach. Leave the kids across the street at the Funspot while you shop through this huge display of woven baskets, furniture, and other items.

Camelot Bookstore (569-1771), 16 North Main Street, Wolfeboro. A fine selection of local books and gifts.

Country Braid House (286-4511), Clark Road, Tilton. Open Monday to Saturday 9–4, Sunday by appointment. Pure wool rugs in a variety of patterns.

Hampshire Pewter (569-4944), 9 Mill Street (just off the main street), Wolfeboro. Open year-round daily, except Sunday, 9–5. Beautiful pewter items, especially their Christmas tree ornaments. This company was founded in 1974 to revive a nearly forgotten early-American craft. Shop and tours.

The Hand and I Craft Center (476-5121), Route 25 (Box 264), Moultonborough. Open every day, casual visitors are welcome afternoons until 5. Robert Wright and Robin Dustin have started a do-it-yourself craft center in a former two-room schoolhouse and teach classes in wood, leather, jewelry, metal work, antique repairs, weaving, and more. Craft center members (from local residents to short-term visitors) can take morning or evening classes or use the facilities to work on their own projects. Special tools and craft supplies for sale.

Pepi Herrmann Crystal (528-1020), 43 Gilford East Drive, Gilford. Fine-quality, handcut crystal and giftware.

Keepsakes Quilting and Country Pleasures (253-4026), Route 25, Senter Marketplace, Centre Harbor (mailing address: Box 1459, Meredith 03253). Open daily. Called New England's largest quilt shop, there is everything and anything a quilter could desire including 3,500 bolts of cotton cloth, stencils, patterns, and kits. For the less ambitious, there are also ready-made quilts for sale. Free catalog.

League of New Hampshire Arts & Crafts. Shops in Center Sandwich (Sandwich Home Industries in the village) and Meredith (Route 3). Open daily late May through Columbus Day. Superb New Hampshire-made crafts of all types including lamps, furniture, prints, carvings, textiles, pottery, and much more. Demonstration programs in July and August. Sandwich Home Industries in Center Sandwich was started in 1926 to promote traditional crafts, and it became the founding member of the League of New Hampshire Arts & Crafts in the 1930s. Its present shop opened in 1934.

The Old Country Store, Route 25, Moultonborough. Open daily. Built as a stagecoach stop in 1781, this rambling old building has a small museum to go along with gifts, books, New Hampshire-made products, and typical country-store items.

The Old Print Barn (279-6479), Winona Road, off Route 104, Meredith. Open Memorial Day to Columbus Day, 10-6 PM, by appointment at other times. The largest display of original prints in New Hampshire includes antique and contemporary work from 1600 to the present. We especially like the old New Hampshire views of the lakes and White Mountains, but one can find etchings, lithographs, and engravings covering virtually any subject from any continent as well as work by locally prominent and world-famous artists. The huge restored barn, with its detailed nineteenth-century craftsmanship, is impressive, too. Free, but it will be hard to resist buying a print!

The Sundial Shops (524-3322), 604 Main Street, Laconia (also in Gilford and Meredith). Local books plus chocolates and gifts.

Farmer's Market, Belknap Mill Plaza, Laconia. An outdoor market open Saturday 9–noon, mid-July through October.

SPECIAL EVENTS   Dozens of events are held each summer in the Winnipesaukee Region, too many to list here in detail, especially since some are one-time events. We suggest checking with the local chambers of commerce (see Guidance), in the several free vacation newspapers found throughout the region, or with such organizations as the Lakes Region Association (569-1117), New Hampshire Farm Museum (652-7840), Belknap Mill Society (524-8813), and Gunstock Recreation Area (293-4341).

Early February: **World Championship Sled Dog Derby**, Opeechee Park, Laconia. Three days of racing by colorful teams of sled dogs.

Mid-February: **Winter Carnival** (569-2758), Wolfeboro Lion's Club. A week of events.

Mid-May: **Annual Winni Fishing Derby** (253-8689), Lake Winnipesaukee. A weekend fishing contest with cash prizes for the largest land-locked salmon or lake trout.

Early June: **Annual Barn Sale and Auction** (652-7840), New Hampshire Farm Museum, Milton. Call for detailed scheduled of many summer events.

Late June: **Annalee Doll Auction and Barbecue** (279-6542), Annalee Dolls, Meredith.

July and August: **Alton Bay Band Concerts**. Several free concerts are held weekly during July and August, plus a week of events during Old Home Week in mid-August. Write the chamber of commerce for a full schedule of summer activities (see Guidance).

Early July: **New Hampshire Music Festival** (253-4331). A six-week regional tradition, all performances at 8. Chamber music on Tuesdays, Boyd Hall, Plymouth State College; orchestral symphony Thursdays at Newfound Regional High School, Bristol, and (repeat of Thursday) Fridays at Gilford Middle-High School.

Fourth of July region-wide celebrations with parades and fireworks, some special events, some events held the night before. Alton, Ashland, Laconia, Meredith, Tamworth, Wolfeboro.

Mid-July: **Arts and Crafts Street Fair**, Downtown Laconia.

Late July: **Annual Antiques Fair and Show** (539-5126), Kingswood High School, Wolfeboro. **Family Fish and Game Day** (271-3254), White Lake State Park,Tamworth. **Antique and Classic Boat Show**, Weirs Beach. **Annual Flea Market and Chicken Barbecue**, East Alton.

Early August: **Huggins Hospital Street Fair** (569-1043), Brewster Field, Wolfeboro.

Mid-August: **Old Home Week** (539-6323), Freedom and Alton. **Miss Winnipesaukee Pageant** (366-4377), Funspot,Weirs Beach.

Late August: **Annual Lakes Region Fine Arts and Crafts Festival** (279-6121), Meredith.

Mid-September: **Annual Winnipesaukee Relay Race** (524-5531). Begins Gunstock Recreation Area and teams of runners circle the lake.

Early October: **Annual Quilter Show** (524-8813), Belknap Mill Society, Laconia.

A Country Road Alternative

An alternative to busy Route 16 is Route 153, a winding and scenic country road connecting Wakefield in the south with Conway in the north. Historic houses, churches, and civic institutions, several ponds, a collection of unique country inns, and even a bit of Maine are part of this quiet drive. For the northbound motorist, follow Route 16 beyond the Spaulding Turnpike to the traffic lights at Sanbornville where Route 109 crosses Route 16. Turn east on 109 a half-mile or so to Route 153 north in the village of Sanbornville. Just out of sight here is Lovell Lake. Heading north, Route 153 next passes through the village of Wakefield Corners, a collection of mostly white-painted eighteenth- and nineteenth-century buildings, 26 of which comprise the Wakefield Corners Historic District. Although Route 153 branches left here, take a short ride through the village to see the rest of the historic district. The road rejoins Route 16, so retrace Mt. Laurel Road back to 153; turn east and follow the winding road through East Wakefield, past several campgrounds, and a convenience store or two, to the sandy shores of Province Lake—a good spot for a swim or a picnic. Here the road crosses into Maine for a short distance as it passes the Province Lake Country Club. Continue north to South Effingham and Taylor City; G. Earle Taylor, mayor; pop. 5. This is actually a small general store located in Parsonsfield, Maine, but just across the street is New Hampshire. There is little commercial activity in the rural countryside of Effingham, but the many nineteenth-century buildings (especially at Lord's Hill) and the landscape (especially when viewed in fall foliage season) are as pretty as anywhere in New Hampshire. Center Effingham has a collection of old structures including the Grange hall, Masonic hall, church, and historical society. Farther north is picturesque Lord's Hill, with another white church, and old country homes including the federal mansion (see listing below) of Isaac Lord. A native of the town, Lord made a fortune in nineteenth-century Portland, Maine, but longed for his birthplace in the country. To convince his wife to move back to Effingham, Lord agreed to build her a country home as fine as any in Portland. And in 1822 he did. A roadside marker proclaims that in 1830 James Bradbury opened the first normal school in

Band concert at Lord's Hill, Effingham.

Photo by Peter E. Randall

America for "instruction and teaching of teachers." Route 153 intersects and joins Route 25 west for a few miles, then branches off north through the villages of Freedom, Madison, Eaton, and, finally, Conway, where it meets Route 16 at the traffic lights in the middle of town.

GUIDANCE   **Greater Ossipee Chamber of Commerce** (539-6201), RD 1, Box 137 CC, Center Ossipee 03814.

   The Greater Wakefield Chamber of Commerce (522-9209), Box 111, Sanbornville 03872.

TO SEE AND DO   From any of the inns along Route 153, it is only a short drive to North Conway and the White Mountains, Lake Winnipesaukee, or the seacoasts of Maine and New Hampshire.

   The Museum of Childhood (522-8073), Wakefield (Mt. Laurel Road, just off Route 16). Open daily, except Tuesday, Memorial Day week to mid-October, 11–4; Sunday 1–4. Adults $3, children under 9 $1.50. Town historian Elizabeth Banks MacRury and her sister Marjorie Banks accumulated more than 2,000 dolls and teddy bears plus music boxes, puppets, stuffed animals, and dollhouses in their lifetimes of collecting. Many of the dolls were picked up in their foreign travels. When this collection outgrew their home, they bought the house next door and in the spring of 1990 they opened this little museum to share their treasures with the public. The garage has been converted into Miss Mariah Plum's 1890 schoolroom, complete with old-fashioned desks, books, chalkboards, and the teacher herself.

Madison Carriage House Wagon and Sleigh Rides (367-4605), Route 113, Madison 03849. An added feature of the B&B (see Dining Out) are buggy and sleigh rides. In any season, with advance notice, Earle Baxter harnesses up the Belgian horses for trips for up to nine people at a time on the farm's 70 wooded acres. $9 adults.

The Freedom Historical Society operates the Allard house and barn on Maple Street. Open Tuesday, Thursday, Saturday, and Sunday 2–4, June through October 15. The collection includes household and barn artifacts and some genealogical items. Refreshments served on Thursdays in July and August.

Madison Historical Society Museum, corner Route 113 and East Madison Road, Madison 03849. Open Tuesday and Sunday 2–4, April through September. A general collection of local artifacts, a turn-of-the-century kitchen, and a complete peddler's wagon with contents intact.

Squire Lord's Great House (539-4803), Rt. 153, Lord's Hill, Effingham 03882. Open by appointment only. $3, ages 12-18, $1.50. Unusual Federal period mansion with distinctive architecture.

SPECIAL VILLAGES   **Wakefield**. This sprawling town is composed of several villages: Union, Brookfield, Sanbornville, and Wakefield Corners. Sanbornville is the commercial center and offers several shops, service stations, churches, and places to eat.

Freedom. The village of this little town is just off Route 153. We wandered through during the August Old Home Week when the many old, white-painted homes and public buildings were festooned with American flags. Apple pie and ice cream were the only missing elements.

Madison. Route 153 bypasses the center of town, which is sort of over-the-hills to the west.

Eaton. Here's another rural village with an idyllic setting beside Crystal Lake. The bustle of North Conway is only 15 minutes' drive north on Route 153. Check out the **Eaton Center Village Store** (groceries and small coffee shop) for local information.

GREEN SPACE   **Madison Boulder Natural Area**, on a side road off Route 113, Madison. Open all year although access is limited to walking in the winter. During the ice age, this massive chunk of rock was plucked off a mountaintop and carried along by a glacier until it reached this spot. Some three stories high and more than 80 feet long, it is one of the largest glacial erratics in the world and has been designated a National Natural Landmark. No facilities and no fees.

SKIING   **King Pine Ski Area** (367-8896 or 800-367-8897 for NE, except NH), Route 153, East Madison 03849. Operated by the Hoyt family and part of the Purity Spring Resort complex (see Lodging and Dining), this is a fine family ski area with snowmaking, night skiing, ski school, equipment rentals, triple and double chairlifts, and two J-bar lifts.

LODGING AND DINING   Purity Spring Resort (367-8896 or 800-367-8897 for NE, except NH), Route 153, East Madison 03849. Open year-round. In the good old days, summer visitors often came to the country for long stays, often a week or more. Automobiles brought motels and the one-night stop, but Purity Spring evokes past travel patterns. Most of their warm-weather guests stay for a week. Many are families, vacationers who enjoy the varied activities which range from swimming, canoeing, boating, water skiing, and fishing in pristine Purity Lake to tennis, volleyball, myriad other outdoor games, and arts and crafts. The inn's van delivers guests to a trailhead for a guided hike or to Tamworth for a performance of the Barnstormers summer theater. There are also trails covering part of the resort's 1,400 acres. Everything, including a nursery, is included in the rates, except for theater tickets and tennis lessons. Some guests leave their autos in the parking lot all week long, and others simply take public transportation to North Conway or Portland, Maine, to be met (by reservation and extra fee) by a car from the resort. Operated since the late 1800s by the Hoyt family, the third generation is now in charge. The fourth generation can be seen scampering around the grounds, helping out the resort's operation. Accommodations are quite varied, furnished country-style, and all rooms have either two twins, two doubles, one double, or a queen-size bed. Most rooms have a full bath, some with half-baths, and others share baths. There are some 70 rooms in 10 separate buildings, some of which are remodeled farmhouses and barns. Several buildings with 5–8 rooms are suitable for groups. The summer season runs from late May through mid-October. Rates vary from AP to MAP depending on the time of the season. The dining room is open to the public in the summer season but serves guests only in the winter. There are also breakfast and dinner cookouts weekly in the summer. Except for groups, the dining room is closed from late October until the end of December when the ski season begins, then closed in April and most of May. There are a variety of winter packages in connection with the King Pine Ski Area (see Skiing). $76 MAP to $132 AP.

Rockhouse Mountain Farm Inn (447-2880), off Route 153, Eaton Center 03832. Open mid-June through October. In an earlier time, farmers often took in summer borders, usually city folks who just wanted to relax in the country, walk open fields, take a canoe trip, and enjoy ample New England cooking. That experience has been possible here since 1946 thanks to the Edge family. With 450 acres of fields and forests to roam and a variety of farm animals (peacocks, llamas, horses, steers, cows, ducks, geese, hens, pigs, etc.), plus a private beach and boats on Crystal Lake, this is a great family spot. Guests often help with haying or feeding the animals or gathering fresh vegetables from the garden for the evening meal. There are 18 rooms, 7 with private baths; the rest share one bath for two rooms. Breakfast and dinner are served daily, and the children are served at an early first course. The single entrée meals are typical country cooking with roasts, scalloped potatoes, homemade breads and cakes, and plenty of farm-picked vegetables, which vary over the course of the summer. Fresh eggs, milk, and cream come from their own animals. There are weekly steak roasts, riverside picnics, and chicken barbecues. Most guests are families who stay for a week (Saturday to Saturday), especially in July and August. $96–$112; reduced rates for children who stay in parents' room, depending on age.

The Inn at Crystal Lake (447-2120), Route 153, Eaton Center 03832. Open all year. Known a few years back as the Palmer House Inn, this large Greek Revival building, with wide porches offering views over Crystal Lake, began as an inn soon after it was built in 1884 and was once a boys' school. Walter and Jacqueline Spink have remodeled the old place into a distinctive Victorian-era furnished inn. All 11 rooms have double, queen, or canopy beds and private baths. There is a library, den, and living room for guests and a lounge where smoking is permitted. Guests may use Crystal Lake for swimming. Walter is a teaching geologist by profession, who apprenticed at a country inn and at a French cooking school before buying this business in Eaton, a town where, coincidentally, he and his wife had summered for decades. He prepares European cuisine for guests and the public by reservation. Sometimes he asks the guests what they would like to eat and prepares the special entrée. Rates vary and include lodging only, B&B, or MAP. Multiple-day discounts also offered. $80–$96 B&B; $120–$132 MAP.

Snowvillage Inn (447-2818), Snowville 03849. Open June 15 through October, December 20 through March. In a "suburb" of Eaton just off Route 153, this inn is located 1,000 feet up Foss Mountain, a hillside setting which offers a panoramic view of Mt. Washington across broad lawns and flower gardens. One of New Hampshire's classic inns, it was built in 1900 as a summer home and has been operated for the last four years by Peter, Trudy, and Frank Cutrone. There are 19 rooms, each named for an author and all furnished with antiques; with private baths in three buildings: the main inn, a remodeled barn, and the new Chimneyhouse which has fireplaced guest rooms. Each building has guest living rooms with books and games, and the main inn has a huge stone fireplace and a spacious porch. The inn has a 14-mile groomed cross-country course. Trudy cooks single entrée gourmet meals, ranging from chicken Madeira to gingered lamb. Vegetarian meals are available on request. Meals are served to the public by reservation ($25 per person). Guests are offered B&B or MAP. There are some package plans and a special cooking school conducted in the off-season by Stephen Raichlen. $100–$120 B&B; $130–$150 MAP.

The Wakefield Inn (522-8272), Mt. Laurel Road (RR 1, Box 2185, Sanbornville 03872). Open all year. A centerpiece of the historic district, this three-story inn is a bed and breakfast with a restaurant. Open to travelers in one form or another since 1890, the inn has been operated for the past five years by Lou and Harry Sisson. The six guest rooms are reached by a unique hanging, spiral staircase. All the rooms, two of which are two-bedroom suites, have private baths, and the attractive furnishings feature Lou's homemade quilts. During the winter, when she is not busy as the six-day-a-week restaurant chef, Lou runs three-day quilt-making workshops. Harry is the host and the bartender in the small lounge, and there is a small common room with a TV. Inquire about special, seasonal package plans. $65 B&B. The restaurant is open 5–9, Wednesday to Monday in summer and autumn, Thursday to Sunday the rest of the year; a light Sunday noon dinner is served year-round. The menu ranges from veal to beef and chicken to seafood. The house specialties include shrimp Grand Marnier with an egg soufflé and chicken Wakefield, a boneless chicken breast stuffed with lobster and shrimp, baked in light pastry, and served with hollandaise.

Freedom House B&B (539-4815), 1 Maple Street, Freedom 03836. Open all year. No smoking. Drive through quaint, quiet Freedom Village and you'll want to stay there for a while. Freedom has a town swimming beach, an antiquarian bookshop, and public tennis courts. The inn has six rooms, all of which share two full and two half baths, are furnished with antiques, and offer twins or double beds. Full country breakfast. Marjorie and Bob Daly. $60.

Madison Carriage House B&B (367-4605), Route 113, Madison 03849. Located in Madison Village, off Route 153 (turn west just below Purity Spring), or turn east on 113 from Route 16 in Chocorua Village. Open all year. Sally Perrow and Earle Baxter have five rooms with TVs and shared baths in her family farmhouse. They serve a full country breakfast. $55.

The Western Lakes

From Canaan Street Lake in the northwest corner to Bradford's Lake Massasecum in the southeast, from Lake Sunapee in the southwest to Newfound Lake in the northeast corner, this region is spotted with lakes big and small, all set in open, rolling countryside, each with a view of one of the area's three mighty mountains: Sunapee, Kearsarge, and Cardigan.

All three summits are rewarding hikes, and all the lakes offer attractive lodging as well as superlative swimming, fishing, and boating. But this entire area is far less well known than the Winnipesaukee region, because the big old hotels here were replaced with second homes instead of with the cottage colonies and motels that took their place around Winnipesaukee. Still these "summer people" continued to patronize summer theater, shops, ski areas, and restaurants. When lodging places began proliferating again—as they have over the past half-dozen years—these amenities were all in place.

But it's still all very low key. The year-round hub of the area is the handsome old college town of New London with a rambling, eighteenth-century inn and Colby-Sawyer College at its center; two small lakes (Little Sunapee and Pleasant) on its arms.

The region's most famous lake is Sunapee. Unusually clear (still a source of drinking water) and unusually high (1,100 feet), Lake Sunapee sits midway between the Connecticut River Valley and the Merrimack River Valley. Ten miles long and three miles wide, still sheathed almost entirely in green, it's unquestionably a special place.

Newfound (8 miles west of I-93), with 22 miles of shoreline, is even more low-key than Sunapee; and Mt. Cardigan looms above its western shore as Mt. Sunapee does above Lake Sunapee. Both Sunapee and Newfound offer sandy state beaches as does smaller Kezar Lake in North Sutton, off I-89 Exit 10 (see swimming). Other lakes accessible to guests at local inns include Canaan Street Lake in Canaan Center; Little Sunapee and Pleasant Lakes, both in New London; Lake Todd and Lake Massasecum in Bradford; Highland Lake in East Andover; and Webster Lake in Franklin.

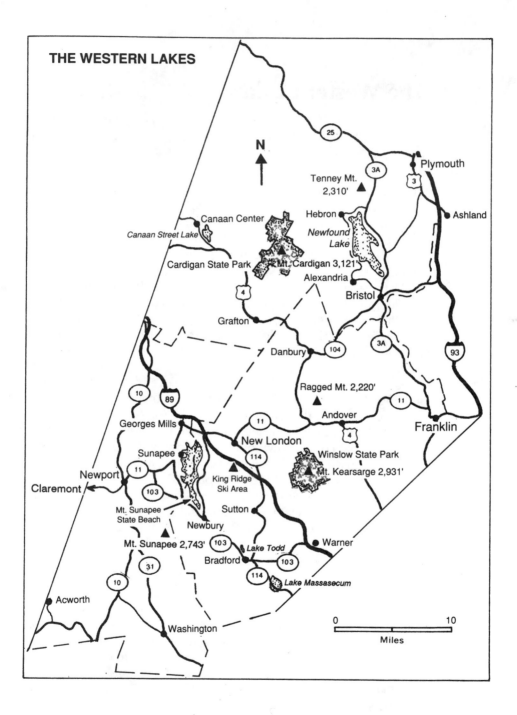

THE WESTERN LAKES

N

25

Plymouth

Tenney Mt.
2,310'

3A

3

Ashland

Canaan Center

Hebron

Canaan Street Lake

*Newfound
Lake*

Cardigan State Park

Mt. Cardigan 3,121'

Alexandria

4

Bristol

Grafton

Danbury

104

3A

93

Ragged Mt. 2,220'

10

89

Andover

11

Georges Mills

11

Franklin

Sunapee

New London

114

Winslow State Park

Mt. Kearsarge 2,931'

4

Newport

11

King Ridge
Ski Area

Claremont

103

Sutton

Mt. Sunapee
State Beach

Newbury

Warner

Mt. Sunapee 2,743'

103

Lake Todd

Bradford

103

31

114

Lake Massasecum

10

Acworth

Washington

0   10

Miles

Since its opening in 1968, I-89 has put New London and Sunapee less than two hours from Boston, but the increase in tourist traffic has not been dramatic. In winter skiers tend to day-trip from Boston as well as Concord; and in summer, innkeepers complain, they whizz right on through to Vermont. Lodging prices are relatively low—even lower in the northern part of this region, backroaded when I-89 replaced Route 4 as the region's major east/west route.

In state of New Hampshire literature you'll find this area under "Dartmouth/Lake Sunapee," but we feel that these "Western Lakes" (west of I-93) deserve more recognition. While it is handy to the cultural happenings around the Dartmouth Green, the area is equally handy to attractions in the White Mountains, the Merrimack Valley, and the Monadnock Region. So these Western Lakes are great spots to explore from. But once visitors have discovered them, most folks just stay put.

GUIDANCE A **Lodging Reservations** number (763-2495 or 800-258-3530) is maintained by the **Lake Sunapee Business Association,** PO Box 400, Sunapee 03782. It's based year-round at Mt. Sunapee Ski Area. This does not represent all lodging, but it is the only umbrella information service for this area.

The **New London Area Chamber of Commerce** (526-6575), PO Box 532, New London 03257, answers phone queries year-round and maintains a helpful, walk-in information booth in the middle of Main Street, June to Labor Day.

The **Newport Chamber of Commerce** (863-1510), PO Box 488, Newport 03773, maintains a seasonal information booth in the center of town.

The seasonal **Sunapee Information Booth** (763-2201), in Sunapee Lower Village, is also a source of lodging and dining advice.

Newfound Region Chamber of Commerce (744-2150), Box 454, Bristol 03222, maintains a seasonal information booth on Route 3A at the foot of the lake.

King Ridge Ski Area also maintains its own seasonal lodging service.

GETTING THERE By bus: **Vermont Transit** (800-451-3292) stops at the New London Pharmacy on Main Street five times a day en route from Boston to White River Junction; direct service from Boston's Logan Airport.

By car: I-89 cuts diagonally across the heart of this region, putting it within 1 1/2 hours of Boston; via I-91 it's also 2 1/2 hours from Hartford.

By air: See the Upper Connecticut River Valley and the Merrimack Valley (Manchester).

MEDICAL EMERGENCY **New London Hospital** (526-2911), County Road, New London, is a major facility. Also see the Upper Connecticut River Valley.

TO SEE AND DO   **Ruggles Mine** (523-4275), off Route 4, Grafton. Open June to October, 9–5; until 6 in July and August. Admission: $9 per adult, $3 per child. Children of all ages will love this place; you don't have to be a mineral buff. The eerie shape of the caves high up on Isinglass Mountain is worth the drive up the access road, and the view includes Cardigan, Kearsarge, and Ragged mountains. Commercial production of mica in this country began here in 1803. The story goes that Sam Ruggles set his large family to work mining and hauling the mica (it was used for lamp chimneys and stove windows) to Portsmouth from where it was shipped to relatives in England to be sold. When the demand for his product grew, these trips were made in the dead of night to protect the secrecy of the mine's location. The mine has yielded some 30 million dollars over the years. It was last actively mined by the Bon Ami Company—for feldspar, mica, and beryl—from 1932 to 1959. An estimated 150 different minerals can still be found; visitors are welcome to take home samples.

Sunapee Harbor Historical Barn (763-9723), Sunapee Harbor. Open mid-June to Labor Day, Sunday 3–5, Monday and Tuesday 9–12, Wednesday 6:30–9. A former livery stable, filled with photos of the grand old hotels and steamboats. You discover that visitors began summering on Lake Sunapee as soon as the railroad reached Newbury in 1849 and that the lake's resort development was sparked by the three Woodsum brothers from Harrison, Maine (another lake resort), who began running steamboats to meet the trains. Soon there were two competing ferry lines (one boat carried 650 passengers) serving dozens of small landings on the shore and islands.

Andover Historical Society Museum is housed in a vintage 1874 Victorian-style railroad station on Route 4 at its junction with Route 11, Andover. Open weekends from Memorial Day to Columbus Day, Saturdays 10–3, Sundays 1–3. The station has been restored and authentically furnished, and it displays local history exhibits. According to a historical marker in the nearby Route 11 rest area: This community takes its name from Richard Potter, a nineteenth-century magician known throughout America. He died in this mansion in 1835 and is buried on his former estate.

Colby-Sawyer College (526-2010), New London. A four-year co-ed college of some 500 students, founded in 1837. The 80-acre campus includes the Marion G. Mugar Art Gallery, with changing exhibits by recognized artists and by college faculty and students.

New London Historical Society Museum and Library (526-4978), Little Sunapee Road, New London. This is an ambitious gathering of eight restored buildings, including an 1835 cape with an attached el and barn; also a schoolhouse, country store, and blacksmith shop on 5 acres. Unfortunately the society has run out of volunteer steam and so is open only by appointment.

The Newport Opera House (863-1111), Main Street, Newport. One of the most prominent buildings on Main Street; the second floor ballroom/theater is the scene of frequent live entertainment: concerts, plays, dances.

The Newport Library Arts Center (863-3040), 58 North Main Street, Newport. Hosts continuous exhibits by local artists. Also note the handsome brick South Congregational Church at the other end of Main Street (it's diagonally across from the Mobil Station), completed in 1823 and almost identical to the Unitarian Church (1824) in Deerfield, MA.

Wilmot Historical Society, just north of Route 11 on Valley Road Extension, Wilmot Flat. This Historical Society Room in the Town Office building (an old schoolhouse) is open Memorial Day weekend to Columbus Day, Saturday 10–noon.

Daniel Webster Homestead, located off Route 127, Franklin. Webster was born here in 1872. A congressman representing Massachusetts, as well as New Hampshire, and a secretary of state, he is best remembered for his landmark Dartmouth College case. Webster was buried at the homestead.

Aerial chairlift (763-2356), at Mt. Sunapee State Park. Weekends Memorial Day to late June and after Labor Day through foliage season; daily 9-3 in the time between. $5.50 per adult, $2.50 per child. Definitely worth the ride. From the 2,700-foot-high summit, lakes spread away to mountains on the north; and on the west, you can see all the way into Vermont—from Killington on down (on a clear day) to Mt. Snow.

COVERED BRIDGES   The **Keniston bridge,** built in 1882, spans the Blackwater River, south of Route 4, one mile west of Andover Village.

The **Cilleyville bridge,** now open to foot traffic only, was built across Pleasant Stream in 1887; it's now at the junction of routes 11 and 4A in Andover.

Bement bridge, built in 1854, is on River Road in Bradford Center.

The 1835 **Newport-Cobin bridge** crosses the Croydon Branch of the Sugar River, 1/2 mile west of Route 10, 2 miles north of Newport Village (Town lattice truss). Inquire abut the two covered railroad bridges in town.

The **Warner-Dalton bridge,** originally built in 1800 and rebuilt in 1963, crosses over the Warner River, south of Route 103 in Warner Village (multiple Kingpost truss).

The **Warner-Waterloo bridge,** rebuilt in 1972, is 2 miles west of Warner Village, south of Route 103 (Town lattice truss).

SPECIAL VILLAGES   **Canaan Center** is a classic hill town: a proud, old agricultural community left high and dry when the railroad came through in the 1860s and the town's business shifted to the area (now the village of Canaan) 3 miles down the road, around the depot. Like Old Deerfield Village in Massachusetts, the old houses here—a few eighteenth-century homes and the rest built before 1850—line one single street, and over the years the community itself has become known as "Canaan Street." Its unusual beauty—and that of its lake—was recognized early on; the train to Canaan soon began bringing summer tourists, hotels opened to accommodate them, and an elaborate pier was built. The **Canaan Historic Museum** (open Memorial Day to Labor Day, Saturday 1–4) displays souvenir dishes with "Canaan Street" and color pictures printed on them. After a long hiatus, this is, happily, one of the places you can once more find lodging. Now Canaan itself is off the beaten track. Look closely and you may find the old depot. A second story has been added, and it's now a laundromat.

Hebron is a classic gathering of white-clapboard houses around a common at the northwestern corner of Newfound Lake. The handsome, two-story meetinghouse was completed in 1803, and the Hebron Village School is housed in a church-like building, its Gothic Revival steeple topped with decorative wooden spikes (peculiar to New Hampshire) resembling upside down icicles.

South Sutton, off I-89, Exit 10 and south on Route 114, or 5 miles north of Bradford. A typical nineteenth-century village center with a 1790s meetinghouse; a former general store, now the Old Store Museum, exhibiting (we're told) no less than 4,000 items; along with the 1863 schoolhouse, open to visitors in July and August, Sundays 1–4 or by appointment (927-4183 or 938-5005).

Bradford Center. Just off the main drag (Route 103), but it feels like a million miles. Coming north the turn for River Road is a left just beyond the junctions of routes 103 and 114. You go through the Bement covered bridge (see Covered Bridges), built in 1854. Continue up the hill, up and up until you come on the old hill town crossroads. Turn left and you will find the old schoolhouse and vintage 1838 meetinghouse with its two doors and Gothic-style (upside down wooden icicles again) tower. The old graveyard is here, too. It's interesting to note that the present town hall was moved down to the present business center of Bradford when the train arrived in the 1860s.

Washington. A tiny gem of a village with a cluster of imposing buildings—a meeting house completed in 1789 (the Asher Benjamin-style steeple was added later); a Gothic Revival, 1840s Gothic-style Congregational church, and a two-story, 1830s schoolhouse—all huddled together on the north side of the common.

Also see Green Space and Hiking.

GREEN SPACE   Cardigan State Park, off routes 4 and 118, 4 1/2 miles east of Canaan. Open mid-May to mid-October. This western approach to the mountain includes a picnic area sited among pines and rocks. For more about the West Ridge Trail, the shortest and easiest route to this 3,121-foot-high summit of Mt. Cardigan itself, see Hiking.

Pillsbury State Park (863-2860), Route 31, 3 1/2 miles north of Washington. Open weekends from Memorial Day, daily from mid-June. Day-use and camping fees. This 9,000-acre near-wilderness was once a thriving settlement with its share of mills. Today the dams are all that survive of "Cherry Valley." Camping is restricted to 20 primitive sites on May Pond, and there's both stream and pond fishing.

Winslow State Park (526-6168), off Route 11, 3 miles south of Wilmot. Open weekends from Memorial Day, daily from early June; fee. An auto road climbs to the 1,820-foot level of 2,937-foot Mt. Kearsarge. There are picnic tables and comfort facilities, and you can inspect the cellar hole of a big nineteenth-century resort hotel, the Winslow House. A steep, mile-long trail leads to the summit for a 360-degree panoramic view. The park is named for Admiral John A. Winslow, commander of the sloop *Kearsarge* when it sank the Confederate gunboat *Alabama* in 1864. (See also Hiking.)

Rollins State Park (239-8153), off Route 103, 4 miles north of Warner. Open weekends from Memorial Day, daily from early June through October. A 3 1/2-mile road, built originally as a scenic toll road in 1874, leads to picnic sites roughly a half mile below the summit. A walking trail accesses the bald summit of Mt. Kearsarge described above.

Knights Hill Nature Park, County Road, New London. Sixty acres of fields and forest, fern gardens and a pond, marsh and stream, all linked by easy trails. No dogs. Inquire at the town information booth about guided hikes.

Cricenti's Bog, Route 11, New London. A genuine bog with a nature trail.

Audubon Society of New Hampshire Paradise Point Nature Center and **Hebron Marsh Wildlife Sanctuary** (744-3516), North Shore Road, East Hebron. This 43-acre preserve includes an extensive, rocky, and unspoiled stretch of shore on Newfound Lake. The property is webbed with trails and includes a nature center (open late June to Labor Day, 10–5 daily; also some spring and fall weekends) with hands-on and wildlife exhibits, a library, and Nature Store. During the summer a natural history day camp and a variety of workshops and special events are also staged. Hebron Marsh is another 1.4 miles down the road towards Hebron Center (drive past the red Ash Cottage and take the next left down the dirt road; park off the road on the left by the sign). The 36-acre property includes the field directly across the road from Ash Cottage down to the Cockermouth River and the field to the southwest of the cottage. The marshes are teeming with bird life; follow signs to the observation tower.

Grafton Pond, off Route 4A. A 935-acre Society for the Protection of New Hampshire Forests preserve. North from Wilmot take a sharp left at the Grafton/Sullivan county line; take first left, then an imme-

Photo by Bill Finney

A beautiful summer day at Sunapee Harbor.

diate right, and park at the dam site. The only amenity is a public boat ramp. The pond has a 7-mile shoreline. Good boating and fishing. (See also Hiking.)

BICYCLING   **Kiernan's** (526-4948), in the New London Shopping Center. Rental bikes: three-speeds to mountain bikes.

The New England Bicycling Center (768-3318), The Inn at Danbury, Danbury. A variety of bicycle loops—from 5 to 11 miles—have been mapped. Touring and mountain bikes are sold, rented, and repaired here; room and board available (see Lodging).

BOATING   **Sargents Marina** (763-5032), Route 11 on Lake Sunapee, Georges Mill. Rents sailboats, canoes, boats, and motors.

Canoe put-ins can be found on Lake Sunapee; Pleasant Lake; Otter Pond in Georges Mills; Rand Pond in Goshen; Lake Todd, Blaisdell Lake, and Lake Massasecum in the Bradford area; Little Sunapee in New London; Kezar Lake in North Sutton; and Kolelemook Lake in Springfield. There are also public boat launches in Sunapee Harbor (fee charged), at Blodgett's Landing (shallow), at Sargents in Georges Mills, and at Sunapee State Park Beach (see Swimming).

BOAT EXCURSIONS   *M/V Mt. Sunapee II* (763-4030), Sunapee Harbor. From weekends in mid-May through foliage season, twice daily from late June through Labor Day: 1 1/2-hour narrated cruises of the lake. $9 per adult, $5 per child. This is unquestionably the best way to see Lake

Sunapee. Capt. Dave Hargboll never seems to tire of telling the history and pointing out the present sites to see. New London's long swath of eastern shore is entirely green with rustic cottages hidden in woods above occasional docks. In Newbury on the south, you see Blodgett's Landing, a tight cluster of gingerbread cottages descended from the tents of the 1890s Sunapee Lake Spiritualist Camp Meeting Association. All children aboard are invited to take a turn at the helm.

M/V Kearsarge **Restaurant Ship** (763-5488), Sunapee Harbor. Summer months. A re-creation of a nineteenth-century steamer offers 1 3/4-hour cruises leaving at 5:30 PM and 7:45 PM.

FISHING   Lake Sunapee is good for salmon, lake trout, brook trout, smallmouth bass, pickerel, perch, sunfish, hornput, and cusk. Otter Pond, Perkins Pond, and Baptist Pond yield bass, pickerel, and perch. Rand Pond, Croydon Pond, Long and Lempster ponds, and Sugar River are good for trout. Pleasant Lake has salmon, trout, bass. Inquire locally about what other lakes offer.

GOLF   **Country Club of New Hampshire** (927-4246), New London. $20 for 18 holes; cart rentals; reservations required.

Eastman (863-4500 or 863-4240), Grantham. $30 for 18 holes; cart rentals; reservations required two days in advance.

John Cain Golf Course (863-7787), Newport. $15 weekdays, $18 weekends for 18 holes; reservations Friday through Sunday.

Maple Leaf (927-9806 or 927-4419), Sutton area. $6 for 9 holes or $10 for all day.

Twin Lake Village Golf Course (526-2034), Twin Lake Village Road, New London. Nine holes, par 3 course by the lake.

HIKING   **Mt. Cardigan.** From Mt. Cardigan State Park (see Green Space) on the western side of the mountain, the West Ridge Trail takes you to the summit in just 1.3 miles. From Old Baldy, the principal peak, the view is of Mt. Sunapee and of Mt. Ascutney in Vermont. A ridge trail runs north to Firescrew Peak and south to South Peak. In all, a network of 50 miles of trails accesses the summit from various directions. Although this western ascent is the shortest and easiest, many hikers prefer the eastern climbs. You might ascend by the Cathedral Spruce and Clark trails (2.5 miles to summit; average time 2 hours, 10 minutes not including stops) or by the more difficult Holt Trail (1.9 miles to summit, NOT to be attempted in wet or icy weather), and return on the Mowglis and Mannin trails (3 miles from the summit). The Appalachian Mountain Club Lodge, high on the mountain's eastern flank (posted from the village of Alexandria), is the departure point for these and other year-round ascents (see Other Lodging).

Mt. Kearsarge. Serious hikers prefer the 2-mile ascent from Winslow State Park on the north side of the mountain to the mere half-mile saunter up from Rollins State Park (see Green Space). The Northside Trail to the summit begins in the southeast corner of the picnic area, climbs through birch and spruce into fir, emerges on smooth ledges then barren rocks. The view is one of the most spectacular in New England, especially for anyone familiar enough with the landscape to know what they're looking at. The sweep is from Mt. Sunapee on the southwest to Moosilauke (the westernmost of the White Mountain peaks) to the Sandwich and Ossipee ranges and Mt. Washington. This is a favorite hang gliding spot. Round-trip time on the Northside Trail averages 1 1/2 hours.

Mt. Sunapee. The lazy man's way up to this outstanding summit view is via the aerial chairlift (see To See and Do) but you can always walk down the 1.6-mile Solitude Trail to Lake Solitude and continue along the ridge to South Peak, then back to the base area via the Rim Trail. The most popular hiking tail up is the Andrew Brook Trail (1.8 miles to Lake Solitude) from a marked trailhead 1.2 miles up Mountain Road, well marked, in turn, off Route 103 roughly 1 mile south of Newbury. The most ambitious approach to Mt. Sunapee is along the 47-mile Monadnock-Sunapee Greenway, which begins atop Mt. Monadnock (see Monadnock Region [Hiking]). The last and perhaps the most rewarding stretch of this trail is from Pillsbury State Park (see Green Space), which offers primitive camping and its own 20-mile system of trails.

HORSEBACK RIDING   See the Concord Area (Horseback Riding).

SWIMMING   **Sunapee State Beach** (263-4642), Route 103, 3 miles west of Newbury. Open weekends mid-May to mid-June and Labor Day to mid-October, daily in between. A 900-foot stretch of smooth sand backed by shaded grass, picnic tables, a snack bar, bathhouse. $2 per person, $2.50 on weekends.

Wellington State Beach (744-2197), Route 3A, 4 miles north of Bristol. Open weekends from Memorial Day, daily mid-June to Labor Day. This is a beauty: a sandy, half-mile-long beach on a peninsula jutting into Newfound Lake. Picnic tables are scattered along the shore, away from the bathhouse and snack bar, under pine trees. $2 per person, $2.50 on weekends.

Wadleigh State Beach (927-4724), on Kezar Lake, Sutton. Marked from Route 114. Open weekends from Memorial Day, daily mid-June to Labor Day. Smaller, less well known, and less crowded than nearby Sunapee; a pleasant beach sloping gradually to the water. Facilities include a shaded picnic area, a bathhouse, and a large playfield. $2 per person, $2.50 on weekends.

Town Beaches. Many more local beaches can be accessed by guests at local inns.

TENNIS   **King Ridge Racquet Club** (526-9293), King Ridge Road, New London.

Colby-Sawyer College (526-2010), New London. Courts (and the Sports Center) are open to the public.

Newport High School courts are open to the public.

WINDSURFING   Mt. Sunapee State Park Beach (763-2356). Rentals and lessons available.

CROSS-COUNTRY SKIING   Norsk (526-6040 or 800-42-NORSK), Route 11 (2 miles east of I-89 Exit 11), New London. One of New England's most ambitious and successful cross-country centers. John Schlosser discovered the sport while attending the University of Oslo in 1972 and with wife Nancy opened Norsk—at the Lake Sunapee Country Club—in 1976. Thanks to its unusual elevation (1,300 feet) and frequent grooming, Norsk's 45-mile trail network frequently offers the best snow conditions south of the White Mountains. A favorite 6-mile loop is to Robb's Hut (open weekends 11–2:30) for lunch, and ambitious types can now take advantage of the 20-km Edge Loop. Trails begin on the golf course (where experiments with snowmaking are underway), but it's possible to quickly get into the woods—and stay there. Better skiers can actually access the system from the Outback parking area, 2 miles east on Route 11. The center itself has been expanded and rebuilt in 1990, and the adjacent country club restaurant caters to skiers. Trail fee $8 adults, $5 juniors; lessons and rentals offered.

Nordic Center (768-3600 or 744-3391), Danbury. Fifteen km of tracked, groomed cross-country ski trails with views of Ragged Mountain and Mt. Cardigan. $5 all day, $3.50 half day; rentals, Nordic and telemark lessons.

Snowhill at Eastman (863-4500), turn right off I-89 (you can't miss the sign), Grantham. Offers 30 km of groomed trails; $8 trail fee on weekends, $5 weekdays.

DOWNHILL SKIING   Mt. Sunapee State Park (763-2356; snow phones: outside NH 800-322-2200, inside NH 763-5626 or 763-4020), Route 103, Newbury. With 32 trails and a vertical drop of 1,510 feet, this is a major ski area that is frequently less crowded than the competition. Perhaps this is because its reputation plummeted while the state took its time making a $7 million investment in snowmaking. The base lodge is no nonsense (no condominium models, either) and pleasant. The Summit Triple Chair accesses a half-dozen swooping intermediate to expert runs, each at least a mile long. Off the North Peak Triple Chair, our favorite is Flying Goose—a quick, steep, and addictive run. In all there are seven lifts (three double chairs, three triple chairs, and one pony). The smaller North Peak Lodge (at the opposite end of the parking lot) and the summit cafeteria help disperse the crowds at lunchtime. When all trails are open, skiers can choose from exposures on three peaks. $29 weekends, $21 weekdays.

King Ridge (526-6966; snow phone 800-343-1312; lodging phone 800-258-3530), off I-89, Exit 11, New London. Founded by the nonprofit New London Outing Club in the late '50s, King Ridge has managed to preserve a no-hassle, welcoming atmosphere despite the I-89 exit just down the road. It caters to families in unusual ways. Rental ski lockers mean you don't have to tote all those skis and boots every weekend, and there is ample, free storage space for day-trippers. Brown baggers, instead of being relegated to the basement, enjoy a large, cheerful space with drink and soup service. The nursery accepts children from four months to six years. The 20 trails are named for Alice in Wonderland characters like Mock Turtle and the March Hare, and a life-size Mad Hatter skis about. Trails are wide, gentle, and well groomed. If the family hotshot gets bored, there is snowboarding, a sport King Ridge takes seriously (rentals and lessons are offered). The base lodge is glass-faced to maximize the top-of-the-hill view, and it's comfortable and separate from the skiers' service lodge which handles tickets, ski school, rentals, and a lodging service. Snowmaking on more than half the trails. Lift tickets: $25 adults, $20 juniors on weekends; $17 and $13 weekdays.

Ragged Mountain Ski Area (768-3475; snow phone 768-3971), off Route 4, Danbury. A pleasant intermediate mountain that's been upgraded in the past few years with snowmaking, a new lift, and a base lodge. Still, it's just enough off the beaten track and little-known enough to be relatively uncrowded. There are 20 trails, a respectable 1,250-foot vertical drop, 72 acres of snowmaking, two double chairs and two T-bars, a nursery, lessons, and rentals. Lift tickets: $25 adults, $20 juniors on weekends; $20 and $15 on weekdays. A genuine family area.

Snowhill at Eastman (863-4241), off I-89, Exit 13, Grantham. Really just a facility for this self-contained condo resort: a 243-foot vertical drop, one double chair and one novice lift, three trails. $14 adults, $9 juniors.

(Also see the Western Whites [Downhill Skiing] and the Concord Area {Downhill Skiing]).

RESORTS   **Twin Lake Village** (526-6460), R.R. 1, Box 680, New London 03257. One 1890s resort that's still flourishing. Opened by Henry Kitter in 1897, it's presently owned and managed by three generations of Kitters and accommodates 180 guests between the rambling "Villa" and a number of Victorian houses scattered through surrounding trees. A 9-hole golf course stretches from the rocker-lined veranda down to the lake. All three daily meals and old-fashioned evening entertainment—maybe a supper-time picnic on Mt. Kearsarge or a talent show by guests' children—are included in the weekly $290–$460 rates. The resort is basically booked throughout its short season, but sporadic openings occur.

Eastman (863-4444), PO Box 1 (just off I-89 Exit 13), Grantham 03753. Developed by an improbable consortium that includes Dartmouth College and the Society for the Protection of New Hampshire Forests; a second home and condo community, scattered in clusters through 3,500 acres on Eastman Lake. Winter facilities include a small ski hill and an extensive ski-touring network. Summer renters can enjoy an 18-hole golf course, tennis, swimming, and boating (sunfish, canoes, and rowboats can be rented). An indoor pool and a recreation barn are available year-round. Units are attractive; individually decorated condos with two to four bedrooms, decks, lofts, and woodstoves. Two-night and weekly rentals: from $345 for two bedrooms in summer, from $370 for winter weekends, from $725 for seven days in summer, from $795 in winter.

INNS   *In the Lake Sunapee area:*   **Dexter's Inn and Tennis Club** (763-5571 or 800-232-5571), Stagecoach Road, Sunapee 03732. Open May through October. This hilltop house dates in part from 1801, but its present look is 1930s when it became a summer home for an adviser to Herbert Hoover. In 1974 Frank and Shirley Simpson turned it into the gracious inn it's been ever since, now owned and managed by their daughter Holly and her husband Michael Durfor. Tennis is a specialty of the house and the three all-weather courts are the stuff of tournaments (there's also a pro). A pool is set in the extensive, beautifully landscaped backyard which also offers croquet and other lawn games. Fields across the road, in front of the house, slope toward Lake Sunapee in the distance. You can also see the lake from porch rockers and from many of the 18 guest rooms (each individually decorated, all with private baths). The best views are from the annex across the road. There's also a great view from the dining room, which is small and open to the public (there are four seatings per night; see Dining Out). Common spaces include a formal living room and a pubby, pine-paneled "cocktail lounge." Altogether this is one of those special places where you tend to want to stay put. $120–$160 double per night, MAP plus 15 percent service. The B&B rate (available May, June, September, October) is $12.50 per person less. Pets are permitted in the annex at $10 per day. Discounts for three nights or longer.

New London Inn (526-2791; outside NH 800-526-2791), PO Box 8, Main Street, New London 03257. Built originally in 1792, this large (30 guest rooms) inn sits in the middle of New London, next to Colby-Sawyer College. It's always busy, but guests can usually find quiet space in a corner of the large, graciously furnished living room. The attractive, shop-studded street invites strolling. Since the Boston-Montreal bus stops at the pharmacy practically across the street, this is one place, theoretically at least, you can come without a car. Rooms are attractive, freshly papered, furnished in real and reproduction antiques. There's a sense of things well-managed by Maureen and John Follansbee. Although he is not "from" this area, John's grandfather built the original Follansbee Inn in North Sutton; his own son, Jeff, is the New London Inn's well-respected chef (see Dining Out). All three meals are served. $60–$90 per room, EP (no meals) plus a 10 percent service charge.

A cozy country inn in the Western Lakes area.

Pleasant Lake Inn (526-6271), PO Box 1030, Pleasant Street, New London 03257. Dating in part back to 1790, this farmhouse acquired its present shape and use in 1878 when it became Red Gables. It's been spiffed up significantly by present innkeepers, Grant and Margaret Rich (all 12 rooms now have private baths) and enjoys a view of Mt. Kearsarge rising splendidly beyond beach-fringed Pleasant Lake. $75–$85 per room includes a full country breakfast. No children under age 8, please.

The Inn at Sunapee (763-4444), Burkehaven Hill Road, Box 336, Sunapee 03782. An 1880s farmhouse set high on the loop road above Sunapee Harbor, facing Mt. Sunapee across a pasture. The lobby walls and ceiling are tin, and the rooms in the main house all have charm; frankly, however, we wouldn't go for the three double rooms in the converted barn out back. Families can take advantage of two- and three-bedroom suites, and there are also double rooms with private baths. The pool is unheated and surrounded by a chain-link fence, and the tennis court is basic (but great for those of us who don't have "whites"; the inn supplies racquets and balls). Both the lounge and dining room overlook the meadow and mountain. $79 double, $110–$140 for a family suite; plus $4 per person per day gratuity.

Seven Hearths Inn (763-5657), old Route 11, Sunapee 03782. Five of the seven hearths are in guest rooms, and yet another (in the Hearth Room) is a focal point for evening cocktails and hors d'oeuvres. The inn is unusually elegant throughout and facilities include a landscaped swimming pool. $108–$138 double including breakfast.

Back Side Inn (863-5161), RFD 2, Box 213, Newport 03773. Open year-round but, unfortunately, closed the day we stopped by. From all reports this is a very pleasant place, set in four acres on a back road (across from our favorite shopping/browsing spot in the region: Nelson Crafts and Used Books [see Selective Shopping]). The 10 guest rooms are each individually furnished (shared and private baths), and there's a fieldstone fireplace in the living room. Mackie and Bruce Hefka are the innkeepers. $41–$51 per double room; weekend packages, midweek specials; Add 15 percent service. No pets. Breakfast and dinner served.

On Newfound Lake: **The Pasquaney Inn** (744-9111), Route 3A, Bridgewater 03222. Open year-round. This 1840s, 26-room inn has been thoroughly rehabbed. Outside the focus is on Newfound Lake across the road (there's a 300-foot sandy beach and dock) and inside it's on the dining room. Chef and co-owner Bud Edrick is known for French/Belgian cuisine (see Dining Out), and French cooking lessons are offered off-season. All but eight rooms have private baths (but many are next door down the hall). $82–$112 double seems a bit high for the size and quality of the rooms and amount of common space; it includes breakfast, but a 15 percent service charge is added. Special packages available.

Near Lakes Todd and Massasecum: **The Bradford Inn** (938-5309), Main Street, Bradford. A genuine 1890s, three-story village inn, complete with mansard roof and wraparound porch. All rooms have private baths and are simply but nicely furnished with a mix of country furniture and antiques. Innkeepers Tom and Connie Mazol also maintain an attractive public dining room, J. Albert's (named for J. Albert Peaselee, the inn's founder). Rates are reasonable: $59 (for an adjoining bath off the hall) to $79 (for a mini-suite with an extra bed in an adjoining room). Special packages available.

In Danbury: **The Inn at Danbury** (768-3318), Route 104, Danbury 03230. Geared to bicyclists and skiers, great for groups (maximum of 35 people). Eight double rooms (two to a bath) and one dorm; ample, comfortable common space and (of all things) an indoor pool in the barn. Handy to Ragged Mountain. (See also Bicycling.) $45.95–$55.95 double with breakfast; $99 per person winter packages with meals; half price for children.

BED & BREAKFASTS   (Dinner is frequently, but not always available.)

Follansbee Inn (927-4221), Route 114, PO Box 92, North Sutton 03260. Open except for parts of November and April. In summer the porch is filled with rockers, festooned with flowers, and a small blackboard displays the message of the day—on our last visit it was "Everyone is ignorant, only on different topics." The low-beamed living room is friendly, the airy dining rooms are comfortably furnished with antiques. On the upper floors the 23 guest rooms are divided by wide halls, and books are scattered around. This classic white, green-trimmed structure was built originally as an annex for the huge but long-gone Follansbee Inn that once stood across the street. The property abuts Kezar Lake, and guests can swim or boat; for those more comfortable with a lifeguard on duty, Wadleigh State Park is just down the road. Many guests also discover the joys of the 3-mile walk, bike, or jog around the lake. In winter there's cross-country skiing out the back door. Innkeepers Dick and Sandy Reilein are knowledgeable about everything and happy to give advice. No smoking and no children under age 10; no TV. $70–$95 includes breakfast. Dinner is also served, and guests are encouraged to sit down together, a practice appreciated by single guests.

Mountain Lake Inn (938-2136 or 800-662-6005), Box 443, Bradford 03221. This inn looks just like most people's idea of what a country inn should be, and it sits just across the road from Lake Massasecum. Inside are nine crisp, antiques-furnished guest rooms with private baths; a TV room wallpapered in Currier & Ives prints; and a low-beamed dining room you want to linger in. Carol Fullerton ran a catering business in her previous life (in Montreal), and dinners (by prearrangement only) as well as breakfasts are something special. Our favorite room is the back living room—a large, informal space with comfortable couches, plenty to read, and a woodstove. In summer the screened-in front porch, with its rockers and view of the lake, is another good spot; but guests tend to spend more time on the private sandy beach (a canoe is also available). The 165 acres out back have been blazed with hiking trails; also good for snowshoeing (snowshoes are available) and cross-country skiing. $75–$85 double includes breakfast. Special weekday and weekend packages available.

The "Inn" on Canaan Street (523-7310), Canaan Street, Canaan 03741. This is the only place to stay on Canaan Street (see Special Villages), and it's a beauty. An early eighteenth-century house with five guest rooms, all with private bath, one with a canopy bed and working fireplace. Downstairs there are two parlors, one with a woodstove, another with a piano. The breakfast room and a side porch overlook the sweep of lawn and sunsets over Pico and Killington far to the west. The view of Mt. Cardigan is out the front door. A path leads through tall pines to the lake and a canoe. $65-$95 for two. Dinners ($16-$20) are served by reservation to inn guests only.

Wonderwell (763-5065), PO Box 128, Philbrick Hill, Springfield 03284. Open year-round except April and Thanksgiving to Christmas. This grand country mansion has been in Susan and Samuel Alexander's family since 1935; they opened it to guests in 1989. Twin granite fireplaces are the focal points in the two-story living room, and an outdoor fireplace warms the side porch when needed. Porches and terraces overlook fields and woods. The eight spacious guest rooms, all with private bath, are furnished with antiques. Guests have a choice at breakfast, although Scottish kippers and cottage fries or baked buttermilk pancakes with peaches, sour cream, and cinnamon sugar are always available. Dinner can be arranged. $115 double includes breakfast.

Webster Lake Inn (934-4050), Webster Avenue, Franklin 03235. A 1920s lakeside lodge right on Webster Lake with a spacious two-story living room, rooms off a second-story balcony (ideal for a group to rent but also good for anyone looking for a reasonably priced lakeside retreat). The eight rooms range from $35 for a small single to $65 for one with working fireplace and private bath; $45 for a comfortable double with shared bath. Prices include breakfast and tax. A sandy town beach is within walking distance.

Jacob's Ladder (456-3494), Main Street, RFD #1, Box 11, Warner 03278. A fine, large, early 1800s house on the main street of this pleasant village, just off I-89. Handy to cross-country ski, and there are snowmobile trails to Mt. Kearsarge. $40 double, with a choice of five different full breakfasts included. Marlon and Deb Baese are your hosts.

The Inn at Coit Mountain (863-3583 or 800-367-2364), Box 3, Newport 03773. The high-ceilinged, oak-paneled living room with its floor-to-ceiling granite fireplace is truly grand, and the master bedroom with its working fireplace is nice. But this fine old summer mansion is too far from the resort amenities and overpriced ($85–$150 double with breakfast) for what it offers.

In the Sunapee area: **Haus Edelweiss** (763-2100), Maple Street, PO Box 609, Sunapee 03782. Up a side street in Sunapee Harbor, this is the best value in the area: a cheerful house with a woodstove in the living room; five upstairs guest rooms from $25 for a single to $50 for a double with a half bath, including complimentary evening wine and snacks and one of Alan's standout breakfasts. You can choose from Traditional (bacon, eggs, French toast), Yankee (fish cakes and baked beans with your eggs and muffins), or Bavarian (eggs, cheeses, German hard rolls, German apple pancakes with whipped cream, sausage . . .). The innkeepers are Lillian and Alan Norton-McGonnigal.

Maple Hill Farm (526-2248), RR 1, Box 1620, New London 03257. Just off I-89, a capacious old farmhouse that once more takes in boarders, the way it did in the nineteenth century. An informal, comfortable place, good for families, with plenty of acreage and access to Little Sunapee Lake. $55–$75 double plus family suite available $85.

Andrew Brook Lodge (938-2920), RFD 1, Box 62, Route 103, Bradford 03221. A find for families and groups (25 people max): an 1860s double house built by brothers, with a variety of rooms—from bunks with shared baths (great for kids) to the $65 room with Franklin fireplace and private bath. Most doubles are $48. The common room has a TV and VCR for evening gatherings; there's a closet full of games and a separate kitchen for guest use. The surrounding 15 acres are split down the middle by Andrew Brook, good for a summer dip. Lake Todd is also handy.

Candlelite Inn (938-5571 or 800-852-1984), Route 114, Bradford 03221. Built in 1897 to be a summer boardinghouse. A friendly, informal place with a TV/VCR in the common room and a corner fireplace between the bay windows in the parlor. $45–$55 double includes a full breakfast.

Blue Goose Inn (763-5519), Route 103B, PO Box 117, Mt. Sunapee 03772. A nineteenth-century farmhouse just up the road from Mt. Sunapee State Park. Three rooms, two with private bath, one handicap accessible; canoe, windsurfer, and bikes available to guests. $50–$65.

1806 House (763-4969), Route 103, Box 54, Mt. Sunapee 03221. Furnished with real flair—an eclectic mix of antiques, colors, unusual spaces. One upstairs room with a porch overlooking woods is very romantic, worth the $99. Other rooms from $69 double, including full breakfast. But you have to like dogs. Wolfgang is lively and big.

The Village House (927-4765), Grist Mill Road, Box 151, Sutton Mills 03221. An 1850s Victorian house with three guest rooms (two baths). Peggy Forand is a quilter herself, and the antique quilts on each bed are carefully chosen; the house throughout is furnished with antiques. You walk out into the village of Sutton Mills, a picturesque country village with a town hall, library, and general store. $45 double, $35 single includes a full breakfast.

In the Highland Lake area: **The English House** (735-5987), PO Box 162, Route 4/11 (next to the Proctor Academy campus), Andover 03216. Brits Gillian and Ken Smith are genial, widely traveled hosts who have skillfully restored this shingled, turn-of-the-century house, making the most of its seven bright, spacious guest rooms, now all with private baths. Full English breakfasts and, of course, 4 o'clock tea are included in $70 per day double, $50 single. Gillian designs and makes clothing that qualifies as art; also quilts. Both Gillian and Ken are delighted to turn guests on to some fine swimming, fishing, skiing, and dining options in this little-touristed area.

The Patchwork Inn (735-6426), Maple Street, PO Box 107, East Andover 03231. Although it dates in part from 1805, this is a very Victorian house whose past owners include a former governor of New Hampshire. Brad and Ethelyn Sherman have carefully restored the guest rooms and fitted them with antiques but (as of the summer of '90) hadn't yet restored the living room to its "halcyon" days (this was called Halcyon House around the turn of the century when it took in boarders). Our corner room with a private bath and view of Highland Lake was $40, including a full breakfast; doubles run $50–$60 and suites are $75–$85. Ethelyn is a quilter and Brad is a magician. Guests are welcome to use the lake, and in winter Ragged Mountain is a short drive.

In the Newfound area: **The Victorian Bed and Breakfast** (744-6157), 16 Summer Street (5.6 miles from I-93 Exit 23), Bristol 03222. Built solidly and elaborately as the town mill owner's mansion in 1902; now offering unusually spacious, nicely furnished guest rooms, two with working fireplaces. Each of the six rooms is carefully decorated and named. Ourfavorites are Spring and Autumn, although Indian Summer is fine, too. A first-floor room is especially designed for elderly and handicapped guests. All six rooms have private baths, and the two loft rooms in the carriage house can each sleep a large family; both have kitchens. In summer Newfound Lake is nearby as are both Ragged and Tenney mountains in winter. Nancy Truitt charges $60–$65 double, $52 single; includes a full breakfast.

 Six Chimneys (744-2029), SR Box 114, Route 3-A, East Hebron 03232. A 1790s tavern that once more welcomes visitors with real warmth. Peter and Lee Fortescue invite guests to make themselves at home in a leather chair in front of the woodstove or the piano or TV in the music room; 12 guests can be accommodated in the six guest rooms—each painstakingly furnished, some with private bath, others with two to a bath. $50–$60 double, $40 single; includes a full breakfast in the low-beamed dining room. Guests enjoy access to a private beach on Newfound Lake, and in winter Tenney Mountain is just up the road.

MOTELS **Lamplighter Motor Inn** (526-6484), PO Box 8, Main Street, New London 03257. A standard motel, but right in New London and offering some kitchen units; cable TV; $50–$60 double.

 Burkehaven Motel (763-2788), PO Box 378, Lake Sunapee 03782. Hidden away high on a loop road above Sunapee Harbor. Roomy motel units with mountain views, kitchen units, a tennis court, and attractive swimming pool. Off-season $50–$75 double; in season $65–$90.

RENTAL COTTAGES **The Daniel George Housekeeping Cottages** (763-2369), Route 11, PO Box 96, Georges Mills 03751. Open year-round. Basic cottages on Otter Lake, will accept two night stays; $65 per night.

 Lakewood Manor Cottages (763-2231), Route 103, Newbury 03255. Chalets and cottages on Lake Sunapee with their own sandy beach; moderately priced weekly and monthly rentals.

 The New London and the Newfound region chambers of commerce (see Guidance) can direct you to local realtors specializing in cottage rentals.

OTHER LODGING **Cardigan Mountain Lodge and Reservation** (744-8011) (mailing: RFD, Bristol 03222), Alexandria. The Appalachian Mountain Club, founded in 1876 to blaze hiking trails through the White Mountains, maintains a number of no-frills, outdoors-oriented huts, lodges, and Family Camps in New Hampshire. This is one of the most interesting, serving three daily meals June to Labor Day; open on weekends for some time before and after, on a care-taker basis the rest of the year. Perched high on the eastern side of Mt. Cardigan, it offers access to and advice on literally dozens of trails to the top. Many of the lower trails are used by cross-country skiers in winter. Rates are per person, in the $40 range, including three family-style meals; rooms range from doubles to five bunks (bring your own sleeping bag). Platform tent sites and campsites are also available.

Stone Rest Bed & Breakfast (744-6066), Fowler River Road, Alexandria 03222. Dick and Peg Clarke have created some comfortable guest spaces in their roadside home, just a mile or so down the road from Cardigan Mountain Lodge. An efficiency unit is just $45 for two people, a two-bedroom cottage is $60, and a studio bedroom sleeping four is $50; one person midweek is $25; all rates include breakfast. Use of the hot tub is extra.

DINING OUT   *In the Lake Sunapee area:*   **Woodbine Cottage** (763-222), Sunapee Harbor. Open May to Columbus Day only (lunch 12–2:30, afternoon tea 3–5, dinner 6–8, Sunday brunch 10–2), but such a landmark deserves top billing. Eleanor and Robert Hill first opened this restaurant in 1928, and Eleanor still works hard every day to provide the food and atmosphere for which she's famous. The atmosphere is classic tea room: polished wood tables, fresh flowers, real woodbine on the face of the white-clapboard cottage. You can lunch on a cheese and nut sandwich ($2.50) or fresh lobster salad ($15.50 with a choice of potato, vedge, muffin, salad, relish tray, tea, and dessert). Afternoon tea—either fresh fruit salad or a tea sandwich and cake with your pot of tea—is $4.95. Full dinners run from $14.95 (the daily special) to $19.95 (steak or lobster), but you can have a cheese and olive sandwich at dinnertime, too. Desserts are the specialty of the house: chiffon pies, strawberry shortcake, Venetian cream torte....

New London Inn (526-2791), Main Street, New London. Dinner except Sunday and Monday, breakfast daily, lunch spring through December. Chef Jeffrey Follansbee prides himself on using fresh, local ingredients imaginatively. The dinner menu changes nightly but might begin with a terrine of spiced pork, spinach and mozzarella, a green salad, and broiled breast of chicken stuffed under the skin with (local) goat cheese and basil, served with cabbage and chilis ($18.95). For lunch you might select an individual strudel with smoked ham, spinach, and Gorgonzola ($6.95).

Seven Hearths (763-5657), Route 11, Sunapee. Dinner Wednesday through Sunday in summer, Thursday through Sunday in winter. Guests are encouraged to come 45 minutes before dinner for drinks around the hearth, then settle into one of the elegant candlelit dining rooms for a leisurely dinner. The handwritten, prix-fixe dinner is $30. Reservations required.

Millstone Restaurant (526-4201), Newport Road, Continental. Open for lunch and dinner daily. A dependable dining landmark with a pleasant atmosphere: skylights, summer terrace dining. The menu is large, and specialties include schnitzel and New Zealand venison, no less.

The Inn at Sunapee (763-4444), Burkehaven Hill Road, Sunapee. Open for dinner Wednesday through Sunday 6–9:30, by reservation. The country dining room in the nineteenth-century inn overlooks a mountain meadow. You might begin with Vietnamese spring rolls (the innkeepers have lived in the Far East), then dine on fresh grilled salmon with the sauce of the day or the daily veal special. All entrées, including fresh baked bread and vegetables, are $16.50.

Dexter's Inn and Tennis Club (763-5571), Stagecoach Road, Sunapee. Dinner served from mid-June through October, except Tuesdays. The dining room is small and the view is sweeping. The set menu ($14.25) usually offers a choice of fish and meat entrées; specialties include fresh poached or grilled salmon.

Schweitzer's Restaurant (863-1820), Route 103, Mt. Sunapee. Lunch and dinner nightly, breakfast Thursday through Monday. A chef-owned dining landmark, specializing in German dishes: schnitzel, sauerbraten, wienerschnitzel. Entrées $9.50–$17.50.

(Also see the *M/V Kearsarge* Restaurant Ship under Boat Excursions.)

In the Newfound area: **The Pasquaney Inn** (744-9111), Route 3A, overlooking Newfound Lake, Bridgewater. Dinner nightly except Mondays, Sunday brunch. The inn's co-owner and chef Bud Edrick is French-trained and takes great pride in the French- and Belgian-accented menu which changes seasonally. Entrées: $12.75–$22.

Abel's Restaurant by the Newfound River (744-8072), Central Square, Bristol. This is one of those delightful places with "eating out" prices and "dining out" atmosphere and quality. The dining rooms fill high, pleasant store-front rooms with back windows overlooking the Newfound River. Shrimp scampi and filet mignon (both $13.95) top the menu and wienerschnitzel is $11.95, but you can dine on a vegetable stir-fry ($7.95) with a choice of imported beers or wine by the glass. A good dinner stop on your way up or home, handy to I-93.

The Homestead (744-2022), Route 104, Bristol. Dinner daily, Sunday brunch. A handsome, white, old roadside mansion with a series of dining rooms inside, ranging from traditional to glass to stone-walled. The menu is traditional American/continental, ranging from pasta to broiled seafood and steak. Entrées are under $16.

Elsewhere: **Potter Place Inn** (735-5141), Route 4/11, Andover. THE dining-out place for Proctor Academy faculty and students. Specialties include roast duckling, veal saltimbocca, grilled jumbo shrimp with garlic; fabulous desserts like cream cheese strudel with chantilly cream. Average entrée is $18.

Flanders Red Horse Restaurant (456-3463), Warner Village (just off I-89 exits 8 or 9). Closed Mondays, otherwise for lunch and dinner. Light fare to a full menu.

EATING OUT   *In the Lake Sunapee area:*   **Peter Christian's Tavern** (526-4042), Main Street, New London. A less pubby, collegiate version of the Hanover landmark, so popular that it's wise to come early or late since there's frequently a line—a consideration if you're planning on a meal before a play (the Barn Playhouse is just down the street). The menu, 11:30-closing stays the same: "Victuals," like a cheese and meat board (plenty for two), for $6.95; onion soup for $2.75; or a hefty sandwich like "Peter's Russian Mistress" (open-faced turkey, bacon, Swiss cheese, spinach, tomato, Russian dressing) for $4.95.

MacKenna's Restaurant (526-9511), New London Shopping Center, New London. Open for breakfast most of the time; lunch 11–3 and dinner 5–7. Every town should be so lucky to have a place like this: clean, friendly, fast, cheap. Homemade soups, great sandwiches on homemade bread (chicken salad was exceptional and just $2.45 with pickles and chips); steak dinners and broiled or fried seafood and chicken (under $8); children's plates.

Bradford Junction Restaurant and Bakery (938-2424), Route 114, Bradford. Open 6 AM–2:20 PM. Great roadfood. Homemade bread, muffins, soups, pot roast for $4.75, baked haddock for $3.95. A counter and cheery dining room, the village gathering place.

Newbury Harbor Restaurant and Pub (763-2525). Open weekends for lunch and dinner, Wednesday through Friday for dinner, too. Good pizza, soups, salads, burgers, basic Italian; takeout.

Appleseed Inn Restaurant (938-2100), Route 103, Bradford. Serving every night but Tuesday; Sunday brunch. Informal, daily specials; pizza.

Elsewhere: **Ryan's Loft at the Whittemore Inn** (744-3518), Route 3A, (just south of Newfound Lake), Bridgewater. Open for lunch and dinner, Sunday brunch. An informal family place, good for veal marsala ($10.95) or baked, stuffed shrimp ($13.95); wine by the carafe and glass.

Merchant's Family Restaurant, Route 104, Danbury. Closed Tuesdays (the day we came by), but we're told it's a clean, cheerful source of good roadfood.

The Foothills Restaurant (456-2140), Main Street, just off I-89, exits 8 and 9, Warner. Open 6 AM–2 PM. The Brewster family has spiffed up this old restaurant, added lace curtains and daily baked specials like breakfast "platter cakes" and soups made from scratch. Good roadfood.

ENTERTAINMENT   **New London Barn Playhouse** (526-6710/4631), Main Street, New London. One of New England's oldest and best summer stock theaters featuring dramatic, musical, and children's productions. June through August.

Music at King Ridge (526-6575), King Ridge Ski Area, New London. Jazz and classical music series July and August. Concerts are Thursday evenings, and patrons are invited to come spread a blanket and picnic beforehand. Occasional performances in the Colby-Sawyer College Auditorium.

Summer band concerts. Springfield Band Concert series held in Sunapee Harbor and Georges Mills on Wednesday evenings. Concerts at New London's Mary D. Haddard Memorial Bandstand on Sargent Common, New London. (call the chamber of commerce for details). Newport band concerts every Sunday evening from late June through August. Held in the Opera House in case of rain. Summer music at Mt. Sunapee, new in '91.

SELECTIVE SHOPPING   Nelson Crafts, Antique Collectibles and Used Books (863-4394), Brook Road, Goshen (Brook Road begins just a mile from the rotary at Sunapee State Park). Open Memorial Day to Labor Day, 10–5 daily, weekends until Columbus Day, then irregularly; call first. "If you stick with one thing you could make a fortune I figure," Audrey Nelson says. "But it gets boring," adds Ms. Nelson, an established local photographer, potter, and weaver. She is explaining the almost organic evolution of her shop to include a wide array of "collectibles" and 40,000 used books as well as a fine selection of crafts.

The Dorr Mill Store (863-1197), routes 11/103 between Newport and Sunapee. Open Monday through Saturday 9–5. No longer an outlet for the woolen mill across the street but a very special place that actually draws bus tours from as far away as Montreal for its line of 100 percent wool used for hooking, braiding, and quilting. Bolts of fabrics, including woolens still made at the mill but a wider selection; also classic clothing: Woolrich, Pendleton, etc. Specializing in sweaters, woolens.

Artisan's Workshop (526-4227), PO Box 124, Main Street, New London. A small but full shop displaying jewelry, pottery, prints, paintings, woodenware, glass, cards, books, and much more in the front rooms of the old inn that now houses Peter Christian's Tavern. Frequent summer demonstrations, special exhibits, concerts.

Nunsuch Cheeses (927-4176), Route 114, South Sutton. This 5-acre, licensed dairy welcomes visitors. Former nun Courtney Haase produces justly famous cheese; also goat milk soap, handmade gift boxes.

The Crafty Goose, Main Street, New London. Open 10–5. A trove of things handcrafted, from aprons and dolls to furniture, toys, ties, and wind chimes.

Antiquing in the Lake Sunapee/New London Region. A map/guide to 16 local antiques dealers is available at local information booths and from the New London Chamber of Commerce (see Guidance).

Pick-your-own farms: **Beaver Pond Farm** (542-7339), Route 103/11, Claremont. Raspberries.

Bartletts Blueberry Farm (863-2583), Bradford Road, Newport. Blueberries.

Eltons Uphill Vegetable Farm (543-0410), Route 103/11, Claremont. Sixteen kinds of vegetables.

King Blossom Farm (863-6125), Dunbar Hill Road, Grantham.

One of the state's most popular events is the annual Craftsman's Fair, held in early August at Sunapee State Park.

Apples and raspberries.

Lavalley Orchard (863-6710), Newport. Apples.

Page Hill Farm (863-2356), Page Hill, Newport. Raspberries, apples.

Sugar Springs Farm (863-1928), Grantham. Strawberries, blueberries, raspberries, apples.

Windy Hill Farm (863-1136), Bascom Road, Newport. Raspberries.

Grandview Farm (456-3822), Walden Hill, Warner. Strawberries, blueberries, apples, peaches, plums.

SPECIAL EVENTS   June: **Annual Inn Tour** of the Sunapee Region.

July: New London Garden Club **annual antiques show.**

August: **New London Hospital Fair. Annual Craftsmen's Fair,** Mt. Sunapee State Park. The biggest event of the year by far. The country's oldest and still one of its best crafts fairs: a nine-day gathering of more than 500 juried artisans. Music, an art exhibit, and a wide variety of crafts demonstrations and workshops is included in the admissions ticket, good for two days—the time you need to take in the full range of exhibits, try your own hand at crafting something, and see the featured demonstrations which vary with the theme of the day. **Old Home Day** in Sutton.

September: **Mt. Sunapee Triathlon.**

October: **Warner Fall Foliage Festival,** Columbus Day weekend. Major crafts show, food, entertainment.

VI. The White Mountains

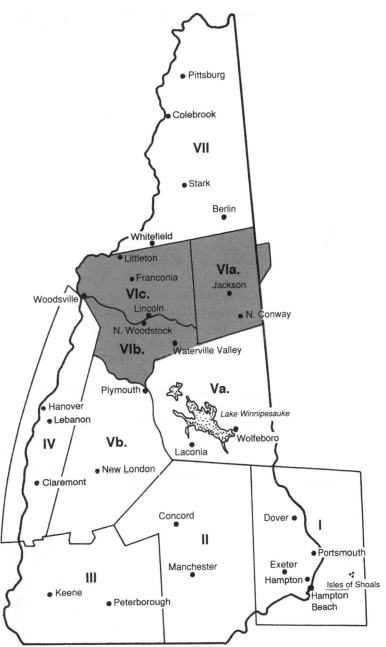

Pittsburg

Colebrook

VII

Stark

Berlin

Whitefield
Littleton
Franconia
VIa.
Jackson
Woodsville
VIc.
Lincoln
N. Woodstock
N. Conway
VIb.
Waterville Valley

Plymouth
Va.
Hanover
Lebanon
Lake Winnipesauke
IV
Vb.
Wolfeboro
Laconia
New London
Claremont

Concord
Dover
I
II
Portsmouth
Manchester
Exeter
Hampton
III
Isles of Shoals
Keene
Hampton
Beach
Peterborough

White Mountain National Forest

The 768,000-acre White Mountain National Forest (WMNF), the largest in the east, was created by the Weeks Act of 1911. Millions of board feet of timber were cut from these mountains in the nineteenth century, and a portion of the Kancamagus Scenic Byway and the Wilderness Trail were the routes of logging railroads, part of an extensive rail system built by the timber companies to harvest the dense stands of mountain trees. The clear-cutting techniques employed by the timber cutters left the steep mountain slopes denuded, leading to massive erosion and downstream flooding. The limbs and branches left behind in the woods quickly dried and fueled huge forest fires which threatened the uncut areas. It was to curtail the clear cutting, reduce the danger of forest fires, provide for reforestation of the mountains, and prevent erosion and flooding that the forest was created.

A ride across the Kancamagus Scenic Byway provides clear evidence of the success of the forest plan. Despite heavy use by visitors, most of the WMNF is again a wilderness. Although the United States Forest Service continues to harvest timber in this huge woodland, the WMNF is also managed for multiple-use activities: hiking, camping, swimming, fishing, nature study, forest research, and scenic beauty. Protection of watersheds and endangered species of plants, insects, and animals also figure into the operation of this forest. So varied is the forest, from lowland bogs to high alpine mountains, so interesting is its history, from Indians to settlers, loggers to scientists, that a whole guide could be written about this wild country.

The WMNF has several self-guided nature trails, is responsible for many miles of backcountry trails, and operates a number of barrier-free day-use facilities and campgrounds. Four congressionally designated wilderness areas within the forest are managed to preserve a wilderness experience. Here no timber cutting is permitted; motorized vehicles (snowmobiles, trail bikes, or bicycles) are prohibited; and campsites are limited to 10 people or fewer. In addition to varied WMNF publications, the best guide to the area is the *AMC White Mountain Guide*, the hiker's 600-page handbook of trail details and also some human and natural history information.

GUIDANCE   WMNF headquarters (528-8721), Box 638, 719 Main Street, Laconia 03247. Contact them, especially in the off-season, for details of campgrounds, fishing, hiking, or other activities.

WMNF Saco Ranger Station (447-5448), Kancamagus Highway, just off Route 16, Conway. Open seven days a week, 8–4:30.

WMNF Androscoggin Ranger Station (466-2713), Route 16, Gorham. Open Monday to Friday 7:30–4:30.

WMNF Ammonoosuc Ranger Station (869-2626), Trudeau Road, off Route 302, Box 239, Bethlehem 03574.

WMNF Evans Notch District (207-824-2134), Bridge Street, RFD 2, Box 2270, Bethel, ME 04217. Open Monday to Friday 7:30–4:30.

AMC Pinkham Notch Camp (466-2725), Route 16, Pinkham Notch. (See also Mt. Washington's Valleys [Mt. Washington and the Notches].)

TO SEE AND DO   Albany Covered Bridge, off Route 112 (Kancamagus Scenic Byway), 6 miles west of Conway. Built in 1858 and renovated in 1970, it is 136 feet long.

SCENIC DRIVES   Kancamagus National Scenic Byway (Route 112). The 34.5-mile paved highway is open all year, weather conditions permitting, but there are no motorist services on the road. More than 750,000 vehicles travel this route every year. On the eastern side of the mountains, the road begins on Route 16, just south of Conway Village. One hundred yards from Route 16 is the Saco Ranger Station, a comprehensive information center open daily year-round. Adjacent to the ranger station is a 10-minute interpretive walk. After a few miles, the road closely parallels the winding, rocky Swift River, offering views across the rushing water to South Moat Mountain. There are plenty of places to stop for fishing or picnicking.

Six miles from Route 16, Dugway Road diverges right, through the Albany covered bridge to the **WMNF Covered Bridge Campground**. Near the bridge the **Boulder Loop Nature Trail** (2.5 miles, allow two hours) leaves Dugway Road and ascends rocky ledges, offering views up and down the river valley. An informative leaflet, keyed to numbered stations, is usually found in a box at the trailhead or at the Saco ranger station. Across the valley is Mt. Chocorua and to its right are Paugus and Passaconaway, named, as was the byway itself, for Indian chiefs who once lived in this region. Dugway Road can be followed east to a junction with the West Side Road, just north of Conway Village. Midway on this route, the road passes the trailhead for **South Moat Mountain** (elevation 2,772 feet), one of our favorite hikes. The 2.3-mile trail (two hours) offers magnificent views in all directions from its open, rocky summit. En route, in-season, can be seen lady slippers and wild blueberries. This trail follows the long ridge to North Moat Mountain, then down to Diana's Baths and the River Road, a total hike of 9.1 miles requiring about six hours.

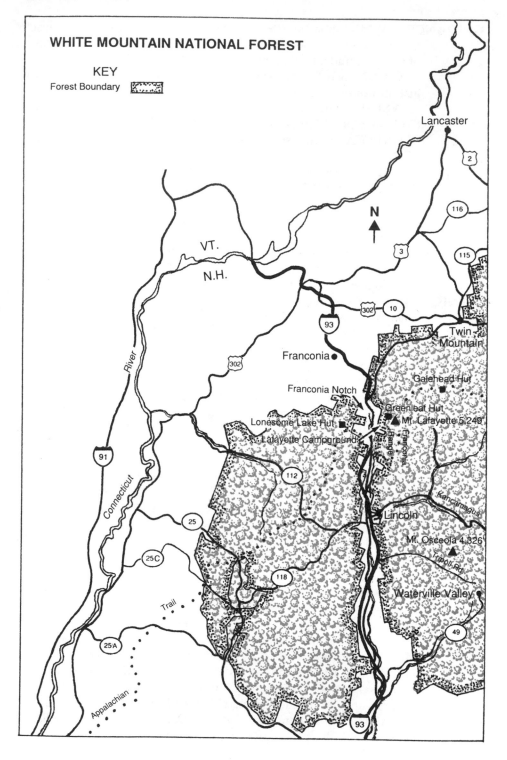

WHITE MOUNTAIN NATIONAL FOREST

KEY

Forest Boundary

Lancaster

VT.

N.H.

N

Franconia

Franconia Notch

Lonesome Lake Hut

Lafayette Campground

Galehead Hut

Greenleaf Hut

Mt. Lafayette 5,249

Twin Mountain

Lincoln

Mt. Osceola 4,326

Waterville Valley

Kancamagus

Tripoli Rd.

Franconia Range

River

Connecticut

Trail

Appalachian

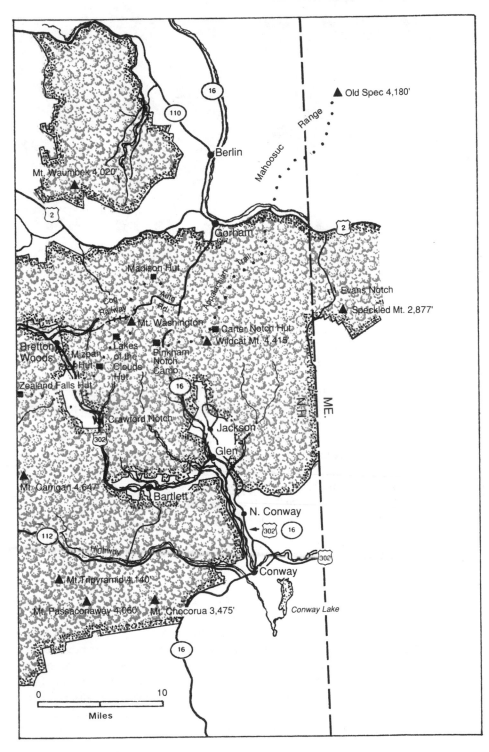

Old Spec 4,180'

Mahoosuc Range

16

110

Berlin

Mt. Waumbek 4,020'

2

Gorham

2

Evans Notch

Madison Hut

Cog Railway

Auto Rd.

Appalachian Trail

Speckled Mt. 2,877'

Mt. Washington

Carter Notch Hut

Wildcat Mt. 4,415'

Bretton Woods

Mizpah Hut

Lakes of the Clouds Hut

Pinkham Notch Camp

Zealand Falls Hut

16

N.H.   ME.

Crawford Notch

Jackson

302

Glen

Mt. Carrigan 4,647'

Bartlett

N. Conway

302   16

112

Highway

302

Conway

Mt. Tripyramid 4,140'

Conway Lake

Mt. Passaconaway 4,060'   Mt. Chocorua 3,475'

16

0   10

Miles

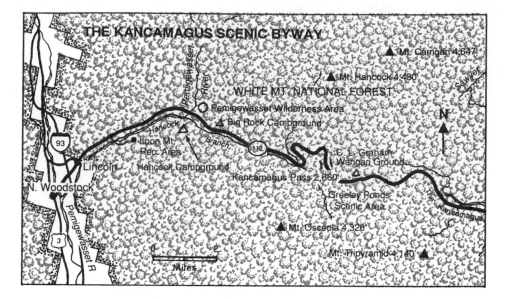

Opposite the junction of the Kancamagus Byway and Dugway Road is the **Blackberry Crossing Campground,** and a half mile west is the **Lower Fall Scenic Area**. Rest rooms, drinking water, and picnic tables. On a summer weekend afternoon you will be amazed at how many people can squeeze onto the rocks at this popular swimming hole. This is not a wilderness experience, but what a treat for people who spend most of their lives in the city!

About 9 miles from Route 16 is the **Rocky Gorge Scenic Area,** an interesting geologic site, where the rushing river has washed its way through the rocks. The footbridge leads to Falls Pond. Barrier-free rest rooms, drinking water, and picnic tables.

About 1.5 miles west is the **Champney Falls Trail** (3.8 miles, 3.5 hours) to Mt. Chocorua. The falls are an easy 3-mile round-trip on the lower section of the trail. The falls are named for Benjamin Champney, founder of the White Mountain School of Painting, who worked in this region of the mountains for more than 60 years.

Twelve miles from Route 16, the **Bear Notch Road** (not winter-maintained) diverges right for Bartlett and Route 302. This 9.3-mile gravel road has several impressive overlooks on its northern end.

At the junction with Bear Notch Road, you are entering Albany Intervale, once the township of Passaconaway. Not far beyond the junction is the **Passaconaway Historic Site**. Here the early nineteenth-century George House is now an information center, a remnant of the isolated farming and logging community that once prospered here (open daily mid-June to Labor Day, weekends from Memorial Day to Columbus Day).The **Rail 'N' River Trail,** a half-mile interpretative loop from this visitors center, is surprisingly varied.

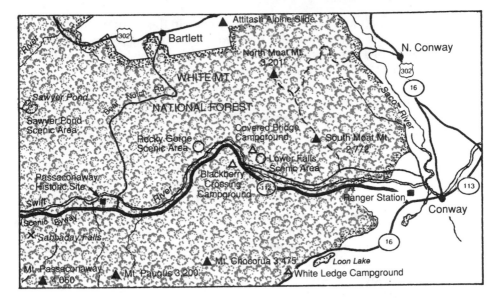

About 15 miles from Conway is the turnoff for **Sabbaday Falls** (the falls are just a 10-minute hike from the highway). Resist temptation; there is no swimming allowed here.

Next along the highway are the **C. L. Graham Wangan Ground**—a picnic spot (a "wangan" was a logging company store) and picturesque **Lily Pond**. Here the highway begins a long climb to **Kancamagus Pass**, the highest point point on this route, where there are scenic lookouts. As you traverse the pass, you leave the valley of the Swift River and cross over to the Pemigewasset River watershed.

West of the pass the highway twists down the mountainside and passes the trailhead for the **Greeley Ponds Scenic Area** (it's an hour's hike in; see Hiking); both ponds are good trout fishing and picnicking spots. (Hardy hikers can continue on into Waterville Valley). Next along the highway is the **Big Rock Campground.**

About 30 miles from Conway on your right is the large parking lot and information center (open on a limited basis year-round, daily mid-June to Labor Day) for the **Pemigewasset Wilderness Area**, one of the largest roadless areas in the Eastern United States. Popular in winter with cross-country skiers, this is a prime access point for year-round backcountry hiking. Stop and walk at least as far as the middle of the suspension bridge across the Pemi, frequently a rushing torrent here. The **Wilderness Trail** follows an old logging rail bed along the East Branch of the Pemi; the Black Pond Trail leads to a trout pond.

Both the Wildnerness Trail and the highway west to Lincoln follow the bed of J. E. Henry's narrow-gauge East Branch and Lincoln Railroad (see Western Whites Introduction). Next along the road is the **Hancock Campground**, and then Loon Mountain Ski Area which is on the left just before the highway ends in the town of Lincoln.

Scenic drives through Crawford, Pinkham, and Evans notches are described later in this chapter under "Mount Washington's Valleys."

FISHING   The WMNF publishes a comprehensive guide to trout fishing in the forest. More than 30 pond sites are listed, plus suggestions for stream fishing. A New Hampshire fishing license is required.

HIKING   The WMNF is crisscrossed with 1,200 miles of hiking trails, some short and quite easy, others longer, and many challenging even to the most experienced backcountry traveler. A long, difficult section of the Appalachian Trail crosses the forest from the southwest to the northeast corner. The weather on the high mountains of the Presidential and Franconia ranges can approach winter conditions in any month of the year so hikers should be well prepared with extra food and proper clothing. Bring your own drinking water since *giardia*, a water-borne intestinal bacteria, is found throughout the mountains. Although trails are well marked, we recommend two guidebooks to make hiking safe and enjoyable. See *Fifty Hikes in the White Mountains* or *Fifty Hikes in New Hampshire*, both by Daniel Doan (Backcountry Publications) and the *AMC White Mountain Guide* (Appalachian Mountain Club). *Waterfalls of the White Mountains*, by Bruce and Doreen Bolnick (Backcountry Publications), is a handy guide for 30 walks to 100 waterfalls. Many of the waterfall hikes are easy and perfect for families. The guide also offers interesting bits of human and natural history.

SNOWMOBILING   Large portions of the WMNF are off limits to snowmobiling, trail bikes, or off-road vehicles. For details contact the Trails Bureau, New Hampshire Division of Parks and Recreation (271-3254), Box 856, Concord 03301, or the New Hampshire Snowmobile Association (224-8906), Box 38, Concord 03301.

CAMPING   The WMNF operates 22 campgrounds. Along the Kancamagus Highway (Route 112) there are 6 campgrounds with a total of 267 sites and one on Route 16 with 28 sites; north of Crawford Notch, just south of Twin Mountain, on Route 302, are 3 campgrounds with 73 sites; and in Evans Notch (Route 113 south of Route 2 east of Shelburne) are 5 campgrounds with 77 sites. Dolly Copp campground in Pinkham Notch has 176 sites, and, adjacent to Interstate 93 between Campton and Lincoln, are 5 campgrounds with 214 sites. Campers should be self-sufficient since these are not fancy campsites (no electrical, water, or sewer connections; camp stores; playgrounds; etc.) Toilets, water, tables, and fireplaces are provided. The sites were designed for tent camping, although trailers and RVs are welcome. Most of the campgrounds are open from mid-May through mid-October, with a few opening earlier and closing later; and several are open all winter though the roads are not plowed. The daily fees range from $7–$9 per person, and many of these sites are filled every summer weekend on a first-come, first-served basis. However, a toll-free reservation system

(800-283-2267) operates for some sites in the following campgrounds: White Ledge (Conway); Covered Bridge (Kancamagus); Sugarloaf I and II (Twin Mountain); Basin, Cold River, and Hastings (Evans Notch); Dolly Copp (Pinkham Notch); and Campton, Russell Pond, and Waterville (I-93). The reservation service operates March through September (Monday to Friday 12–9, weekends 12–5) and costs $6 in addition to the camping fee. Reservations may be made 120 days before arrival, but 10 days before arrival is the minimum time.

Backcountry camping is permitted in many areas of the WMNF but generally not within 200 feet of trails, lakes, or streams or within 1/4 mile of roads, most designated campsites or huts, at certain trailheads, or along certain trails. There are also many designated backcountry camping sites, some with shelters, others with tent platforms. The WMNF promotes a carry in-carry out, low impact, no-trace policy for backcountry hikers and campers and suggests (requires in some cases) the use of portable cooking stoves. Restricted-use areas, which help to protect the backcountry from overuse, are located in many parts of the forest. For backcountry information consult the *AMC White Mountain Guide* or contact the WMNF.

Mt. Washington's Valleys

The first recorded "tourist" in the White Mountains was Darby Field, who walked into the so-called "crystal-hills" in 1642 and climbed the highest peak—probably the first person ever to climb the mountain since the indigenous Indians considered it the home of the Great Spirit, a holy place to be feared and avoided by mortals. Some 350 years have passed since Field's first visit, and now approximately 250,000 people a year walk and ride to the summit of Mt. Washington, the highest point in the northeast and the focal point of the valleys east, south, and west of the mountain.

Despite Field's early visit, it was to be more than 150 years before tourism had an impact on this region. The industry began in the early 1800s when small inns served only a few visitors among the commercial travelers, men who hauled goods and supplies by wagon from the seacoast to the villages south of the mountains and through Crawford Notch to the settlements beyond. The roads were rough, and the accommodations worse so those early travelers had to be adventurous by nature. Many of them sought out Mt. Washington, attracted by scientific reports from geologists and botanists. The Crawford family, for whom the notch is named, might be called the first developers of tourism in the mountains. Abel Crawford and his sons, Tom and Ethan Allen, aware that increasing numbers of people were coming to the mountains for pleasure, built inns in the notch, constructed bridle paths into the mountains, led guided hikes (sometimes carrying guests over portions of trails), and advertised their services in Boston newspapers.

Because it was on the major route to the mountains which followed the Saco River through Crawford Notch, the village of Conway began catering to visitors. A sleepy farming community, Conway had five inns by 1825, becoming the hotel center of the region. Tourists reached the mountains by stage and private coaches, but it was the extension of railroads into the region that opened up the mountains to vast numbers of visitors and created the basis for the hospitality we enjoy today. By 1876, for example, when the west was still wild and settlers and

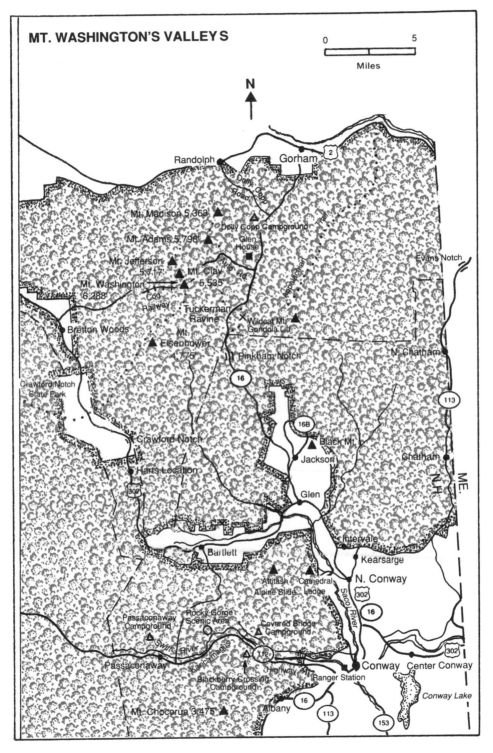

MT. WASHINGTON'S VALLEYS

0 5
Miles

N

Indians were at war, formally dressed ladies and gentlemen from the eastern cities could ride by train to luxurious hotels in the mountains, transfer to the Cog Railway to ride up Mt. Washington, spend a night in a summit hotel, then travel by carriage down the eastern side of the mountain to connect with a stage for a trip back to the railroad line. The three-day journey cost $17. The golden age of White Mountains hotels was under way, and the region had more beds for overnight visitors than at any time since, except for the past few years when development has again boomed. Years ago it was a prosperous summer business, and many guests came with trunks for vacations of a month or more.

The work of well-known artists and writers spread the fame of the White Mountains, and religious leaders set up tents and preached to crowds daily. Trenchermen, industrialists of the day, clad in suits and bulging at the waist, sat down to three huge daily meals and rocked away their days in wide verandas before the high mountain peaks. Several hotels accommodated 500 or more guests, and hotel owners bought farms to raise their own produce; generated their own lights and power; built ponds, hiking trails, golf courses, and tennis courts; and maintained post offices.

Fires and automobiles changed the business after a few decades. Many large hotels regrettably burned and were not replaced, and the auto provided mobility. It was no longer necessary to stay at one resort for a month; and, although the rates seem low by today's prices, many visitors couldn't afford to stay at the fancy hotels. The budgets of the middle-class travelers led to the development of cabin colonies and eventually motels. Those hotels that didn't burn were eventually closed and torn down, and none of the major hotels of the Victorian era in the White Mountains remains today, except for the Mt. Washington Hotel, which was built in 1912.

A few hardy folks used to enjoy the mountains in the winter, especially for snowshoeing, skating, or sleigh rides. Clubs and other groups came by train for winter weekends, often staying with farmers or in small inns since the large hotels were closed. It was great sport for a few but nothing on which to build an industry. In the 1920s New Englanders "discovered" skiing, a way of life and a sport enjoyed in Europe for centuries. Later, in 1938, businessman Harvey Gibson built the famous Mt. Cranmore Skimobile and a year later brought Austrian ski instructor Hannes Schneider to North Conway. Soon the region had another season for tourists, and since then the mountains have never been the same. There are now six downhill ski areas and two cross-country areas within 20 miles of North Conway.

Not to be overlooked in the development of tourism is the impact of folks who appreciate the outdoors and the mountains themselves. During the nineteenth century most of the mountains were owned by logging companies who clear-cut their way up one ridge and down another. While unsightly, the clear-cut areas were also subject to frequent forest fires, and rains and melting snows on the denuded mountainsides eroded the slopes and caused flooding downriver. Organizations such as the Appalachian Mountain Club (AMC), formed in 1877, and the Society for the Protection of New Hampshire Forests, formed in 1903, led the way to the protection of mountains as natural areas; and they continue to work for these purposes. The Weeks Act of 1911 established the White Mountain National Forest as the largest forest in the east. While the AMC hardly invented hiking, many of its early members were instrumental in constructing trails in the White Mountains; today it not only maintains trails but sponsors group hikes and seminars, publishes guidebooks, and operates a series of high mountain huts open to the public.

Today North Conway is the regions' liveliest resort town. A summer haven for nearly 200 years and one of the country's first ski destinations, it's now a major shopping center—with more than 200 shops and factory outlets. And it represents the White Mountains' largest concentration of inns, motels, and restaurants.

The Mount Washington Valley—as North Conway and surrounding villages are generally known—is a particularly appealing winter destination. Its four ski areas—Mt. Cranmore, Attitash, Black Mountain, and Wildcat—are each very different and all honor interchangable tickets. With more than 200 kilometers of cross-country trails between North Conway and Jackson, this is also one of the top places to ski-tour in the East.

The village of Jackson by contrast, is strictly zoned and far quieter. Here the winter accent is on cross-country skiing, and while there are plenty of inns and a few restaurants, nightlife tends to consist of reading by the fire, relaxing in a hot tub, or skiing under a full moon.

Pinkham Notch, just up Route 16 from Jackson, is the most dramatic pass in the mountains and is less developed than Franconia Notch. There is plenty to do here, especially for those who are able to do some walking. The most popular Mt. Washington trail begins at the Appalachian Mountain Club's Pinkham Notch Camp, a center for year-round hiking since the 1920s.

Between Jackson and North Conway is Bartlett. The Route 16 end of Bartlett, the area called Glen, and nearby Attitash Ski Area, with motels, commercial attractions, and restaurants, seems more like North Conway; yet Bartlett Village is in decline from a more prosperous past.

North of Bartlett is Crawford Notch, the least developed and among the most magnificent of New Hampshire's high mountain passes. Above of this notch, at the western base of New England's highest mountain, the vast white, red-roofed Mt. Washington Hotel still stands, a reminder of the other huge summer hotels–the Crawford House, Fabyan's, the Mt. Pleasant House and Twin Mountain–which have vanished with the railroad that used to bring guests. At present Mt. Washington Hotel's own future is unclear but it is open for the summer season. In winter the Bretton Woods Resort offers one of New Hampshire's most attractive and least crowded ski areas and one of its most extensive and dependable cross-country trail networks. Year-round the resort offers a choice of restaurants and condominiums, an inn, and a motor lodge. In summer Bretton Woods offers golf, horse-back riding, and the Mt. Washington Cog Railway, which has been chugging up the western flank of the mountain since 1869 (see Mt. Washington and the Notches).

Bretton Woods is technically a village in the town of Carroll for which the commercial center is Twin Mountain, a crossroads villlage at the junction of routes 3 and 302. Its motels cater to hikers, skiers, and snowmobilers.

Because there are so many places to stay and dine and things to do in the Mt. Washington Valley, this chapter has been broken into several sections: North Conway and vicinity, Jackson and Bartlett, Mt. Washington and Pinkham Notch, and Crawford Notch and Bretton Woods. For Twin Mountain see the Franconia and North of the Notches chapter; for Gorham and Jefferson, see the North Country chapter.

GUIDANCE   Mt. Washington Valley Chamber of Commerce (356-3171 or 800-367-3364), Box 2300, North Conway 03860. Free vacation guide, visitor information, and central reservation service. By calling the toll-free number, you can get information and make reservations at 90 lodging properties including condos, resorts, inns, bed & breakfasts, and motels.

State of New Hampshire Information Center, Route 16, Intervale, just north of North Conway. Rest rooms and telephones. Open all year.

Country Inns of the White Mountains (356-9460, outside NH 800-562-1300), Box 2025, North Conway 03860. Fifteen inns (Tamworth, Eaton, Snowville, Conway, North Conway, Intervale, Bartlett and Jackson) are part of this service. Your call is answered in one of the inns, and you can make a reservation with that inn, receive information about the other inns, or have your call transferred to one of the other inns in the group.

(See under Guidance within each section of this chapter for other chambers of commerce.)

GETTING THERE   By car: Route 16 threads through the valley, bringing visitors north from Boston and places south to Conway, Glen, Jackson, and Pinkham Notch and connecting with Route 2 in Gorham. Route 302, from Portland, joins Route 16 south of North Conway, then at

Photo by Peter E. Randall

North Conway.

Glen branches west through Bartlett and Crawford Notch to Bretton Woods and connects with Route 3 at Twin Mountain.

By bus: **Concord Trailways** (800-852-3317), provides scheduled service from Boston's Logan Airport to central and northern New Hampshire via Manchester, Concord, and Meredith. Mt. Washington Valley stops, via Meredith, Centre Harbor, Moultonborough, West Ossipee, and Chocorua, include Conway, North Conway, Jackson, Glen, and Pinkham Notch. Daily service varies.

NORTH CONWAY AND VICINITY

The town of Conway is composed of the villages of Conway, Intervale, and North, East, Center, and South Conway. It is North Conway, however, that dominates the community and this region. Long a summer tourist spot, it was placed on the winter map when Mt. Cranmore opened in the 1930s, but even that development is overshadowed by the commercial growth of the 1980s. North Conway was once a village roughly bounded by the Victorian railroad station and Cranmore. One could walk to most anywhere, from inns and restaurants to skiing to shopping.

As late as the 1930s, the strip along Route 16 south of town was a dirt road; but it was the only area left for development, and business began to establish there. With no zoning, commercial enterprises began to line the strip, slowly at first; then in the 1980s the factory outlet craze took over and North Conway became one of the major shopping destinations in New England. This development has worsened an already serious traffic situation on Route 16. With one exception, it is the only north-south way through the town, and on summer weekends and most holidays, the traffic is likely to be stop-and-go for several miles north and south of North Conway Village, especially in the afternoons. Current plans call for a Route 16 bypass, but it will not be completed until 1994, so the traffic inconvenience will continue until that time. Visitors can always plan nonweekend travel when the problem is reduced. Since the stores are open all year, it also makes sense to shop here off-season when sales are common, traffic is lighter, and accommodations are easy to get.

Shopping aside, North Conway is a bustling village with plenty of inns, resorts, and restaurants. Many of these places have nightly entertainment. Downhill skiing is as near as Cranmore, and the newly organized Mt. Washington Valley Ski Touring Association has trails that connect many of the inns listed below. Hiking trails are abundant offering both challenging hikes and short, easy ones. There is always the Saco River for swimming and canoeing. North Conway is what you make of it.

GUIDANCE **Conway Village Chamber of Commerce** (447-2639), Conway 03818. A summer information booth is on Route 16 located south of town adjacent to the railroad tracks.

Mt. Washington Valley Visitors Bureau (356-3171 or 800-367-3364), Box 2300, North Conway 03860. Free vacation guide, visitor information, and central reservation service. A year-round visitors center is located on Main Street opposite the railroad station.

GETTING AROUND **Taxi service** (356-5577 or 374-2453).

MEDICAL EMERGENCY **Memorial Hospital** (356-5461), Route 16, north of North Conway Village. As you might imagine, this facility has great experience in treating skiing injuries!

Ambulance (356-6911, North Conway; 447-5522, Conway).

TO SEE AND DO **Conway Historical Society** (447-5551), the Eastman-Lord House, 100 Main Street, Conway. Open Tuesdays 5–7, Wednesdays 2–4 and 6–8. This historic house contains local memorabilia plus special exhibits including items related to White Mountain artist Benjamin Champney, a Victorian parlor, and a 1940s kitchen.

Conway Scenic Railroad (356-5251), Box 1947, North Conway 03860. Open daily from the second weekend in June through the fourth Saturday in October, weekends in May and early June. Also runs on Thanksgiving weekend; Santa Claus specials on December

Photo by Eric Sanford, courtesy State of New Hampshire

The view from Cathedral Ledge includes Echo Lake State Park, North Conway Village and surrounding mountains.

weekends until Christmas. Usually four trips daily, except sunset runs Tuesday through Saturday in July and August. Ride behind the steam engine for an 11-mile round-trip between North Conway's 1874 railroad station and Conway Village. There are also exhibits such as a diesel engine, the large turntable, and an old depot; gift shop. Adults $7, ages 4-12 $4.50, under 4 free.

COVERED BRIDGES   **Saco River Covered Bridge,** on Washington Street (turn north at the Route 16 lights), Conway Village. Just rebuilt, this 240-foot two-span bridge is the one you see from the modern Route 16 bridge just north of Conway Village.

Swift River Bridge, West Side Road (turn north at the Route 16 lights), Conway Village. No longer used for traffic, this 144-foot 1869 bridge is now being restored (after being threatened with demolition) by the town and a citizens' group.

FOR FAMILIES   **Fun Factory Amusement Park** (356-6541), Route 16, North Conway. Open daily and evenings May through October, water slide Memorial Day to Labor Day, arcade open all year. A minipark with miniature golf, water slides, an arcade, and a snack bar.

GREEN SPACE   **Echo Lake State Park,** off River Road, 2 miles west of Route 16 in North Conway. Open weekends beginning Memorial Day, then daily late June to Labor Day. A swimming beach with picnic tables and bath house plus dramatic views across the lake to White Horse (can you see the horse?) Ledge and Cathedral Ledge. Drive the mile-long road to the top of **Cathedral Ledge State Park** for broad views across the valley of the Saco. Rock climbers ascend these steep ledges, and they can be seen from the road as they pick their way along the cracks and crevasses. Rare peregrine falcons nest on the ledges and sometimes can be seen soaring on the updrafts.

Whitaker Woods, Kearsarge Road, North Conway. A wild area with trails for walking or winter cross-country skiing.

Davis Park, Washington Street, Conway. A great swimming beach with picnic tables next to the Saco River covered bridge, plus tennis and basketball courts.

Diana's Baths, River Road, 2.2 miles west of North Conway. Watch for a dirt road on the left and park beside the road. A short walk to the stream. No swimming since this is a public water supply. Lucy Brook has eroded and sculpted the rocks in this beautiful place. Moat Mountain Trail (4.2 miles, 3.5 hours) leads to the summit of North Moat Mountain (elevation 3,201 feet).

Outdoor Explorations in Mt. Washington Valley, by Ned Beecher (Tin Mountain Conservation Center), is a marvelous handbook for adults and children providing information about the natural environment of this entire region.

SCENIC DRIVES   **West Side Road,** running north from the Conway Village traffic lights to River Road in North Conway, is not only a scenic road that passes two covered bridges, working farms, and mountain views, it is also the best and only way to avoid much of the Route 16 traffic snarl between Conway and North Conway. About a mile north of Conway, Still Road turns left, eventually joins Dugway Road in the White Mountain National Forest, and connects with the Kancamagus Scenic Byway at Blackberry Crossing. At the intersection with River

Road, turn west past Echo Lake State Park, Cathedral Ledge, Diana's Baths, and Humphrey's Ledge, and travel along the Saco River to join Route 302 west of Glen.

Route 153, also beginning at the Conway Village lights (turn south), is another country ride (see the Lake Winnipesaukee chapter).

East Conway and Chatham. Off the main roads, both of these towns are great for an afternoon's ride. East Conway, with its many dairy farms, recalls Conway's framing past. Chatham, nearly completely surrounded by the National Forest, has a small population and is the south gateway to Evans Notch. Near Redstone on Route 302 between Center and North Conway, turn north for East Conway. Eventually this road joins Route 113, just above Fryeburg, Maine, which meanders through rural Chatham. The road is not winter-maintained through Evans Notch, but it is a smoothly graded road used in other seasons. Hurricane Mountain Road, paved but not winter-maintained, turns east from Intervale above North Conway and steeply winds and twists across a mountain ridge to connect with Route 113 in Chatham.

CANOEING   The Saco is a popular canoeing river. Many people like to put in where River Road (turn west at the traffic lights at the north edge of North Conway Village) crosses the river, then paddle about 8 miles downstream to the Conway Village covered bridge. In the summer the river is wide and slow, except for light rapids between the Swift River covered bridge and the Conway (second) covered bridge. Take out after the second bridge at Davis Park.

Saco Bound (447-2177), Box 119, Route 302, Center Conway 03813. Rentals, sales, instruction, canoe camping, and guided trips. They also have a seasonal office on Main Street, North Conway. (Also see the North Country.)

Rentals also available at **Canoe King** (356-5280) and **Northbound** (356-3820), North Conway; **Saco River Canoe and Kayak** (207-935-2369), Fryeburg, Maine; **Down East Rafting Company** (447-3002), Center Conway.

FISHING   Brook and brown trout, lake trout, bass, and salmon are the target fish for anglers in this area. Try your luck in the Saco or Swift rivers, Conway Lake, Crystal Lake, and at a number of ponds in the White Mountain National Forest.

North Country Angler (356-6000), Route 16, north of North Conway Village. Specialists in trout and Atlantic salmon fishing, they sell equipment and clothes and offer local fishing information. There is also a small wildlife art gallery, a professional fly-tying school, and multi-day fly-fishing instruction programs in combination with Nereledge Inn.

GOLF   **North Conway Country Club** (356-9391, pro shop), in the center of the village, North Conway. Eighteen holes.

The White Mountain Hotel and Country Club (356-6377), on the West Side Road, Hale's Location. A new 9-hole course.

HIKING   **Mt. Kearsarge North Trail** (3.1 miles, 2.75 hours). Mt. Kearsarge (elevation 3,268 feet) is just north of North Conway, and this hike has been popular since the turn of the century. At Intervale, north of North Conway Village, Hurricane Mountain Road diverges east. Follow this road for 1.5 miles to the trailhead. From the summit fire tower there are views across the Saco River Valley to the Moat Range and north to Mt. Washington and the Presidential Range. (Also see Green Space.)

ROCK CLIMBING   Here is one sport that is definitely for the well-equipped and well-trained individual. Cathedral Ledge is famous for its many challenging routes, and from the base you can observe climbers inching up cracks and crevasses. For those who would like to join the climbers, **Eastern Mountain Sports Climbing School** (356-5433), **International Mountain Equipment Climbing School** (356-7064 or 447-6700), or **Mountain Guides Alliance** (356-5287), offer instruction and guided climbs. **Cranmore Mountain Recreation Center** (356-6301) has an artificial, indoor climbing wall and offers instruction programs.

WAGON RIDES   **Horse n' Around** (356-6033). In the summer, horse-drawn excursions and wagon rides to Echo Lake and Diana's Baths from Schoeller Park, North Conway; winter sleigh rides from Mt. Cranmore and the White Mountain Hotel, Hale's Location.

   Mt. Cranmore (356-5543), has sleigh rides all year. Also **Nestlenook Farm** (383-0845), Jackson, or **Madison Carriage House Wagon and Sleigh Rides** (367-4605), Madison.

CROSS-COUNTRY SKIING   **Mt. Washington Valley Ski Touring Foundation** (356-9304, outside NH 800-282-5220, ski info 356-9920), Route 16A, Intervale 03845. Formerly the Intervale Nordic Center, this is a new (1990–91) nonprofit operation with new grooming equipment featuring 60 km of groomed trails, rentals, lessons, wax clinics, instruction, lighted night-skiing, and a large backcountry loop for the experienced skier. A 30-km loop connects a number of inns with Mt. Cranmore, and you can set up an inn-to-inn ski package. Weekday, weekend, and season rates.

DOWNHILL SKIING   **Mt. Cranmore** (356-5543, lodging package information outside NH 800-543-9206, ski info 800-SUN-N-SKI), Kearsarge Road, North Conway 03860. The grandaddy of New England ski areas and still a favorite for its in-town location, moderate slopes, night skiing, and extensive snowmaking. The 28 trails and four open slopes are served by a triple chairlift and four double chairlifts, with 100 percent snowmaking. A family area with kids programs plus trailside condos, ski school and rentals, a sports center, and a variety of ski and lodging packages. (Also see Attitash and Black Mountain under Jackson and Bartlett and Wildcat under Mt. Washington and Pinkham Notch.)

LODGING   North Conway has a large number of motels, most of which are located along Route 16, south and north of the village. (Also see Lake Winnipesaukee [A Country Road Alternative] for inns in nearby Eaton, Snowville, and Madison.)

INNS   The New England Inn and Resort (356-5541, outside NH 800-826-3466), Route 16A, Box 428, Intervale 03845. Open all year. This is a large country complex now owned by an inn chain. It offers a variety of accommodations, all with private baths; beds are queens or doubles; and some have two doubles. The main inn, built in 1809, has 11 rooms plus the dining room, tavern, and three fireplaced living rooms. There are 10 cottage suites with king-size beds, phones, and fireplaces; 3 private cottages with queen-size brass beds, phones, and fireplaces; and 14 more rooms in the Hampshire House, which has a large meeting room suitable for a conference. Rooms are well furnished in a country-style, some with four-poster canopy beds. There are tennis courts, a swimming pool, a wading pool for children, and cross-country skiing from the door. Anna Martin's Tavern serves a country-style dinner (see Eating Out). Kathy Witbeck, innkeeper. MAP for two, $114–$192, depending on the season and accommodation; deduct $15 per person for EP. Various package plans available.

The 1785 Inn (356-9025, outside NH 800-421-1785), Route 16 (mailing: Box 1785, North Conway 03860), Intervale. Open all year. Perhaps the most scenic vista in all the White Mountains is the view across the Saco River intervale to Mt. Washington. Celebrated by the artists of the White Mountain School, the view was once threatened with plans for condos, but the land is now protected. This inn, part of which was built in 1785, is one of the oldest buildings in the valley and sits on a knoll overlooking the intervale where the dining room and guest rooms benefit from the panorama. The inn's 16 rooms, 12 with private baths, have king and double beds. Rooms are comfortably country-furnished, and some have two beds. Their dining room, considered one of the best restaurants in the valley, serves continental cuisine nightly (see Dining Out). Check out the extensive wine list and the desserts. There is a swimming pool and many trails for walking in the summer or cross-country skiing in the winter. Part of the Mt. Washington Valley Ski Touring Foundation circuit, the inn serves lunch during the cross-country season. Becky and Charlie Mallar, innkeepers. $60–$115, depending on the season and accommodations.

Scottish Lion Inn and Restaurant (356-6381), Route 16, North Conway 03860. Open all year. Scottish decor is the accent here, with bright tartan rugs to accent the seven country guest rooms, all with private baths and air-conditioning. Five rooms have double beds; the other two have twins. New owners have spruced up the rooms. A full Scottish-style breakfast (to guests), lunch, and dinner are served daily. A no-smoking inn. Michael and Janet Procopio, innkeepers. $65–$75.

Stonehurst Manor (356-3113), Route 16, Box 1937, North Conway 03860. Open all year. This three-story inn, accented with stonework, fine oak woodwork, and gables, is located on a 33-acre site off Route 16. The 24 large rooms (all but two with private baths) have TVs and are well furnished, many with antiques. Beds are queens and doubles, and some rooms have two beds. Fourteen of the rooms are in the manor, and ten are in an attached motel section. Townhouse accommodations are also available. There are tennis courts and an outdoor swimming pool. Dinners nightly, with a continental menu (see Dining Out). $85–135, continental breakfast priced additional. A variety of special weekend and holiday MAP plans available.

The Darby Field Inn and Restaurant (447-2181, outside NH 800-426-4147), Bald Hill Road, Conway 03818. Open all year. Another New Hampshire classic. Operated by Marc and Maria Donaldson since 1979, the place is named for that intrepid first climber of Mt. Washington, whose summit and other high peaks can be seen from the inn. The secluded hilltop location only adds to the charm of this place, surrounded by woods and landscaped grounds, including a large vegetable garden. All but 2 of the 17 antiques-furnished rooms have private baths, and the beds range from kings to doubles to twins. There is a two-room suite and a large room with a queen bed and air-conditioning. All the rooms are lovely, but those on one side have the broad mountain views. The common room is spacious and cozy with a fireplace and lots of books. Adjacent is the lounge with a woodstove and hanging plants. Guests may use the swimming pool or the cross-country ski trails. Dinner served nightly (see Dining Out). MAP $100–$180, depending on the season and accommodations. Three- and five-day package plans available.

BED & BREAKFASTS **The Buttonwood Inn** (356-2625), Mt. Surprise Road, Box 817, North Conway 03860. Open all year. One-entrée dinners are served on Saturday nights in the winter. This genteel inn has nine guest rooms, three with private baths. Beds range from queens to doubles with some twin beds, and many furnishings are antiques. Two common rooms, one downstairs with a fireplace, wet bar, and games to play. An outdoor swimming pool for summer fun or cross-country skiing from the door in winter. Not far from Mt. Cranmore or Route 16, the inn is located on a quiet country road—just the right place to relax. Full breakfast. Ann and Hugh Begley, innkeepers. $50–$80, depending on the season and accommodations. Special multi-day packages also available.

Cranmore Inn (356-5502, outside NH 800-822-5502), Kearsarge Street, Box 1349, North Conway 03860. Open all year. A traditional village inn, opened 125 years ago, this is the oldest continuously operating inn in the valley. It has 23 rooms including several two-room suites. Nine rooms have private baths; beds are mostly doubles and queens and some rooms have two beds. Country decor with matching bedspreads and curtains, stencilled wallpaper, and antique bed frames. Seasonal drinks are served in the afternoons; the common room is cozy with a fireplace and a piano; and there is a separate TV room. This inn has a pool and lawn games, and guests have membership privileges at nearby Mt. Cranmore Recreation Center. A big plus is the inn's location, just a block from North Conway's main street. Full breakfast served; dinner (choice of three entrées, price varies) available in ski season. No smoking in guest rooms. Chris and Ginny Kanzler, innkeepers. $35–$86, depending on the season and accommodations.

Cranmore Mountain Lodge (356-2044), Kearsarge Road, Box 1194, North Conway 03860. Open all year. Everyone is welcome here, but families and active folks especially will enjoy the facilities. This seems appropriate since Babe Ruth's daughter once owned the place; and, if it's not taken, you can ask for the Babe's old room (#2, with his original furniture). The main inn has 11 rooms and a two-room suite, all with shared baths, although most of these rooms have sinks. Next door is the barn with four loft rooms, all with antiques, private baths, air-conditioning, and TVs. A dorm sleeps 40 in two bunkrooms, popular with groups of bicyclists, hikers, skiers, and church members. This area includes its own recreation room with fireplace. Outside is a swimming pool; tennis, volleyball, and basketball courts; farm animals; a pond, which doubles as a winter (lighted) skating rink; a mountain stream; plus an outdoor Jacuzzi hot tub. Try the toboggan run, cross-country skiing from the door, or downhill skiing nearby at Mt. Cranmore. Cross-country and downhill rentals to guests. Innkeepers Dennis and Judy Helfand moved here from Alaska, and they brought enthusiasm from the last frontier with them. Full breakfast year-round, single-entrée dinners during ski season. Spring, summer, and fall: B&B $56–$85; winter: MAP $89–$109. Inquire about mid-week packages and group rates for the dorm.

Nereledge Inn and White Horse Pub (356-2831), River Road, North Conway 03860. Open all year. Nine rooms, three with private baths, one with a half bath. Two comfortable sitting rooms, one with a woodstove. This inn appeals to active people, and many of their guests are hikers, rock climbers, and cross-country skiers. Walk to the village or to Saco River swimming. They serve dinners to groups by reservation, and their English-style pub (with dart board) serves beer and wine on weekends. This is also the headquarters for the Mountain Guides Alliance, offering instruction and guide service (locally and internationally) for mountaineering, rock and ice climbing, and skiing. With North Country Angler, the inn hosts a fly-fishing program. A no-smoking inn. Full breakfast. Valerie and Dave Halprin, innkeepers. $60–$75.

The 1787 Center Chimney B&B (356-6788), River Road, Box 1229, North Conway 03860. Four comfortable rooms, all with shared baths, are situated around the huge center chimney in this old Cape. Rooms have king, double, or two or three twin beds. One large room has a TV and balcony. Farley Whitley, innkeeper. $49 per room with continental breakfast (fresh fruit and muffins, coffee and tea).

Victorian Harvest Inn (356-3548), Locust Lane, Box 1763, North Conway 03860. Open all year. Situated on a side south of the village, this inn has mountain views from each of its six well-furnished rooms. Four rooms have private baths, three rooms have king beds, one has a queen, and two have double beds. Radios and books in rooms; swimming pool; common rooms with TV, games, and wood fire. Full breakfast. A no-smoking inn. Bob and Linda Dahlberg, innkeepers. $60–$75.

Sunny Side Inn (356-6239), Seavey Street, North Conway 03860. Open all year. Ten rooms, two with private baths. Most rooms have a double and a twin bed. Walking distance to North Conway Village shopping, near Mt. Cranmore. Fireplace in the common room. Full breakfast. Chris and Marylee Uggerholt, hosts. $45–$65, depending on the season and accommodations.

The Forest Inn (356-9772), Route 16A, Box 37, Intervale 03854. Open all year for B&B; MAP in ski season and for some special weekends. This antiques-furnished inn celebrated its 100th anniversary in 1990. Its 13 rooms, 10 with private baths, include a special two-room stone cottage with a fireplace, and four two-room suites. Beds are doubles and twins. Afternoon tea is served, and rooms have complimentary wine and sherry. The Victorian-furnished common rooms have a fireplace and woodstove. Swim in their pool or cross-country ski from the door. Full breakfast. Ken and Rae Wyman, innkeepers. $50–$80 depending on the season and accommodations. Special multi-day package plans available.

Riverside Country Inn (356-9060), Route 16A, Intervale 03845. Open all year, dinner served Friday and Saturday evenings. Built in 1906 by the innkeeper's grandfather, this large Victorian home has been tastefully decorated and furnished with antiques, art, and plenty of books. Seven rooms, three with private baths; beds are doubles and twins. Two third-floor rooms could be a cozy suite. Located beside a rushing mountain stream, the inn offers cross-country skiing from the door. Full breakfast. Geoff and Anne Cotter, innkeepers. $45–$95, gourmet dinners plus unusual appetizers and rich desserts (see Dining Out).

Wildflowers Guest House (356-2224), Route 16, Box 802, Intervale 03845. Open May through October. Six large rooms, two with private baths, beds are doubles and twins, some rooms with both. Designed as the summer home of a famed Victorian Boston architect, this delightful place is enhanced by period antiques, bright wildflower wallpaper, and the original douglas fir moldings and doors plus an exquisite front porch flower garden. Flowers, fresh and pictured, are everywhere. Innkeepers Eileen Davis and Dean Franke serve a continental breakfast. $50–$92 depending on the season and accommodations.

Mountain Vale Inn (356-9880), Route 16A, Box 482, Intervale 03845. Open all year. Three large rooms—two with double beds, one with twins—and shared baths. Swimming pool; pool table; common room with TV, VCR, and fireplace. Many furnishings collected during the innkeeper's travels to exotic countries. Full breakfast. Helen and Rusty Cook, innkeepers. $45–$60, depending on the season, plus package plans.

Mountain Valley Manner (447-3988), West Side Road, Box 1649, Conway 03818. Open all year. In Conway Village, this inn is just across the street from the Swift River covered bridge and only a short walk to swimming and tennis at Davis Park. Furnished with Victorian antiques, the inn has four cozy guest rooms, all with air-conditioning and private baths. Beds are king, queen, and double. One room is a suite with a king waterbed. Ask about their antiques shop. A no-smoking inn. Full breakfast. Bob, Lynn, and Amy Lein, innkeepers. $55–$68.

HOUSEKEEPING UNITS   Wilderness Cabins (356-8899), Bear Notch Road, Box 1289, Conway 03818. Open all year. Here's a unique opportunity to live in the middle of the White Mountain National Forest. Located on Bear Notch Road (off the Kancamagus Byway, 22 miles from Lincoln, 8 miles from Bartlett, or 12 miles from Conway), this is a five-cabin complex, three of which are open all winter. The nearest town is Bartlett, but you can't drive there in the winter because the road is unplowed from these cabins north through Bear Notch. You supply all food plus sheets, pillowcases, and towels. They have completely equipped cabins for four to six people and folding cots to add another one or two. Since the place is beyond power lines, they generate their own electricity, generally from dusk to 9:30 PM. Since electricity is limited, there are no electrical appliances permitted. Gas powers the stove, refrigerator, lights, and heaters. All cabins have at least one double bed, the rest are twins. Nearby is mountain stream swimming, fishing, snowshoeing, cross-country skiing, hiking, or hunting, and the solitude of a wilderness setting. Most guests stay for a week or more, and many return for years, but overnight guests are welcome as well. Two of the winter cabins have outhouses (with inside showers), but these are being upgraded to inside facilities. Jim and Marsha Smith, hosts. Daily, $45–$83; weekly, $190–$390. Rates vary depending on the number of persons and are slightly higher in winter; special family rates.

DINING OUT   Bellini's (356-7000), Seavey Street, North Conway. Open daily at 5. The Marcello family has more than fifty years' experience in the

Italian food business, and they use all of their talents in this restaurant. The pasta is imported, but everything else is freshly prepared. All the well-known southern and northern Italian specialties are offered here, including chicken, veal, and vegetarian entrées with homemade soups, salads, and cannolis and other rich desserts. Prices range from $5.95–$14.95.

The 1785 Inn (356-9025), Route 16 at the Intervale (mailing: Box 1785, North Conway 03860). Nightly, except Monday, 5–9 or 10; lunch during the cross-country season. A recent newspaper poll awarded this inn first place for best restaurant, wine list, and dessert. They list more appetizers (14, priced from $5.85–$9.85) than many restaurants have entrées. Filet mignon, duck liver pâté, crab imperial, smoked salmon, or Caesar salad for two (made at your table) could make a delightful meal by themselves. But then you would miss such entrées as veal and shrimp in a rum cream sauce with artichoke hearts, sherried rabbit, raspberry duckling, rack of lamb, scallops in a cream sauce with garlic and leeks, or tournedos bordelaise (pan-broiled tenderloin with a burgundy sauce). The fine dining is enhanced by a wine list of some 200 titles, a roaring fireplace, and a comfortable colonial atmosphere ($14.85–$21.85).

Scottish Lion Inn and Restaurant (356-6381), Route 16, North Conway 03860. Lunch Monday to Saturday 11:30–2; Sunday brunch 10:30–2; dinner 5:30–9. A longtime favorite with valley visitors, this dining room has Scottish decor and menu offerings to match. Finnan Haddie, Edinburgh broil (prime rib), Highland game pie (beef, hare, pheasant, venison, and goose), or beef Wellington are enough to make Scots of us all. The lunch ($4.95–$7.95) and dinner ($12.50–$18.95) menus also have a variety of traditional chicken, fish, and beef offerings. Relax before or after dinner in the Black Watch pub.

Stonehurst Manor (356-3113), Route 16, Box 1937, North Conway 03860. Dining nightly 6–10; reservations required. Victorian splendor with tuxedoed waiters in an English-style country house complete with exquisite woodwork and leaded stained-glass windows. The cuisine is classic continental to match the decor. Beef Wellington, veal Oscar, salmon steak, Turkish shish kebab, and paella Valparaiso for two (must be ordered in advance) are among the house specialties, along with various pastas and something called gourmet pies ($9.50–$14.95). The latter, 9" in diameter, include basil pesto and grilled eggplant, homemade pork sausage, and smoked salmon with lobster, caviar, and Marscapone cheese. Appetizers lean to seafood with oysters, salmon, and shrimp plus escargot, pâté, and warm pasta salad. There is a fine selection of domestic and imported wines, rich desserts, and espresso. Prices range from $12.95 to $42 (for chateaubriand for two).

Riverside Country Inn (356-9060), Route 16A, Intervale 03845.

Dinner served Friday and Saturday evenings 6–9. Cozy European-style gourmet dining in a country setting. The menu is limited and changes weekly since Anne Cotter cooks to match seasonal specialties and the freshest available ingredients. The menu always offers three appetizers (such as shrimp with Thai dipping sauce), three or four desserts, and, with entrées, a choice of two salads, two vegetables, and two starches. Chicken, beef, fish, and veal are always offered. A recent menu included hot and sour chicken, sirloin tips with horseradish sauce, veal à la creme, and salmon fillet dressed with dill. Finish with lemon cake with blueberries, strawberries, and oranges, or chocolate ginger mousse! Prices from $11.50–$15.50.

The Darby Field Inn and Restaurant (447-2181, outside NH 800-426-4147), Bald Hill Road, Conway 03818. Dinner served nightly 6–9; reservations recommended, especially on weekends. Candlelight dining is a pleasure with appetizers such as country pâté and baked stuffed mushroom caps, followed by lamb chops, veal scaloppini, roast duckling (a house specialty with Grand Marnier orange sauce), or chicken marquis (breast of chicken sautéed with garlic, mushrooms, tomatoes, scallions, white wine, and lemon juice). The fish dish changes daily and there are three to four nightly specials. A favorite dessert is Darby cream pie. Prices range from $14.95–$18.

EATING OUT   **Anna Martin's Tavern** (356-5541, outside NH 800-826-3466), Route 16A, Box 428, Intervale 03845. Anna Martin's Tavern serves a country-style dinner. The house specialty is Shaker cranberry pot roast; other entrées include seafood imperial, swordfish, turkey, pork chops, and other New England favorites.

Horsefeathers (356-2687), Main Street, North Conway. Open daily 11:30–11:30. Comfortable and affordable dining in the middle of the village marks this longtime favorite, the original on a small chair. Soups, salads, sandwiches, pastas, and nightly specials ($3.50–$12.50).

Carriage Inn Restaurant (356-2336), Route 16, north of North Conway Village. Open all year 5–9, until 10 on weekends in summer and fall. A large, reasonably priced ($11.95–$15.95) family restaurant featuring steaks, seafood, and veal. They also have an extensive children's menu.

Peking Restaurant (356-6976), Route 16, North Conway. Open all year, daily from 11:30. Called the best Chinese restaurant in Carroll County, this place has all of your favorites to eat in or take out, including Polynesian dishes and hot and spicy Peking and Szechwan ($8.95–$13.45).

Mario's (356-9712),Route 16, south of North Conway Village. Open all year 11–9. A longtime favorite family Italian restaurant. Italian sandwiches, fried chicken, seafood marinara, spaghetti, lasagna and ravioli, baked tortellini, and more.

The Homestead (356-5900), Route 16, south of North Conway

Village. Open all year 4:30–10. Traditional New England fare served in a restored 1793 homestead. Susan's mother's fish chowder, broiled brook trout, baked shrimp, rack of lamb, broiled scallops, and seafood Newburg are featured ($12.95–$19.50) along with rich desserts such as Indian pudding and hot cherry crisp with ice cream. Fresh baked treats from the Homestead kitchen. For children under 12, half portions at half prices. No smoking.

A Step Above Bakeshop and Cafe (356-2091), Main Street, North Conway Village. Open daily 8–3, Sundays 8–1. Breakfast and lunch ($3-$5.25) featuring creatively prepared eggs such as frittatas, an Italian version of the omelet with lightly sautéed ingredients (broccoli, tomato, pepper, potatoes, and onions), eggs added, and baked in the oven.

Studebaker's (356-5011), Route 16, south of North Conway. Open all year 11–9, until 10 on weekends. A touristy, family spot focusing on the '50s with tunes from that era on the juke box, dancing waitresses, and decor to match the times. Some menu items are named beatniks (Chinese dumplings), green bow ties (Farfalle pasta), and Caddy wings (spiced chicken wings). Sandwiches, salads, and light dinners plus a kids' menu (meals are $2.95–$12.50, but most items are $5–$7). Pick up a coupon for a discount visit to the Grand Manor, an antique car exhibit a few miles north of North Conway.

Grammy Macintosh Village Cafe (447-5050), 151 Main Street, Conway Village. Open year-round; dinners served late June through October, Thursday through Monday until 8. Summer and fall 7–8:30, winter and spring 7–3. Bountiful breakfasts including pancakes and blintzes, fresh salads, subs, burgers, clubs, Mexican dishes, and a New York deli. Inexpensive.

ENTERTAINMENT   **Arts Jubilee** (356-9393), offers summer musical performances, weekly afternoon children's programs, and fall art show.

SELECTIVE SHOPPING   From the traffic lights on Route 16 in Conway Village north through North Conway, this is a shopper's heaven. This has always been a good shopping destination, but now there are more than 200 specialty shops and outlet centers. A longtime favorite is **Yield House**, at the south end of the Route 16 strip, offering reproduction-finished and unfinished furniture and kits. In North Conway Village are two original **Carroll Reed** shops (clothing and ski rentals); **Eastern Mountain Sports** (outdoor clothing and equipment), located in the Eastern Slope Inn; and **Joe Jones Shop** (more clothing and ski rentals).

The **factory outlet** boom hit in the 1980s, and most of the leading manufacturers have opened stores along Route 16, especially south of North Conway Village. Everything from clothing and luggage to shoes and boots to tools, dishes, and jewelry can be found in one shop or another. Most of the outlet stores are open daily 9–6. Everyone has favorite shops; we like the **L.L. Bean Factory Store** (clothing and outdoor equipment, the only Bean store outside of its home base in Freeport, Maine), the **Globe Corner Book Store** (a wonderful New England and travel book store where most of the guidebooks we mention are available), **J. G. Hook** (clothing), **Timberland** (shoes and boots), and **Brookstone** (every kind of tool imagined, some needed and others just intriguing). You might like **Ralph Lauren** or the only **Bugle Boy** (jeans) outlet in New England.

Art galleries and antiques shops: There are many art galleries and antique shops in the region, most open daily in the summer and by appointment the rest of the year. Check with the Chamber of Commerce information center for listing brochures.

Arts and crafts and special shops: **League of New Hampshire Craftsmen** (356-2441), North Conway Village. Quality handmade crafts including pottery, jewelry, clothing, and furnishings. Open all year.

Abenaki Indian Shop, Route 16 (across the street from the state information center), Box 73, Intervale 03845. Open June 15 to October 15 daily 10–12 and 3–5. Stephen Laurent and his wife operate a small Abenaki Indian crafts shop, begun by his father in 1884. The Abenakis were the original settlers in this place, fled to Canada to escape the white settlers, and over a century later returned each summer to sell sweetgrass and other handmade items. Stephen has kept alive the tradition by selling authentic moccasins, sweetgrass baskets, gifts, jewelry, toys, and books, and sharing his vast knowledge of Indian culture and language.

Handcrafters Barn, Route 16, North Conway. Open all year. A collection of 35 stalls where artists from throughout New England display their handmade items including pottery, quilts, jewelry, clothing, wooden items, and paintings.

Peter Limmer and Sons (356-5378), Route 16A, Box 88, Intervale 03845. Closed Sunday. If anything is a craft item, it is a pair of handmade mountain boots, fabricated by the third generation of the Limmer family. The boots are expensive ($245 per pair), and you may wait a year or more to have a pair custom-made to fit your feet; but our pair, purchased 25 years ago, is on its third set of soles and, after hundreds of miles of mountain trails, is still in great shape. "Limmers" have gone from Mt. Washington to Mt. Everest, and many hikers wouldn't enter the woods without a pair. You'll also find street and golf shoes.

SPECIAL EVENTS   We have listed primarily annual events but not specific dates since the exact dates change each year. Contact any of the places listed under Guidance for more details about these and many other one-time events held throughout the year. Cranmore Recreation Center is often the host for professional tennis tournaments, and world-class skiing races are often held at valley ski areas.

Late June: **Conway Village Festival**, Conway.

July through Labor Day: **Mt. Washington Valley Band** plays free concerts on Tuesdays at 7:30 at the Conway Recreation Center, Main Sttreet, Conway Village, and Sundays at 6:30 at the gazebo in North Conway village.

Fourth of July Carnival, North Conway. Fireworks and parade.

Early September: **World Mud Bowl**, North Conway. Some people enjoy this annual football game, played in knee-deep mud. At least local charities benefit from the proceeds.

Late September: **Annual Arts Jubilee**, North Conway.

First week in October: **Fryeburg Fair**, Fryeburg, Maine. This is a large agricultural fair with horse- and cattle-pulling, livestock exhibits and judging, midway, and pari-mutuel harness racing. Just across the border from Mt. Washington Valley, this annual fair attracts a huge crowd in the middle of foliage season.

JACKSON AND BARTLETT

From its covered bridge and rushing river flowing through the middle of town to its 1847 white community church, Jackson is one of New Hampshire's special villages. It has been hosting guests for more than a century; yet it has little of the glitz found farther south. Careful zoning and a strong community spirit have resulted in a tourist atmosphere that is relaxing and comfortable for guests as well as for residents. As a group, its inns and restaurants are as nice as can be found anywhere, and they are especially pleasant in the quieter, non-winter seasons.

The town is perhaps best known now for cross-country skiing, a sport promoted by the Jackson Ski Touring Foundation, a nonprofit organization founded in 1972 when the sport was in its infancy in America. The foundation maintains the 154-km trail system, rated by *Esquire* magazine as one of the top four areas in the world. On winter weekends the town bustles with skiers who bring enough business to keep the inns and restaurants busy and make last-minute reservations difficult, except for midweek. The ski center is right in the middle of the village and so are golf and tennis. In summer one could also hike the local trails or climb among many mountains near the village or just up the road in Pinkham Notch. Jackson also has several art galleries and a few antiques shops to keep the shopper happy, and there is always North Conway just a few minutes away.

Meanwhile Bartlett appears as two villages—one the residential center stretched along Route 302, the other a commercial center located between Attitash Ski Area and the junction of routes 302 and

16. The town of Harts Location, primarily a strip of land situated between Bartlett and Crawford Notch, has a small population and a couple of commercial establishments; it is surrounded by the White Mountain National Forest. Its few voters can meet in a private home to hold town meetings. Crawford Notch is described under the Mt. Washington section of this chapter.

GUIDANCE   **Jackson Resort Association** (383-9356, outside NH 800-866-3334), Box 304, Jackson Village 03846. Information and a reservation system.

Mt. Washington Valley Visitors Bureau (356-3171 or 800-367-3364), Box 2300, North Conway 03860. Free vacation guide and visitor information.

State of New Hampshire Information Center, Route 16, Intervale, just north of North Conway. Rest rooms and telephones. Open all year.

TO SEE AND DO   **Heritage New Hampshire** (383-9776), Route 16, Box 1776, Glen 03838. Open Memorial Day to mid-June and Labor Day to mid-October, 10–5; mid-June to Labor Day, 9–6. Heritage New Hampshire evokes the history of this state as you travel from England on a seventeenth-century vessel, visit with important individuals from the past such as Daniel Webster, and enter the twentieth century on a train ride through Crawford Notch. Designed around an 1,800-foot walkway, which is handicapped-accessible, this attraction is a 300-year review of New Hampshire history through photographs, dioramas, rides, and talking mannikins. Created long before the more technologically advanced but essentially similar attractions at Epcot, this is, nevertheless, a fine introduction to the state's past. Adults $7, ages 4-12 $4.50, under ge 4 free .

Grand Manor Antique and Classic Car Museum (356-9366), Route 16, Glen 03838. Open daily in the summer 9:30–5; weekends in the spring and fall. A changing collection of some 50 older, restored autos and some newer classics. Some cars are for sale or can be rented for weddings or special events. Gift shop. Reduced admission available with a coupon, given when eating at Studebaker's in North Conway.

FOR FAMILIES   **Attitash Alpine Slide and Waterslides** (374-2368), Route 302, Bartlett 03812. Open weekends 10–5, late May to mid-June and Labor Day to early October; open daily, 10–6, late June through Labor Day. Great fun for the kids and adults too. The Alpine Slide includes a ride to the top of the mountain on the ski lift, then a slide down a curving, bowed .75-mile chute on a self-controlled sled. Then cool off in the Aquaboggin water slide. Fees: Alpine Slide, Adults $5, ages 6-12 $4.50; two rides all ages $8; all day includes unlimited Alpine Slide and one hour Waterslide, all ages, $14; Waterslide, ages 6-adult, one half hour, $5. Under age 4 and over 70 ride free.

Story Land (383-4293), Route 16, Box 1776, Glen 03838. Open Father's Day to Labor Day 9–6; weekends from Labor Day through

Columbus Day 10–5. Created more than 35 years ago and regularly expanded, Story Land is a leading family theme park, organized around well-known fairy tales and children's stories. Fifteen rides range from a pirate ship, railroad, and antique autos to an African safari, voyage to the moon, and Dr. Geyser's remarkable raft ride. Cinderella, the Old Woman Who Lived in a Shoe, the Three Little Pigs, and Billy Goat's Gruff are all here along with Heidi of the Alps, farm animals to pet and feed, and dozens of other favorites. There is a restaurant, gift shop, and free parking. Ages 4-adult $12 which covers all rides. Operated, along with Heritage New Hampshire next door, by the Morrill family.

SCENIC DRIVES   When you are in the middle of the mountains, most any road is a scenic drive. The **Five-Mile Circuit** drive begins in Jackson Village. Follow Route 16B at the schoolhouse, up the hill, and, eventually, past farms and views across the valley to Whitney's; then turn left for a couple of miles to Carter Notch Road where you turn left again, past the Eagle Mountain House and Jackson Falls before reaching the village. For another variation of this drive, turn right at Whitney's, and right again at Black Mountain on **Dundee Road**, which changes to gravel now and again as it passes abandoned farms and mountain scenery en route to Intervale at Route 16A. Turn right and pick up Thorn Hill Road to return to Jackson.

GOLF   **Wentworth Resort Golf Club** (383-9641), Jackson Village. Eighteen holes, with pro shop, club and cart rentals, full lunch available. Call for tee times.

Eagle Mountain House (363-9111), Carter Notch Road, Jackson. Nine holes, full hotel facilities.

HIKING   The Jackson Resort Association publishes a small folder describing short walks in and around the village. Note: While some cross-country trails are suitable for hiking, many of them are on private land and not open to the public except for the ski season.

Eagle Mountain Path (1 mile, 50 minutes). Begins behind the Eagle Mountain House.

Black Mountain Ski Trail (1.7 miles, 1.6 hours). Begins on Carter Notch Road, 3.7 miles from the village. Leads to a cabin and a knob which offers a fine view of Mt. Washington.

North Doublehead, via the Doublehead Ski Trail. Begins on Dundee Road, 2.9 miles from the village. Follows an old ski trail to the WMNF Doublehead cabin on the wooded summit. A path leads to a good view east, and by using the Old Path and the New Path, one can make a round-trip hike from Dundee Road over both North and South Doublehead and back to the road. To North Doublehead, 1.8 miles, 1.6 hours; a round-trip to both summits is about 4.3 miles and 4 hours.

Rocky Branch Trail makes a loop from Jericho Road off Route 302 in Glen to Route 16 north of Dana Place. We suggest walking the Jericho Road end (turn off 302 in Glen and follow the road about 4.3 miles to the trail head), which follows the brook for a couple of miles to a shelter. Allow two hours round-trip on a smooth trail. The Rocky Branch is one of the better trout fishing brooks, and in the spring it is prime wildflower country (look but don't pick!).

SWIMMING   There is nothing like an old swimming hole, and there are several here. The best is probably at Jackson Falls in Jackson Village. Here the mountain-cool Wildcat River tumbles over rocky outcrops just above the village. There are several pools and picnic spots along the falls. Another favorite spot is on the Rocky Branch Brook, just off Route 302 in Glen. Driving west, watch for Jericho Road on the right and follow it to the Rocky Branch trailhead. Walk about 50 yards along the river back toward Route 302 for the swimming place.

CROSS-COUNTRY SKIING   **Jackson Ski Touring Foundation** (383-9355), Box 216, Jackson Village 03846. This nonprofit organization promotes the sport of cross-country skiing and maintains some 154 km of groomed trails in and around the village. The trails range from easy to difficult so be sure to consult the map before heading off for a ski. On the trail system one can ski from inn to inn for lunch or après ski activities. Foundation members get free instruction on technique and waxing, invitations to such special club events as a gourmet ski tour, ladies tours, and the end-of-the-season barbecue plus unlimited use of the trails. Every winter weekend there are events such as citizens' races and workshops. Trail fees/memberships pay for trail maintenance and such improvements as the northeast's newest covered bridge, built to provide easier access to the Ellis River Trail, a 10-km route from the village north to Dana Place Inn, where lunch is served and there is a warming hut. All trail users must be a daily or seasonal member of the foundation.

    Jack Frost Ski Shop (383-9657), Jackson Village 03846. Cross-country rentals and instruction; also alpine and telemark rentals. Rent a pulk (sled) and pull the baby on the trail.

    Nestlenook Farm (383-9443), Dinsmore Road, Jackson Village. Open daily in-season. Rentals and instructions plus a groomed trail network which connects to the Jackson system (additional charge for the Jackson trails).

DOWNHILL SKIING   **Attitash Ski Area** (374-2368, outside NH 800-223-7669), Route 302, Bartlett 03812. A family area, Attitash has 27 trails ranging from beginner to intermediate to expert, all on a 1,700-foot vertical drop, served by two triple and four double chairlifts. A new trail, opened in 1990, claims to be the longest, steepest lift-serviced trail east of the Rockies. The area makes 8–10 feet of snow per year on most of its trails, insuring good conditions throughout the season. Individual and group lessons are offered plus rentals. Package plans include skiing, lessons, and lodging at motels, condos, resorts, or country inns.

Black Mountain (383-4490, lodging 800-252-5622), Route 16B, Jackson 03846. Another of the historic New Hampshire ski areas, dating from the 1930s when Bill Whitney made a tow with shovel handles. There are some 20 trails served with a t-bar and a double and triple lift, with 95 percent snowmaking. Country views enhance the fun of this quiet, family area. Dining and lodging at the base in Whitney's Inn plus ski school, rentals, and a connection to Jackson's 154 km of cross-country trails.

ICE SKATING   A town-maintained ice-skating rink is located in the center of the village across from the grammar school, and Nestlenook Farm has skating for a fee or free to guests.

SLEIGH RIDES   **Nestlenook Farm** (383-9443), Dinsmore Road, Jackson Village. Daily except Wednesday. Sleigh rides last 25 minutes and taking you through the woods beside the Ellis River in a 25-person rustic sleigh or a smaller Austrian-built model. Oil lamps light the trails at night. Wheels are added for summer rides.

Horse Logic (383-9876), Jackson Village. Open seasonally for horse-drawn sleigh rides and hayrides around the village.

LODGING   Glen, Bartlett, and Jackson have a number of motels situated along routes 302 and 16.

RESORTS   **Eagle Mountain Resort** (383-9111, outside NH 800-777-1700), Carter Notch Road, Jackson 03846. Open all year. Not many of the old Victorian White Mountain hotels remain; but this is one of them, completely renovated and now managed by Colony Hotels/Resorts. All 94 rooms, including several suites, have private baths, phones, and cable TV. Most rooms have double beds and are furnished in a country style, not in typical hotel fashion. There is a 9-hole golf course, lighted tennis courts, health club, and heated pool. Winter guests can schuss right out on a large cross-country trail network. Unwind in the Eagle Landing Lounge where lunch is served in-season. Breakfast, Sunday brunch, and dinner are served in Highfields, the hotel dining room. The dinner menu is quite varied, featuring seafood, beef, chicken, and veal plus Cornish game hen and pork Zingara (a tenderloin with ham, artichoke hearts, black olives, mushrooms, and a white wine demiglaze). Appetizers include fried calamari and smoked trout. Joseph Antonelli, manager. $60–$135 per room depending on season and accommodations. MAP adds $30 per adult, $16 per child; also a variety of B&B package plans, especially in ski season.

Wentworth Resort Hotel (383-9700), Jackson Village 03846. Another old-timer, built in the 1880s and once known as Wentworth Hall, the core of this hotel has been renovated and modernized, the rest of the hotel was razed. Its 62 rooms are identically furnished, with king, queen, and twin beds; private baths; wall-to-wall carpeting; and cable TV. The hotel has an outdoor pool, or guests can walk to the river for a dip in the cool mountain water of the Wildcat River. From the hotel's location right in the middle of the village, guests can walk to skiing, golf, tennis, or lunch. Breakfast and dinner are served in the hotel dining room, which is also open to the public. Dinner entrées range from quail, roast duckling, and rack of lamb to Atlantic salmon, grilled shrimp in red pepper sauce, and scallops sautéed with leeks in a cream sauce. Fritz Koeppel, innkeeper. $49–$99, depending on season and day of the week; MAP add $23.

INNS   **The Bernerhof** (383-4414, outside NH 800-8007), Route 302, Box 240, Glen 03838. Open all year. Breakfast for house guests, lunch and dinner to the public. Another New Hampshire classic inn and one of the premier restaurants in the region as well as a cooking school. The inn has 11 rooms, four of which share baths. The best rooms, however, are four large new ones in a recent addition. Beautifully decorated, each has a private bath with a Jacuzzi in a separate alcove, air-conditioning, TV, and a brass king, queen, or double bed. Oak paneling accents the lounge (named for the Zumsteins, the longtime former owners) and adjacent dining room where lunch is served. Dining is European with six veal entrées as specialties. Try weiner schnitzel, schnitzel cordon bleu, or jaegerschnitzel (sautéed veal with shallots, mushrooms, and fresh herbs served with brown sauce). Cheese and beef fondues for two and roast duckling are other highlights, but if you fancy something else, just give the chef 48 hours' notice and he will prepare it especially for you. Cooking flexibility is easy here since general manager and chef Richard Spencer and Stephen James direct A Taste of the Mountains Cooking School. Three- and five-day, hands-on classes are conducted in spring, winter, and fall; and a special fifteen-week Wednesday class is taught from January through April by a variety of New England chefs. Ted and Sharon Wroblewiski, owners. B&B $64–$100; MAP $120–$133; a complimentary champagne breakfast in bed is served to guests on the third morning of their stay. Cooking school: three days, $300–$375 per person; five days, $825–$975 per person. Cooking school prices include five-course gourmet lunches and dinners with suitable wines and lodging.

Christmas Farm Inn (383-4313, outside NH 800-HI-Elves), Route 16B, Jackson 03846. Open all year. Celebrate Christmas here all year in rooms named for Santa's reindeer while relaxing in the Mistletoe Lounge or dining in the holiday-decorated dining room. Since purchasing the old place in 1976, the Zeliff family has transformed the property into one of the state's more imaginative inns. The main inn, a portion of which was built 200 years ago, has 10 regular rooms, all with private baths and king, queen, double, or twin beds. Five deluxe rooms also have Jacuzzis. Adjacent buildings include the Saltbox House, with nine new rooms; the Barn, with four deluxe suites; and the two-bedroom Log Cabin and Sugar House, each with a sun deck, fireplace, refrigerator, and telephone.

All rooms have clock radios and are furnished country-style with a Christmas accent. Spacious gardens surround the outdoor pool; and, for winter visitors, a cross-country trail passes right by the inn, connecting it with a large trail network. Longtime innkeepers Bill and Sydna Zeliff might not be so much in evidence now that he has been elected to Congress, but son Will remains as host and the inn's chef. Baked salmon, shrimp scampi, chicken Kiev, lamb kabob, steak, pasta, and vegetarian dishes highlight the menu, along with fresh-made desserts and such appetizers as "a warm slice of duck with diced vegetables and fresh greens." MAP $136–$180, plus a variety of package plans.

Dana Place (383-6822), Route 16, Jackson 03846. Open all year. Unlike most of Jackson's other inns, this one is by itself on 300 acres, just below the rugged walls of Pinkham Notch. Serving travellers since 1890, the inn has been changed, renovated, and expanded several times; but the heart of the place is a center-chimney colonial. There are 35 country-style guest rooms, all but four with private baths. Beds are kings, queens, and doubles; and some rooms have two doubles or one double and a day bed. Families are encouraged, and children under 18 stay free in parents' rooms (children's meals are additional). The dinner menu is broad with imaginative dishes such as salmon fillet in puff pastry with a spinach and herb beurre blanc; chicken with wine, herbs, and mixed vegetables steamed in parchment; and chicken Gloria, sautéed breast of chicken with apricots and finished with brandy, a selection of *Ford Times* magazine. Old favorites include rack of lamb, veal Oscar, steak au poivre, and roast duckling, plus daily seafood and pasta specialties. A blazing fireplace and candlelight in the colorful dining room enhance the distinctive dining. It is a treat to start the day in the breakfast room where large windows overlook a host of birdfeeders. Relax in the inn's pub or in the cozy library before the fireplace. Many of the rooms overlook the rushing Ellis River where a natural pool welcomes summer guests. There is also an indoor pool with Jacuzzi, and there are tennis courts. A rolling 10-km cross-country trail connects the inn with Jackson Village. Skiers can follow the route in either direction, then ride back in a shuttle bus. Since the inn serves lunch in cross-country season, many people ski up to the inn for lunch, then ride the shuttle back. Afternoon tea is served to guests who also can have a box lunch in ski season. The Levine family, innkeepers. B&B off-season $59, MAP $110–$175; plus a variety of package plans.

The Notchland Inn (374-6131), Route 302, Harts Location (Bartlett 03812). Open all year. Located near the site of Abel Crawford's early White Mountain Hotel, once called the Inn Unique (this place is still unique). Situated on a mountainside and surrounded by wilderness, it was built of granite in 1852 by Samuel Bemis, a Boston dentist and pioneering photographer. Maps and photographs feature local history. There are 11 rooms (including four two-room suites), each with private bath and a working fireplace. Beds are queen, double, and twin size. Two cozy sitting rooms also have fireplaces and for summer guests a sun room with wicker furniture overlooks the swimming pool. The inn grooms cross-country ski trails for guests only, and there is ice skating on their pond, snowshoeing, rock and ice climbing, and many nearby hiking trails. Innkeepers John and Pat Bernandin raise llamas and miniature horses and also maintain a refuge for rare and endangered species, primarily wool-producing animals. A professional chef, Pat prepares five-course, three-entrée dinners, generally for guests but also to the public by reservation and when space permits. A typical menu might include beef Wellington; baked haddock; pan-fried veal with vegetables, shrimp, and onion in a cream-and-cheese Czarina sauce; or Cajun-style chicken; plus homemade soups, appetizers, and rich desserts. MAP (two-night minimum, reservations usually required for weekends) $136 per night; B&B weekdays only, $90.

Inn at Thorn Hill (383-4242 or 383-6448), Thorn Hill Road, Jackson Village 03846. Open all year. Another of New Hampshire's classic inns, this 1895 mansion was designed by famed architect Stanford White, and it has been furnished to reflect its Victorian heritage. It has 20 rooms, all with private baths. The 10 Victorian rooms in the main building vary in size, but most beds are queens; a few have canopies. There are seven rooms in the Carriage House plus three cottages. The main inn has several common areas, including a pub with a fireplace, the dining room, a Victorian sitting room with TV, plus a drawing room with a view down the valley to the village and across the hills to Mt. Washington. Catering to artists, the inn offers special three- and five-day art workshops. Dine at the common table with other inn guests at 7 PM, or select your own individual table. The menu changes daily but includes several appetizers, four entrées, and several desserts. Some specialties include Lobster Pie Thorn Hill, roast duck, and prime rib plus unusual offerings such as grilled quail or Atlantic salmon. Swim in the inn pool or cross-country ski from the door. The village is just a short walk down the hill. No smoking except in the pub. Peter and Linda LaRose, innkeepers. MAP $110–$192, depending on season and accommodations; plus various package plans. For B&B, deduct $15 per person.

Whitney's Village Inn (383-6886, outside NH 800-252-5622), Route 16B, Jackson 03846. With Black Mountain (one of the state's oldest ski areas) in the backyard, this old inn is a popular destination for winter vacationers; but its country location is a relaxing spot in other seasons as well. The inn's 32 rooms offer a variety of accommodations from regular rooms to deluxe rooms with private sitting areas, plus eight family suites in a separate building (where children under 12 stay and eat free from May through August), two cottages with fireplaces, and the four-room Brookside Cottage, also with fireplaces. All the rooms are bright and colorful with private baths and king, queen, or double beds. Rooms in the deluxe section overlook the ski slopes. The lounge and dining room have fireplaces, and there is also a separate common room for guests. The remodeled barn, used for lunch during ski season, has recreation rooms for teens and younger children; there are lawn games, a mountain pond for swimming, tennis and volleyball courts plus outdoor skating in winter. Begin a dinner with apple and butternut squash bisque, then try rack of lamb for two, roast duckling, broiled scrod, broiled venison steak, or daily pasta or veal specialties. The Tannehill and Kelley families, innkeepers. MAP $120–$175, but various package plans are available.

Wildcat Inn and Tavern (383-4245), Jackson Village 03846. Open all year. If you would like to be in the middle of everything, try this long-time favorite. Walk to cross-country skiing, shopping, golf, or tennis; plus their tavern offers folk music on weekends. There are 12 rooms, 10 with private baths. This is not an ideal family inn since the rooms are not large, but they are cozy with country furniture and some antiques, and most of them can be arranged as suites for families. There is also a large TV and game room and a separate living room with a fireplace, plus the tavern. Three country gourmet meals are served daily in one of the area's most popular restaurants. Dinner ranges from lasagna and baked scallops to lobster fettucini, roast lamb, tavern steak, and scampi. Marty and Pam Sweeney are the longtime innkeepers. He is the dinner chef while she bakes and serves lunch (consider Lobster Benedict or one of many unusual sandwiches). B&B $70–$90; MAP $130–$140; plus theatre, tennis, and golf package plans.

BED & BREAKFASTS   **The Blake House** (383-9057), Route 16, Jackson 03846. Open all year. Sara Blake Maynard's father built a portion of this place as a ski cabin in the 1930s, but more recently it has been expanded and now offers five rooms with two shared baths. One room has a king bed, one a double with a separate screened porch; others have twins. The guests' living room has cozy chairs, TV, VCR, books, games, and a fireplace while the dining room features a huge window overlooking the forest and the rushing Ellis River, which nearly surrounds the wooded property. Located north of town and surrounded by white birches, this is a quiet, woodsy place. Breakfast is an expanded continental offering with fresh fruit and breads, hot and cold cereals, and hard- or soft-boiled eggs. Sara and Jeff Maynard, innkeepers. $50–$60.

Covered Bridge House (383-9109, outside NH 800-232-9109), Route 302, Box 358, Glen 03838. Open all year. This restored turn-of-the-century home has five guest rooms, most with private baths and each with a king, queen, or double bed. Fresh flowers and fruit accent the homey decor. Rollaways and cribs are available for the kids. Two comfortable sitting rooms, one with a guest refrigerator, and wine and cheese served at 5 PM daily. Guests have privileges at a nearby health club, and you can swim in the cool Saco River behind the inn. Visit the inn's recently restored, circa 1850, covered bridge which has gift and antiques shops. Full breakfast served. Marc and Mary Ellen Frydman, innkeepers. $58–$68; multi-day package plans available.

The Country Inn at Bartlett (374-2353), Route 302, Box 327, Bartlett 02812. Open all year. Just west of Bartlett Village, this place has 6 inn rooms with shared baths and 11 cottage rooms, each with private bath and TV. The living room has a large fireplace, and there is an outside hot tub. The inn appeals to hikers, skiers, and lovers of the outdoors—folks with whom innkeeper Mark Dindorf worked when he was an AMC employee. B&B $56–$72.

Ellis River House (383-0330, outside NH 800-233-8309), Route 16, Box 656, Jackson 03846. Open all year. Situated just off the main road, backed up to its namesake river, this renovated turn-of-the-century farmhouse offers cozy, comfortable accommodations. Five antiques-furnished rooms share two baths and access to two new sun decks. A separate three-room suite has a private bath, a single with a TV, one room with a queen bed; and the other has twins. In a two-room cottage for four people, there is a sitting room with TV, private bath, and a second-floor room with a queen. A recent addition is a Jacuzzi in a bright atrium overlooking the river. You can swim or fish in the river, play volleyball, or cross-country ski from the door. Hot toddies are served in the afternoon. The dining room is one of several sitting areas and has easy chairs, a woodstove, and a grand piano. The full breakfast includes fresh eggs and sausage and bacon from the inn's farm animals. A full-course dinner is also available to guests only by request ($22.50 pp), and it features six entrées: duckling, Cornish game hen, lobster, rainbow trout, haddock, and linguini with marinara sauce. Vegetables from the inn garden are featured. Barry and Barbara Lubao. B&B $50–$120, depending on the season and accommodations; plus package plans.

The Inn at Jackson (383-4321), Jackson Village 03846. Open all year. This old summer mansion overlooks the village from its hillside lot. There are eight large, well-furnished rooms, all with private baths; most beds are queens; three rooms have fireplaces. There is a second-floor common room and a panoramic view of the village and the mountains from the breakfast sun porch. Cross-country ski from the door or walk to lunch or dinner. Full breakfast. Lori Tradewell, innkeeper. B&B $56–$78.

Jackson House (383-4226), Route 16, Jackson 03846. Open all year. Peter and Laraine Hill have spent seven years transforming this circa 1868 country home into a comfortable inn. They have 14 rooms, 9 with private baths, each with a double or a double and a twin. Several rooms are new with bright comforters, handmade items, and custom-built Shaker beds. Swing in the hammock or jump into the hot tub in the solarium. Full breakfast. B&B $50–$90.

Nestlenook Farm (383-9443), Dinsmore Road, Jackson Village 03846. Open all year. Elaborately furnished and decorated, this recently renovated Victorian inn (one of Jackson's original houses) is for couples only. Painted peach and green, the inn is part of a million-dollar development with extensive gardens, a gazebo, a pond, and a location beside the Ellis River. Each of the seven guest rooms has a private bath with a Jacuzzi. Some rooms have working fireplaces or parlor stoves. Rooms have queen-size beds, many with canopies, and separate sitting rooms. The rooms are named for local artists (some famous ones from the nineteenth century), and many feature an original painting as part of the decor. Guests may enjoy complimentary sleigh rides and skating, and they have free use of the inn's cross-country rentals, instruction, and trails, which connect to the extensive Jackson trail network. You can also pet the inn's herd of reindeer. A no-smoking inn. The inn has offered dinner in the past, but the restaurant was closed when we were preparing this report. B&B $99–$216 for a two-room suite (depending season and accommodations), including an expanded continental breakfast.

Paisley and Parsley (383-0859), Route 16B, Box 572, Jackson 03846. Open all year. Bea and Chuck Stone have turned their contemporary home into a cozy, three-room B&B. One downstairs room (with a king-size bed and Jacuzzi) has a private entrance. Upstairs are two rooms, each with its own sitting room—one with two doubles, the other with a canopy bed. All have private baths and are furnished with antiques. Don't miss the beautiful rock gardens. Full gourmet breakfast. $65–$95.

The Village House (383-6666), Box 359, Jackson Village. Open all year. This old cozy inn is right in the village where you can walk to tennis, cross-country skiing, golf, lunch, or dinner. Ten rooms, all but two with private baths, furnished country-style with braided rugs on the floors. They have an outdoor swimming pool, and the common room has a fireplace, TV, and games. Continental breakfast in summer, full breakfast in winter. Robin Crocker, innkeeper. $40–$100.

DINING OUT   Dining out in Jackson and Bartlett is limited primarily to one of several inns or resorts, all of which are described above, or you could dine at one of the following:

The Thompson House (393-9341), Jackson Village. Daily 11:30–10, closed November and April. This popular restaurant is now open ten months a year after offering summer-only dining for 15 seasons. Owner/chef Larry Baima prepares a host of distinctive and imaginative combination sandwiches, soups, salads, and dinner entrées in a 1790 farmhouse. Try something Italian, Mexican, or traditional American, from pastas to chicken, veal, and seafood; and it's all made fresh daily, to order, and can be prepared to suit dietary needs. A few lunch choices: a Reuben with turkey, sauerkraut, cheddar cheese, and

Russian dressing,; knockwurst marinated in beer and grilled with tomatoes, Swiss cheese, and spicy mustard sauce; or cheese tortellini with sun dried tomato and basil vinaigrette, served atop fresh greens with artichoke hearts, prosciutto, tomatoes, and lots more. Dinner choices range from saffron scallops and pork picatta to beef tenderloin or gulf shrimp stir-fried with veggies in an oriental marinade flavored with sherry; or Chicken San Remo, a specialty of white chicken sautéed with eggplant, sweet peppers, onions, and sun dried tomatoes in a garlic herb wine sauce, garnished with prosciutto. Sandwiches $2.50–$6.95; entrées $11.25–$14.95. Full bar plus sangria, hot-buttered rum, and spiced cider. Patio dining in the summer, a roaring wood-stove in the winter.

I Cugini (374-1977), Route 302, Bartlett. Open 4:30–9, weekends until 10. Cousins (cugini) Michael DiLuca and Anthony DiStefano operate this Italian restaurant, featuring many old recipes passed down from family members. Several veal dishes are featured along with a seafood marinara with shrimp, calamari, scallops, and clams, simmered in a spicy marinara sauce and served over linguini. The lounge, open until midnight, serves lighter fare, such as pizza and calzones. Prices range from 5.95–$15.95.

The Red Parka Pub (383-4344), Route 302, Glen. Open daily 4–10. A favorite with the locals and for aprés ski, this is a traditional ski tavern, with skis dating back to the 1930s adorning the walls and ceilings. Famous for steak and prime rib, the Red Parka Pub also features baked seafood, barbecued spare ribs and pork, shrimp, and six varied chicken dishes. An extensive salad bar rounds out the meal; special kids' menu. Prices range from $7.95–$18.95 (for a 22 ounce t-bone). Next door is the Black Diamond Grill, a summer-only restaurant with burgers, shakes, and lighter fare.

EATING OUT   Stanley's Restaurant (383-6529), Route 16, Glen. Tom and Helen have been serving their breakfast menu all day (plus fried foods and sandwiches for lunch) since 1949.

Glen Junction (383-9660), Route 302, Glen. Open for breakfast, lunch, and dinner. Takeout sandwiches, deli, and home-style cooking in a family atmosphere. Kids (and adults) are fascinated with the two large-scale model trains that circle the dining rooms on tracks near the ceiling.

SPECIAL EVENTS   AMC Pinkham Notch Camp (466-2725), organizes and hosts weekend activities and workshops throughout the year.

Cross-country Skiing, Jackson Village. Throughout the ski season weekend citizens races are held, and often special international events use the Jackson trails.

May: Queen Victoria Festival and Clambake, Jackson Village. A weekend festival for Canadian and American visitors alike.

Late May: Quacktillion and Wildquack River Festival, Jackson

The summit of Mt. Washington in winter. The historic Tip Top House is in the foreground.

Village. A weekend of dancing, then cheer on one of 2,000 rubber duckies as they race down the river. Rent your own for $5.

Early June: **Jackson Covered Bridge 10 km**, Jackson Village. One of the most demanding 10-km road races in New England. **Wildflower Guided Tour and Barbecue**, Jackson Village. See more than 400 wildflowers and ferns, and classic eighteenth- and nineteenth-century gardens plus a chicken barbecue.

Fourth of July: **Family in the Park**, Jackson Village. An old-fashioned Fourth of July celebration.

Mid-July: **Jackson Jazz Festival**, Black Mountain Ski Area.

Mid-August: **Attitash Equine Festival** (374-2372), Attitash Ski Area, Bartlett. World-class riders and horses compete for $100,000 in prizes at a weekend of show jumping, plus an international food fair and a country fair exposition.

Photo by Peter E. Randall

MT. WASHINGTON AND PINKHAM NOTCH

Rising 6,288 feet above sea level, Mt. Washington is the highest peak in the northeast and one of the most popular scenic attractions in the state. It offers varied recreational opportunities for the most hardy to the most sedentary visitor. P. T. Barnum called the mountain and its attractions the second Greatest Show on Earth. Since the days of Darby Field's first climb in 1642, the mountain has been the source of recreation, adventure, scientific research, and not a few tragedies. Annually some 250,000 people of all ages visit the summit, the location of Mt. Washington State Park, the Mt. Washington Observatory, and the transmitter facilities for a television station and several radio stations. There are three ways to reach the summit, each described in more detail below: hiking, the Mt. Washington Auto Road, and the Mt. Washington Cog Railway.

Perhaps the most impressive aspect of the mountain is its weather. Mt. Washington Observatory records prove that the mountain has the worst combination of wind, cold, and ice of any regularly inhabited place on earth. It can, and often does, snow every month of the year although summer snowstorms are somewhat rare, and the snow usually melts quickly. Winds over 100 mph are common although not usual in the summer when the July breeze averages 25 mph and the temperature averages about 49 degrees. February is the coldest month, averaging 5.6 degrees; and January is the windiest, averaging 35 mph. Hurricane force winds (over 75 mph) occur more than 100 days annually, and the highest recorded wind velocity, 231 mph, blew over the mountain in April 1934. The highest recorded temperature is just above 70 degrees while the low approaches –50 degrees. In addition, it is foggy more than 300 days per year, although this condition can appear and dissipate rapidly over the course of a day. Visitors should be patient if the summit is in the clouds—it might, and often does, clear suddenly. At other times, the valley is cloudy and the summit is open. When the weather is clear, the view extends some 130 miles to New York, Canada, Maine, and the Atlantic Ocean. However you reach the summit, take along an extra jacket or sweater since it is always cooler there than at the base of the mountain.

Because of the elevation and the weather conditions, Mt. Washington's vegetation is also unusual. Squatty, spreading evergreens, called krummholz, are seen as one approaches tree line and are actually balsam fir and black spruce which grow as tall as normal trees lower on the mountain. The trees grow as krummholz as a defense against the harsh weather conditions, especially the wind. Many tiny, flowering alpine plants found here are more common to Labrador while some other species are unique to this mountain alone. Mid-June is the prime season for flower viewing; and while the best approach is by hiking, the flowers also grow along the Auto Road. The study of these plants brought scientists to the mountains in the early nineteenth century, and many of the mountain's features are named for these individuals. The AMC offers annual guided walks to the best viewing areas and also publishes the *Mountain Flowers of New England*, the best flower handbook available. Another AMC book is *At Timberline, A Nature Guide to the Mountains of the Northeast*.

GUIDANCE   **WMNF Androscoggin Ranger Station** (466-2713), Route 16, Gorham. Open Monday to Friday 7:30–4:30.

AMC Pinkham Notch Camp (466-2725 for weather, trail, or general information; 466-2727 for overnight or workshop reservations; 617-523-0636 for membership details), Route 16, Box 298, Gorham 03518. Opened in 1920 and expanded several times since, this is the North Country headquarters for an organization of some 37,000 members. The main office is at 5 Joy Street, Boston, and chapters serve members from the mid-Atlantic states to New England. Members receive discounts on hikes, books, workshops, accommodations, and meals; but everyone is welcome to use the facilities and participate in their programs.

Photo by Peter E. Randall

Appalachian Mountain Club headquarters in Pinkham Notch, with the summit of Mt. Washington behind the clouds.

The club offers a variety of special weekend programs throughout the year, ranging from hiking, skiing, snowshoeing, woods crafts, and canoeing to bird study, photography, art, and writing. The AMC publishes annual and monthly publications and a variety of books and operates eight full-service, high-mountain huts, to which you must walk on trails ranging from 1.7 miles to over 4 miles in length. Write to the address above for a brochure describing the huts and fees. A recent innovation is a shuttle bus system for hikers, which provides service between popular trailheads in Pinkham, Crawford, and Franconia notches. The organization, especially its North Country headquarters, trail maintenance crew, and hut crews, is staffed primarily with young men and women who love the outdoors and who are hired for their energy and willingness and ability to relate to the public. They are a source of information and advice for the novice and more experienced hiker alike. These staffers cook all meals, maintain trails, guide hikes, teach workshops, and, when needed, participate in all manner of mountain rescue missions. This facility includes the full-service Joe Dodge Center (see Lodging); the Trading Post, which sells snacks, books, postcards, and some equipment and has rest rooms with showers; and administrative offices. The AMC, with its trained staff and large membership, is one of New England's strongest conservation voices, urging careful use of and protection for the mountains.

GETTING THERE   Daily **Concord-Trailways bus service** (800-852-3317) to Pinkham Notch Camp from Boston's Logan Airport.

TO SEE AND DO   Mt. Washington Cog Railway (846-5404, advance reservations recommended), off Route 302, Bretton Woods 03589. (See Crawford Notch and Bretton Woods.)

Mt. Washington State Park, on the summit of the mountain. Open daily, Memorial Day through Columbus Day. Although most of Mt. Washington is part of the White Mountain National Forest, there are several other owners. One is the state of New Hampshire, which operates the Sherman Adams Summit Building, named for the former governor who was the chief of staff for President Eisenhower. This contemporary, two-story curved building sits into the northeast side of the mountain, offering a sweeping view across the peaks of the Presidential Range. Park facilities include a gift shop, snack bar, post office, rest rooms (all handicapped-accessible), and a hiker pack room. The mountain and its summit have a fascinating history, too detailed to be explained here, but the old Tip Top House, originally built as a summit hotel in 1853, has been restored and is open daily as a reminder of the past. Free. Other summit buildings include the transmitter and generator facilities of Channel 8, WMTW-TV, which provides transmitter service for radio stations and relays for state and federal government agencies.

Mt. Washington Museum, on the summit. Open daily when the building is open. Located one flight below the main building, the museum is operated by the Mt. Washington Observatory and offers historical exhibits and a wealth of scientific information on the meteorology, geology, botany, and biology of the mountain. A small gift shop helps support the activities of the observatory. Fee charged.

Mt. Washington Observatory, on the summit, Gorham 03518. Closed to the public, but members may tour the facility. This private, nonprofit, membership institution occupies a section of the Sherman Adams Summit Building and is staffed all year by rotating crews of two to three people who change each week. Weather observations are taken every three hours, providing a lengthy record of data which extends back to the 1930s when the institution was formed. The staff endured the highest wind ever recorded, 231 mph, in April 1934. The original building was the old Stage Office, a replica of which is on the summit. Various on-going research projects study the effects of icing, aspects of atmospheric physics, and related subjects. It has conducted research for a variety of commercial, institutional, and governmental organizations. Facilities include crew quarters, a weather instrument room, a radio room, a photography darkroom, and a library. The observatory publishes a quarterly bulletin. The staffers provide live morning weather reports on several area radio stations, including WMWV 93.5 FM in Conway. Write for membership information.

Mt. Washington Auto (Carriage) Road (466-2222 or 466-3988), Route 16, Pinkham Notch, Box 278, Gorham 03518. Open daily, weather permitting, mid-May to mid-October, from 7:30 AM to 6 PM most of the summer, with shorter hours earlier and later in the season. Opened in 1861, originally for mountain stagecoaches or carriages, this 8-mile auto graded road climbs steadily without steep pitches, but with an average grade of 12 percent, from the Glen to the summit. Although the road is narrow in spots and skirts some steep slopes, it has a remarkable safety record and annually carries some 100,000 visitors. En route, there are many places to pull off and enjoy the view, and it is crossed by several hiking trails. At various times the road is used for annual foot and bicycle races (each record is about 1 hour) and, once again, for auto races. While it's a long way compared to hiking trails, some people prefer to walk its smooth grade to the summit. The route is the year-round supply line for the summit facilities and is followed by tractor-treaded snowcats in the winter. You may drive your own passenger car to the summit or take a 1.5-hour guided tour in one of the chauffeur-driven vans, called stages, to keep alive a historical tradition. At the base is a gift shop and snack bar. Passenger car rates: $11 for car and driver, $3 each additional passenger. Guided tour: $15 for adults, $10 for children.

HIKING   Mt. Washington is crisscrossed with trails, but there are two popular routes. The **Tuckerman Ravine Trail** (4.1 miles, 4.5 hours) begins at the AMC Pinkham Notch Camp on Route 16. It is nearly a graded path most of the first 2.5 miles where it approaches the ravine; then it climbs steeply up the ravine's headwall and reaches the summit cone for the final ascent to the top. The ravine has open-sided shelters for up to 86 people, and each person has to carry up everything needed for an overnight stay. (Register at the AMC Pinkham Notch Camp, no reservations.) This is the trail used by spring skiers, and it can be walked to the ravine by anyone in reasonably good condition. The beginning of this trail is an easy .5-mile walk on a graded path to the pretty Crystal Cascade.

On the west side of Mt. Washington is the **Ammonoosuc Ravine Trail** (in combination with Crawford Path; 3.86 miles, 4.5 hours). It begins at the Cog Railway Base Station, located off Route 302 north of Crawford Notch. About 2.5 miles from the start is the AMC Lakes of the Clouds Hut, a full-service facility, serving two meals daily and complete with bunk rooms and blankets. (Make reservations with the AMC, 466-2727.) Near this hut are the best areas to view the alpine flowers. Here also is a junction with popular **Crawford Path**, the oldest continuously maintained hiking trail in the country, built in 1819 by the Crawford family. This trail is 8.2 miles long and requires 6 hours to reach the summit of Mt. Washington. It begins just above Crawford Notch, and at about 2.5 miles is the AMC Mizpah Spring

Hut, another of the full-service facilities. In the vicinity of the AMC Pinkham Notch Camp are many short hiking trails or paths suitable for family groups. Ask for suggestions and directions at the camp.

A few words of caution about hiking on Mt. Washington and the Presidential Range. Most of these trails lead above tree line and should be attempted only by properly equipped hikers. Winter weather conditions can occur above tree line any month of the year. Annually some 50,000 hikers safely reach the summit, many in the winter, but hiking is a self-reliant activity so even fair-weather summer hikers are warned to climb well prepared with extra clothing and food in addition to maps and a compass. Most of the trails to the summits are 4–5 miles in length and require 4–5 hours to reach the top. Although these trails are not exceptionally long, there is an elevation gain of some 4,000 feet, a distance which becomes painfully evident to those who are not in reasonably good physical condition. Western hikers, used to the higher Rockies, soon appreciate the ruggedness and the elevation change when climbing this mountain. About 100 people have died on the slopes of the mountain, some from falls while hiking, rock or ice climbing, or skiing; but others have died in the summer when they were caught unprepared by rapidly changing weather conditions. Since the weather can be most severe above tree line, cautious hikers will assess the weather conditions when reaching that point on a climb. The AMC (466-2725) provides daily weather information. Also call 466-5252 for recorded weather information.

Since AMC staffers often volunteer for mountain rescues, they are careful to give considered advice to beginning and more experienced hikers. The *AMC White Mountain Guide* has the most comprehensive trail information available for hikers, but also see Daniel Doan's *Fifty Hikes in the White Mountains.*

CROSS-COUNTRY SKIING   AMC Pinkham Notch Camp There are a number of trails in the notch near the AMC headquarters although they are not groomed and would be considered backcountry trails. One expert trail, part of the Jackson system, goes down the back side of Wildcat.

DOWNHILL SKIING   Wildcat Mountain (466-3326, lodging 800-255-6439), Route 16, Pinkham Notch, Jackson 03846. One of the east's biggest ski mountains, Wildcat was first used in the 1930s when skiers had to climb to the top of the ski run. Now it has some 30-plus trails with 97 percent snowmaking and a 2,100-foot vertical drop; its six lifts can handle 8,500 skiers per hour, the largest capacity in the valley. The gondola goes to the top of the 4,000 foot mountain, which is just across the valley from towering Mt. Washington, offering the best view for skiers in the east. This high-mountain location, which makes Wildcat colder than some lower elevation areas, also provides a season from mid-November to April. Although considered a world-class area with challenging expert runs, Wildcat's easier Polecat trail offers a 2.75-mile run from the top of the hill. Telemark, cross-country, and downhill rentals; ski school; and snack bars at the base and summit. Wildcat's gondola is also open for passengers in the off-season. The two-person cars make a half-hour round-trip to the summit. The cars stop at stationary platforms making boarding and exiting easy for all ages. At the summit is a snack bar, picnic tables, and hiking trails plus that great view across the valley to Mt. Washington. The gondola is open weekends Memorial Day to late June, then daily until early October.

Tuckerman Ravine (call Appalachian Mountain Club 466-2725), off Route 16, Pinkham Notch. Spring skiing has become an annual rite for many skiers, and there is nowhere better than the steep slopes of Tuckerman Ravine. There are no lifts, so you have to walk over 3 miles to reach the headwall of this cirque, a little valley carved out of the eastern side of Mt. Washington by glaciers during the ice age. Winds blow snow from the mountain into the ravine where it settles to a depth of 75 feet or more. When snow has melted from traditional ski slopes, it still remains in the ravine; and skiers by the thousands walk the trail from the AMC Pinkham Notch Camp to reach the slopes. Skiing begins in early April, and we have seen some diehards in June skiing the small patches of snow remaining in the ravine.

Early in the season when there is plenty of snow, the steep John Sherburne Ski Trail provides a brisk run from the ravine back to Pinkham Notch Camp. Spring sun warms the air, and many people ski in short-sleeved shirts and shorts, risking sunburn and bruises if they fall. Skiing here is for experts since a fall on the 35- to 55-degree slopes means a long, dangerous slide to the bottom of the ravine. A volunteer ski patrol is on duty, and WMNF rangers patrol the ravine to watch for avalanches. The three-sided Hermit Lake shelters offer sleeping-bag accommodations for 86 hardy backpackers, who must carry everything up to the site for overnight stays. Winter-use only (November to March) tent platforms are also available in the ravine. Register for shelters or tent platforms through the AMC Pinkham Notch Camp (466-2727, no reservations; first-come, first-served only).

PINKHAM NOTCH   Pinkham Notch Scenic Area, Route 16, between Jackson and Gorham. This 5,600-acre section of the White Mountain National Forest covers the eastern side of Mt. Washington and includes several spectacular ravines and other natural features and a most important human resource, the Appalachian Mountain Club Pinkham Notch Camp. Tuckerman Ravine is famous for spring skiing and hiking while adjacent Huntington Ravine is a challenge to winter ice climbers. The Great Gulf Wilderness is a larger glacial valley surrounded by the state's highest peaks.

Approaching from the Jackson end of the notch, Route 16 begins a long, gradual ascent, passing the beginnings of several hiking trails and a few pullouts adjacent to the Ellis River. Watch the ridge of the mountains on the west side, and gradually the huge Glen Boulder becomes silhouetted against the sky. This glacial erratic was dragged to this seemingly precarious spot eons ago by an ice-age glacier. Situated at an elevation of about 2,500 feet, the boulder is a steep 1.5-mile, two-hour hike from the highway, a short but steep climb to tree line. At the top of the notch, the mountainside drops steeply to the east and allows a panoramic view south down the Ellis River Valley toward Conway and Mt. Chocorua. Across this valley rises the long ridge of Wildcat Mountain. Just ahead is a parking lot for Glen Ellis Falls, one of the picturesque highlights of the notch. To see the falls, cross under the highway by the short tunnel, then walk .2 mile down a short trail to the base of the falls.

North along Route 16, as the highway skirts under the side of Mt. Washington, are the AMC Pinkham Notch Camp, an information center with rest rooms and snacks for sale, then Wildcat Mountain Ski Area (with summer and fall mountain gondola rides), and the Mt. Washington Auto Road at the Glen. Here is one of the most magnificent views in all the mountains. At left can be seen the summit of Mt. Washington although it doesn't appear to be the highest spot around. Rising clockwise above the Great Gulf, another glacial valley, are mounts Clay, Jefferson, Adams (the state's second highest peak), and Madison. Route 16 continues north to Gorham, passing en route WMNF Dolly Copp campground and the entrance to Pinkham B (Dolly Copp) Road which connects to Route 2 at Randolph. Just north of Pinkham Notch, several hiking trails head east into the Carter Range. One, the Nineteen Mile Brook Trail (3.8 miles, 2.5 hours) leads to the AMC Carter Notch Hut, another full-service facility. It is also open on a self-service, caretaker basis in the winter.

LODGING   See the North Country (Gorham and Jefferson) and Western Whites (Twin Mountain) for additional lodging listings.

CAMPS   **Appalachian Mountain Club Pinkham Notch Camp** (466-2727), Route 16, Pinkham Notch, Box 298, Gorham 03581. The headquarters of the AMC is in a lodging class by itself. This is a full-service facility offering two meals a day, bunk beds, and shared baths. Bunk rooms for two, three, and four people accommodate 106 guests in the Joe Dodge Center. It appeals mostly to outdoorsey people (hikers, skiers and such), since it is not fancy; but it is clean and comfortable, with a library and a huge fireplace in the living room and another in the main lodge dining area. Families are encouraged. Meals are served family-style, and no one goes hungry here since the one-entrée offerings are huge. Operated primarily for club members, nonmembers are welcome as guests and can participate in club activities. B&B $64; MAP $84; members save $7 per night. (Also see Pinkham Notch.)

Appalachian Mountain Club High Huts (466-2727), Pinkham Notch, Box 298, Gorham 03581. The AMC maintains eight full-service mountain huts which are only reached by walking. You supply your clothes and towels; they provide meals, bunks, and blankets. Some AMC programs involve guided hikes to the huts. Contact the AMC for rates and other information and see the *AMC White Mountain Guide* for trail routes.

CAMPING   **WMNF Dolly Copp Campground** (466-3984, July through Labor Day), Route 16, Pinkham Notch, Gorham. Open mid-May through mid-October. Some of the 176 sites are available through a **toll-free reservation system** (800-283-2267). The reservation service operates March through September (Monday to Friday 12–9, weekends 12–5) and costs $6 in addition to the camping fee. Reservations may be made 120 days before arrival, but 10 days before arrival is the minimum time.

SPECIAL EVENTS   **AMC Pinkham Notch Camp** (466-2725), organizes and hosts weekend activities and workshops throughout the year.

Late June: **Mt. Washington Auto Road Foot Race and Auto Hill Climb**, Mt. Washington Auto Road, Pinkham Notch. On consecutive weekends, first runners, then autos race from the Glen to the summit over the steep winding course. For foot race details call 863-2537; for auto race details 466-3988.

Mid-September: **Mt. Washington Bike Race** (466-3988), Mt. Washington Auto Road, Pinkham Notch. This event attracts some of the top United States racers.

CRAWFORD NOTCH AND BRETTON WOODS

Crawford is the least developed of New Hampshire's mountain passes although historically it has been important since the eighteenth century when settlers followed today's Route 302 from Conway north to establish towns above the mountains. The notch was "discovered" by white men in 1770, but, undoubtedly, it was the location of an earlier Indian trail. It was in this narrow notch, flanked by steep mountains, that the Crawford family began taking in travelers, and thus created the tourist industry which dominates the White Mountains today. At the turn of the century some of the region's largest and best hotels were located just above the notch; now only the Mt. Washington Hotel remains.

Although Crawford Notch itself has few attractions, there are many sights to see, including fine waterfalls and one of the best views in all the mountains.

"Look at me gentleman...for I am the poor fool who built all this!" coal baron Joseph Stickney is reported to have exclaimed on the July day in 1902 when the Mt. Washington first opened. It's noted that he "laughed heartily at this own folly." By-and-large the 174-room hotel has been lucky. Although Stickney died in 1903, it remained in his family until World War II and was then lavishly refurbished by the United States government for the 1944 Bretton Woods Monetary Conference, which set the gold standard and created both the World Bank and the International Monetary Fund. In ensuing decades it's had its ups and downs. A Philadelphia group added the ski area, and a subsequent owner added the motor lodge and condos across the road. Its most recent owners, however, went bankrupt, and, as we put this book to bed, its future is unclear. It will be open for the summer season, but owned by FDIC. Happily the ski area, the extensive cross-country trail system, the condos, motor lodge, and a small inn continue to thrive. We wish this resort luck. It's a gem in one of the country's most magnificent settings.

GUIDANCE   **Twin Mountain Chamber of Commerce** (846-5407 or 800-245-TWIN), Box 194, Twin Mountain 03595, produces a brochure and operates a summer information center at the junction of routes 2 and 302.

TO SEE AND DO   **Mt. Washington Cog Railway** (846-5404, advance reservations recommended), off Route 302, Bretton Woods 03589. Open weekends in May, daily until mid-October. Opened in 1869, this is the world's first mountain-climbing cog railway, and it remains one of the few places where you can observe steam locomotives at work. At one time regular trains followed a spur line to the Base Station where passengers boarded the cog railway directly for the summit. So unique and ambitious was the plan to build the railroad that its promoter, Sylvester Marsh, was told he might as well "build a railway to the moon." The eight little engines, each made for this purpose by this railroad company, have boilers positioned at an angle because of the steep grade up the mountain. On the three-hour round-trip, which permits a visit at the summit, each engine pushes a single car up, then backs down in front of the car to provide breaking. Unique cog wheels fit into slots between the rails to provide traction and breaking. The average grade along the 3.25-mile track is 25 percent, but at Jacob's Ladder trestle it rises to 37.5 percent. Several switches permit ascending and descending trains to pass en route. The Base Station, a short drive on a paved road from Route 302, includes a restaurant, gift shop, B&B, and an RV park. Adults $32, children 6–12 $22.

GREEN SPACE   **Crawford Notch State Park** This large state park is located in the middle of the White Mountain National Forest, some 12 miles north of Bartlett. The park headquarters is located at the Willey House Memorial, the site of an unusual mountain tragedy. In August 1826 a terrible rainstorm blew through the notch, frightening the Willey family, who operated a small inn. Hearing an avalanche sliding down the steep side of the mountain, the family and two employees ran from the inn only to be swallowed up in the debris as the avalanche split above the inn, leaving it intact. Seven people died; the avalanche scar can still

Cross country skiing at Bretton Woods with Mt. Washington in the background.

be seen on the mountain. This park was established in 1911 when the state purchased the virgin spruce forest to save it from loggers' axes. Today there is a seasonal gift shop (selling New Hampshire-made craft items), a waterfowl pond, and a self-guided nature trail. Several major hiking trails begin within the park's borders.

Eisenhower Memorial Wayside Park is on Route 302, 2 miles above Crawford Notch. This small park is a tribute to the former president in whose honor one of the nearby mountains in the Presidential Range was named. A short walk leads to a magnificent view of mounts Eisenhower, Monroe, Washington, Jefferson, Adams, and Madison. The tracks of the Mt. Washington Cog Railway can be seen ascending the side of Washington, and sometimes a bit of smoke can be seen as one of the little engines puffs up the steep track.

GOLF   **Bretton Woods Golf Course** (278-1000), Route 302, Bretton Woods (at the Mt. Washington Hotel). Offers a total of 27 holes.

HIKING   Many hiking trails cross and parallel the notch. One is the Appalachian Trail—follow it north to Maine or south to Georgia. Consult the *AMC White Mountain Guide* for details of the many trails. Below are some less ambitious alternatives.

Arethusa Falls Trail is a 1.3-mile, one-hour, easy-to-moderate walk to New Hampshire's most impressive and highest waterfall, at its best in the spring and early summer when water is high. The well-marked trail begins on the east side of Route 302 near the southern entrance to the park. Silver Cascade, also a pretty waterfall, can be seen from your vehicle at the top of the notch where there is a parking lot and a scenic outlook.

Mt. Willard Trail begins at the AMC Crawford Notch Information Center, a year-round facility with rest rooms located in a restored railroad station just above the top of the notch. It is a 1.4-mile, one-hour walk, most of which is easy along a former carriage road. It leads to rocky ledges with a panoramic view down through Crawford Notch. The railroad station once served the old Crawford House, one of the earliest of the old hotels. It was closed in the 1970s and finally burned.

Saco Lake Trail (.4 mile, 15 minutes) is across the street from the information center. Saco Lake is the source of the river that flows through Crawford Notch, and behind it is Elephant Head, a rocky ridge shaped like a pachyderm.

Crawford Path, from Route 302 (opposite the Crawford House site) to Mt. Washington, is the oldest hiking trail in the country, built in 1819 by the Crawford family and used as a bridle path in the 1870s. Mt. Washington is a long 8.2-mile, six-hour walk. The AMC Mizpah Spring Hut (466-2727 for reservations) is a 2.5-mile, two-hour walk over the well-worn trail.

Ammonoosuc Ravine Trail (See Mt. Washington and Pinkham Notch [Hiking].)

HORSEBACK RIDING   Mt. Washington Hotel (278-1000), Route 302, Bretton Woods.The Mt. Washington Hotel's impressive stables offer unusually scenic trail rides, pitched to riders with at least some experience.

SNOWMOBILING   Large portions of the WMNF are off limits to snowmobiling, trail bikes, and off-road vehicles, but there are marked trails in Crawford Notch. A popular ride is along Mt. Clinton Road (begins opposite the Crawford House site on Route 302) to the Base Station Road and over the Jefferson Notch Road to Jefferson. (See the North Country [Scenic Drives].) For details contact the Trails Bureau, New Hampshire Division of Parks and Recreation (271-3254), Box 856, Concord 03301, or the New Hampshire Snowmobile Association (224-8906), Box 38, Concord 03301.

CROSS-COUNTRY SKIING   Bretton Woods Touring Center (278-5181) at the Mt. Washington Hotel, across Route 302 from the ski area. A shuttle service operates back and forth. The 86-km network is considered one of the best in New England and it's groomed for both touring and skating techniques. There are 39 trails, all mapped and marked, divided in three linked trail systems. One trail leads down from the summit of the alpine area.

Backcountry skiing is popular in the Zealand Valley, off Route 302 between Bretton Woods and Twin Mountain. Well-equipped and prepared skiers can schuss from Route 302 some 2.5 miles into the AMC Zealand Hut (466-2727), which is open all winter on a caretaker basis. Bring your own sleeping bag and food; use their cabin and cooking facilities.

DOWNHILL SKIING   Alpine Skiing Bretton Woods Ski Area (278-5000), Route 302, Bretton Woods. While it's not the most challenging ski area in New Hampshire, this is certainly one of the most enjoyable, and its 26 predominantly intermediate trails command magnificent views of the Mt. Washington Range. The vertical drop is 1,500 feet, and the longest run is 2 miles. Snowmaking covers 98 percent of the terrain, and the five lifts include two double chairs, a triple chair, and a detachable quad. Night skiing is offered every weekend, and the multi-tiered base lodge is unusually attractive.

LODGING   Lodging in Bretton Woods is all accessed by phoning 800-334-3910 or 278-1000 or 278-4000. The mailing address is Bretton Woods 03575. Additional lodging is available at Twin Mountain (See the Western Whites [Franconia and North of the Notch].)

The Mt. Washington Hotel, Route 302, Bretton Woods. Open Memorial Day to October. Everything about this hotel mirrors the scale of its majestic surroundings. The 174-room hotel rises like a white cruise ship from a surrounding sea of green woods, dwarfed only by its backdrop: New England's highest mountains. Its approach is up a mile-long drive, and the veranda is vast, the lobby high and columned, and the dining room grand, the menu immense. Amenities include indoor and outdoor pools, tennis courts, and a 27-hole golf course. $87.50-$275 per person. (See the introduction to this section for more about its history and present status.)

The Bretton Arms, Bretton Woods. A former annex of the Mt. Washington Hotel is a small, attractive inn with 34 rooms. $95-$150 per night.

The Lodge at Bretton Woods. The 50 rooms are all motel-style, large and pleasant with two double beds and TV. Amenities include an indoor pool, a spa pool and sauna, and comfortable common rooms with fireplaces. Its restaurant, Darby's (see Dining Out), serves breakfast as well as dinner. $60-$95 per night; $225 for five nights.

The Townhomes at Bretton Woods. A variety of one- to five-bedroom condominiums. $70-$305 per night.

BED & BREAKFAST   Mt. Washington Cog Railway B&B Chalet (summer 846-2256, year-round 846-5404), off Route 302, Bretton Woods 03595. Open all year, although call for details about lodging in the winter. Located at the Base Station of the Cog Railway, this chalet has five rooms, some with private baths. Various bed combinations allow some rooms to sleep four to six people. Surrounded by the national forest, with great views, this is a unique place to stay.

HOSTEL   Appalachian Mountain Club Shapleigh Hostel (466-2727), Route 302, north of Crawford Notch. Located in one of the remaining outbuildings of the old Crawford House, the hostel is open year-round on a caretaker basis with accommodations for 20 people plus 8 people each in two cabins which are heated with woodstoves. There is a self-service kitchen with cookware and utensils; bring a sleeping bag and food.

CAMPING   Camping is prohibited along the roadside in Crawford Notch State Park, but there are two campgrounds.

Dry River Campground, Route 302, Crawford Notch. A state-owned facility, open mid-May through mid-October, with 30 tent sites. No reservations.

Crawford Notch General Store and Campground (374-2779), Route 302 (south of Crawford Notch), Harts Location. The store sells gas, groceries, and hiking and camping supplies and is open all year; the campground, with wooded sites, tables, fireplaces, and hot showers, is open May through October.

EVANS NOTCH

Evans Notch is one of the lesser known of the White Mountain passes. Route 113 through the notch (not winter-maintained) connects Hastings, Maine (on Route 2 west of Shelburne, New Hampshire), with Chatham, New Hampshire, on the south. The best views in this notch are seen traveling from north to south. There are four campgrounds (see Camping) in the notch, many hiking trails, and good fishing along the Wild River.

GUIDANCE   **WMNF Androscoggin Ranger Station** (466-2713), Route 16, Gorham. Open Monday to Friday 7:30–4:30.

WMNF Evans Notch District (207-824-2134), Bridge Street, RFD 2, Box 2270, Bethel, ME 04217. Open Monday to Friday 7:30–4:30.

CAMPING   **WMNF Campgrounds,** Evans Notch. Seventy-seven wooded sites. Four of the campgrounds are open all year; and three—Hastings, Cold River, and Basin—are part of the toll-free reservation system (see Mt. Washington and Pinkham Notch [Camping]).

The Western Whites

New England's highest mountains march in a ragged line, heading diagonally northeast across New Hampshire, beginning near the Connecticut River with Mt. Moosilauke. This spectacular mountain region divides simply into "The Mt. Washington Area" and "The Western White Mountains."

The heart of these "Western Whites" is Franconia Notch, a high pass between the granite walls of Cannon Mountain and Mt. Lafayette. Here I-93 narrows into the Franconia Notch Parkway, and visitors frequently spend a day viewing the stony profile of Old Man of the Mountain, exploring the "Flume," the "Pool," and Avalanche Falls, maybe taking the aerial tram to the top of Cannon Mountain or taking a swim in Echo Lake, ideally hiking at least up to Lonesome Lake.

A footpath from the Notch to the top of Mt. Lafayette is said to have been blazed as early as 1825, the year the area's first hotel opened. By the 1880s it was served by a narrow gauge railroad; and The Profile House, the largest of several hotels here, could accommodate 500 guests. The villages of Franconia and Bethlehem—just north of the Notch and of North Woodstock, just east of Kinsman Notch as well as south of Franconia Notch—also had their share of elaborate summer hotels.

The area's steep, heavily wooded mountains were even more enticing to loggers than to tourists. While early conservationists fought to preserve the "notches" and "gorges," lumber companies built wilderness railways and employed small armies of men to clear-cut vast tracts. Legendary lumberman James E. Henry transformed the little outpost of Lincoln, with 110 residents in 1890, into a booming logging center of 1,278 by 1910. His J. E. Henry Company owned 115,000 acres of virgin timber along the East Branch of the Pemigewasset River, reducing much of it to pulp.

This Pemigewasset ("Pemi") area became part of the White Mountain National Forest in the mid-1930s. It was still being logged in 1923 when Sherman Adams came to Lincoln to work for the Parker-

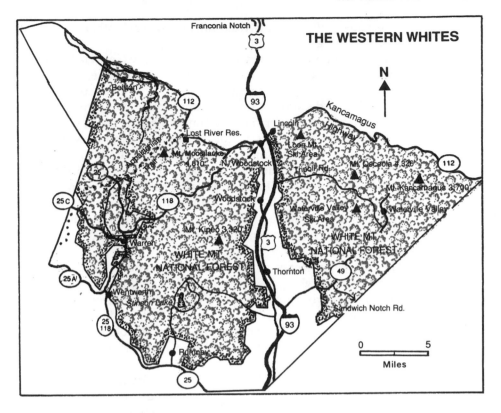

THE WESTERN WHITES

Young Co., J. E. Henry's successor. Over the next 20 years Adams came to know the valley intimately, and when he returned to Lincoln in the 1960s—after having served as New Hampshire's governor and President Eisenhower's chief of staff—Adams opened Loon Mountain Ski Area.

In that same month another public figure—young ex-Olympian skier Tom Corcoran—opened another ski area less than a dozen miles away (as the crow flies) in Waterville Valley. Up in Franconia Notch state-run Cannon Mountain's aerial tramway and steep slopes had been attracting skiers since 1938, but these newcomers both represented something new—rather than just "ski areas," both were "ski resorts," spawning new communities.

Dictated both by the personalities of their founders and the lay of their land, Loon Mountain and Waterville Valley have, however, developed differently.

Conservative Adams saw his business as running a ski area and left condominium development to others. Corcoran, fresh from Aspen, planned a self-contained, Rockies-style resort from the start. Loon's facilities, moreover, lined a narrow shelf of land above the Pemigewasset River on the edge of a mill town, while Waterville was in an isolated valley with two ski hills facing each other across 500 acres just waiting to be filled.

Loon Mountain and Waterville Valley are now New Hampshire's largest, liveliest ski resorts. The abundance of attractive, reasonably priced, off-season condo-lodging is contributing to an interesting phenomenon: After decades as a pass-through place, this area (still with Franconia Notch as center ring and myriad hiking trails, waterfalls, and other natural attractions as sideshows) is once more becoming as popular a summer destination today as it was in the 1890s.

But the "beaten track" through the Western Whites remains delightfully narrow. The quiet old resort villages of Bethlehem, Franconia, and Sugar Hill have changed little in many decades, and the Ammonoosuc Valley has a distinctly hidden-away feel. Farther south, the Baker River Valley offers another little-traveled, scenic byway through the mountains.

The full magnificence of the mountains themselves can only be appreciated by climbing (or riding) to their summits, but the beauty of their high, narrow notches and hidden valleys is accessible to all.

GUIDANCE   **The White Mountains Visitor Center** (745-8720), Route 112 (mailing: PO Box 10, North Woodstock 03262), Lincoln. Open 8:30–5 daily. A walk-in facility (just off I-93 Exit 32) displaying brochures and offering information for this entire area.

Ski 93 Association (745-8101), PO Box 517, Lincoln 03251. Based at the White Mountains Visitor Center. Promotes Cannon, Loon, and Waterville Valley ski areas; also Bretton Woods (see Mt. Washington's Valleys). Its reservation service works with some 75 local lodging places and specializes in combined ski and lodging packages.

Chambers of commerce are also listed under Guidance within each section of this chapter: Lincoln and North Woodstock, the Waterville Valley, and Plymouth and the Baker River Valley.

LINCOLN AND NORTH WOODSTOCK

North Woodstock is a sleepy village. Lincoln, a mile east, is one of New Hampshire's liveliest resort villages. But until relatively recently, the opposite was true.

Around the turn of the century, Lincoln boomed into existence as a company town with a company-owned school, store, hotel, hospital, and housing for hundreds of workers, all built by the legendary lumber baron J. E. Henry. And it remained a smoke-belching "mill town" well into the 1970s.

North Woodstock, set against two dramatic notches—Kinsman and Franconia—boasted a half-dozen large hotels, among them the Deer Park, accommodating 250 guests.

Photo by Dorothy Crossley

Ski trails and condominiums at Loon Mountain, Lincoln.

Today Deer Park is still a familiar name but only as one of the dozen major condominium complexes that have recently become synonymous with this area. With Loon Mountain as its centerpiece, Lincoln/Woodstock now has a bed base (the buzz word for visitors' pillows) of 13,000, more than eight times what it offered a decade ago.

Loon Mountain was a success from the start, opening in 1966 with a gondola, two chairlifts, an octagonal base lodge, and the then unheard-of policy of limiting lift ticket sales. Then in 1973, I-93 reached Lincoln, depositing skiers 3 miles from the lifts. But it wasn't until the early 1980s that the town of Lincoln itself began to boom.

"Three things came together then," observes Phil Gravink, President and General Manager of Loon Mountain Recreation Corp. All the land owned by the paper mill (see the Western Whites Introduction), which had closed in 1979, suddenly became available. Loon itself had grown into a substantial ski area, and a real estate boom was sweeping New Hampshire's lakes and mountains. Positioned just south of Franconia Notch and surrounded by national forest, Lincoln was a developer's dream: relatively cheap land with no zoning.

A heady few years ensued, but now they're over. Zoning has since been imposed, and Lincoln is adjusting to its new status as a major, year-round destination—one that can accommodate as many visitors as any resort in northern New England.

GUIDANCE   **Lincoln-Woodstock Chamber of Commerce** (745-6621 or 800-227-4191), Box 358, Lincoln 03251. A helpful, walk-in information center on Main Street, middle of the village; also a reservation service for the area.

White Mountains Visitors Center (745-8720), Route 112 just off I-93, North Woodstock. Open daily 8:30–5. A walk-in information center for the entire western White Mountains region.

GETTING THERE   By bus: **Concord Trailways** (800-852-3317) provides daily service to and from Concord, Manchester, and Boston, stopping at the **Hobo Railroad** (745-2135), Main Street, Lincoln.

For **Vermont Transit,** offering east/west service to St. Johnsbury, VT and Portland, ME, see Franconia Notch and North (Bethlehem).

GETTING AROUND   Shuttle service within Lincoln makes coming by bus a viable option, especially during ski season when the **Loon Mountain Shuttle** serves most inns and condo complexes around town.

The Shuttle Connection (745-8888 or 800-648-4947) requires 24-hour advance notice but serves Manchester Airport as well as local destinations year-round.

MEDICAL EMERGENCY   **Speare Memorial Hospital** (536-1120), Hospital Road, Plymouth, or **Littleton Hospital** (444-7731), 107 Cottage Street, Littleton.

TO SEE AND DO   **Lost River Reservation** (745-8031), Route 112, 7 miles west of North Woodstock. Open mid-May to late October, weather permitting, 9–5:30. This was the first acquisition of the Society for the Protection of New Hampshire Forests, purchased from a local timber company in 1912. The Nature Garden here is said to feature over 200 varieties of native plants, and the glacial meltwater gorge is spectacular. Boardwalks thread a series of basins and caves, past rock formations with names like Guillotine Rock and Hall of Ships. Now maintained by the White Mountains Attractions, the complex includes a snack bar and gift shop. $5.50 per adult, $2.75 for children ages 6–12.

Indian Head. Like the Old Man of the Mountains, this craggy profile on Mt. Pemigewasset, visible from Route 3, is an old local landmark. Admittedly it needs a chin trim: fir trees have grown up, partially obscuring it. Best seen from the Route 3 parking lot of the Indian Head Resort. The summit is accessible via the Mt. Pemigewasset Trail, which starts off the Franconia Notch bike path just north of the Flume Visitors Center (see Franconia and North of the Notches).

Clark's Trading Post (745-8913), Route 3, Lincoln. Open daily July through Labor Day, 10–6; weekends Memorial Day through mid-October. One of the country's oldest theme parks, begun in the '20s as a dog ranch (Florence Clark was the first woman to reach the summit of Mt. Washington by dog sled). Still owned and managed by the Clark family, known for trained bear shows (July and August); also featuring a haunted house, Avery's old-time garage and the 1890s fire station, a photo parlor, bumper boats, and Merlin's Mystical Mansion. $6 adults, $4 children.

Upper Pemigewasset Historical Society (745-2268 745-2281), Church Street, Lincoln. June 15 to Columbus Day, Sunday 2–4; call for other hours. A small museum with photographs and artifacts dramatizing the logging history of the Upper Pemi Valley.

FOR FAMILIES   **The Whale's Tale Waterpark** (745-8810), Route 3, Lincoln. Open late June to Labor Day daily, weekends from Memorial Day. Wave pool, speed and curvy slides, wading pool for small children, tube rentals. $14 per person. Children under 35 inches tall and seniors over age 70, free.

GREEN SPACE   **Agassiz Basin,** west of North Woodstock on Route 112, just below Govoni's Italian Restaurant. Natural steps lead down to a suspension bridge across Moosilauke Brook, a great picnic spot.

Beaver Pond, Route 112 west from North Woodstock in Kinsman Notch, beyond Lost River. A beautiful pond with a rock promontory for picnicking or sunning and a view of Mt. Blue.

(For Franconia Notch see Franconia and North of the Notches.)

SCENIC DRIVES   *The Kancamagus National Scenic Byway:*   Open year-round, this is the 34 1/2-mile stretch of Route 112 east from Lincoln to Conway (Route 16) through the White Mountain National Forest. Officially recognized as one of the most scenic highways in the country, it climbs to 2,855 feet in elevation at the Kancamagus Pass, the ridge line dividing two watersheds. (Streams run downhill west to the Pemigewasset and east into the Saco.) This is also the point considered the heart of the White Mountains, which, we're told, stretch for a radius of 35 miles in all directions.

The highway was completed in 1959 after 25 years in the building. It offers four scenic overlooks, four picnic sites, a half-dozen campgrounds (see Camping), several scenic areas, and access to myriad hiking trails ranging from the .5-mile Rail 'N' River Trail to multi-day treks into the Pemigewasset Wilderness.

Before setting out from Lincoln, you might want to stop at the White Mountains Visitors Center (see Guidance) where you can pick up a map/guide to the highway and detailed sheets on specific trails and campgrounds. July fourth through Labor Day, Forest Service visitor information specialists are also here on weekends to steer would-be campers to vacant sites and hikers to appropriate trails.

For a detailed description of the highway see "The White Mountain National Forest" chapter.

For detailed descriptions of longer hikes from the "Kanc" consult the *AMC White Mountains Guide;* descriptions of individual trails are available from the White Mountains Visitors Center and the Saco Ranger Station.

Tripoli Road: Pronounced "Triple Eye," this shortcut from I-93 (Exit 31) Woodstock to Waterville Valley accesses a number of hiking trails and campsites. It is also a fine foliage season loop, returning to Woodstock via routes 49 and 175. See the Waterville Valley section.

Kinsman Notch: Route 112 west from North Woodstock is less traveled but as beautiful as the Kancamagus, climbing quickly into Kinsman Notch, past Beaver Pond (see Green Space) and Lost River (see To See and Do), crossing the Appalachian Trail. You can continue on by the Wildwood Campground to Mt. Moosilauke (see Hiking) or cut up Route 116 to Easton, Sugar Hill, and Franconia and back down through Franconia Notch. Another option is to take the dirt "North/South" road off Route 116 beyond Kinsman Notch, through the National Forest to Long Pond where there is a boat launch and, we're told, good fishing; also picnic sites. You can return to Route 116 or continue on to Route 25.

Route 118 west from North Woodstock climbs steeply through the national forest, then down into the Baker River Valley. You may want to stop at the **Morse Museum** in Warren and **Polar Caves** in Plymouth and cut back up I-93; or take Route 25 to Haverhill with its handsome old village center (just south of the junction of routes 25 and 10), returning via routes 116 and 112 through Kinsman Notch.

AERIAL RIDES   Loon Mountain Gondola Ride (745-8111). Ride to the summit where there's an observation tower, a summit cafeteria, summit cave walk, hiking trails. $7.50 per adult, $3 per child ages 6–12.

Also see Franconia and North of the Notches (Green Space) for Cannon Mountain's Aerial Tramway.

BICYCLING   Loon Mountain Bike Center (745-8111), Lincoln. Open Memorial Day to late October. Mountain bike rentals, guided group tours, 30 kilometers of cross-country trails along the Pemigewasset River ($5 trail fee), inn-to-inn tours.

The Franconia Notch Bike Path is a favorite loop (12 miles round-trip).

CAMPING   The campgrounds along the Kancamagus Highway are among the most popular in the White Mountain National Forest and accessible only on a first-come, first-served basis.

Russell Pond Campground (800-283-CAMP), off Tripoli Road, 3.7 miles east of Exit 31, North Woodstock. Open April through October. Eighty-seven sites on a 40-acre pond, good for swimming (no lifeguard) and fishing; Saturday evening interpretive nature programs. Reservations may be made up to 120 days in advance. $8 per day.

In the Pemigewasset Region (536-1310). **Hancock** (4 miles east of Lincoln) is open year-round with 56 sites, $8 per day; and **Big Rock**

(6 miles east of Lincoln) is open year-round with 23 sites, $8 per day.

In the Saco Region (447-5448). **Passaconaway** has 33 sites, $8 per day; **Jigger Johnson** has 75 sites, $8 per day; **Covered Bridge** has 49 sites, $8 per day; and **Blackberry Crossing** has 26 sites, $7 per day.

In the Ammonoosuc Region (869-2626). **Wildwood** is open mid-April through early December. Offers 26 campsites, good fishing.

(See the Waterville Valley section and the Franconia and North of the Notches chapter for more White Mountain National Forest campsites.)

FISHING   The free *Freshwater Fishing Guide* is available at local information centers. Fishermen frequent the East Branch of the Pemi, Russell Pond, and many mountain streams.

HIKING   **Mt. Moosilauke.** The Benton Trail and Tunnel Brook Trail ascend the northwest flank of Mt. Moosilauke at a steady, moderate grade. It's 3.5 miles to the summit (4,802 feet), which offers one of the most extensive views in New Hampshire. The trail begins in a parking area off the Tunnel Brook Road; take Route 112 west from North Woodstock, 1.5 miles.

Greeley Ponds. This easy trail is 4 1/2 miles round-trip, beginning on the Kancamagus Highway, 9 miles east of Lincoln. As local hiking guru Steve Smith describes it: The trail climbs gradually to the high point of Mad River Notch, then dips down to Upper Greeley Pond, a deep tarn hemmed in by the cliff-studded slopes of Mt. Osceola's East Peak and Mt. Kancamagus. A half mile farther you reach the south shore of boggy Lower Greeley Pond, where you can look north into the cleft of the notch.

Also see Scenic Drives, the Waterville Valley section, and the Franconia and North of the Notches chapter for other brief trail descriptions.

Detailed descriptions of these hikes are found in *Fifty Hikes in the White Mountains* by Daniel Doan (Backcountry Publications) and in the *AMC White Mountain Guide*.

HORSEBACK RIDING   **Loon Mountain** (745-8111). July and August. Trail rides offered.

GOLF   **Jack O'Lantern Country Club** (745-3636), Route 3, Woodstock. Eighteen-hole, par 70 course, instruction, rental clubs, golf carts, and pull carts.

MINIATURE GOLF   **White Mountain Miniature Golf** (745-2777), Route 3, Lincoln. Open mid-June to Labor Day, daily 1–10; weekends and mid-week evenings during shoulder seasons. Grass-carpeted, 18-hole course.

Hobo Hills Adventure Golf (745-2135), Main Street, Lincoln. Open daily June to Labor Day, weekends in spring and fall. Eighteen holes with hills and water.

RAILROAD EXCURSIONS   **Hobo Railroad** (745-2135), Hobo Junction (just east of I-93), Lincoln. Open Memorial Day through Halloween; daily

July to Labor Day, otherwise weekends; again weekends Thanksgiving to Christmas. A 15-mile round-trip excursion along the Pemigewasset River in "dining coaches" with velour seats and tables. $7 per adult, $4.50 per child. Optional breakfast, picnic lunch, dinner.

Café Lafayette, the deluxe dining car service on the Hobo Railroad, leaves Lincoln at 6:30 PM during summer months (see also Dining Out).

SWIMMING   The Mountain Club Fitness Center at Loon Mountain (745-8111), Route 112, Lincoln. Open 7 AM–10 PM daily. Indoor lap pool, outdoor pool in summer.

Swimming holes. "The Lady's Bathtub," in the Pemi, Lincoln. Maybe 15 feet deep, fringed with a little sand, accessible through the parking lot at Lincoln Station.

In North Woodstock **the Cascades** is a favorite dunking spot in the Pemi right behind Main Street. Other spot along the Pemi can be found along Route 175 in Woodstock. One is just across from the Tripoli Road, I-93 interchange.

TENNIS   Indian Head Resort (745-8000). Outdoor tennis courts.

Mountain Club. Loon also offers outdoor courts.

CROSS-COUNTRY SKIING   Loon Mountain (745-8111). Thirty-five km of trails, some winding part way up the mountain, others following the river bed. Rentals, instructions, special events. Trail fee $7.

Wilderness Trail. Off the Kancamagus, a large parking lot on the left is your clue to a major ungroomed cross-country system maintained by the Forest Service. The visitors center here is maintained on a limited basis in winter.

DOWNHILL SKIING   Loon Mountain (745-8111), 2 miles from I-93 Exit 32, Lincoln. With its long cruising trails and easy access, Loon attracts more skiers per year than any other New Hampshire ski area. It is a nicely designed mountain with dozens of intermediate trails streaking its face and a choice of steeply pitched trails, served by their own high altitude East Basin chairlift, on North Peak. Beginners have the Little Sister chair and slope to themselves, then graduate to a choice of equally isolated (from hot-rod skiers) runs in the West Basin. The only hitch is that the main base area and West Basin are separated by a long, stringbean-shaped parking lot. The lay of the land dictates the strung-out shape of Loon's base facilities—which line a narrow shelf along the Pemigewasset River—which in turn has cut this steep Upper Pemi Valley.

The one big hitch to skiing Loon is securing a lift ticket. Since 1966 its limited ticket policy has insured that lift lines are kept to 15 minutes or under, but this means that tickets are frequently unavailable by 8:30 AM on weekends and holidays. Tickets are available in advance through local inns and condos, by ordering on a "Loon Reservation Card" ($35), through Ticketron, and in Lincoln the day before (2–10 PM). Next-day tickets may also be purchased daily at the ticket window from 3–5 PM weekdays, 3–9 PM Friday, Saturday, and vacations.

Obviously the demand for Loon to expand is large, but the corporation's long-standing plans to double its ski terrain (with an eventual buildout on some 900 acres of national forest on adjacent South Mountain) have been stymied by National Environmental Protection Agency review boards. At this writing a scaled-down expansion is expected to be approved in 1991.

Trails number 41 with 25 percent easiest, 55 percent more difficult, 20 percent most difficult (22 miles total); vertical drop of 2,100 feet; snowmaking covers 85 percent of total top-to-bottom terrain. Lifts include a four-passenger gondola, two triple chairs, five double chairs, and one surface. Facilities include two base lodges, three lounges, two rental shops, summit cafeteria, and mid-mountain lodge (Camp 3) at the base of North Peak. Slopeside lodging at the 234-room Mountain Club includes condo units, indoor pool, game rooms, and restaurants; ice skating, cross-country skiing..The ski school has 170 full- and part-time instructors, modified ATM system, freestyle, mountain challenge, and NASTAR. For children there is the Loon Mountain Nursery for ages six weeks to six years; Honeybears SKIwee (ages 3–5), Bear Cubs SKIwee (ages 6–8), Mountain Explorers (ages 9–12). Rates: $34 adult weekends (all chairs), $38 for gondola; $30 adult weekdays; $20 junior; also multi-day rates.

ICE SKATING   Loon Mountain Recreation Corporation (745-8111) maintains a lighted rink near the main base lodge.

SLEIGH RIDES   Sleigh Rides (745-3603) depart regularly from the front of the Millfront Marketplace. See also Franconia and North of the Notches.

SNOWMOBILING   Trail maps available locally detail the extensive local system.

RESORTS   All resorts listed are in Lincoln 03251.

The Mountain Club on Loon (745-8111 or 800-433-3413), With 234 rooms, this is New England's largest, most elaborate slopeside hotel. Bellmen hover and the front desk is always covered. The two-tiered lobby has a crackling hearth and a concierge. Cars are parked in the garage on arrival and needn't budge until departure. Guests can wake up to a room service breakfast and ski in at noon to pop a frozen pizza in the microwave, drop by the sauna and pool, play some racquetball before dinner. The skating rink and cross-country trails are also within walking distance. In summer a full program of activities is also available. Babysitters are available, and older children keep busy enough with video games and table tennis in the game room, then a movie on the VCR in their "unit" to free parents to dine in Rachel's, the hotel dining room. From $65 (for a standard, double room) to $120 (for a "studio" with kitchen) in spring and early summer; $145–$225 for a Mountain Club Suite (up to four people) during ski season; less in summer, packages available.

The Mill House Inn (800-654-6183), Route 112. A 95-room hotel built from scratch but connected (a luxury in winter) to the Millfront Marketplace (see Selective Shopping), a complex that incorporates three of the old paper mill buildings. Positioned to be at the entrance to the proposed South Mountain addition to Loon Mountain, it is connected to the ski area in winter by its own, as well as by Loon's, shuttle. Amenities include indoor and outdoor pools, saunas, Jacuzzis, and exercise room. Some suites have kitchen facilities but most are simply spacious one- or two-room, nicely designed spaces with phones and color cable TVs. Downstairs public spaces include a library and ample comfortable corners. Doubles are $49–$79 in spring and $69–$109 during ski season; family suites (with a separate room with bunks for children, sleeping up to six) are $109–$169 in ski season; $119–$189 on weekends. Five-day summer vacation packages are $595 for a family of four, including selected daily meals and other perks. Many packages.

Rivergreen Condominiums at The Mill (754-2450 or 800-654-6183), PO Box 1056, Route 112. A separate building, unattached to the Mill House Inn or the marketplace but part of the same complex. Kitchen units $80 (sleeping two people), $120 (sleeping four), $125 (sleeping six); more on weekends; weekly and package rates available.

The Village of Loon Mountain (745-3401 or 800-258-8932). Of the 650 units here, 200 are in the rental pool. Positioned directly across the road from Loon Mountain, this development is nicely designed to blend into the hillside. Amenities include 2 indoor pools, 12 outdoor tennis courts (2 flooded to form a skating rink in winter), a kids' game room with arcade, and table tennis. From $75 per person with a two-night minimum on winter weekends.

Deer Park (745-9040), PO Box 1177. Just 30 units in the elaborate complex are in the rental pool, but the sports facilities, although due to reopen, are closed at this writing. From $195 for a one-bedroom unit (sleeping four) on winter weekends, minimum two-night stay.

RESORT MOTELS   **Indian Head Resort** (745-8000 or 800-343-8000), Lincoln 03251. First opened in the 1920s, gradually evolving to its present 90 motel rooms, 50 cabins (with fireplaces). Indoor and outdoor heated pools, tennis courts, game room, coffee shop, and dining room. From $109 double MAP or from $58 weekdays and $76 weekends per room only.

Woodward's Motor Inn (745-8141), Route 3, Lincoln 03251. Closed between foliage and ski season and in spring. An 80-room complex that has grown gradually over the past 39 years, carefully managed by the Woodward family. Amenities include indoor and outdoor pools and an indoor racquetball court. In summer there are also lawn games. The Colonial Dining Room serves breakfast daily, and dinner is served nightly in the Open Hearth Dining Room; there's also a lounge. $78 per room; MAP rates, packages, off-season prices.

Jack O'Lantern Resort (745-3636), North Woodstock 03262. Closed between foliage and ski season, again in spring. Another landmark local motel that has evolved into a resort with 25 motel rooms, 50 one- to three-room cottages and condominiums. Amenities include a pool, tennis, Jacuzzi, 18-hole golf course. $117–$152 double in summer with breakfast and dinner; $74–$152, no meals, in winter.

INN   **The Woodstock Inn** (745-3951), PO Box 18, Main Street (Route 3), North Woodstock 03262. Known for both its formal dining (on the glassed-in front porch) and informal dining (in Woodstock Station out back; see Dining Out), this is also a comfortable inn with six, antiques furnished rooms (sharing three baths) in the main house; another eight in Riverside, each with private bath and access to a porch overlooking the river; most of these have separate living room and bedroom areas. From $45 for "Agassiz," a large front room with twin beds and a sitting room in the house, to $56 for the tower room in Riverside. $68–$78 at peak times; packages available.

BED & BREAKFAST   **The Birches** (745-6603), Route 175, Box 59, North Woodstock 03262. Former schoolteacher Ruth Ballmer offers her guests a sense of what it's like to live in an unusually spacious, sun-filled house on the banks of the Pemigewasset. But you must like dogs—Ms. Ballmer breeds large, well-behaved Bernese Mountain dogs. Request the tower room. Rates for the three rooms range from $60–$70 most of the year, $70 during ski season; 10 percent from three nights.

MOTEL   **Franconia Notch Motel** (745-2229), Route 3, Lincoln 03251. The nicest kind of family-run motel: 6 two-room cottages (summer only) and 12 standard motel units, backing on the Pemigewasset River where picnic tables and grills are in place. Franconia Notch State Park is a half mile up the road. Each unit is different; most have twin beds. One small single with a view of the river is $38; room with twins is $48–$65. Board games and morning coffee are available.

OTHER LODGING   **The Ledges Hostel** (745-8433), Route 3, Woodstock 03293. A cheery and companionable lodging place for hikers to find ample information about local trails as well as a comfortable bunk, kitchen privileges, canoe rentals; bikers and skiers also welcome. $25–$30 weekends, less midweek.

DINING OUT   **The Woodstock Inn** (745-3951), Route 3, North Woodstock 03262. Open nightly and for Sunday brunch. The Clement Room, a glassed-in porch set crisply with white linen tablecloths and fine china, is the setting for the finest dining in Lincoln-Woodstock. The menu is several pages. Poultry includes roast duckling ($16.95) and a half dozen chicken dishes. Beef Wellington ($19.25) is a specialty along with nine versions of veal and fresh seafood (where else in northern

New Hampshire can you find fresh Norwegian salmon poached in herb cream with sun-dried tomatoes and fresh asparagus?). Other specialties include fresh wild game and charbroiled lamb chops. The entrée price includes a house appetizer, salad, sorbet, breads, and starch.

Rachel's (745-8111) in the Mountain Club at Loon Mountain. Open daily 11:30–9. Named for Mrs. Sherman Adams and decorated with her paintings. Standard crowd pleasers like broiled scallops ($12.95), veal marsala ($12.95), and daily specials (Friday and Saturday: prime rib, governor's cut for $14.95). Burgers, salads, and nachos also available—choose from Franconia, Crawford, and Kinsman "Notchos."

The Tavern at the Mill (745-3603), Millfront Market Place, Route 112, Lincoln. Family restaurant prices but a pleasant, brick-walled, dimly lighted, multi-tiered place in a part of the original mill; a piano bar that's the liveliest place in town on ski weekends. The vast menu ranges from pasta to blackened prime rib to fresh poached salmon to chicken teriyaki to Fajita Falmeado (huge, gloppy, and delicious) to lemon pepper chicken salad. Most entrées are under $10.

Dickens at the Village of Loon Mountain (745-6335), Route 112, Lincoln. Open nightly from 5 PM. A family-priced restaurant with some real flare: the French onion soup comes in a crock and the cheese topping is seasoned with wine. Entrées include veal dijonnaise (sautéed medallions of veal finished with white wine, shallots, cream, and Dijon mustard. Entrées average $12. The children's menu includes meatballs and pasta for $2.95.

Gordi's Fish and Steak House (745-6635), Route 112, Lincoln. The decor is glitzy Victorian mixed with photos of ski heros past and present (the owners include two past members of Olympic ski teams). The specialties are lobster (note the tank), seafood, and beef. You can also make a meal of the salad bar. Most entrées are under $14.

The Common Man (745-3463), at the corner of Pollard Road and Main Street, Lincoln. Open nightly except Thanksgiving and Christmas. The winning formula here is a limited menu stressing simplicity and fresh ingredients: broiled and grilled swordfish, freshly made pastas, spare ribs, steaks, chicken Kiev. Most entrées under $14.

Eugenio's Italian Cuisine (745-6798), Lincoln Center North, Main Street, Lincoln. Open daily for lunch and dinner. A great place for pasta lovers—real pasta that is. Try the seafood pesto. The large menu ranges from burgers at lunch to steak au poivre at dinner, and the decor is elaborate: etched-glass, stenciling, tiffany lamps.

Govoni's Italian Restaurant (745-8042), Lost River Road, Route 112 west of North Woodstock. Open nightly from Memorial Day to Labor Day. Northern Italian specialties served in a traditional New Hampshire house overlooking Agassiz Basin.

Café Lafayette (745-2135 or 745-3500), on the Hobo Railroad, Hobo

Junction, Lincoln. The typical set menu on this excursion run in a vintage 1924 Pullman Railroad Car begins with caviar or pâté, proceeds through maison and sorbet to a choice of "poulet," salmon or filet mignon. (See also To See and Do.)

EATING OUT **Woodstock Station** (745-3951), at the Woodstock Inn, Main Street, North Woodstock. This railroad station was built in the late 1800s in Lincoln, continuing to serve tourists—including skiers bound for Cannon Mountain—in the 1930s and 1940s. In 1984 it was sawed in half and moved to its present location; the old freight room is now the bar and the passenger waiting room is the lower dining room. This large, eclectically furnished space is one of the liveliest dining spaces in the North Country, and the menu is immense: everything from escargot ($5.75) and frogs' legs ($5.95) to Peking ravioli to quesadilla to nachos and burritos (lots of Mexican) to a wide choice of original sandwiches (the croute route sandwiches cheeses, ham, and smoked turkey with garlic cheese sauce between layers of puff pastry) to pastas to baked scrod to ribs and burgers. The children's menu includes a $2.50 hot dog. Beverages fill four more pages of the menu and include a wide variety of imported beers.

Truants Taverne (745-2239), Main Street, North Woodstock. Open daily from 11:30 AM–10 PM ("or so"). Hung over the river in a back-behind kind of space, part of an old millyard. Polished pine tables and a large menu that's fun to read: for lunch choose from the Class Bully, the Salutarian, the Class Clown, the Elementary Burger, or maybe the Exchange Student (a flour tortilla stuffed with spicy beef, cheese, and sour cream, etc.). At dinner the Dan's List includes veal marsala ($11.50) but you can also scrape by with that old Exchange Student or Elementary Burger. A good place.

Jasmann's in the Millyard Marketplace. Despite its location in a corner of the mill mall, there is an obvious sense of someone hard at work caring about what they produce here, everything from BLTs with avocado ($3.25) and tuna salad (made with albacore tuna only) to a nifty spinach salad and freshly roasted turkey melt. Twenty gourmet coffees are offered.

Donny G's, in the Millfront Marketplace. A '50s-style place with a good family-priced menu.

Elvio's Pizzeria (745-8817), 117 Main Street, Lincoln. "Best pizza north of the Bronx." The best pizza in town; subs and basic Italian dinners to go, too.

Breakfast in North Woodstock: **Woodstock Inn** (745-3951), Main Street, Lincoln. A wide range of waffles, omelets and other memorable breakfast fare—like homemade red flannel hash, poached egg, and home fries.

Wilderness Inn and Cafe (745-3890). Freshly ground coffee, homemade muffins, selected hot crêpes, omelets.

ENTERTAINMENT   North Country Center for the Arts (745-2141), The Mill at
Loon Mountain Late June through mid-October. Musicals, comedy,
classics, children's theater, Wednesdays at 11 AM and 1:30 PM ($3.50
tickets). Machine Room #1 of the old Franconia Paper Mill is now a
250-seat theatre, and plans call to convert the former Finishing Room
into a 475-seat theater. Tickets for Main Stage productions run $11–$16.

Lincoln Cinemas 4 (745-6238), Lincoln Center North, Main Street,
Lincoln. Four screens.

Summer band concerts. Wednesday evenings at the Gazebo,
Lincoln. Also regularly on the common in North Woodstock.

Loon Mountain Lecture Series (745-8111). Saturday evenings during the summer. The North Country Chamber Players also perform
regularly at the Governor's Lodge during summer months.

SELECTIVE SHOPPING   Pinestead Quilts (745-8640), 99 Main Street, Lincoln.
An unusual selection of locally made quilts, machine-pieced but hand-
tied, traditional designs. From $65 for quilted wraps to $650 for king
size.

Lahout's Country Clothing and Ski Shop, Inc., Main Street,
Lincoln. Open daily. A branch of the Littleton store opened in 1922
and was billed as "the oldest, continually operated ski shop in New
England." Operated by the three sons of the original Lahout and dedicated to "beating anyone's price," this is unquestionably one of THE
places in the North Country to shop for ski gear, sturdy footwear, long
johns, etc., etc.

Rodgers Ski Outlet, Main Street, Lincoln. Open daily 7 AM–9 PM.
"Lawho?" the competition may well ask if you mention Lahout's.
Over 1,500 pairs of skis in stock at any time; tune-ups, rentals, repairs
are the specialties. Billed as "Northern New England's largest volume
ski shop."

The North Face, Main Street, Lincoln. This Berkeley, California-
based company claims to be the largest manufacturer of its kind of
sports equipment—tents, skiwear, backpacks, etc.—in the world.
While its products are available in all major sports stores, this is its
only outlet in the northeast: a large space filled with sportswear, skiwear, sleeping bags, and technical outerwear at savings of 20 to 50
percent.

League of New Hampshire Craftsmen (745-2166), Main Street
Marketplace, Lincoln. Open daily 10–6. A nonprofit gallery showcasing quality crafts.

Fadden's General Store, Main Street, North Woodstock. Open
daily 7 AM–12 PM. One of the few genuine old-time general stores left
in New England (now run by the third generation of Faddens), filled
with genuine relics of storekeeping past; also an amazing assortment
of current stock.

Antiques, Crafts and Collectibles (745-8111), at Loon Mountain.

Open daily late May through October. More than 50 dealers exhibiting furniture and furnishings, stained glass, pottery, crafts, and more.

Deke's Sport House, Route 112, Lincoln. Ski, bike, and tennis sales; rentals; fishing, hiking, and camping equipment.

Dick's Dugout, Main Street, North Woodstock. A baseball card collector's oasis.

The Depot, Route 112, Lincoln. Factory outlets here include All Seasons (sportswear), Kids Port USA, and Timberland.

Millfront Marketplace. Twenty-three shops and restaurants in a complex incorporating three turn-of-the-century mill buildings. The complex includes:

The Country Carriage. "Country" gifts, reproduction furniture, tinware, collectible dolls, etc.

Innisfree Bookshop (745-6107). The only full-service bookstore in the region, specializing in New England titles, White Mountain guides and trail maps, ski titles, field guides, and children's books.

Carroll Reed Ski & Sport Shop. Ski gear and skiwear, ski rentals and service, tennis equipment, clothing.

SPECIAL EVENTS   January: **Mid-winter Snowfest,** Lincoln/Woodstock. A full week of festivities.

February: **Snowmobile Easter Seal ride**.

March: **Spring Fling** at Loon Mountain.

June: **Annual Fiddlers Contest,** sponsored by Lincoln-Woodstock Lions Club.

July: **Fourth of July Celebration,** Lincoln-Woodstock. **Arts and Crafts Fair** at Loon Mountain.

September: **New Hampshire Highland Games,** Loon Mountain.

October: **Fall Foliage Festival** at Loon Mountain

THE WATERVILLE VALLEY

This valley is a 10-mile deep cul-de-sac cut by one of New England's many Mad Rivers and circled by majestic mountains, many of them more than 4,000 feet tall.

Since 1835, the year the village's population peaked, urbanites have been coming here for R & R. By 1868 there were enough people to fill a green-shuttered inn. Less luxurious than most of the White Mountains summer hotels, it appealed to high-minded teachers and ministers who brought their families here to enjoy "sweet Christian living" (no smoking or drinking, lots of hiking). These families, including their children and grandchildren, became devoted to the valley, buying the inn when it came up for sale in 1919, donating all but a few hundred of their 26,000 acres in 1928 to the White Mountain National Forest. These same families founded and filled the ski clubs that kept the inn going in winter, beginning in 1935 when a few trails were etched on Snow's Mountain. And in 1937 the Civilian Conservation Corps (CCC) cut a precipitous mile-and-a-half trail down the southern shoulder of Mt. Tecumseh, across the valley from Snow's.

It was to ski the Tecumseh Trail that a Phillips Exeter Academy student named Tom Corcoran first came to Waterville Valley in 1949. Corcoran went on to race with the Dartmouth College ski team, and then the US Olympic ski team, and eventually went to work for the Aspen Corporation for which he did the feasibility study recommending acquisition of nearby Buttermilk Mountain. By 1965 when Corcoran was ready to buy his own ski mountain, the Waterville Valley Inn was up for sale along with 425 acres—virtually all the town that wasn't in the national forest.

Corcoran's Waterville Valley—complete with four chairlifts, a T-bar, even some snowmaking—opened for Christmas of 1966. The inn burned that first season, but two new ski lodges were ready for the following year—as were some condominiums, then as new to the eastern ski scene as snowmaking.

Something new—a condo hotel here, a new lift or sports center there—has been added to Waterville Valley every year since. It's been a steady, controlled growth all dictated by Corcoran's original plan which, in just the past few years, has finally clicked into place.

What's made it click is Town Square: three interconnected clapboard buildings 4 1/2 stories high with traditional saltbox lines softened by modern touches like an occasional round window and 100 dormers. A variation on the lines of a massive old White Mountains hotel this complex does something that no other New England ski resort building has achieved: it actually heightens the beauty of its setting, a circle of majestic peaks.

With its shops, restaurants, and frequent special events, Town Square serves as a year-round centerpiece for the resort's 500 or so condominiums, its five lodges, and two ski areas. It's adjacent to Corcoran Pond and the amphitheater, in which summer concerts are performed and which serves as a weather-proofed ice-skating rink in winter. Year-round it's a short walk from the Sports Center.

Future plans call for more lifts on Snow's Mountain, some coming right to Town Square; but, at present, shuttle buses fill the bill of ferrying skiers from their rooms and condos to ski trails, shops, and restaurants. Some 6,000 guests can bed down in the valley's lodging places, ranging from '60s-era ski lodges to the Adirondack-style Golden Eagle Lodge with its seven-story towers. Modest, traditional B&Bs can also still be found in the nearby village of Campton.

GUIDANCE   Waterville Valley Central Reservations (236-8371 or 800-GO-VALLEY), Waterville Valley 03215. A walk-in information center, a source of information on local activities as well as lodging and services.

Photo by Joan Eaton

Famous for skiing, Waterville Valley is also a popular summer destination.

I-93 White Mountain Gateway Chamber of Commerce (726-3804 or 800-237-2307), RFD #1, Box 1067, Campton 03223. Open 9–5 daily. A walk-in visitors information center primarily for the Campton, Plymouth, Thornton, and Waterville Valley areas. Rest rooms, brochures, phones.

GETTING THERE   By bus: **Concord Trailways** from Boston's Logan Airport stops in Plymouth, 25 miles away. Check with lodging to arrange a pickup or cab.

By car: I-93 to Exit 28, then 10 miles up Route 49.

GETTING AROUND   Buses circulate throughout the resort December to March, 7:30 AM–4:30 PM.

MEDICAL EMERGENCY   For the local rescue squad call 236-4377. For the **Plymouth ambulance service** call 524-1545.

TO SEE AND DO   **Blair Bridge.** The easiest way to find this is I-93 to Exit 27; at the bottom of the exit ramp, follow Blair Road to the blinking light, then go straight across.

Turkey Jim's Bridge. At I-93 Exit 28 follow Route 49 west. After about 1/2 mile (as you cross over the metal bridge) look for a sign on your right for Branch Brook Campground. You must drive into the campground to see the bridge.

Bump Bridge. At I-93 Exit 28, follow Route 49 east for about 1/2 mile. Turn right at the traffic lights and go over the dam. Turn right again on Route 175 south. After 3 or 4 miles, you come to a sharp left turn; bear to the left and stay straight, down the dirt road. Take the first right and the covered bridge is about 1/2 mile on the left.

Waterville Valley Sports Center (236-8311). Offers indoor tennis, racquetball and squash courts, 25-meter indoor and outdoor swimming pools, jogging track, fitness evaluation facilities, Nautilus exercise equipment, aerobics, whirlpools, saunas and steam rooms, tanning booths, massage service, restaurant/lounge and game room.

Day Camp. In summer the town sponsors a supervised day camp for children ages 4 to 7 and there are activities for children 8 and older. Waterville Valley Resort also sponsors midweek activities.

SCENIC DRIVES   (Closed in winter.)

Tripoli Road. A shortcut from Waterville Valley to I-93 north: roughly 10 miles, paved and unpaved, up through Thornton Gap (a high pass between Mt. Osceola and Mt. Tecumseh) and over a high shoulder of 4,326-foot Mt. Osceola. Begin on West Branch Road (a left before the Osceola Library); cross the one-lane bridge and turn right into the national forest. Note the Mt. Osceola Trail (see Hiking) 3 miles up the road. Continue through the Thornton Gap. Note trailheads for the Mt. Tecumseh and East Pond Trails.

Sandwich Notch Road. We have fond memories of this steep, roughly 10-mile dirt road from Center Sandwich to Waterville, built one rod wide for $300 by the town of Sandwich in the late eighteenth century. When we described it glowingly in the *Boston Globe*, however, we did get a few complaints from readers who attempted it in large, low cars. Be prepared to make way for any vehicle coming from the opposite direction. The road follows the Bearcamp River, and stone walls tell of long-vanished farms. Center Sandwich offers a crafts center, museum, and dining (see the Lake Winnipesaukee Area).

BICYCLING   Mountain Valley Bikes (236-4666), in Town Square. Rents mountain bikes, tandem bikes, or bicycle buggies for toddlers. Mountain bike clinics, special events utilizing cross-country trails and logging roads.

BOATING   Corcoran Pond (236-4666), at Waterville Valley Resort. Paddleboat, canoe, and sunfish rentals on 6 acres

CAMPING   Sites in the White Mountain National Forest campgrounds in this area can be reserved up to 120 days in advance by phoning 800-283-CAMP.

Campton, on Route 49, 2 miles east of I-93 Exit 28, Campton. Open mid-April to mid-October. Fifty-eight sites. Interpretive programs on weekends June through Labor Day. $8 per night; pay shower available.

Russell Pond, Exit 31 off I-93, 3 miles northeast on the Tripoli Road. Eighty-one sites. $9 per night.

Waterville, 8 miles northeast of I-93 on Route 49, Waterville. Open year-round, 27 sites. $7 per night; half-price in winter.

FISHING Stream fishing was one of the first lures of visitors to this valley, and the fish are still biting in Russell Pond (Tripoli Road) and all along the Mad River, stocked with trout each spring. Campton Pond (at the lights) is a popular fishing hole.

GOLF **Waterville Valley Resort** (236-4805). Nine-hole golf course, rental carts.

HIKING Trail information for short hikes can be found in summer months at Jugtown, the general store in Waterville's Town Square.

Cascades Path begins at the base of Snow's Mountain Ski Area and follows a brook for 1 1/2 miles.

Mt. Osceola. A 7-mile, 4 1/2-hour hike beginning on the Tripoli Road (see Scenic Drives). The Tripoli Road crests at the 2,300-foot-high Thornton Gap; the Mt. Osceola Trail begins some 200 yards beyond. Follow an old tractor road up through many switchbacks and along Breadtray Ridge, then across a brook, up log steps, by another ridge to the summit ledges. This is the highest of the mountains circling Waterville Valley, and the view is spectacular. For details consult *Fifty Hikes in the White Mountains* by Daniel Doan, also the source of a detailed description to the trail up Mt. Tripyramid, accessible from the Livermore Road out of Waterville Valley.

Welch Mountain. Open ledge walking at a surprisingly low elevation overlooking the Mad River Valley. It's a challenging 4-mile round-trip hike but well worth the sweat. According to local hiking guru Steve Smith, the broad sheets of granite offer views and blueberries in abundance. The panorama from the open summit includes Sandwich Mountain, Mt. Tripyramid, Mt. Tecumseh, and Mt. Moosilauke. You can extend the hike into a loop by continuing over the slightly higher Dickey Mountain and its fine north viewpoint (the ledges on this hike may be slippery when wet). The trailhead for this loop is on Orris Road, off Upper Mad River Road between Campton and Waterville Valley.

HORSEBACK RIDING **Waterville Valley Resort** (236-8311). Guided trail riding during summer months; pony rides for children.

The Sugar Shack (726-3636), Route 175, North Thornton. Offers riding over the cross-country trails and old logging roads on its 180 acres.

ROLLERBLADING **Valley Sports** (236-4075), Town Square, Waterville. Rentals.

SWIMMING **Waterville Valley Resort's Sports Center** offers an indoor pool. Several lodges also offer indoor pools.

Corcoran's Pond with a sandy beach is the resort's principal summer swimming area.

On Route 49 look for **Smart's Brook Trail.** An easy mile's hike over logging and dirt roads to a swimming hole among the pools of a mountain brook.

TENNIS **Waterville Valley Resort** (236-4841). Eighteen clay, outdoor courts, two indoor courts at the Sports Center.

CROSS-COUNTRY SKIING   Waterville Valley Cross-Country Center (236-4666), in Town Square. Ski school, warming/waxing areas, rentals. More than 100 km through the valley and surrounding national forest; 70 km groomed. The center's move to Town Square has its pros and cons: easy access but too many condos to go by before you get up into the woods. We look forward to the day when it's easier to access the area's many beautiful high and backcountry trails. $10 weekends, $8 midweek ($7 juniors and seniors weekends, $5 midweek).

   The Sugar Shack (726-3867), Route 175 North, Thornton. The Sugar Shack itself is a working, third-generation maple sugaring operation (muffins, sandwiches, and soups are served in the warming hut daily 7 AM–4 PM); trails are across rolling pasture along the Pemigewasset River and up through the hardwoods around the King's Chair Ledge, a natural stone seat said to be used by Indians. The view extends up and down the valley, from Franconia Notch to Campton. $8 trail fee weekends, $6 midweek; $6 and $4 for children.

DOWNHILL SKIING   Waterville Valley (236-8311) is a family-geared resort featuring family-style lodging (including roughly 1,000 kitchens), great children's skiing, and summer programs. A limited ticket policy insures lift line waits of no longer than 15 minutes. It's a policy that discourages day-trippers since tickets frequently sell out early on a good ski day. With the new detachable quad it's now just a 7 1/2-minute ride to the summit of Mt. Tecumseh, and the way down is via a choice of long, wide cruising trails like Upper Bobby's Run and Tippecanoe. Mogul lovers will find plenty to please them on True Grit and Cia, and beginners have their own area served by the Lower Meadows Double Chair. Fifty-three trails on two mountains, 13 lifts (one high-speed detachable quad, three triples, five doubles, four surface), vertical drop of 2,020 feet, and snowmaking covers 96 percent. Facilities include the Schwendi Hutte near the top off Mt. Tecumseh, Sunnyside-Up Lodge (mid-mountain cafeteria), Base Lodge Cafeteria, and the World Cup Bar and Grill. The ski school specializes in clinics for all ages and all abilities. There is a nursery for children from age six weeks. The ski area has one of the country's first and still one of its most outstanding SKIwee programs: Petite SKIwee, ages 3–5; Grand SKIwee, ages 6–8; Mountain Scouts, ages 9–12. Children have their own hill, with its own lift and terrain garden. Also evening children's programs. Lift rates: $35 adult weekend, $65 for two days; $20 junior, $36 for two days; two-day and multi-day rates; ages 70 and over ski free midweek and nonholidays.

ICE SKATING   An indoor, hockey-sized ice-skating rink maintained throughout the winter. Complete with skate rentals, maintenance, and repairs.

SLEIGH RIDES   Throughout the winter, horse-drawn sleigh rides depart afternoons from Town Square, Waterville.

SNOWBOARDING   Snow's Mountain, 150-meter half pipe.

LODGING   In Waterville Valley 03215. Central reservations numbers are 236-8371 or 800-GO-VALLE.

> **The Golden Eagle.** A 1990s version of an 1890s grand hotel: 139 condominium suites, 5 1/2 stories with four seven-story towers. The shingles and fieldstone facing and sloping roofs suggest a classic Adirondack lodge, and the dramatic two-story lobby with its ornate woodwork, large sash windows, and hearths underscore that feel. Designed by Cambridge architect Graham Gund (who also designed the Town Square), it's a whimsical combination of old and new. The tower suites have 360-degree views, and even the least expensive units are beautifully executed. Suites include kitchens, sleep four to six. Amenities include an indoor pool, whirlpools, saunas. Rates include access to Sports Center. From $129–$290 per night on winter weekends; weekend, midweek, off-season rates all cheaper.

> **Snowy Owl Inn** (236-2383). An attractive lodge with a central, three-story fieldstone hearth and a surrounding atrium supported by single log posts; there's a cupola you can sit in. This is a family-geared place with lower-level game rooms adjoining a pleasant breakfast room. There are also indoor and outdoor pools. Of the 80 rooms, more than half have a wet bar, fridge, and whirlpool tub. Rates include a breakfast buffet, afternoon wine and cheese, and Sports Center access. From $79–$99 single per night in winter; cheaper multi-days and off-season.

> **Black Bear Lodge.** Less exciting architecturally than the other two lodges but perfectly comfortable with 107 one- and two-bedroom suites that sleep four to six people. Each suite has a kitchen, dining area, a sitting area with queen-size bed and cable TV, and a separate bedroom; indoor/outdoor pool, whirlpool, sauna, and game room on the lower level. Rates include Sports Center access. From $89 single in ski season; cheaper for multi-days and off-season.

> **Valley Inn and Tavern.** An attractive, 45-room lodge with an indoor/outdoor pool, giant whirlpool, and saunas; also a dining room with candlelight dining, a health spa, and game rooms. Rates include après-ski hors d'oeuvres, ski movies, and live entertainment in the lounge. From $93 single; cheaper for multi-days and in summer.

> **Silver Squirrel Inn.** One of the first, still the simplest and smallest of the resort's lodges. Thirty rooms, some with lofts; a pleasant common area with plants and flowers, reading nooks. Rates include Sports Center access and morning tea or coffee. From $69 single per night during ski season ($434 for seven days).

CONDOMINIUMS   The quality of Waterville's 500 or so condominiums is uniformly high, but since these units lack the indoor pools and game rooms enjoyed by lodge guests, it's important to make sure rentals include access to the Sports Center's pool, exercise rooms, game rooms, etc. The nearer to the Sports Center and to Town Square, the better.

Rates begin at $135 for a one-bedroom condo on a ski-season weekend, from $310 for a one-bedroom unit for five days; cheaper in summer.

BED & BREAKFASTS   The Mountain-Fare Inn (726-4283), Box 553, Campton 03223.   An old-style ski lodge run year-round by Susan and Nick Preston, both ski coaches at Waterville Valley. Ten rooms, half with private bath, some dorm-style spaces sleeping up to six, other cozy rooms for two; caters to both families and groups. A large yard, good for cross-country skiing in winter, volleyball in summer. From $24–$32 single, includes a full breakfast; MAP rates in winter.

Osgood Inn (726-3543), Box 419, Campton 03223.   A gracious old home with a comfortable living room and two large upstairs guest rooms sharing a bath. In an adjoining wing, a two-bedroom suite sleeps up to six people, with its own delightful small sitting room with woodstove and a full kitchen. $55 in the main house, $110 weekends during ski season; less midweek and off-season. All rates include a full country breakfast.

Amber Lights Inn (726-4077), RFD 1 Box 828, Route 3, West Thornton 03223.   An attractive roadside house with five carefully furnished guest rooms, seven-course breakfasts served in front of an elegant fireplace. No smoking and no children under seven. From $55–$70 double.

DINING OUT   The Yacht Club Restaurant (236-8885). Open daily for lunch and dinner, light bar menu until midnight. Entertainment Thursday through Saturday in July, August, and ski season. Multi-tiered dining space with a fully rigged sailboat dangling from the ceiling; casual atmosphere. Big, moderately priced menu: fish and chips and spaghetti with Italian sauce to poached salmon with scallions and ginger ($8.95–$17.95).

William Tell (726-4103), Route 49, Campton. Newly reopened under previous and well-respected ownership. Specializing in Swiss and German dishes.

Mad River Tavern & Restaurant (726-4290), Route 49 (just off I-93 Exit 28), Campton. Closed Tuesdays, otherwise open from lunch through dinner. Serving until 11 PM Fridays and Saturdays. A large, varied menu; specialties include a mixed grill ($11.95) and BBQ ribs ($8.95). Children's portions available.

Valley Inn and Tavern (236-8336), Waterville Valley; candlelight dining, standard continental menu, the most elegant dining room in Waterville Valley.

Sunset Grill (726-3108), corner of routes 3 & 49. Open daily from 11:30 AM, Sunday brunch 11:30–3. Burgers and grilled cheese for lunch but an ambitious dinner menu. Specialties include boneless loin of lamb ($17.95) and thick prime rib ($13.95), a variety of steaks and pasta.

Brookside Bistro (236-4309), in Town Square, Waterville. Good for breakfast, lunch, dinner. Quite elegant for dinner, entertainment on weekends. Italian and great kids' menu.

EATING OUT   Finish Line Cafe at the base of Snow's Mountain. Family fare for lunch.

Jugtown Country Store and Deli (236-8662), the heart of Town Square, Waterville. Open daily. A grocery store with an extensive deli—in warm-weather months you just step outside with salads and sandwiches to the tables in the square. Fresh bagels and breads baked daily.

Waterville Valley Coffee Emporium, Town Square, Waterville. Gourmet coffees, continental breakfast and afternoon tea, gourmet jelly beans.

Alpine Pizza and Ice Cream Shoppe (236-4173). Open daily 11 AM–10 PM. Pizza, ice cream.

Chile Peppers, in the Sports Center. The same cheerful, reasonably priced Mexican fare found at Chile Peppers in the Millfront Marketplace in Lincoln.

SELECTIVE SHOPPING   Daphne's (236-4200). Tom Corcoran's wife Daphne's choice of gifts, cookware, accessories.

Toad Hall (236-4165), Town Square, Waterville. Toys and games for children of all ages.

The Book Monger, Town Square. Paperbacks, games, CDs, magazines, general titles.

Adornments, Town Square. Unusual jewelry, all prices.

SPECIAL EVENTS   Easter Sunday: Sunrise service on Mt. Tecumseh.

Late June through August: **Music Festival Concert Series,** in Town Square Concert Pavilion. Every Friday and Saturday nights at 8:30 PM **Periodic block parties,** Town Square.

July Fourth: **Parade and Fireworks.**

Early August: **"You've Gotta Regatta,"** on Corcoran Pond. Boat parade and beach party.

September: **Labor Day Festivities Craft Show.**

October: **Oktoberfest** on Columbus Day weekend.

November: **Ski area** opens by mid-month. **Fireworks and tree lighting,** Thanksgiving weekend.

PLYMOUTH AND THE BAKER RIVER VALLEY

From I-93 what you see of Plymouth are the high-rise dorms of Plymouth State College, a clue to the existence of shops and restaurants catering to the needs of 4,000 students. Billing itself as the gateway to both the Lakes Region (heading south) and the White Mountains (heading north), Plymouth is also the way into the Baker River Valley (heading west), a relatively little-touristed route through this neck of the mountains heading either for the Connecticut River Valley up around Mt. Moosilauke and back to North Woodstock or past Tenney Mountain to Newfound Lake. The picturesque village of Wentworth, with its choice of B&Bs, is actually well positioned as a hub from which to explore in all directions.

GUIDANCE   I-93 White Mountain Gateway Chamber of Commerce (726-3804 or 800-237-2307), RFD #1, Box 1067 (just of I-93 Exit 28), Campton 03223. Open 9–5 daily.

Baker Valley Business Association, PO Box 145, Rumney 03266, publishes a useful map/guide.

GETTING THERE   By bus: Concord Trailways (800-852-3317) from Boston, stops in Plymouth at Volpes Market (536-4430), 83 Main Street.

MEDICAL EMERGENCY   Speare Memorial Hospital (536-1120), Hospital Road (off Highland Street), Plymouth.

TO SEE AND DO   Polar Caves (536-1888), Route 25, 4 miles west of Plymouth. Open mid-May through mid-October, 9–5. Discovered by neighborhood children around 1900 and opened as a commercial attraction in 1922, this is an extensive property with a series of caves connected by passageways and walkways with taped commentaries at stations along the way. The name refers to the cold air rising from the first "Ice" cave where the temperature in August averages 55 degrees. There's much here to learn about minerals and geology, much that's just fun. The complex includes picnic tables and a snack bar. $7 for adults; $3.50 for children ages 6–12.

Smith Covered Bridge, Airport Road off Route 25/3A west of Plymouth. A long, truss-style bridge built originally in 1850, rebuilt in 1958.

Mary Baker Eddy House (786-9943), Stinson Lake, Rumney. Open May to October, daily except Mondays and holidays. A home of the founder of the Christian Science Church.

Morse Museum (764-9407), Route 25C, Warren. Open June through Labor Day. A trove of mementos from India and Africa collected on trips and safaris by the Morse family early in this century. The town of Warren is also known for the space rocket booster with "USA" painted on its side, a gift of New Hampshire astronaut Alan Shepard (who is not from Warren).

GREEN SPACE   Quincy Bog (786-9465), off Route 25/3A west. Left on Airport Road, through Smith Bridge, and left on Quincy Road. Turn right at the sign for Quincy Bog (just beyond Quincy State Forest), left at the first fork to the parking area. This 40-acre peat bog is a place to find frogs in April and May, to hunt for salamanders and newts, and to bird-watch. The Nature Center here is open mid-June to mid-August. Also good for cross-country skiing. You can continue on from here to Quincy Village and back out to Route 25/3A.

Stinson Lake. An isolated lake, deep in the national forest, circled by road; good fishing (trout, perch, pickerel) year-round; powerboats allowed, access available for a fee.

Stinson Mountain Trail is marked, beginning with a dirt road, then left through the woods and right at the brook, up through spruce and fir to the summit ledges. Great views. Note that you can continue east on this road out to I-93 Exit 28.

DOWNHILL SKIING   Tenney Mountain (536-1717), Route 3A, Plymouth. This long-established, family ski area was sold in 1990 to a Japanese-backed California group. It offers 29 trails; 90 percent snowmaking; one triple chair, one double chair, two surface lifts; a vertical drop of 1,400 feet, and condominium lodging.

LODGING   Hobson House (764-9460), Town Common, Wentworth 03282. An 1815, Federal-style, "four-square" house that's been run as an inn since 1979 by Kay and Bob Thayer. It's sited in the center of Wentworth's tiny, picture-perfect village, and the Thayers are knowledgeable about the countryside for miles around—where to find a swimming hole, cross-country trails, or an antiques shop. $55 double B&B, $75 in winter; minimum two-night stay; rates include dinner.

Crab Apple Inn (536-4476), Route 25, RR 4, Box 1955, Plymouth 03264. A classic 1835, brick, Federal-style, roadside mansion with four antiques-furnished guest rooms, some with fireplaces, all with private bath. The common rooms are fairly formal and elegant, and the grounds are several acres deep with an English garden and paths leading back into woods. No children. A full breakfast is included in the rates: $70–$85.

Wentworth Inn and Art Gallery (764-9923), Ellsworth Hill Road, Wentworth Village 03282. A handsome, old country mansion with some elaborate detailing and stained-glass windows, within sound as well as sight of Baker Pond Brook. The seven guest rooms have frilly touches, some with canopy beds. $60–$80 double includes a full breakfast; a variety of packages are offered including dinner.

Mt. Laurel Inn (764-9600), Route 25 at 25A, Wentworth 03282. Open June to October. This is a consciously "romantic" place: Laura Ashley wallpaper, heaps of pillows on large beds, no TV. The attractive house overlooks surrounding fields. Three of the five rooms have private baths. $65–$75 includes a full breakfast.

Hilltop Acres (764-5896), Hilltop Acres, East Side and Buffalo Road, Wentworth 03282. A pleasant old farmhouse; rooms with private and semi-private bath from $50–$60; also traditional housekeeping cottages with fireplace and screened porch ($150 per weekend, $400 per week).

DINING OUT   Glove Hollow (536-4536), Route 3, Plymouth. Open for dinner Tuesday through Sunday and Sunday brunch; just Thursday through Sunday in winter. Generally considered the best restaurant around, worth the drive down from Loon or Waterville Valley. The decor is Victorian and heavy on gloves (there once was a glove factory here).

The menu might include Maine crabcakes and rack of lamb with Dijon, garlic and rosemary. Sunday brunch is a specialty; Italian night every Friday.

The Downunder (536-3983), 3 South Main Street, Plymouth. Open for lunch Monday through Saturday, dinner nightly. A bright, collegiate atmosphere with photo murals, skylights, a big aquarium, and a zaney menu to match: Cajun fried chicken, veggie kabobs, goulash, veal parmigiana. Most entrées under $12.

Jigger Johnson's (536-4FUN). Lots of atmosphere, friendly service, great food. Parties a specialty.

The Backyard (536-1994), 105 Main Street, Plymouth. Open for dinner, Wednesday through Sunday 5–9. Back behind and under the Trolley Car Restaurant, this small trattoria features homemade pastas and Italian classics like veal marsala and chicken parmigiana. The wines are all Italian, too.

EATING OUT   *In Plymouth:* **Suzanne's Kitchen** (536-3304), 36 South Main Street. Open daily 7 AM–9 PM. Flour is ground right here and only natural sweeteners are used in the dozen kinds of bread and fairly elaborate desserts. Bulky sandwiches and vegetarian dishes are also specialties. A coffeehouse atmosphere with folk music Wednesday and Saturday nights, but beer and wine are served. No smoking.

Biederman's Deli (536-3354). Sandwiches featuring Boar's Head meats; every beer imaginable; hang-out for college crowd and business folk.

Trolley Car Diner (536-4433). A local gathering place for lunch and dinner; genuine '50s atmosphere.

In the Baker River Valley: **Steve's Restaurant** (786-9788), just off Route 25 on Stinson Lake Road, Rumney. Open 6 AM–9 PM daily, until 9:30 Friday and Saturday; open Sunday for brunch. One of those little family restaurants that's so good it just keeps growing. The menu is big now, too, ranging from burgers and Greek salad to veal picatta, Cajun-baked chicken, and filet mignon; the specialty is seafood: fried, baked, broiled. Most entrées are well under $10.

Moosilauke View Restaurant, Route 25, Warren Village. Open daily 9 AM–8 PM, Sunday 8–7. A clean, friendly eatery with daily specials like hamburger vegetable soup and hot turkey sandwich. We spent $1.75 for lunch.

ENTERTAINMENT   **Plymouth Theater** (536-1089), Main Street, Plymouth. A '30s movie palace that's recently been restored; screens a broad assortment of films.

(Also see the New Hampshire Music Festival under Special Events.)

SELECTIVE SHOPPING   **Shanware Pottery** (786-9835), Route 25, Rumney. A working studio in a rustic barn; distinctive, functional stoneware pottery.

SPECIAL EVENTS   January: **Winter Carnival**.

July and August: **New Hampshire Music Festival** (253-4331), in Silver Hall on the Plymouth State College Campus (a new Cultural Arts Center is due to be completed in '92). Tuesday evening chamber music concerts; Wednesday evening concerts on the Common; Thursday evening concerts at Silver Hall.

August: **Plymouth State Fair,** Plymouth.

December: **Christmas Parade.**

Franconia and North of the Notches

Wrapped in forest and dominated by granite White Mountain peaks, the Franconia-Bethlehem area seems to be the distilled essence of northern New Hampshire. Northwest of this high, wooded country, the landscape changes suddenly, flattening around Littleton, the shopping town for this region. For views of both the Green Mountains and the White Mountains, follow this Ammonoosuc Valley south to Lisbon and Bath, then back up to Sugar Hill and Franconia on memorable back roads.

The town of Franconia alone packs into its 65 square miles more splendid scenic vistas and unusual natural attractions than many states or provinces can boast. Curiously, while annual visitors to Franconia Notch are said to outnumber New Hampshire residents, relatively few stray into the delightful neighboring valley, which seems happily trapped in a 1950s time warp.

Franconia and its small satellite towns of Sugar Hill and Easton have been catering to visitors of one sort or another for more than 150 years. Travelers were first attracted to Franconia Notch by its convenience as a north-south route through the mountains; but they were invariably impressed by the scenery and their tales of natural wonders like the granite profile of the Old Man of the Mountain circulated widely.

Sightseers and health seekers began trickling into the Notch after the War of Independence, and a few inns and taverns catered to them along with more conventional travelers. Then in the mid-nineteenth century the railroad arrived, inaugurating a grand resort era. Such literary notables as Nathaniel Hawthorne, Washington Irving, John Greenleaf Whittier, and Henry Wadsworth Longfellow were all Franconia summer visitors whose enthusiastic accounts of the region fanned its fame. Hawthorne even wrote a story about the Old Man, "The Great Stone Face."

One of the most celebrated hotels in America in its day, and a symbol of the White Mountains' golden age, was the 400-room Profile House, which stood in the heart of Franconia Notch. Besides elegant

Photo by Peter E. Randall

The Old Man of Mountain and Profile Lake.

service in a rustic setting, the hotel offered its guests a superb view of the Old Man. An institution for 70 years, Profile House burned down in 1923, just as the automobile began permanently altering America's vacation habits and the grand hotel era was ending. The hotel site is now part of Franconia Notch State Park.

Grand hotels also appeared in Bethlehem, known for its pollen-free air. It became headquarters for the National Hay Fever Relief Association, which was founded here in the 1920s, and at one time Bethlehem had 34 hotels, some large and luxurious indeed, and a two-mile-long boardwalk for their guests to stroll along.

Although many once-famous grand hotels closed their doors in the 1920s and 1930s, a few lasted until the 1950s when railroad service to the White Mountains ended and a resort way of life ended with it. A few traces of Bethlehem's glory days remain, such as the impressive fieldstone and shingle clubhouse of the Maplewood Golf Course (formerly The Casino), an outbuilding of the very grand but long vanished Maplewood Hotel.

Summer residents and hotel guests, outraged at what unrestricted logging was doing to their beloved mountain scenery, founded the still active Society for the Preservation of New Hampshire Forests. The efforts of this pioneering conservation organization eventually led to the creation in 1911 of the 768,000-acre White Mountain National Forest, the first national forest in the country.

When the summer resort scene began to fade in the White Mountains, a winter one commenced, thriving as Americans discovered skiing. The Franconia area can claim a number of skiing firsts. Among them: the nation's first ski school (which opened at Pecketts-on-Sugar Hill in 1929) and this country's first aerial tramway (constructed in 1938), which ran to the summit of state-owned Cannon Mountain. Cannon also hosted America's first racing trail in the 1920s and its first World Cup race in the 1960s.

In 1945 a flamboyant Austrian aristocrat, Baron Hugo Von Pantz, founded Mittersill, a Tyrolean-style resort adjacent to Cannon. The baron's resort attracted high society types from New York and Boston, and, for a time, Franconia was the New England equivalent of Aspen or St. Moritz. Cannon remains a popular ski area, and its expansion plans include reopening the (now dormant) Mittersill ski slopes.

Times change. The current winter hot spot is south of the Notch (see the Western Whites [Lincoln and North Woodstock]), and the socialites have gone the way of the old hotels. An unusual number of craftsmen have settled in—graduates of Franconia College, a liberal institution of the '60s that was housed in the (since demolished) old Forest Hill Hotel but that died with the '70s. Some of New Hampshire's most pleasant inns and bed & breakfasts are scattered throughout the folds of the valleys and gentler hills north and west of Franconia Notch.

GUIDANCE   **Franconia-Easton-Sugar Hill Chamber of Commerce** (823-5661), Box D, Main Street, Franconia 03580. Downtown information booth is open through foliage season; another is open at the Cannon Mountain tramway base station through ski season.

Bethlehem Chamber of Commerce (444-9921), PO Box 748, Bethlehem 03547. Seasonal information booth on Route 302 near the intersection of I-93.

Littleton Area Chamber of Commerce (444-6561), 141 Main Street, Box 105, Littleton 03561. Seasonal information booth located in front of the office.

Twin Mountain Chamber of Commerce (846-5407), Box 194, Twin Mountain 03595, produces a brochure and operates a summer information center at the junction of routes 3 and 302.

WMNF Ammonoosuc Ranger Station (869-2626), Trudeau Road, off Route 302, Box 239, Bethlehem 03574. Open Monday through Friday 7–4:30.

GETTING THERE   By bus: **Concord Trailways** (228-3300 or 800-852-3317) has daily service from Boston, Manchester, Concord, Lincoln, and Littleton.

By car: From north or south, take I-93 to Franconia Notch Parkway

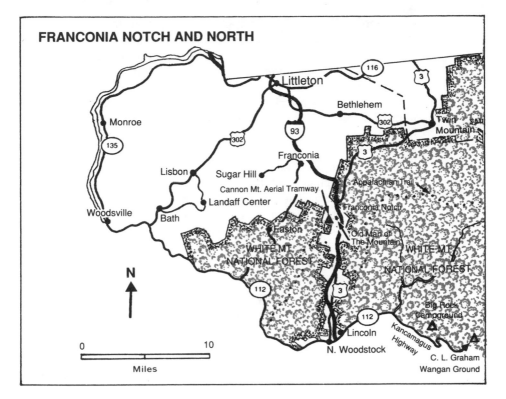

FRANCONIA NOTCH AND NORTH

(Route 3). Route 116 west leads to Franconia and the adjacent towns of Sugar Hill and Easton. Route 302 east leads into Bethlehem from the north, Route 142 east from the south.

MEDICAL EMERGENCY **Littleton Hospital** (444-7731), 107 Cottage Street, Littleton.

Franconia-Easton rescue: **Franconia Life Squad** (823-8123).

Bethlehem Volunteer Ambulance (869-2232).

TO SEE AND DO **The Robert Frost Place** (823-8038), Ridge Road, off Route 116, Franconia. Former home of the noted poet, now a town-run museum and center for poetry and the arts. Displays of rare editions of Frost's books, photos, and memorabilia and a slide presentation about Frost's life and work in Franconia. A nature trail behind the house is signposted with quotations from appropriate Frost poems. In summer there are frequent poetry readings and workshops. Open weekends spring and fall; daily except Tuesday in July and August. Admission $3 adults, $2 seniors, $1.25 children.

Sugar Hill Historical Museum (823-8142), Main Street (Route 117), Sugar Hill. Interesting, small local museum with changing exhibits about aspects of the town from its pioneer settlement in 1780 until the present. Open Thursday, Saturday, and Sunday afternoons. Admission $1.

Littleton Historical Society, One Union Street (lower level of the 1894 town office building), Littleton. In summer open every Wednesday and Saturday 1:30–4:30. A large collection of local items include stereoscopic slides (unique photographs published by the famous Kilburn Brothers of Littleton).

Crossroads of America (869-3919), corner of Trudeau Road and Route 302, Bethlehem. Open June through foliage season 9–6; closed Monday. A must stop for rail fans: the world's largest 3/16 scale model railroad on public exhibit. Tours offered every hour. Admission fee.

Mt. Washington Cog Railway (see Mount Washington's Valleys [Crawford Notch and Bretton Woods]).

SPECIAL VILLAGES   **Bath.** The village of Bath itself is known for its vintage 1832 covered bridge and for its 1804 Old Brick Store, billed as the country's oldest general store. Upper Bath Village, a few miles north on Route 302, is a striking cluster of Federal-era brick homes set against surrounding fields.

Landaff Center. Set well back into the hills east of Route 302, this is one of New Hampshire's most photographed old hill towns. The town hall commands a superb view. The latest population count is 286. You can't help wondering what it would be if Dartmouth College had been sited here the way Governor John Wentworth suggested in 1770.

GREEN SPACE   **Franconia Notch State Park** (823-5563). This 6,440-acre park runs between the Franconia and Kinsmen mountain ranges and contains many of the White Mountains' most notable natural sights. As it passes through the 8 miles of the notch, I-93 is scaled down to the Franconia Notch Parkway (Route 3), built (after a 25-year controversy) to funnel traffic through with minimum scenic and environmental impact. The principal sights of the Notch are all within the park and easily accessible from the parkway.

The **State Park Visitors Center** by the entrance to the Flume provides information and shows interpretive films of the area. It also has a snack bar, rest rooms, and a souvenir shop A $10 combination ticket is available—good for a round-trip tramway ride and admission to both the Flume and Echo Lake beach.

The Flume. An 800-foot-long, deep and narrow gorge—no more than 20 feet wide but up to 90 feet high—through which Flume Brook flows. A system of staircases and boardwalks takes visitors through the Flume to Ridge Path, which leads to Liberty Cascade and on to Sentinel Pine covered bridge that overlooks a clear mountain pool. The Wildwood Path loops past giant boulders brought down by the glaciers and returns to the flume entrance. Admission charge is $5.50.

Echo Lake. A 28-acre lake at an elevation of 1,931 feet, the mirror-like surface of which perfectly reflects Mt. Lafayette and Cannon Mountain. There are picnic tables, a swimming beach, and a boat launching area. Admission is $2 per adult weekdays, $2.50 weekends.

The Flume, Franconia Notch State Park.

Photo by George Sylvester

Cannon Mountain. One of New Hampshire's most popular ski areas and the site of America's first aerial tramway The present tramway, which replaced the 1938 original in 1980, carries 80 passengers to the summit of the 4,180-foot-high mountain where there is an observation tower and the panoramic Rim Trail. Besides operating during ski season, the tram runs from late May through Columbus Day when autumn colors are usually at or near peak. A round-trip tram ticket is $7 (see also Alpine Skiing).

New England Ski Museum. Adjacent to the tramway base station, the privately operated museum tells the story of New England skiing with exhibits of skis, clothing, and equipment dating from the nineteenth century to the present, along with vintage still photos and film. Open daily May 27 through October 16 and December 15 through March 31. Admission $2 adults; $1 children ages 12 to 18.

The Old Man of the Mountain. The famous 40-foot-high rock formation—the state's official symbol—resembles the profile of a craggy-featured male. (The pioneers who discovered the profile in 1805 thought it looked like Thomas Jefferson.) The great stone face juts out from a sheer cliff above Profile Lake, and the best view and photograph is from the lake shore.

The Basin. A deep glacial pothole or natural pool almost 30 feet in diameter created over eons by the churning action of water rushing down from the nearby waterfall.

The Rocks (444-6228), Route 302, RFD 1, Bethlehem 03574. Owned by the Society for the Protection of New Hampshire Forests (SPNHF), this estate with its huge barns is the northern headquarters for the state's largest and most active conservation organization. The estate's 1,200 acres are managed as a tree farm by the SPNHF; a large area is reserved as a Christmas tree plantation. Trees are sold during the annual Christmas tree celebration held in December. There are various conservation and family programs (see Special Events) held through the year plus a self-guided nature trail and cross-country skiing.

Bretzfelder Park (444-6228 or 869-2683), Prospect Street, Bethlehem. Owned by the SPNHF, this 77-acre site is managed as a community park with various summer programs plus picnic tables, fishing, and a nature trail.

AIR RIDES   **North Country Flying Service** (823-8881), Route 116, Franconia. Open daily late May through October. Glider rides and scenic bi-plane rides. Flights from $10.

Twin Mountain Airport (846-5505), 300 yards off Route 302, Twin Mountain. Year-round, weather permitting, Joe O'Brien offers sightseeing flights over Mt. Washington and the surrounding area.

BICYCLING   An 8-mile-long bicycle path, used in winter as a cross-country ski trail, traverses Franconia Notch.

GOLF   **Bethlehem Golf Course** (869-5745), Main Street (Route 302), Bethlehem. Eighteen holes.

Maplewood Golf Course (869-5745), Main Street (Route 302), Bethlehem. Eighteen holes.

Sunset Hill Golf Course (823-5522), Sugar Hill. Nine holes.

Profile Club (823-9568), Franconia. Nine holes.

HIKING   Hiking information is available at the Franconia-Easton-Sugar Hill Chamber of Commerce and the Bethlehem Chamber of Commerce information booths (see Guidance); the Franconia Notch State Park Visitors Center by the entrance to the Flume (see Green Space); Cannon Mountain; the park's Lafayette Campground; and the national forest's Ammonoosuc Ranger Station (869-2626), Trudeau Road, Bethlehem. Franconia Notch offers some of the most rewarding short hikes in the White Mountains. They include:

Artist's Bluff and Bald Mountain. From Route 18 in Franconia Notch State Park, 0.5 miles north of its junction with Route 3. The parking lot is across from Cannon Mountain's Peabody Ski Slopes. Favored by nineteenth-century guests at the Notch's former hotels, Bald Mountain is an easy ascent with sweeping views. First you follow an old carriage road to a saddle between two summits, then branch left to Bald Mountain, right to Artist's Bluff. You should investigate both. The round-trip is 1 or 1.8 miles.

Basin-Cascades Trail (3 miles). Start at the Basin, marked from Route 3 in Franconia Notch State Park, and ascend along Cascade Brook leading to the Cascade Brook Trail.

Lonesome Lake Trail. From Lafayette Place on Route 3 in Franconia Notch, an old bridle path leads to an 80-acre lake which sits at an elevation of 2,734 feet and is warm enough in summer for swimming. The Appalachian Mountain Club's Lonesome Lake Hut offers overnight lodging and a variety of family-geared programs. Contact the AMC Pinkham Notch Camp (466-2725).

Mt. Lafayette via the Old Bridle Path. This is a full day's hike, and you should pick up a detailed map before attempting it. After 2.5 miles you reach the AMC Greenleaf Hut (for lodging phone 466-2725); the summit—with magnificent views—is another 1.1 miles. If the weather is good and your energy high, continue along the Franconia Ridge Trail south over Mt. Lincoln to Little Haystack. This narrow, rocky route is spectacular, but there are steep drops on both sides of the trail. At Little Haystack turn right (west) on the Falling Waters Trail. This trail passes more waterfalls in 2.8 miles than any other trail in the mountains; it ends back at Lafayette Place.

HORSEBACK RIDING   **Franconia Inn** (823-5542), Route 116, Franconia.

Mittersill Riding Stable (823-5511), Mittersill Resort, Route 18, Franconia.

ALPINE SKIING   **Cannon Mountain** (823-5563), Route 3, Franconia. One of New

Hampshire's oldest ski mountains, state-owned Cannon has a whopping 2,146-foot vertical drop. Its aerial tram (the country's first in the 1930s) was replaced in the 1980s, and snowmaking has since been substantially increased to cover 85 percent of the 28 trails. Lifts include two quad chairs, a triple, and two doubles as well as the tram. While its image remains "The Mountain That'll Burn Your Boots Off!," in reality many trails have recently been softened—broadened and smoothed as well as carpeted with snowmaking. In addition to runs in Franconia Notch itself, more than a dozen intermediate and beginner runs meander down the mountain's gentler northern face to the Peabody Slopes base area. The only trails still "au naturel" are Taft Slalom (a remnant of that '20s racing trail) and the Hardscrabbles—both of which command their own following. In 1990/1991, season lift tickets are $34 per adult on weekends, $21 midweek.

CROSS-COUNTRY SKIING   *White Mountain National Forest:*   Detailed maps of all these trails are available from the Franconia-Easton-Sugar Hill Chamber of Commerce, at Cannon Mountain, and from the Ammonoosuc Ranger Station (see Guidance).

Lafayette Trails, Route 3, Franconia Notch. The Notchway Trail is the old Route 3 road bed, accessed from Route 141 just east of I-93 Exit 36. It's identified by a metal sign with a skier symbol. The trail is 2.1 miles, and side loops include the short Bog Trail, the more difficult Scarface Trail (1.2 miles), and the Bickford Trail (0.3 mile).

The Pemi Trail, Franconia Notch. Just over 6 miles long, this trail extends from Profile Lake to the Flume Parking Lot and is open to cross-country skiers, snowshoers, and hikers. It can also be accessed from the Echo Lake, tramway, and Flume parking areas. Pick up a map at the information booth at Cannon's base lodge in Franconia Notch.

Beaver Brook Cross Country Trails begin at the Beaver Brook Wayside on Route 3 between Twin Mountain and Franconia Notch. The Beaver Loop is 2.3 kilometers, Badger is a more difficult 3.1 kilometers, and Moose Watch is classified as "most difficult," a total of 8.6 kilometers with some spectacular views. These trails are ungroomed and not regularly patrolled so be sure not to ski alone.

Zealand Valley Trails. See Mt. Washington's Valleys (Bretton Woods and Crawford Notch).

In the town of Franconia: **Franconia Inn** (823-5542), Easton Road, maintains 29 miles of trails, and an additional 15 miles meander across this 1,100-foot-high valley. Rentals and lessons available.

Sunset Hill House (823-5522), Sugar Hill, maintains 15 miles of trails, theoretically connecting with those maintained by Franconia Inn. Rentals and lessons available.

SNOWMOBILING   In Franconia Notch the bike path serves in winter as a corridor connector for the 100-mile network of snowmobile trails in this area. Twin Mountain is a popular snowmobiling center. Some winter weekends are as busy as those in the summer. Many motels and lodges have trails right from the door that connect to a large trail network. For maps and other information write **Twin Mountain Snowmobile Club**, Box 179, Twin Mountain 03595; **The Trails Bureau** (271-3254), NH Division of Parks and Recreation, Box 856, Concord 03301; or the **New Hampshire Snowmobile Association** (224-8906), Box 38, Concord 03301. (Also see Mt. Washington's Valleys [Crawford Notch and Bretton Woods].)

LODGING   Lovett's Inn (823-7761 or 800-356-3802), by Lafayette Brook, Franconia 03580. Built in 1784, the inn today is a rambling collection of rooms and cottages, most with fieldstone fireplaces and some with exposed 200-year-old hand-hewn beams. Rates for a room are from $86 for a couple, from $116 for a cottage.

Franconia Inn (823-5542), Route 116, Franconia 03580. Founded just after the Civil War, the 34-room Franconia inn was rebuilt after a fire in 1934; and its decor and ambience remain that of about a half-century ago. It is a pleasant period piece that appeals to active people who like genteel, old-fashioned surroundings. Available activities include horseback riding, tennis, cross-country skiing, sleigh rides, and gliding. Amenities include a paneled library and a heated pool. Rates are from $65 per couple.

The Ammonoosuc Inn (838-6118), Bishop Road, Lisbon 03585. Open year-round. A nineteenth-century farmhouse positioned on a knoll above the Ammonoosuc River. In the 1920s its fields were smoothed into golf links, and in recent years an outdoor pool and clay tennis court have been added. In winter Cannon Mountain is just a 15-minute drive and Bretton Woods, 30 minutes. The inn maintains cross-country trails on its own 136 acres. Innkeepers Steven and Laura Bromley have renovated the nine rooms (each with private bath) and turned the old carriage house into attractive condominiums ranging in size from one to three bedrooms. Cobblers, the inn's restaurant, is popular locally (see Dining Out). Common space includes two spacious parlor rooms, a lounge with a full bar, and a big wraparound porch. Rates are $50–$70 per room, $90–$200 for condominiums. Rates include a continental breakfast; MAP rates also available.

Sunset Hill House (823-5522), Sugar Hill 03585. A 36-room, mansard-roof building facing the Sunset Hill Golf Course, the inn is imposing but was actually built in the last century as the employees' quarters of the original and far more grand Sunset Hill House. It boasts that it is "a skyline resort above the fogline," and the view from the dining room is indeed splendidly panoramic. Among the preserved White Mountain traditions are the Thanksgiving "work bee" at which guests pitch in to prepare for winter; and a "country Christmas" celebration, complete with Yule log and Wassail bowl. Rates for a double from $65.

Ledgeland Inn and Cottages (823-5341), Sugar Hill 03585. Built as a rustic private home, the inn itself has nine rooms and is open from June until mid-October. The 14 cottage units are open year-round and have fireplaces, kitchens, and fine views of the Franconia range. Daily rates start at $60 for double inn rooms; $74 for cottages.

Horse & Hound Inn (823-5501), Wells Road, Franconia 03580. Built in the 1830s as a farmhouse, the 10-room Horse and Hounds was converted to an inn just after World War II by an enthusiastic horseman who was master of a hunt, hence the name. Lots of pine paneling and fireplaces; the dining room specializes in continental cuisine. Rates for a double room are from $60 with full breakfast.

Thayer's Inn (444-6469), 136 Main Street, Littleton 03561. Open year-round. Listed on the National Register of Historic Places, this hotel has been welcoming White Mountain travelers since it was built in 1843. Most of the 40 rooms have private baths, TV, and telephones. Each room is individually furnished so guests are invited to select their own room on arrival. The two-bedroom suites are great for families. Coffee shop, restaurant, and lounge on the premises. Don and Carolyn Lambert, innkeepers. EP $30–$40, two-bedroom suites $70 for up to four people.

Rivagale Inn (823-7044), Main Street, Franconia 03580. Built at the turn of the century as a combination clinic and doctor's residence, the rambling Rivagale was later a dormitory for the now-defunct Franconia College. Its pubby Taverne Restaurant, which always has five spicy and substantial Mexican entrées on the menu, is a popular spot (see Eating Out). Rates for a couple start at $75, except in foliage season when all rates are MAP and start at $135 with two meals.

Wayside Inn (869-3364 or 800-448-9557), Route 302 at Pierce Bridge, Bethlehem 03574. A historic eighteenth-century inn building with an attached modern motel. The inn's Riverview Restaurant is one of the area's best (see Dining Out). Room rates from $42, suites start at $65.

The Red Coach Inn (800-COACH-93), PO Box 40, Franconia 03580. The 60-room Red Coach Inn is the newest and largest hostelry in the area. Amenities include a heated indoor swimming pool, sauna, and Jacuzzi. There is also a gift shop and a small coffee shop-style restaurant. Rates for a couple start at $65.

BED & BREAKFASTS   The Beal House Inn (444-2661), 247 West Main Street, Littleton 03561. Open year-round. Another New Hampshire classic, this inn has 14 rooms, all furnished with antiques, and all rooms but two have private baths. The rooms vary in size; the smaller ones are cozy and comfortable. Beds range from doubles to kings, and some have canopies. Two common rooms with plenty of books. Browse in their adjacent antiques shop. Hot tea is available any time and complimentary drinks and refreshments are served in the afternoon and evening. Continental breakfast includes fresh popovers; full breakfast served a la carte. $40–$90, depending on season and accommodations.

Bungay Jar (823-7775), Easton Valley Road, PO Box 15, Franconia 03580 An enlarged eighteenth century barn, moved to a wooded riverside and mountain-view site, that owners Kate Kerivan and Lee Strimbeck have filled with an eclectic antique collection. Amenities include king-sized suites, a sauna, huge old-fashioned tubs (one belonged to Benny Goodman), a two-story common room, afternoon tea, and a full country breakfast. Rates are from $60 per couple.

Sugar Hill Inn (823-5621), Route 117, Franconia 03580. A gracious, restored colonial-era farmhouse with 10 rooms in the main house and 6 in adjacent cottages. Non-smoking. Afternoon tea and full breakfast. Rates $92–$124 per couple.

Blanche's B&B (823-7061), Box 75, Easton Valley Road, Franconia 03580. A homey last-century farmhouse. Owners Brenda Shannon and John Vail got turned onto B&Bs in England—observe the amiable British custom of tea and conversation that are always available. No smoking. Rates from $55 per couple.

The Homestead (823-5564), on Route 117, Sugar Hill 03585. The main building of this 20-room inn is a former farmhouse in the same family for seven generations. Rooms are filled with family antiques and heirlooms; the dining room is decorated with hand-painted plates depicting local scenes and events. Full three-course country breakfast. Rates from $70 per couple.

The Hilltop Inn (823-5695), Main Street, Sugar Hill 03585. A pleasant atmospheric Victorian inn in the middle of sleepy Sugar Hill. Owners Meri and Mike Hern usually welcome guests in their scented kitchen dominated by a cast iron, wood-burning oven. Amenities include period antiques, English flannel sheets, sunsets from the deck, and very large breakfasts. Children and pets welcome. Private or shared baths. Rates from $50 per couple.

Evergreen Bed & Breakfast (747-3947), Route 302, Bath 03740. An 1820s house in Bath Village has been Victorianized by innkeepers John Ray and Tom Koda. Two guest rooms have working fireplaces, and two more have been carefully furnished with Victorian-era antiques. All rooms share two nicely fitted bathrooms. Common rooms are comfortable, filled with an amazing variety of Victoriana. A full breakfast is included in $50 double.

The Bells (869-2647), Strawberry Hill Street, Bethlehem 03574. A pagoda-shaped Victorian mansion with three pleasant, antiques-filled mini-suites with private baths. One room, arguably the most romantic in the White Mountains, occupies the pagoda cupola and has a walka-round balcony and splendid views on four sides. Rates from $60 per couple.

Maplewood Inn (869-5869), Main Street, Bethlehem 03574. Six rooms, four with bath. No smoking, pets, or children under 12. Two-day minimum. Rates are $65–$80 per couple.

The Mulburn Inn (869-3389), Main Street, Bethlehem 03574. Two sisters and their husbands run this spacious mansion that has been converted into a seven-room B&B. All rooms have private baths with king or queen beds. Large wraparound porches and spacious grounds. Full country breakfast. Bob and Cheryl Burns, Moe and Linda Mulkigian, innkeepers. Rates from $50–$60.

The Old Homestead Bed and Breakfast (869-9794), Main Street, Box 698, Bethlehem 03574. Open year-round. This rustic place was built in the 1800s as a blacksmith shop. The Chenevert family has converted it into an eight-room B&B. Two rooms have private baths; the others share three baths. Two rooms have woodstoves, most have double beds, and one has bunks. Full breakfast with homemade muffins and breads. The rate of $35 per couple makes this the local bargain.

Partridge House Inn (846-2277), Route 302, Twin Mountain 03595. A remodeled farmhouse, this B&B has ten rooms, eight with private baths. Common area, music room, and library plus hammocks and swings; continental breakfast. Ray Lamoueux, innkeeper. $55.

Northern Zermatt Inn and Motel (846-5533, outside NH 800-535-3214), Route 3, Twin Mountain 03595. Seventeen rooms (eight rooms in the inn have a queen or a double bed, nine rooms in the motel have two doubles), all with private baths, TV, and air-conditioning. Two motel rooms have kitchens. Swimming pool, picnic area, and lawn games. Country breakfast bar. Joe and Sheila Terra, innkeepers. Rates from $35–$75.

MOTELS   **Gale River** (823-5655 or 800-255-7989), Route 18, Franconia 03580. The motel building has 10 rooms, and there are 3 cottages with one to five bedrooms, rentable by the week. Amenities include heated pool, whirlpool, and hot tub. Rates for a double from $52. Cottages start at $85 with a five-day minimum.

Raynor's Motor Lodge (823-9586, 800-634-8187), at junction of routes 18 and 142, Franconia 03580. Thirty rooms, about half air-conditioned. Heated pool, coffee shop, and bar. Doubles from $36.

Stonybrook Motor Lodge (823-8192 or 800-722-3552), Route 18, Franconia 03580. Two heated pools. Doubles from $51, June to mid-October. Kids free.

Twin Mountain has many motels. Among them are **Carlson's Lodge** (846-5501), **Paquette's Motel and Restaurant** (846-5562), and **Profile Deluxe Motel** (846-5522).

LODGES   **Pinestead Farm Lodge** (823-8121), Route 116, Franconia 03580. Pinestead has been taking in guests since 1899 but is still a working farm run by the Sherburn family. The locally renowned Pinestead quilts are made and sold on the premises. The nine rooms are in clusters of three with shared baths and kitchens. Easy access to fishing, hiking, downhill, and cross-country skiing. Room rate for a couple from $30.

CONDOMINIUMS   **Village at Maplewood** (869-2111 or 800-873-2111), Main Street (Route 302), Maplewood 03574.Twenty condo townhouse units are available for daily or weekly rental. Rates from $100 a night.

CAMPS   Several **Appalachian Mountain Club High Huts** (466-2727, Box 298, Gorham 03581) are located in this area. Nearest to Route 302 off Zealand Road is the Zealand Hut; adjacent to I-93 in Franconia Notch are Lonesome Lake on the west side of the highway and Greenleaf Hut on the east. Lonesome Lake is the nearest AMC hut to a road, just 1.7 miles and an easy one-hour walk (our five-year-old daughter made it with ease); there is swimming and fishing in the lake. On the trail between Greenleaf and Zealand is Galehead. You must hike to the huts and supply your clothes and towels; they provide meals, bunks, and blankets. Some AMC programs involve guided hikes to the huts. Contact the AMC for rates and other information, and see the *AMC White Mountain Guide* for trail routes.

CAMPGROUNDS   **WMNF campgrounds** are located along Route 302, east of Twin Mountain. Sugarloaf 1 and 2 have 62 sites, and Zealand has 11 sites. The Sugarloaf sites are part of the toll-free reservation system (see White Mountain National Forest chapter).

Lafayette Campground (823-5563), a popular state park facility just off the parkway in the heart of Franconia Notch, has 97 wooded tent sites available on a first-come, first-served basis. A central lodge has showers and a small store with hiking and camping supplies. Site fees are $8–$17.

Local private campgrounds include **Fransted Campground** (823-5675), Route 18, Franconia, with 65 wooded tent sites and 26 trailer sites; and **Apple Hill Campground** (869-2238), Route 142 north, Bethlehem, with 45 tent sites, 20 trailer hookups, a store, and a bathhouse.

OTHER LODGING   **Mittersill** (823-5511), Franconia Notch 03580. A 500-acre, Tyrolean-style resort developed as part of a once fashionable but now defunct ski area adjoining Cannon Mountain. Plans call for a new lift to connect Mittersill with the Cannon trail system. There is a dining room and lounge in the central Alpine Lodge and riding stables on the grounds. Accommodations include hotel rooms, efficiency units, one- and two-bedroom suites, and free-standing chalets. Room rates start at $45, efficiencies $60, suites $75, and chalets $180.

DINING OUT   **Franconia Inn** (823-5542), Easton Road, Franconia. Dinner nightly 6–9. Long considered the local restaurant for elegant dining and special occasions, the Franconia Inn's handsome candlelit dining rooms offer black-tie service and a mountain view. Cocktails are served in the cozy, paneled Rathskeller Lounge. The a la carte menu ($15–$20) features American and continental cuisine and changes frequently. Typical entrées are saltimbocca, filet mignon with smoked veal breast, shrimp primavera, and veal medallions au champagne.

Lovett's by Lafayette Brook (823-7761), Profile Road, Franconia. Dinner nightly 6–8. A venerable inn, parts of which date to the eighteenth century. Lovett's has a fine view of Cannon Mountain and an established reputation for food and wine. Drinks are served in an intimate lounge, with a marble bar from a Newport, RI mansion, and the notable three-course table d'hôte ($20) is served in three connecting, open-beamed dining rooms. Soups are frequently unusual and may include cold bisque of fresh watercress, black bean soup with Demarara rum, and wild blueberry soup. Entrées might include chicken with apples and calvados, curried lamb with grape chutney, and sautéed Norwegian salmon or poached Colorado trout.

Tim-bir Alley (444-6142), 28 Main Street, Littleton. Dinner Wednesday to Sunday 5:30–9:30; Sunday brunch 9–1. Cash or check only, no reservations. Fine dining has come to the North Country with this seven-table gourmet restaurant, serving an eclectic menu that changes weekly and features six nightly entrées and homemade desserts. Entrées might include salmon with Brie and walnut cream; scaloppine with date and pecan sauce; or mixed grill with lamb, veal, and beef, each one enhanced separately with herbs and sauces. Each entrée is beautifully presented making the dining experience as exciting for the eye as it is for the palate. Prices range from $13–$17.

Cobblers (838-6118), Bishop Road, Lisbon. Open for dinner nightly except Mondays in winter. The pleasant dining room in the Ammonoosuc Inn offers entrées like chicken alfredo (chicken pieces with broccoli and artichokes tossed in noodles, cream, and Parmesan cheese) for $9. 95 or seafood Wellington (shrimp, scallops, scrod, and crabmeat in a cream sauce, baked in a pastry shell) for $13. 95. It's a large menu.

Horse & Hound Inn (823-5501), off Route 18, Franconia Open nightly, except Tuesday, from 6–9. The dining room of this small, traditional inn is paneled and warm; drinks are served in the cozy, book-lined combination library and lounge.The nightly menu includes beef, chicken, lamb, and seafood dishes, prepared with a French flair. Prices from $12–$20.

The Riverview Restaurant (869-3364 or 800-448-9557), Route 302 at Pierce Bridge, Bethlehem. Open nightly spring through fall, Thursday through Sunday in winter, from 6–9. The dining room of the Wayside Inn, the Riverview has long been regarded as the town's toniest restaurant. The inn's Pierce Lounge is also a popular drinking spot. The European-born owners, Victor and Kathe Hoffmann, emphasize continental cuisine. Swiss specialties are served every Friday night, but fondue is always available in ski season. Prime rib tops the menu on Saturdays.

EATING OUT   Polly's Pancake Parlor (823-5575), Route 117, Sugar Hill. Housed in an 1830s former carriage house with a grand mountain view, Polly's is a local institution with a menu that includes cob-smoked bacon and just about every kind of pancake known, from blueberry to walnut. Nice atmosphere. Reasonable prices.

Dutch Treat Restaurant (823-8851), Main Street, Franconia Village. A local standby. The dining room features Italian entrées and the adjoining Sports Lounge serves homemade pizza and screens sports events and classic movies on its giant TV screen.

Taverne Restaurant (823-7044), Main Street, Franconia. The dining room of the Rivagale Inn. Paneled, old-shoe atmosphere, fireplace, and a menu that always includes five spicy but inexpensive Mexican entrées as well as standard American fare.

Lloyd Hills (869-2141), Main Street, Bethlehem. Pleasant, informal, pub-style restaurant. Moderate.

Rosa Flamingo's (869-3111), Main Street, Bethlehem. Cheery and informal, serving a variety of Italian dishes. Moderate.

Cannonball Café and Deli (823-7478), Main Street, Franconia Village. Sandwiches, salads, and specialty dishes to eat in or take out. Unusual sandwiches include Brie, apple, and walnut on French bread. The menu also features offbeat international dishes such as "Himalayan Hen," a Cornish game hen marinated in fresh garlic, ginger, coriander, and other exotic spices.

The Clamshell (444-6445), Dells Road, Littleton. Monday to Saturday 11:30–4; Monday to Thursday 5–9, Friday and Saturday until 10; Sunday brunch 11–2. Just off Exit 42 of I-93, this is a popular seafood restaurant serving lobster, steaks, and prime rib; also sandwiches and a salad bar. They also have a fish market.

SELECTIVE SHOPPING   Franconia Marketplace, Main Street, Franconia. Selling only products made in Franconia, this complex in the heart of town houses the **Grateful Bread Quality Bakery** (823-5228), which makes whole grain and organic breads; **Cannonball Café and Deli** (823-7478), serving fresh sandwiches, salads, and international dishes; **Gale River Outlet,** with more than 100 styles of cotton clothes and sleepwear; and **Tiffany Workshop** (823-5539), featuring crystal jewelry, candles, and air-brushed shirts.

Sugar Hill Sampler, Route 117, Sugar Hill. A 1780s barn with a folksy pioneer museum and a large selection of candies, cheese, crafts, and antiques.

Harmons Cheese and Country Store (823-8000), Route 117, Sugar Hill. The specialty is well-aged cheddar, but the store also stocks maple sugar products and gourmet items.

Bungay Jar (823-7775), Route 116, Easton. An eclectic collection of antiques in an eighteenth-century barn; also a B&B (see Bed & Breakfast).

Abigail's Antiques (869-5550), Bethlehem Flower Farm, Main Street (Route 302), Bethlehem. Antiques and reproductions. Also on Main Street are a number of seasonal antiques shops.

The Village Bookstore (444-5263), Main Street, Littleton. Open daily. The largest and most complete bookstore (and one of the state's best) north of the mountains.

SPECIAL EVENTS   February: **Forest Festival** (444-6228), the Rocks Estate, Route 302, Bethlehem. A mid-February day in the woods with logging demonstrations plus snowshoeing and cross-country skiing. **Frostbite Follies:** A week-long series of events around Franconia, including sleigh rides, ski movies, broom hockey, ski races, community suppers. April: **Maple Season Tours** (444-6228), the Rocks Estate, Route 302, Bethlehem. Early April weekend features a workshop about maple trees plus learn about gathering sap and boiling it down to make maple syrup.

June: **Wildflower Festival** (444-6228), the Rocks Estate, Route 302, Bethlehem. Guided walks, workshops, demonstrations, and a children's walk on a Sunday in early June. **Open for the Season Celebration,** Bethlehem. Old-fashioned festival that includes golf tournament, crafts fair, and ball. Last weekend of the month. **Old Man in the Mountains USA and Canada Rugby Matches,** Cannon Mountain House Field, Route 116, Franconia.

July: **North Country Chamber Players,** Sugar Hill. Classical concerts Fridays at 8 PM in the Sugar Hill Meeting House. **Hayseed Blue Grass Festival** Dow Strip, Franconia. Bluegrass and fiddle music played outside. **Day Lily Festival,** Bethlehem.

August: **Horse Show,** Mittersill Resort, Franconia.

September: **Franconia Scramble,** Franconia. A 6.2-mile footrace over Franconia roads. **New England Boiled Dinner,** the town house, Franconia. Corned beef and all the fixings. **Annual Antique Show and Sale,** Sugar Hill Meeting House. Selected dealers of antiques and collectibles.

October: **Quilt Festival,** Franconia. **Durrell Methodist Church Bazaar,** Franconia. On Saturday of Columbus Day weekend. **Crafts Fair,** Elementary School, Bethlehem. On Sunday of Columbus Day weekend. **The Halloween Tradition** (444-6228), the Rocks Estate, Route 302, Bethlehem. Ghosts and goblins haunt the estate in a program co-sponsored by local Boy and Girl Scouts, plus apple bobbing, pumpkin carving, and ghost stories told around the fire.

December: **Oh! Christmas Tree** (444-6228), the Rocks Estate, Route 302, Bethlehem. Weekends in early December . Celebrate Christmas with wreath-making, ornament-making, and a hay-wagon tour of the Christmas tree plantation. Pick your own tree from the stump. Tree sales daily in December.

VII. The North Country

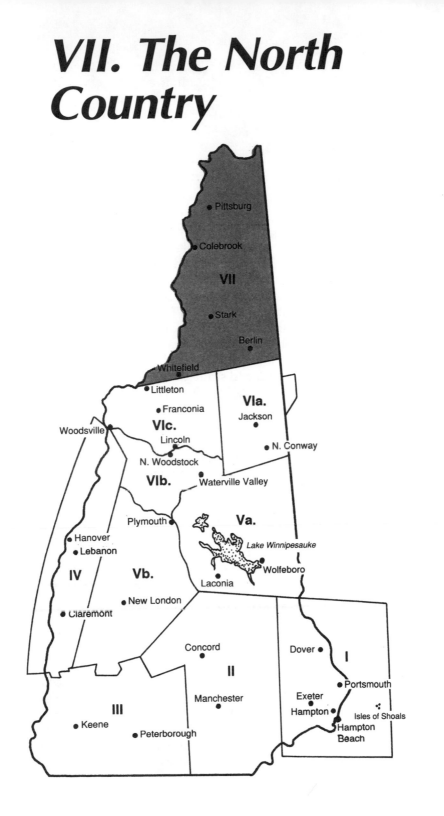

Introduction

The vast region north of the White Mountains, an area larger than Rhode Island, is New Hampshire's remaining frontier. Route 2, which connects Gorham in the east and Lancaster in the west, is considered the southern boundary of the North Country. Route 16, from Gorham to Errol; Route 26, from Errol to Colebrook; and Route 3, from Lancaster north through Colebrook to Pittsburg are the main, and sometimes the only, roads for travelers. The broad forests, fast-running rivers, and rugged mountains are cut by only a few roads, and many of the towns are small and scattered. Although most of the privately owned woodlands have been cut more than once to feed the voracious paper mills, the overall impression is one of wilderness. Trees are harvested as a cash crop, but cutting is usually back from the highways and only the sight of huge, heavily loaded logging trucks gives evidence of how much wood is cut annually. The paper and timber management companies, who own most of this forested country, allow recreational use of their property for hunting, fishing, hiking, and snowmobiling while managing the woods for a continuous yield.

This system has worked well for decades, but there are signs that changes are coming. Huge sections of land were sold to developers in 1988; and even though the state of New Hampshire, various conservation groups, and the federal government were able to buy some environmentally critical acreage, other parcels may be used for vacation homes or other types of developments.

Economically, this is the poorest section of the state; and while New Hampshire is the fastest growing state in the northeast, the North Country is losing population as many young people are forced to seek employment elsewhere. Working in the woods and in the paper mills are important occupations; but with woodlands being sold for development and the three large paper mills currently for sale, residents are naturally concerned about the future. Land sold for development is lost for outdoor recreation, yet when acreage is acquired by the state or federal governments, these small towns lose badly needed tax revenues.

Tourism is becoming more important to the economy. Hunting and

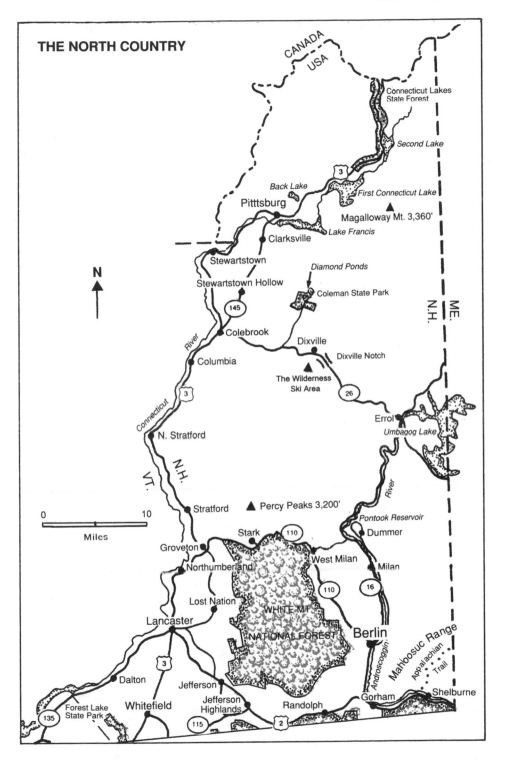

THE NORTH COUNTRY

CANADA
USA

Connecticut Lakes
State Forest

Second Lake

3

Back Lake

First Connecticut Lake

Pitttsburg

Magalloway Mt. 3,360'

Clarksville

Lake Francis

Stewartstown

Stewartstown Hollow

N

Diamond Ponds

145

Coleman State Park

Colebrook

Dixville

Columbia

Dixville Notch

The Wilderness
Ski Area

26

3

Errol

Umbagog Lake

N. Stratford

VT.   N.H.

ME.
N.H.

Stratford

▲ Percy Peaks 3,200'

Pontook Reservoir

0   10

Miles

Stark

110

Dummer

Groveton

West Milan

Milan

Northumberland

110

16

Lost Nation

WHITE MT.

Lancaster

NATIONAL FOREST

Berlin

Mahloosuc Range

Appalachian   Trail

Dalton

Jefferson

Androscoggin

Gorham

Shelburne

3

Whitefield

Jefferson
Highlands

Randolph

115

2

Forest Lake
State Park

135

Connecticut   River

fishing are leisure-time activities for residents and visitors alike. Trapping remains a winter occupation for a few people, and others make a living as hunting and fishing guides.

All of the North Country is part of Coos County (to sound like a native pronounce it as "Co-oss"). Although the Kilkenny District of the White Mountain National Forest occupies a large section of the North Country, campers are reminded that most of the North Country is private property, and open fires and camping are not permitted except at campgrounds.

Travelers in the North Country are reminded that lodging and dining establishments are few and far between, especially on Route 16 north of Berlin. This is great country for taking along a picnic to enjoy as you fish, canoe, or just relax in New Hampshire's northern wilds.

GETTING THERE   With only limited bus service, no taxis, and no scheduled air service, a private vehicle is the best way to travel in the North Country.

By car: Routes 16, 302, or I-93 to Route 3 from the south; Route 2 from Maine or Vermont; Route 257 from Montreal; and Route 147 from Quebec City.

By bus: **Concord Trailways** (800-852-3317) provides scheduled service from Boston's Logan Airport to central and northern New Hampshire via Manchester and Meredith. Western North Country stops, via Plymouth and Franconia, include Littleton, Whitefield, Lancaster, Groveton, North Stratford, Colebrook, and the Balsams. Eastern North Country stops, via Meredith and West Ossipee, include Conway, North Conway, Jackson, Glen, Pinkham Notch, Gorham, and Berlin. Daily service varies.

By air: There is no scheduled air service anywhere near the North Country. Fly to commercial airports in Lebanon or Manchester, New Hampshire; Portland, Maine; or Boston, Massachusetts, and get rental cars at the airports. **Dave-L Limousine Service** (752-5112), Berlin, runs to Logan Airport in Boston and the Portland Jetport in Maine by reservation only. Several private airports are listed below (see Airplane Rides), but there are no taxis. Some inns and lodges arrange for pickup on request.

MEDICAL EMERGENCY   See towns below for hospitals, or call the State Police (800-852-3411).

Along Route 2

Gorham has been catering to tourists since 1851 when the newly built Atlantic and St. Lawrence Railroad (now the Canadian National) began to bring thousands of tourists from southern and central New England via Portland to the White Mountains. Today it is a prime crossroads where east-west Route 2 intersects north-south Route 16. Strung out along the Androscoggin River, Shelburne is famous for its stand of white birches that straddle Route 2 a few miles east of Gorham. Large in land area, small in population, the two towns of Randolph and Jefferson stretch out along Route 2 bordering the northern peaks of the Presidential Range of the White Mountains. Randolph is a center for White Mountain hiking, while Jefferson has long been a popular resort community.

GUIDANCE   **Northern White Mountains Chamber of Commerce** (752-6060), 164 Main Street, Box 298, Berlin 03570.

Town of Gorham Information Center (466-2340), Main Street, Gorham. Open weekends Memorial Day through June, then daily from July to Columbus Day weekend. **Gorham Resort Bureau** (466-2520).

A seasonal **New Hampshire Information Center**, with rest rooms and picnic tables, is located on Route 2, Shelburne.

White Mountain National Forest, Androscoggin Ranger Station (466-2713), Route 16, Gorham. Open Monday through Friday 7:30–4:30.

TO SEE AND DO   **Six Gun City** (586-4592), Route 2, Jefferson. Open daily 9–6, mid-June to Labor Day; weekends until Columbus Day. Cowboy skits and frontier shows are combined with 35 western town buildings; a 100-piece, horse-drawn vehicle museum; miniature horses and other animals; animal rides; and a water slide. Food and gift shops. Admission includes unlimited rides and shows. Age 4 to adult $8, age 3 and under free with an adult.

Santa's Village (586-4445), Route 2, Jefferson. Open daily 9:30–7, Father's Day to Labor Day; weekends 9:30–5 until Columbus Day. Santa and his elves, along with the reindeer, make this Christmas in the summer for children and adults. Ride the Yule Log Flume, the railroad, Ferris wheel, or roller coaster; watch the trained macaw show;

see the new animated Twelve Days of Christmas kiosk; and, of course, sit on Santa's lap. Food and gift shops. Admission includes unlimited rides and shows. Age 4 to adult $10, age 3 and under with an adult free as Santa's guest.

Gorham Historical Society, Railroad Street, Gorham. The Railroad Station Museum contains displays on local history and especially railroading, tourism, and logging.

White Mountain Llamas (586-4598), Route 115, Jefferson Meadows 03583. Something new for the hiker is a trek with these unusual animals hauling the gear and your experienced guides pointing out the flora and fauna and preparing a mountainside gourmet lunch. One- to four-day treks with accommodations at **Stag Hollow Inn and Llama Keep** (see Bed & Breakfasts) and two meals daily is $150–$500 per couple; without accommodations, $55 per person.

SCENIC DRIVES   **Pinkham B Road** (formerly Dolly Copp Road) is a mostly unpaved wilderness road running from Dolly Copp Campground on Route 16, past the base of Mt. Madison to Route 2. Several hiking trails begin on this road. Not winter-maintained.

Jefferson Notch Road is a historic route beside the western edge of the Presidential Range. Not winter-maintained, this winding gravel road reaches the highest elevation point of any public through road in New Hampshire at Jefferson Notch (3,008 feet). Drive with care because snow and mud leave late in the spring, and ice returns early in the fall; it is best used in the summer. The Caps Ridge Trail, at the 7-mile point on Jefferson Notch, offers the shortest route to any of the Presidential Range peaks: 2.5 miles to Mt. Jefferson. From the north, Jefferson Notch Road leaves Valley Road (which connects routes 2 and 115) in Jefferson and runs south to the Cog Railway Base Station Road. At that intersection paved Mt. Clinton Road continues on to the Crawford House site on Route 302.

Shelburne's North Road is a winding country byway with great views of the Presidential Range across the Androscoggin River.

AIRPLANE RIDES   **Screaming Eagle Aviation** (466-3431 or 356-5809), Gorham Airport, routes 16 and 2, Gorham. Airplane rides over the White Mountains in a vintage 1941 Fairchild 24, a classic luxury design of the 1930s. The windows roll down for picture taking. Rates begin at $20 per person for three passengers.

GOLF   **Androscoggin Valley Country Club** (466-9468; pro shop 466-2641), Route 2, Gorham. Eighteen holes, bar and food service.

The Waumbeck Country Club (586-7777), Route 2, Jefferson. The 18-hole course, overlooked by the Presidential Range, is about all that remains from one of the largest nineteenth-century resort hotels. Food and beverages, also tennis.

HORSEBACK RIDING   **Philbrook Farm Stables** (466-2993), North Road Shelburne 03581, offers lessons and trail rides.

HIKING   **White Mountain Adventures** (466-2363), Route 2, Shelburne 03581, is a guide service for hiking, backpacking, and snowshoeing in the White Mountains. All food and group equipment is provided for day hikes or two- to three-day overnight trips. Trips are organized to suit hikers' abilities. All participants receive detailed lists of needed personal gear. Rates vary for type and length of trip.

Presidential Range Hiking. For any White Mountain hiking consult the *AMC White Mountain Guide* for details about trailheads, routes, distances, hiking time estimates, and special information. (Also see *Fifty Hikes in the White Mountains* or *Fifty Hikes in New Hampshire*, both by Daniel Doan, Backcountry Publications). A map is vital here since there are myriad trails interconnecting on the north side of the rugged Presidential Range peaks. There are three parking areas on Route 2 and another on Pinkham B (Dolly Copp) Road, connecting routes 2 and 16, which are at the most popular trailheads for climbing the northern peaks of Madison, Adams, and Jefferson. Most of these trails lead above tree line and should be attempted only by properly equipped hikers. Winter weather conditions can occur above tree line any month of the year. Most of the trails to the summits are 4–5 miles in length and require 4–5 hours to reach the top. The lower portions of the trails pass through wooded areas along streams and are suitable for short walks.

High on the side of **Mt. Adams,** the **Randolph Mountain Club** (Randolph 03570) maintains two cabins and two shelters for hikers. Overnight fees of $1–$2.50 per person are charged. The cabins have cooking utensils and gas stoves in July and August, but hikers must supply their own food and bedding.

The **Appalachian Mountain Club** (reservations 466-2727) has operated Madison Hut since 1888 , a full-service, summer-only, facility at tree line on **Mt. Madison** (see full listing under Mt. Washington's Valleys).

A less-rigorous hike to **Pine Mountain** offers fine views of the Presidential Range. Off Pinkham B (Dolly Copp) Road (2.4 miles from Route 2 or 1.9 miles from Route 16), a private road that is open to public foot traffic only leads to the summit and connects to a loop trail. Estimated hiking time is two hours for a 3.4-mile round-trip.

Pinkham Notch; AMC Pinkham Notch Camp, headquarters for Mt. Washington hiking; **Wildcat Ski Area;** and The **Mt. Washington Carriage Road** are just south of Gorham on Route 16. See Mt. Washington's Valleys chapter for details.

North of Route 2 in Jefferson, **Waumbek** and **Starr King** mountains are popular hikes. The climb is 3.8 miles and requires just over three hours to the top.

LODGING   **Philbrook Farm Inn** (466-3831), North Road, Shelburne 03581. Open May 1 to October 31 and December 26 to March 31. This unique inn has been operated by five generations of the Philbrook family since it began in 1861. A treasure of White Mountain historical artifacts, the inn retains its old-time character; a visitor from 100 years ago probably would still feel right at home even though there have been changes and additions over the years. Situated in a quiet spot a mile and a half from Route 2, the place has been popular with artists and writers who enjoy the solitude and with hikers who can wander the inn's 1,000 acres that back up to the national forest. Swim in the barnyard pool, rock on the porch or beside a huge fireplace in the living room with its historical treasures, take a trail ride at the stables next door, or play a variety of indoor and outdoor games. There is snowshoeing or cross-country skiing from the door. The country-style accommodations vary. The large main inn has 19 rooms—some have private baths, others share baths. There are twin-, double-, and king-size beds. Five outbuildings offer more private accommodations with from one to five bedrooms, fireplaces, living rooms, porches, and kitchens—just right for a family or small groups. MAP rates include a full breakfast and single entrée New England dinner. The inn can accommodate those with special diets with advance notice. Most of the vegetables come from the inn's or its neighbor's gardens. Fresh breads and pastries are cooked daily in a huge commercial-size woodstove. Rates are $100–$120 MAP for two, full American plan available to weekly guests; housekeeping cottages for up to eight persons are $400 a week.

BED & BREAKFASTS   **The Gorham House** (466-2271), 55 Main Street, Box 267, Gorham 03581. This 1891 Queen Anne-style Victorian B&B has four rooms with shared baths. Rooms have double beds or a double and a twin. Innkeepers: Ronnie, Maggie, and Sam. Rates are $50 for two people.

The Jefferson Inn (586-7998), Route 2 (at the junction with Route 115a), Jefferson 03583. Open year-round, except parts of November and April. This fine, old (built in 1896), 10-room inn has a new breakfast room and two new guest rooms. Five rooms have private baths, a two-room suite accommodates four people, and three rooms share a bath. A trail for nearby Waumbek and Starr King mountains leaves from the inn, and just across the street is a wonderful old stone swimming pool with a beach for children. Afternoon tea with homemade baked goods is served at 4 PM. Rates are $40–$70, breakfast is an additional $4.

The Davenport Inn (586-4320), Route 2, Jefferson 03583. Located on Davenport Road, east of Jefferson Village and 500 yards off Route 2, this five-room B&B offers quiet and solitude. All five rooms, including one with a king-size bed, have private baths. Enjoy the antique claw-foot tubs, and relax on the wraparound porch. Rates are $58, full breakfast included.

Applebrook B&B (586-7713), Route 115a, Box 178, Jefferson 03583. Open year-round. A rambling old Victorian building, this inn has seven rooms—two with private baths, the others share three baths. The two large dorm rooms with three and seven beds each are great for groups. A full breakfast is included and dinner is available to groups by advance reservation. Innkeeper Martin Kelley charges $50 per couple..

Stag Hollow Inn and Llama Keep (586-4598), Route 115, Jefferson Meadow 03583. Three rooms, one with two double beds, share a single bath. Large living room with fireplace, cross-country skiing from the back door, a nearby natural swimming hole in the Israel River plus 11 llamas (see **White Mountain Llamas** under To See and Do). Innkeeper Joanna Fryon charges $45–$65 per couple.

MOTELS   Motels line Gorham's Main Street, two of which are open year-round: **Tourist Village Motel** (466-3312) and **Gorham Motor Inn** (466-3381).

Town and Country Motor Inn (466-3315), Route 2, Shelburne 03581. Open year-round. Situated in the midst of the famous birches, this 160-room resort includes a health club, indoor pool, whirlpool, and steam bath. Rooms have air-conditioning, phones, and color cable TV. Rates are $52–$72 for two. The restaurant has a diverse menu for breakfast and dinner and Sunday dinner. Lounge with entertainment. Moderately priced.

Evergreen Motel (586-4449), Route 2 (Box 33), Jefferson. Open mid-May through Columbus Day weekend. Eighteen units, air-conditioning, TV, swimming pool, coffee shop, and across the street from Santa's Village. Rates are $34–$48 for two.

Lantern Motor Inn (586-7151), Route 2 (Box 97), Jefferson. Open mid-May through October. Thirty units, air-conditioning, TV, pool, and playground. Rates are $38–$48 for two.

CAMPING   **Moose Brook State Park,** Route 2, Gorham. Open daily June to Labor Day, on weekends from mid-May. This small park has a large outdoor pool (known for its cold water), a small beach, and 42 tent sites. No reservations. Camping and day-use fees charged.

Also see Mt. Washington's Valleys (Crawford Notch and Bretton Woods).

DINING OUT   **Yokohama Restaurant** (466-2501), Main Street, Gorham. Serves lunch and dinner, closed Monday. A longtime, popular American–Oriental eatery. Moderately priced.

Via Sorrento (466-2520), Main Street, Gorham. Closed Sunday. Serves lunch and dinner. An Italian restaurant where everything is homemade. Moderately priced.

Also see Motels (Town and Country Motor Inn).

Berlin and Route 16 North

Called "the city that trees built," Berlin is the industrial center of the North Country. While the heavy aroma often emitted from the paper mills offends the nostrils of visitors, natives call it the smell of money since the mills are the chief employers in the region. Actually millions of dollars have been spent in recent years to clean up the water pollution in the Androscoggin River. There's a strong French-Canadian influence here because many residents are descended from Quebec immigrants who came to work in the woods and in the mills. French remains a second, and sometimes the primary, language of many people. Though not considered a tourist destination, Berlin is the largest community in the North Country and a service center for a wide area.

Milan, Dummer, and Errol are small towns north of Berlin along Route 16 that are known for outdoor opportunities—especially on the Androscoggin River, which flows through the communities.

Not so much a town as it is a place (since its tiny population is mostly connected with the Balsams Resort), Dixville gets a moment of fame every four years when all of its 30 voters stay up past midnight to cast the first early votes in the presidential election. The most northerly of New Hampshire's notches, Dixville is worth the ride just for the views of this narrow pass and the picturesque Balsams as you drive through the steep, rugged mountains.

GUIDANCE **Northern White Mountains Chamber of Commerce** (752-6060), 164 Main Street, Box 298, Berlin 03570.

MEDICAL EMERGENCY **Androscoggin Valley Hospital** (752-2200), 59 Page Hill Road, Berlin. Ambulance: 752-1020.

TO SEE AND DO View the **James River Corporation's paper mills** along the Androscoggin River from Cascade to Berlin—once the largest complex of its type in the world—still producing a variety of paper products.

Holy Resurrection Church, 20 Petrograd Street, Berlin. An unusual Eastern Orthodox church, complete with onion domes, built by Russian immigrants in 1915.

Berlin Public Library (752-5210), Main Street, Berlin, has a collection of stone Indian implements, some dating back 7,000 years.

GREEN SPACE **Nansen Wayside Park,** Route 16, 4 miles north of Berlin. The state-owned ski jump is across the street from this small park beside

Photo by George Sylvester

The Androscoggin River offers some of New Hampshire's best fishing
and canoeing.

the Androscoggin River. Several picnic sites and a boat-launching ramp.

The **Androscoggin River** is one of New Hampshire's natural treasures. It enters the state from Maine at Wentworth Location, just north of the village of Errol, and flows south through Dummer and Milan to Berlin, where, unfortunately, it picks up wastes from the paper mills before turning sharply west and flowing back into Maine. In recent years millions of dollars have been spent on treatment plants in Berlin, and the river is now much cleaner than it has been for decades. North of Berlin, the river is one of the state's most popular canoeing and fishing waters. There is plenty of history here as well. The river was used to float logs down to the mills. Just above the Berlin city center are large pilings in the river, once used to anchor booms which kept the logs moving swiftly to the mills. The most beautiful stretch of the river is the **Thirteen-Mile Woods Scenic Area**, just south of Errol, where the road and river curve along side by side through a wild area. At about the midpoint is the riverside **Androscoggin Wayside Park**, situated on a bluff overlooking the river with picnic tables. No fee.

Lake Umbagog, a largely undeveloped lake, is one of the finest wild areas in northern New England. Here live the only known nesting New Hampshire bald eagles, sharing the skies with osprey, loons, and varied waterfowl. Moose amble the shorelines, and the fishing is great. Most of the surrounding land is owned by timber management companies.

Currently, federal and state agencies are working with conservation organizations to acquire enough acreage to establish a wildlife refuge. The
need for a refuge became apparent several years ago when developers
announced a plan to mine diatomaceous earth (composed of microscopic
animal skeletons, which cover the bottom of the lake), which is used for
industrial filtering and abrasives. The northern end of the lake is most
interesting, especially in the extensive freshwater marshes where the
Androscoggin and Magalloway rivers meet. Inexpensive, primitive
campsites make this an ideal destination for a family or group canoeing.
Boats and canoes may be launched north of Errol on Route 16 and south
of Errol on Route 26 at Umbagog Lake Campground, where arrange-
ments can be made to rent the campsites (see Campgrounds).

   Dixville Notch State Park, Route 26, Dixville Notch. There are two
roadside picnic areas and pretty waterfalls here. For the hardy, there
is a steep, 30-minute, 0.3-mile climb up the south side of the notch to
Table Rock, which offers a panoramic view of the Balsams and Lake
Gloriette.

AIRPLANE RIDES   Mountain Rain (482-3323), Errol Airport, Errol 03579. David
Heasley operates the airport, offers sight-seeing rides and charters; also
flies canoeists, kayakers, and fishermen into backcountry areas.

CANOEING   Androscoggin River paddlers are advised to check with the *AMC
River Guide* or *Canoe Camping Vermont and New Hampshire Rivers*
(Backcountry Publications). **Northern Waters** in Errol Village has
rentals, instruction, guided trips, or other canoeing information. They
offer raft float trips every Wednesday in July and August from their
location beside the river, and they also coordinate flat-water kayak
trips on the Magalloway River and Lake Umbagog. For information
or reservations, contact **Saco Bound** (447-2177), Box 119, Route 302,
Center Conway 03813.

FISHING   The **Androscoggin** is a popular trout stream. New Hampshire fishing licenses, required for adults, are sold at many stores throughout
the region. Another recommended fishing spot is **South Pond
Recreation Area,** located off Route 110 in West Milan. It also has a picnic and swimming area.

GOLF   Panorama Golf Course (255-4961), part of the Balsams Resort,
Dixville Notch. This 18-hole, par-72 course, rolling over beautiful
mountain slopes, was designed by Donald Ross in 1912. Adjacent is
an executive par-3 course. Pro shop, lessons, and cart rentals; tee times
are required.

HIKING   There are plenty of hiking opportunities in the area north of Route
2, but trails are not well marked and some are obliterated as a result
of logging operations. Consult the *AMC White Mountain Guide,* or
Walks & Rambles in the Upper Connecticut River Valley (Backcountry
Publications), or ask locally for trail details.

   Mahoosuc Range. Stretching from Shelburne northeast to Grafton

Notch in Maine, this rugged range offers some of the most difficult hiking on the Appalachian Trail (the mountains are not high, but the trails steeply ascend and descend the peaks). Many of the peaks as well as rocky Mahoosuc Notch, where the ice stays in crevasses year-round, are most easily reached by Success Pond Road, a smooth logging road on the north side of the mountains. In the middle of Berlin, turn east at the traffic lights across the river, through the log yard of the paper company, then travel up to 14 miles along the road to get to the various trailheads. Watch for logging trucks on this road. (See the *AMC White Mountain Guide* for hiking details.)

SKIING   Wilderness Ski Area (800-255-0600; in NH 800-255-0800), Route 26, Dixville Notch 03576. The most remote ski area in New Hampshire, Wilderness gets most of its business from local day trippers (some from nearby Quebec) or from guests at the nearby Balsams Resort, owners of the ski area—so rarely are there any lift lines. There are 12 trails on easy to difficult terrain, and the abundant natural snow is backed up with snowmaking. For the cross-country skier there are 50 km of developed trails, most of which are groomed and tracked. Ski school, rentals, and nursery are available. Skiing is free for hotel guests and package plans include free ski lessons.

SNOWMOBILING   The North Country is the state's most popular snowmobiling area. On hundreds of miles of woods roads and some specially maintained trails, the snowmobile enthusiast can travel to Quebec, Vermont, and Maine. Some winter weekends are as busy as those in the summer. Many motels and lodges, especially in Colebrook and Pittsburg, have trails right from the door that connect with a lengthy trail network. For maps and other information, write **North Country Chamber of Commerce** (237-8939), Box 1, Colebrook 03576; **The Trails Bureau** (271-3254), NH Division of Parks and Recreation, Box 856, Concord 03301; or the **New Hampshire Snowmobile Association** (224-8906), Box 38, Concord 03301.

RESORT   The Balsams Resort (800-255-0600; in NH 800-255-0800), Route 26, Dixville Notch 03576. Open mid-May to mid-October and mid-December through March. A four-star, grand resort, this is New Hampshire's (and arguably New England's) finest hotel. Dating back to 1866, this rambling French-provincial style castle-like hostelry, on the shore of Lake Gloriette and overlooked by the jagged spires of Dixville Notch, appears like a piece of the Alps in America. With more staff members than guests (up to 400 for 232 rooms) and 15,000 acres of mostly wilderness, the Balsams is an American-plan destination resort offering tennis, golf, swimming, and hiking in the summer and an exclusive downhill and cross-country ski area plus skating in the winter. Guests are offered seasonal natural history programs, children's activities and nursery, nightclub entertainment, movies, and dancing. All the guest rooms are well-appointed, but the superior rooms offer better views of the countryside. The award-winning dining fits the deluxe character of this resort, and the extensive menu is attractively displayed for guests to view before ordering. The rates cover everything, including lodging, dining, skiing, golf, and all other facilities. Summer season: AP, from $250; winter season: MAP, from $158. Ski weeks from $355 per person.

OTHER LODING   Except for the Balsams Resort, there is not much in the way of lodging in this section of New Hampshire. The **Errol Motel** (482-3256), Route 26, Errol, is open year-round and has three housekeeping units. Snowmobile trails from the motel connect with all local trails. Rates are $43 per couple.

Stark Village Inn (636-2644), just across the covered bridge off Route 110, west of Milan or east of Groveton (mailing: RFD 1, Box 389, Groveton 03582. (See Bed & Breakfasts in Littleton, Stark, etc. chapter.)

CAMPGROUNDS   **Milan Hill State Park,** Route 110B (off Route 16), Milan. A small park with 24 primitive camping sites, picnic tables, and a playground. A fire tower atop the 1,737-foot-high hill offers sweeping views of the North Country and into Canada. Camping and day-use fees charged.

13-Mile Woods Campgrounds (482-3373), Box 34, Errol 03579. Open mid-May through hunting season, depending on the weather. Ed "Moose" Damp operates the 50-site Mollidgewock Campground, located about 4 miles south of Errol Village, in the 13-Mile Woods Scenic Area. He also has a few other campsites along the river. These are somewhat primitive sites with picnic tables, fireplaces, water, and outhouses, but they are beside the river and perfect for fishing and canoeing. $6 per adult per night.

Umbagog Lake Campground and Cottages (482-7795), Route 26, PO Box 181, Errol 03579. Open late May to mid-September. Umbagog is a large, mostly wilderness, 14-mile-long lake that straddles the New Hampshire–Maine border. Around the lake and on some of its small islands are 25 primitive camping sites that are reached by your own canoe or boat (rentals available). Campers must bring tents and food; there are picnic tables and fireplaces. Here you can see moose, eagles, osprey, and a variety of waterfowl. Fall asleep to the sounds of loons calling in the night. At the base camp, just south of Errol on Route 26, there is also a family campground, with a camp store for supplies and some housekeeping cabins.

DINING OUT   See the Balsams Resort under Lodging.

EATING OUT   **The Northland Dairy Bar and Restaurant** (752-6210), Route 16, Berlin. Located just north of the city and popular with canoeists and hikers, the eatery features fresh seafood, sandwiches, and their own fresh-made ice cream and pastries.

Errol Restaurant (482-3852), Errol Village. Open daily at 5 AM, year-round. Country menu, seafood to steaks; breakfast, lunch, and dinner. Home of the mooseburger.

Littleton, Whitefield, Lancaster, Groveton, and Stark

Lancaster is the Coos County seat and the place to visit for people searching deeds or probate records. It is the local shopping center for a wide area. A hilly community midway between Littleton and Lancaster, with a perfect village square surrounded by shops, homes, and churches, Whitefield looks like everyone's all-American town.

Groveton is the business center of the town of Northumberland. Coming upon the town from the south, one is greeted with a perfect tableau combining North Country history and the region's prime industry. Before the large James River Company paper mill is Groveton covered bridge and beside it an old logging engine, dating to the days when logging railroads spread over the North Country and the White Mountains. Rising high in the background are the distinctive Percy Peaks, a reminder perhaps that the future of the North Country lies in its wilderness. Tiny Stark village, on routes 110 and 110a/110b between Groveton and Milan–Berlin, is best known for a picturesque covered bridge and Union church, both built in the 1850s, just beside the highway. During World War II German prisoners-of-war were brought to a prison camp here to work in the woods.

GUIDANCE **Lancaster Chamber of Commerce** (788-2578), Main Street, Lancaster 03584. Summer-only information booth.

Whitefield Chamber of Commerce (837-2609), Whitefield. Information booth on the square.

MEDICAL EMERGENCY **Weeks Memorial Hospital** (788-4911), Middle Street, Lancaster.

TO SEE AND DO **Weeks State Historic Site**, Route 3, 2 miles south of Lancaster. Open daily late June to Labor Day and weekends in September, weather permitting. Situated atop Mt. Prospect, this was the summer home of Lancaster native John Sinclair Weeks, a Massachusetts congressman responsible for the bill that established the White Mountain National Forest and all national forests in the eastern United States. By the turn of the nineteenth century, logging companies were clear-cutting the northern forests, destroying wildlife

Stark covered bridge.

habitat and the forest wilderness. Without trees on the steep mountain slopes to hold back rainwater, soil erosion was increasing and down-river flooding threatened communities every spring. Weeks's love of the wilderness led him to file the legislation that passed in 1911 and which resulted in the 768,000-acre White Mountain National Forest of New Hampshire and Maine. The house and a nearby observation tower offer broad views of the Presidential Range. Fee charged.

Wilder-Holton House (788-3004), 226 Main Street, Lancaster 03584. The first two-story house built in Coos County (1780), this is the museum of the Lancaster Historical Society. Open by appointment.

COVERED BRIDGES   The **Lancaster, NH–Lunenburg, VT,** covered bridge crosses the Connecticut River 5 miles southwest of Lancaster off Route 135. The **Mechanic Street** bridge is east of Routes 2/3 in the village of Lancaster. The **Groveton** bridge is just south of the James River Company paper mills. The **Stark** bridge is just off Route 110, west of Milan or east of Groveton.

GREEN SPACE   **Forest Lake State Beach,** Dalton, on a side road off Route 115 between Littleton and Whitefield. Open weekends from Memorial Day, daily late June through Labor Day. One of the original state parks dating from 1935, this 50-acre site has a 200-foot-long swimming beach, bathhouse, and picnic sites. Handicapped accessible. Fee charged.

SCENIC DRIVES   **North Road** (Route 116) connects Lancaster with Jefferson and offers country views of the mountains, especially Mt. Cabot and the Kilkenny Wilderness Area east of Lancaster. Just south of Lancaster, **Lost Nation Road** departs from North Road and runs north to Groveton. According to one tradition, this area was named by a traveling preacher, who, when he could get only one person to attend church, likened the local folks to the lost tribes of Israel. **Route 110 and Routes 110a/110b** from Groveton to Milan and Berlin are picturesque in any season, but also try the secondary road that runs parallel to Route 110, north of the Upper Ammonoosuc River, from Groveton Village, through Percy and Stark, to rejoin Route 110 just west of the 110/110a intersection.

AIRPLANE RIDES   **White Mountain Regional Airport** (837-5505), off Routes 3, 115, or 116, Whitefield. Sight-seeing rides.

GOLF   **Mountain View House Country Club** (837-3885), Whitefield. Nine-hole course operated by the Spalding Inn (see Resorts). This golf course served the Mountain View House, still standing but now closed. On a clear day the summit of Mt. Washington seems but a long 2-iron shot away.

HIKING   The best hiking area is the Kilkenny District of the White Mountain National Forest although the trails are not so well marked as in the mountains farther south. One popular climb is **Mt. Cabot** (4 miles, 3 hours), east of Lancaster. The **Percy Peaks** (2 miles, 2 hours), north of

Stark, offer views across the North Country and are not likely to be crowded with other hikers. Check the *AMC White Mountain Guide* for directions to Cabot and the Percy Peaks.

White Mountain Trekkers (837-2285 evenings), Kimball Hill Road, Whitefield 03598. Mike Purcell and Joseph Simard lead three- to seven-day hikes in the White Mountains for four to eight people. They supply all food and gear needed; hikers bring their own clothes, legs, strong back, and good physical condition. Trekkers carry a 25- to 30-lb. backpack and camp out in tents in sleeping bags. Distances and walking pace are geared to wilderness enjoyment and are not a survival test. Rates vary on type and length of trip.

RESORTS   The Spalding Inn Resort (837-2572), Mountain View Road, Whitefield 03598. Open Memorial Day to mid-October. Since 1926 this has been one of the state's finest resorts, offering a relaxed country location, personal service, and a host of amenities. The inn is famous for its lawn bowling, and it has often hosted the United States singles and doubles championships. There is also tennis, golf (9-hole and par-3), a swimming pool, and organized activities if desired. The inn and adjacent lodge have 42 rooms, with twin, double, and queen-size beds, all with private baths and phones. Six separate cottages have a total of 16 rooms, and some of these have fireplaces and kitchenettes. Three meals are served daily (see Dining Out). Richard Hamilton and Paul Truax, innkeepers. B&B $130–$190; MAP $180–$240. EP is also available.

INNS   Kimball Hill Inn (837-2284), Kimball Hill Road, Box 74, Whitefield 03598. Open year-round. Situated at an elevation of 1,400 feet, on a hill overlooking the mountains of the North Country, this inn has nature trails, a large comfortable living room, and Preston's Pub, a small bar with games to play. There are nine rooms with private baths plus four efficiency cottages. Expanded continental breakfast served to guests only; dinner served to the public by reservation (see Dining Out). Penny and Rick Preston, innkeepers. Inn rates are $45–$60; cottages are $350 per week.

BED & BREAKFAST   Stark Village Inn (636-2644), just across the covered bridge off Route 110, west of Milan or east of Groveton (mailing: RFD 1, Box 389, Groveton 032582). Open year-round. The Upper Ammonoosuc River ripples between this inn and a picturesque church and under the covered bridge. It is a classic location to spend the night or a few days. Nearby is trout fishing, hiking, bicycling, cross-country skiing, skating on the river, or snowmobiling. The old restored farmhouse, furnished with antiques and comfortable furniture, has three rooms—two with double beds and all with private baths. A full breakfast is cooked on the woodstove. The Spaulding family, innkeepers. Rates are $45 for two; single room is $30.

DINING OUT   The Spalding Inn Resort (837-2572), Mountain View Road,

Whitefield. Open Memorial Day to mid-October. The menu changes daily, and the five-course dinner usually offers beef, chicken, and seafood, all cooked in a continental style. Breakfast is $10, luncheon $14, and dinner $25, all fixed prices.

Kimball Hill Inn (837-2284), Kimball Hill Road, Box 74, Whitefield. Open year-round. Five entrées served nightly. Steak to chicken to fresh seafood, homemade desserts. Moderately priced.

EATING OUT   **Barbara's** (837-3161), Route 3, north of Whitefield Village. Open daily 6 AM to 9 PM. A varied menu from sandwiches to full dinners. Inexpensive.

ENTERTAINMENT   **Weathervane Theatre** (837-9322), Route 3, Whitefield. Open July and August. A repertory theater (since 1966) featuring old favorites, especially musicals.

SPECIAL EVENTS   Late June: **Old Time Fiddler's Contest** (636-1325), Whitcomb Field, Stark. Bring a picnic lunch, blanket or lawn chairs and enjoy the music of dozens of fiddlers. Food available. Admission fee.

Labor Day weekend: **Lancaster Fair** (837-2770) is a real old-fashioned country fair, highlighted by nonbetting harness racing. A large midway, food, and thrill rides plus 4-H animal judging competition, Grange exhibits, displays of vegetables and handicrafts, and oxen and horse pulling. Admission fee, children under 12 free.

Colebrook, Pittsburg, and vicinity

Bustling, friendly little Colebrook on the Connecticut River is a service oasis for people traveling north from Berlin over routes 16 and 26, north from Lancaster on Route 3, or south from Canada and Pittsburg. It is a recreational center, especially for hunting, fishing, and winter snowmobiling; and it is the shopping center for a number of small towns including Pittsburg, Columbia, Stewartstown, Dixville Notch, Errol, and adjacent Vermont communities.

New Hampshire's largest (190,000 acres) and most northerly community, Pittsburg retains a frontier atmosphere appreciated by anyone who enjoys the outdoors. Many residents work in the woods and spend their spare hours hunting and fishing, often displaying a spirit of independence which goes back to 1832 when portions of this town became an independent nation called the Indian Stream Republic. The name comes from a tributary of the Connecticut River, but the nation evolved when local settlers, disgruntled by boundary squabbling between Canada and the United States, solved the problem by seceding from both countries. They created their own stamps, coins, and government, but their independence lasted only a few years before the Treaty of Washington in 1842 made the republic part of New Hampshire.

Pittsburg is where the foliage begins to change first in the fall, snow arrives early, and it gets down to 30 below zero in the winter. It is closer to Montreal than it is to Boston, and a four-wheel-drive vehicle is the favorite family car. Route 3 is the main road through Pittsburg, and it connects with Canada at the north end of the town. Although Pittsburg is mostly wooded wilderness, no overnight camping or open fires are permitted except at campgrounds.

GUIDANCE **North Country Chamber of Commerce** (237-8939), Box 1, Colebrook 03576. Serves Colebrook, Pittsburg, and surrounding towns. Open summer through early fall, and sometimes winter weekends, the information center is located south of town on Route 3.

New Hampshire Information Center, Route 3, north of Colebrook. Open daily from Memorial Day to Columbus Day, with rest rooms and picnic tables.

East Colebrook farms.

The folks at **Trading Post General Store** (538-6533), in the middle of Pittsburg can probably answer most local questions, and there is a small **information booth** also in the center of town.

GETTING AROUND   Crossing the border. The United States Customs and Immigration Service maintains a point of entry station in Pittsburg on Route 3 at the International Border (819-656-2261). Hours: April 2 to June 15, 8–8; June 16 to Labor Day, 8–midnight; the day after Labor Day to November 30, 8–8; December 1 to April 1, 8–4. The border may be crossed from Canada to the United States when the station is closed, but federal law requires individuals to proceed directly without stopping to the Beecher Falls, Vermont, station (Customs 802-266-3336, Immigration 802-266-3320) to report in. Follow Route 3 to West Stewartstown and across the Connecticut River to Vermont Route 114 to Beecher Falls. Failure to report directly may result in a seizure of the vehicle and heavy fines for individuals.

MEDICAL EMERGENCY   Upper Connecticut Valley Hospital (237-4971), Corliss Lane (off Route 145), Colebrook. This little, well-equipped hospital is the health care center for a large area of northern New Hampshire, Quebec, Vermont, and Maine. At least one doctor has a private plane and makes house calls by air.

TO SEE AND DO   Pittsburg Historical Society, Pittsburg. The society maintains a museum in the town hall. Open July 4 and Saturdays in July and August.

Shrine of our Lady of Grace (237-5511), Route 3, Colebrook. Open Sundays, May through October, for a guided tour and a short ceremony beginning at 1 PM; groups are welcome by appointment, individuals anytime. A shrine and outdoor monuments of sculpture depict the Way of the Cross. Maintained by the Oblates of Mary Immaculate.

COVERED BRIDGES   **Columbia Bridge** crosses the Connecticut River just south of Colebrook in Columbia Village. Pittsburg has three covered bridges. The **Pittsburg-Clarksville bridge,** 91 feet long, is off Route 3, 1/4 mile west of Pittsburg Village. **Happy Corner bridge,** 86 feet long, is south of Route 3, 6 miles northeast of the village. **River Road bridge,** 57 feet long and one of the state's smallest covered bridges, is south of Route 3, 5.5 miles northeast of the village.

GREEN SPACE   Throughout this section of the North Country, and especially in Pittsburg, moose are quite common and are often seen wandering along beside Route 3. The Connecticut Lakes are great for bird-watching.

Coleman State Park is in Stewartstown, but it is most easily reached from Route 26 east of Colebrook. Open May to mid-October. There are 30 tent camping sites, a recreation building, and picnic tables. Fishing is good in the Diamond Ponds and surrounding streams. No reservations. Fee charged.

Lake Francis State Park, off Route 3 on River Road, 7 miles north of Pittsburg Village. Open from mid-May through Columbus Day. This small park beside the 2,000-acre, man-made lake has 40 primitive campsites, a boat-launching ramp, and a picnic area. A popular camping site for anglers and canoeists. No reservations. Fee charged.

Connecticut Lakes State Forest is a wooded corridor on both sides of Route 3 from the north end of the First Connecticut Lake to the border. Most of the rest of the wilderness is owned by large timber companies. In 1990 the Champion International Corporation gave the Nature Conservancy a 78-acre parcel of land that includes the tiny Fourth Connecticut Lake, the source of the longest river in New England. To see this small woodland lake, park and sign in at the Customs Station on Route 3, then follow a steep, rough .05-mile trail (which is on the border) to the lake.

SCENIC DRIVES   **Route 26,** from Colebrook through Dixville Notch to Errol and down Route 16 to Milan is one of the prettiest drives in the state. Just east of Colebrook, Fish Hatchery Road departs Route 26 north for the Diamond Ponds and Coleman State Park. The road is paved most of the way, but several gravel side roads wind over and around the hills of East Colebrook, and one continues on to Stewartstown Hollow on Route 145, which connects Colebrook and Pittsburg. This is one of the most picturesque and least-known parts of the state. Red-barned dairy farms are impressive, dotting the hillsides and views, especially during foliage season. **Beaver Brook Falls**, just north of Colebrook on Route 145, is popular with photographers.

Route 3, north from Pittsburg Village, is 22.5 miles to the border. The evergreen forest stretches as far as you can see, broken only by the several lakes and streams. Drive to the border station, perched high on a hill, if only to see the views north into Canada and south over the North Country.

Route 145 from Pittsburg south to Colebrook is best driven from north to south, especially for the sweeping view from Ben Young Hill. En route to and from Pittsburg, you will cross the 45th parallel, halfway between the North Pole and the equator.

CANOEING   The **Connecticut River** is popular for fishing and canoeing although its rather placid flow makes paddling it less challenging than the Androscoggin. The upper Connecticut watershed, including Hall and Indian Streams, forms the border between New Hampshire and Quebec, and, farther south, it is the border between New Hampshire and Vermont. Actually the boundary between the two states is the low-water mark on the Vermont shore so the river is in New Hampshire until it crosses into Massachusetts. This river also has a long history of log drives and was infamous for destructive flooding before many dams, most of which were built as hydroelectric power sources, tamed the river. Most canoeists start at the Vermont end of the Canaan-West Stewartstown Bridge off Route 3 The only difficult rapids (class 2) in this area are below Columbia. They run for about 7.5 miles and cannot be navigated when the water is low. Paddlers are advised to check with the *AMC River Guide* or *Canoe Camping Vermont and New Hampshire Rivers*. No canoe rentals available in this section of the river, but see Berlin and Route 16 North (Canoeing) or the Upper Connecticut River Valley (Canoeing).

FISHING   Fishing is the prime warm-weather attraction in Pittsburg, and operators of most of the 14 or so lodges, motels, and campgrounds depend on seekers of trout and salmon for their livelihoods. The several Connecticut lakes; Lake Francis; Back Lake; Hall, Indian, and Perry streams; and the Connecticut River provide miles of shoreline and hundreds of acres of world-class fishing, more than enough fishing waters to satisfy the most ardent angler. Many of the older lodges have guests who have returned annually for decades, and likely some of these folks still find new places to wet a line each year. The trout season runs from the fourth Saturday in April through October 15, but the best fishing months are May, June, and early fall. Most of the lodges provide guides, sell licenses, sell or rent tackle, rent boats, and will give fishing information.

Grant's Fly Shack (237-8137), RR 1, Box 142, Colebrook 03576. Open mid-May to October. Although Grant Woodbury no longer has a retail shop, he does guide up to two people at a time in boats (for fly-fishing only) on the Connecticut and Androscoggin rivers. Full day or afternoon/evening trips. By reservation only, rates vary.

Yankee Sportsman (237-8867), Route 1, Box 357, Colebrook. Open on Lake Winnipesaukee from ice-out until May 20, then on Lake Francis and the First and Second Connecticut lakes until September 30; also Connecticut River trips from spring through October 15. Registered guides Bud Pierce and Jackie Cass have a fully equipped 22-foot commercial lobster boat, with a trailer, for up to four passengers for four- and eight-hour (including dinner) trips. A small boat is used for Connecticut River fishing. By reservation, rates vary.

HIKING   Overlooking Colebrook from the Vermont side of the river is **Monadnock Mountain** which rises steeply and offers a nice view from the summit fire tower. The trail begins in a driveway off Route 102 near the bridge between Colebrook and Lemington, Vermont. You may have to inquire at a residence to find the exact location of the trail.

Walks & Rambles in the Upper Connecticut River Valley (Backcountry Publications) lists a number of hikes in this area including **Mt. Magalloway** (4.5 miles, 3.5 hours), at 3,300 feet the highest peak in the North Country.

GOLF   **Colebrook Country Club** (237-5566), on Route 26, east of Colebrook Village. A 9-hole, par-36 course.

The Panorama Golf Course (255-4961), at the Balsams Resort, Dixville Notch (see Berlin and Route 16 North [Lodging]).

SNOWMOBILING   More than 125 miles of groomed trails connect all areas of the North Country and even provide access to Maine, Vermont, Quebec, and southern New Hampshire. From the Pittsburg lodges and Colebrook motels, the snowmobiler can head off after breakfast and have lunch in Maine or Canada, then return to the lodge for dinner. For maps and other information, write the **North Country Chamber of Commerce** (237-8939), Box 1, Colebrook 03576; **The Trails Bureau** (271-3254), NH Division of Parks and Recreation, Box 856, Concord 03301; or the **New Hampshire Snowmobile Association** (224-8906), Box 38, Concord 03301.

RESORTS   See The Balsams Resort (Berlin and Route 16 North [Resort]).

BED & BREAKFAST   **Monadnock B&B** (237-8216), corner Monadnock and Bridge streets, Colebrook 03576. Open year-round. Built in 1916 in the bungalow architectural style, this B&B retains its exquisite natural woodwork. Its eclectic furnishings were gathered by Barbara and Wendell Woodard during their many travels when he was in the armed services. There are three main guest rooms—one with a double and two single beds, the others with double beds. There is a crib and a small room with a sink and coffeemaker. All share a single bath. A basement section has four bedrooms (two singles, one with a double bed, one with twins), an open area with a TV and table tennis, and a living room. A full breakfast is served. $43.20 double; $32.40 single.

MOTELS   There are several Colebrook motels including the **Northern Comfort** (237-4440); the **Colebrook Country Club and Motel** (237-5566), which also has a dining room and a lounge; and the **Colebrook House** (237-5521), a small village hotel with motel section, lounge, and dining room.

SPORTING LODGES   Most of the lodges are open for deer, moose, and game-bird hunting season and cater to snowmobilers in the winter.

Tall Timber Lodge (538-6651), Back Lake, off Route 3, Pittsburg 03592. Open year-round. Founded in 1946 by the legendary guide Vernon Hawes and his wife Pearl, and now operated by the Caron family, this is one of New England's most popular sporting lodges. Many guests have returned for the same week annually for decades; and while some families come just to relax in the wilderness and swim at the nearby beach, the business here is fishing, hunting, and snowmobiling. The lodge maintains 28 rental boats and motors, some on Back Lake and others on local ponds. Guides are also available, and fishing tackle is sold. Accommodations are comfortable, not fancy, so it is probably not the spot for a honeymoon weekend unless fishing is the priority. The lodge has 8 rooms sharing three baths, and there are 2 two-bedroom cabins and 12 other housekeeping units on the lake plus three units just across the street. There are dorm rooms and some separate units sleep eight to ten people. Home-cooked meals are served in the knotty pine dining room overlooking the lake, and box lunches are available on request. Most guests stay for a week or longer; and since many return annually leading to a strong repeat business, make reservations as far in advance as possible. MAP, one to three nights, $35–$42 per person per night; housekeeping cabins begin at $25 per person.

Other popular Pittsburg sporting lodges include **Powder Horn Lodge and Cabins** (538-6300), **Wander Inn** (538-6535), **Timberland Lodge and Cabins** (538-6613), and **Partridge Cabins** (538-6380). Reservations are suggested, especially in prime hunting and fishing seasons.

DINING OUT   **Sutton Place** (237-8842), 152 Main Street, Colebrook. Open daily year-round 5:30–9, except closed Sundays in the winter. Here's fine, intimate dining in the front rooms of a Queen Anne-style house. Chicken cordon bleu to steak au poivre, with seafood, a few Italian specialties, and a light menu with smaller portions for the diet-conscious. Reservations suggested, especially on weekends. Moderately priced.

EATING OUT   **Howard's Restaurant** (237-4025), Main Street, Colebrook. Open daily 5 AM–8 PM; Sundays at 6 AM, Friday night until 9 PM. A full-service restaurant with a large menu, daily specials, and homemade pies and puddings. A longtime favorite with the locals.

Wilderness Restaurant (237-8779), Main Street, Colebrook. Open 4 AM–9 PM daily. All homemade cooking; lounge and entertainment on weekends.

Also try the **Colebrook Country Club** (237-5566), Route 26, east of Colebrook Village, and the **Colebrook House** (237-5521), Main Street, Colebrook Village.

SPECIAL EVENTS   North Country visitors should be self-sufficient, since, unlike other areas of the state, there are few activities designed to entertain them. Exceptions are:

Late January: **North Country Sled Dog Races** (237-8939). A 100-mile race begins Friday morning in Rangely, Maine, and finishes in East Colebrook on Saturday; a 70-mile race begins Saturday morning at Murphy Dam in Pittsburg and finishes in Errol.

February: **Pittsburg-Colebrook Winter Carnival,** Kiwanis Club. Activities and events daily during the week of February school vacation.

June: **Blessing of the Motorcycles** (237-5511), Shrine of our Lady of Grace, Colebrook. Held the weekend after Father's Day.

Late June: **Family Fly-Fishing Weekend, Coleman State Park,** (271-3254), Stewartstown.

Fourth of July Celebration, Kiwanis Club, Colebrook. Parade, barbecue, and mud volleyball tourney.

Third Sunday of August: **Annual Pittsburg Guide's Show** (538-6984), on Back Lake, Pittsburg. The area's working guides show off their skills in log rolling, canoe and kayak competition, and fly casting. Admission.

Index

Agricultural fairs, 5
  Concord area, 92
  Durham/Dover area, 64
  Lancaster area, 345
  Manchester area, 80
  Mt. Washington's Valleys, 254
Air rides
  Berlin/Route 16 North area, 338
  Franconia-Bethlehem area, 316
  Lake Winnipesaukee region, 173
  Lancaster area, 343
  Mt. Washington's Valleys, 288
  North Country/Route 2 area, 332
  Peterborough/Keene area, 106
  Upper Valley Towns, 141
Air service, 5
Alexandria, 219-220
Allenstown, 75
Alpine skiing. See Downhill skiing
Alstead, 100-101, 110, 115-116
Alton, 7, 164, 167-168, 194
Alton Bay, 162, 175
AMC. See Appalachian Mountain Club
Amherst, 78
Amusement parks. See Theme parks
Andover, 205, 218, 221
Annual events
  Colebrook/Pittsburg area, 352
  Franconia-Bethlehem area, 326
  Hampton/Exeter area, 57-58

Lake Winnipesaukee region, 194-195
Lancaster area, 345
Manchester area, 79-80
Mt. Washington's Valleys, 253-254, 265-266, 275, 297, 305, 308-309
Peterborough/Keene area, 130
Portsmouth area, 44-45
Upper Valley Towns, 156-157
Western Lakes region, 224-225
Antiquarian bookshops, 5-6
  Peterborough/Keene area, 130
  Portsmouth area, 44
Antiques, 6
  Concord area, 91
  Mt. Washington's Valleys, 253
  Peterborough/Keene area, 127
  Upper Valley Towns, 154
  Western Lakes region, 223
Antrim, 110, 113, 116, 123, 130
Appalachian Mountain Club (AMC), 10-11, 13, 219-220, 268-269
Area code, 6
Art galleries, 6
  Manchester area, 74
  Mt. Washington's Valleys, 253
  Peterborough/Keene area, 127-128
  Upper Valley Towns, 154
Art museums, 6, 100
  Manchester area, 71-73
  Upper Valley Towns, 136-138
  see also Art galleries
Ascutney, Vt., 144

Ashland, 167-168, 176, 184, 190, 194
Atkinson, 50
Audubon Society of New Hampshire, 7, 11, 86, 207
Automatic teller machines, 6-7
Auto racing. See Stock car racing

Bakeries. See Eating
Baker River Valley, 305-309
Bands, 7. See also Entertaiment
Banking, 6-7
Barrington, 61, 63
Bartlett, 237, 254-255, 257-258, 260-261, 263, 265-266
Bath, 11, 314, 321
Beaches
  Hampton/Exeter area, 47, 52-53
  Lake Winnipesaukee region, 173
  Lancaster area, 343
  Portsmouth area, 34
  Western Lakes region, 210
Bed & Breakfasts, 7. See also LODGING INDEX
Bedford, 76-77, 79
Belmont, 175
Bennington, 106, 123, 125
Berlin, 336-337, 340
Bethlehem, 284, 311-317, 320-322, 324-326
Bicycling, 7
  Concord area, 87
  Franconia-Bethlehem area, 316
  Mt. Washington's Valleys, 288, 300-305
  Peterborough/Keene area, 106
  Upper Valley Towns, 141
  Western Lakes region, 208

Birding, 7
Boat excursions. *See* Cruises
Boating, 7-8, 208
  Mt. Washington's Valleys, 300
  Peterborough/Keene area, 106
  see also Canoeing; Cruises
Boat rentals, 174-175
Books about New Hampshire, 8, 13-14, 20, 268, 272
Bradford, Vt., 153, 156-157, 201, 215-218, 222
Bradford Center, 205-206
Brentwood, 48
Bretton Woods, 14, 238, 270, 275-280
Breweries
  Manchester area, 75
  Upper Valley Towns, 156
Bridges, covered. *See* Covered bridges
Bridgewater, 215, 221-222
Bristol, 192, 194, 203, 219, 221
Brownsville, Vt., 141, 144
Buggy rides, Portsmouth area, 29
Bus service, 8

Caanan Center, 205-206
Campgrounds, 8-9. *See also* LODGING INDEX
Camping
  Mt. Washington's Valleys, 288, 300
  White Mountain National Forest (WMNF), 232-233
Camps, for adults, Peterborough/Keene area, 109
Camps, for children, 10
  Mt. Washington's Valleys, 300
Campton, 172, 300, 304
Canaan, 157, 216
Canaan Center, 201
Candia, 76
Canoeing, 9
  Berlin/Route 16 North area, 338
  Colebrook/Pittsburg area, 349
  Concord area, 87
  Manchester area, 76

Mt. Washington's Valleys, 243
  Upper Valley Towns, 141
  Western Lakes region, 208
Canterbury, 17, 81, 89-92
Carroll, 238
Cemeteries, Portsmouth area, 32
Center Barnstead, 88-89
Center Conway, 239, 243
Center Effingham, 195
Center Ossipee, 164, 167, 175, 177
Center Sandwich, 6, 167, 169, 180, 188, 192-193
Central lakes region, 159-224
Centre Harbor, 6, 17, 164, 167, 169, 176, 182-184, 189, 193
Charlestown, 134-145, 147-148, 151
Chatham, 243
Chesterfield, 104, 111-112, 120
Chichester, 88
Children
  activities for, 9. *See also* Family activities
  museums, Portsmouth area, 27-28
  summer camps, 10
Chocorua, 179, 181, 187
Chocorua Village, 181
Christmas trees, 10
Churches. *See* Historic houses and sites
Claremont, 16, 135, 148, 151-154, 223
Claremont Junction, 151
Colebrook, 328, 346-352
Colleges and universities, 10
  Concord area, 85-86
  Durham/Dover area, 59-64
  Hampton/Exeter area, 47
  Mt. Washington's Valleys, 305
  Upper Valley Towns, 136-138
  Western Lakes region, 204
Columbia, 346
Concord, 6, 12, 15-16, 66, 81-92
Concord area, 81-92
Condominiums, 18. *See also* LODGING INDEX
Conservation groups, 10
Continental, 220-221

Contoocook, 6
Conway, 7, 12, 195-196, 227, 234-236, 239-240, 242, 246, 249, 251, 254
Conway Village, 242
Cornish, 11, 132, 135, 142-143, 147, 155, 157
Cottages, rental, 18. *See also* LODGING INDEX
Covered bridges, 11
  Colebrook/Pittsburg area, 348
  Concord area, 86
  Lake Winnipesaukee region, 168
  Lancaster area, 343
  Manchester area, 75
  Mt. Washington's Valleys, 242, 299-300, 306
  Peterborough/Keene area, 100
  Upper Valley Towns, 135-136, 138-139
  Western Lakes region, 205
  White Mountain National Forest (WMNF), 227
Crafts, 11
  Concord area, 91
  Mt. Washington's Valleys, 253, 296-297, 308
  Peterborough/Keene area, 128
  Upper Valley Towns, 154-156
Craft workshops, Peterborough/Keene area, 109
Crawford Notch, 237-238, 275-280
Cross-country skiing, 19
  Berlin/Route 16 North area, 339
  Franconia-Bethlehem area, 318
  Lake Winnipesaukee region, 177
  Mt. Washington's Valleys, 244, 257, 272, 279, 290, 302
  Peterborough/Keene area, 111
  Upper Valley Towns, 143-144
Cruises, 11
  Hampton/Exeter area, 52

Lake Winnipesaukee
region, 173
Portsmouth area, 34-35
Upper Valley Towns, 141
Western Lakes region, 208-
209

Dalton, 343
Danbury, 7, 208, 211-212, 215,
222
Dance. *See* Entertainment
Danville, 48
Deerfield, 5, 80
Derry, 74
Dining out. *See* Eating
Dixville, 336
Dixville Notch, 338-340, 346,
348, 350
Dover, 12, 16-17, 59-64
Dover Point, 61
Downhill skiing, 19
Berlin/Route 16 North
area, 339
Concord area, 87
Franconia-Bethlehem area,
317-318
Lake Winnipesaukee
region, 197
Mt. Washington's Valleys,
244, 257-258, 272-273,
279, 290-291, 302, 307
Peterborough/Keene area,
112
Upper Valley Towns, 144
Western Lakes region, 211-
212
Dublin, 9, 101, 104, 106, 109,
120, 122
Dummer, 336
Durham, 59-63
Durham/Dover area, 59-64

East Alton, 194
East Andover, 201, 218
East Conway, 239, 243
East Hebron, 219
East Kingston, 53
East Madison, 198
Easton, 310, 325
East Thetford, Vt., 155
East Wakefield, 176, 195
Eating
Berlin/Route 16 North
area, 340

Colebrook/Pittsburg area,
351
Concord area, 88-90
Durham/Dover area, 62-63
Franconia-Bethlehem area,
323-325
Hampton/Exeter area, 55-
57
Lake Winnipesaukee
region, 186-191
Lancaster area, 344-345
Manchester area, 77-78
Mt. Washington's Valleys,
249-252, 264-265, 293-295,
304-305, 307-308
North Country/Route 2
area, 335
Peterborough/Keene area,
120-126
Portsmouth area, 27-43
Upper Valley Towns, 149-
153
Western Lakes region, 220-
222
Eaton, 196, 197
Effingham, 195
Emergencies, 11
Enfield, 136, 142, 145, 147, 151,
155, 157
Entertainment
Durham/Dover area, 63
Hampton/Exeter area, 57
Lake Winnipesaukee
region, 191-192
Lancaster area, 345
Manchester area, 78-79
Mt. Washington's Valleys,
252, 296
Peterborough/Keene area,
126-127
Portsmouth area, 43-44
Upper Valley Towns, 153-
154
Western Lakes region, 222-
223
Epping, 48
Epsom, 6
Errol, 328, 336-338, 340, 346,
348, 352
Errol Village, 340
Etna, 146
Evans Notch, 280-281
Events. *See* Annual events
Exeter, 7, 12, 15, 47, 50-51, 53-58

Factory outlets, 12
Mt. Washington's Valleys,
252-253
Factory tours
Berlin/Route 16 North
area, 336
Manchester area, 75
see also Breweries; Mine
tours
Fairlee Vt., 146, 149
Family activities
Concord area, 86
Lake Winnipesaukee
region, 168
Manchester area, 75
Mt. Washington's Valleys,
242, 255-256
Peterborough/Keene area,
104
Farmer's markets, 12
Durham/Dover area, 59
Hampton/Exeter area, 52
Portsmouth area, 29
Fishing, 12
Berlin/Route 16 North
area, 338
Colebrook/Pittsburg area,
349-350
Concord area, 87
Hampton/Exeter area, 52
Mt. Washington's Valleys,
243, 289, 301
Portsmouth area, 35
Upper Valley Towns, 141-142
Western Lakes region, 209
White Mountain National
Forest (WMNF), 232
Fitzwilliam, 6, 101, 113-114,
116, 120, 127-128, 130
Foliage, 12
Forts
Portsmouth area, 33
Upper Valley Towns, 134-
135
Francestown, 101, 106-107,
114, 122-123, 127, 129-130
Franconia, 284, 310-326
Franconia-Bethlehem area,
310-326
Franconia Notch, 237
Franconia Village, 325
Franklin, 175, 201, 205, 217
Freedom, 194, 196-197, 200
Fremont, 48, 50-51

Fruit farms, 6
    Hampton/Exeter area, 52
    Western Lakes region, 223-224
Fryeburg, Me., 243, 254

Gardens, Hampton/Exeter area, 47-48
Georges Mills, 208, 219
Gilford, 168, 171, 173, 175, 177, 186, 192-194
Gilsum, 105, 128, 130
Glen, 9, 255, 259, 262-263, 265
Goffstown, 78
Golf, 12-13
    Berlin/Route 16 North area, 338
    Colebrook/Pittsburg area, 350
    Concord area, 87
    Durham/Dover area, 61
    Franconia-Bethlehem area, 317
    Hampton/Exeter area, 53
    Lake Winnipesaukee region, 175-176
    Lancaster area, 343
    Manchester area, 76
    Mt. Washington's Valleys, 243, 256, 278, 289, 301
    North Country/Route 2 area, 332
    Peterborough/Keene area, 106-107
    Portsmouth area, 35-36
    Upper Valley Towns, 143
    Western Lakes region, 209
Gonic, 61
Gorham, 268, 270, 328, 331-332, 334-335
Goshen, 223
Grafton, 18, 203
Grantham, 209, 211-213, 223
Greenfield, 102, 110, 116, 130
Greenland, 32, 35-37
Green space, 33-34
    Berlin/Route 16 North area, 336-338
    Colebrook/Pittsburg area, 348
    Concord area, 86-87
    Durham/Dover area, 61
    Franconia-Bethlehem area, 314-316

Hampton/Exeter area, 52-53
Lake Winnipesaukee region, 171-172, 197
Lancaster area, 343
Manchester area, 75-76
Mt. Washington's Valleys, 242, 276-278, 287, 306-307
Peterborough/Keene area, 104-105
Upper Valley Towns, 141
Western Lakes region, 206-208
see also Natural areas; State beaches; State parks
Greenville, 105
Greyhound racing
    Hampton/Exeter area, 53
    Peterborough/Keene area, 107
Groveton, 341
Guide books, 8, 13-14, 20, 268, 272, 338

Hampton, 12, 46, 50, 53-58
Hampton Beach, 7, 22, 49, 53-54, 56-58, 446
Hampton Falls, 48, 51-52
Hampton Harbor, 57
Hampton River, 46-47, 50
Hancock, 102, 106, 114, 116, 130, 288-289
Hancock Village, 122
Hanover, 6, 15, 20, 132-134, 136-138, 142-144, 148-157
Hanover Center, 156
Harrisville, 94, 102, 109, 116-117, 128
Haverhill, 11, 138-139, 147
Hebron, 206
Henniker, 14, 82, 85-92, 109
High huts of the White Mountains, 13. See also LODGING INDEX
Hiking, 13-14
    Berlin/Route 16 North area, 338-339
    Colebrook/Pittsburg area, 350
    Franconia-Bethlehem area, 317
    Lake Winnipesaukee region, 176-177
    Lancaster area, 343-344
    Mt. Washington's Valleys,

244, 256-257, 271-272, 278, 289, 301
North Country/Route 2 area, 333
Peterborough/Keene area, 107-109
Western Lakes region, 209-210
White Mountain National Forest (WMNF), 227-232
Hillsboro, 6, 105-106, 110
Hillsborough, 99, 117, 130
Historical societies
    Colebrook/Pittsburg area, 347-348
    Concord area, 84-85
    Durham/Dover area, 61
    Franconia-Bethlehem area, 314
    Hampton/Exeter area, 50
    Lake Winnipesaukee region, 167-168, 197
    Manchester area, 74-75
    Mt. Washington's Valleys, 240, 287-288
    North Country/Route 2 area, 332
    Peterborough/Keene area, 99
    Portsmouth area, 32
    Western Lakes region, 204-205
Historic houses and sites, 14
    Berlin/Route 16 North area, 336
    Concord area, 85
    Durham/Dover area, 60-61
    Franconia-Bethlehem area, 313
    Hampton/Exeter area, 47, 50-51
    Lake Winnipesaukee region, 166-169, 197
    Lancaster area, 341-342
    Manchester area, 73-75
    Mt. Washington's Valleys, 240-241, 306
    Peterborough/Keene area, 98-104
    Portsmouth area, 28-32
    Upper Valley Towns, 135-141
    Western Lakes region, 204-206

White Mountain National Forest (WMNF), 230
Holderness, 164, 166, 174-175, 182-184, 189-190
Hollis, 76
Honey, 14
Hopkinton, 5-6, 86, 89, 91
Horseback riding, 14
    Concord area, 87
    Franconia-Bethlehem area, 317
    Mt. Washington's Valleys, 279, 289, 301
    North Country/Route 2 area, 332
    Peterborough/Keene area, 109
    Western Lakes region, 210
Horse racing, Manchester area, 76
Housekeeping units. See LODGING INDEX
Hunting, 14

Ice cream, 14. See also Eating
Ice skating
    Mt. Washington's Valleys, 258, 291, 302
    Upper Valley Towns, 144
Information, 14-15
Intervale, 239, 244-245, 248-251
Isles of Shoals, 32

Jackson, 237, 254-266, 272-273
Jackson Village, 256-258, 261-266
Jaffrey, 98-99, 105-107, 110, 112-113, 115, 117, 125
Jaffrey Center, 102-103, 107, 110-112, 114-115, 122
Jefferson, 9, 15, 331-332, 334-335
Jefferson Meadows, 332, 335

Keene, 15-16, 20, 94-100, 107, 110, 117-118, 120, 124, 128-130
Kensington, 48
Kingston, 53, 58
the Kingstons, 48

Laconia, 12, 16, 164, 173, 175, 177, 185, 190, 194-195

Lakes, 15. See also Lake Winnipesaukee region; Western Lakes region
Lake Sunapee, 219
Lake Winnipesaukee region, 160-200
Lancaster, 5, 328, 341-343, 345
Lancaster area, 341-345
Landaff Center, 314
The League of New Hampshire Craftsmen, 11
Lebanon, 16, 142-144, 153-154
Lectures. See Entertainment
Lee, 61, 64
Libraries, 15
    Berlin/Route 16 North area, 336
    Concord area, 84-85
    Portsmouth area, 28
    Upper Valley Towns, 137
    Western Lakes region, 204
Lincoln, 7, 12, 17, 19, 284-297
Lisbon, 319, 324
Litchfield, 78
Littleton, 320-321, 324-326, 341
Llama treks, 15
    North Country/Route 2 area, 332
Lobsters. See Eating
Lodging
    Berlin/Route 16 North area, 339-340
    Colebrook/Pittsburg area, 350-351
    Concord area, 88
    Durham/Dover area, 61-62
    Franconia-Bethlehem area, 319-323
    Hampton/Exeter area, 53-55
    Lake Winnipesaukee region, 178-186, 198-200
    Lancaster area, 344
    Manchester area, 76-77
    Mt. Washington's Valleys, 245-251, 258-264, 274-275, 279-280, 291-292, 303-304, 307
    North Country/Route 2 area, 333-335
    Peterborough/Keene area, 112-120
    Portsmouth area, 36-37
    Upper Valley Towns, 144-149

Western Lakes region, 212-220
    see also LODGING INDEX
Lord's Hill, 195-196
Lottery, 15
Lyme, 139, 145-147, 149-150, 156-157
Lyme Center, 144

Madison, 196-197, 200, 244
Magazines, 15-16
Manchester, 6, 12, 15-16, 66, 68-74, 76-80
Manchester area, 68-80
Maple sugaring, 16
    Peterborough/Keene area, 109-110
    Upper Valley Towns, 143
Maplewood, 323
Marlborough, 118, 127, 130
Mason, 103, 110, 124, 126, 129
Melvin Village, 167-168, 175
Meredith, 6, 14, 160, 164, 166-167, 175, 183-185, 190-194
Merrimack, 75, 77
Merrimack Valley, 65-92
Milan, 336, 340, 348
Milford, 12, 20, 75
Milton, 17, 165-166, 194
Mine tours, 204
Miniature golf, Mt. Washington's Valleys, 289
Mirror Lake, 178-179
Monadnock region, 93-130
Moultonborough, 165-166, 181, 188-189, 193
Mountaintops, 16
Mountonborough Neck, 180
Mt. Sunapee, 218, 221, 224
Mt. Washington/Pinkham Notch area, 267-275
Mt. Washington's Valleys, 234-281
Munsonville, 118, 128
Museums, 16-17
    Concord area, 83-85
    Durham/Dover area, 59-60
    Franconia-Bethlehem area, 313, 316
    Hampton/Exeter area, 50-51
    Lake Winnipesaukee region, 165-166, 169, 196-197

Manchester area, 73-75
Mt. Washington's Valleys, 255, 270, 306
Peterborough/Keene area, 98-100, 104
Portsmouth area, 27-29
Upper Valley Towns, 136, 139-140
Western Lakes region, 204, 206
see also Art museums; Museum villages
Museum villages, 17
Concord area, 83
Lake Winnipesaukee region, 165-167
Upper Valley Towns, 136
Music, 7, 17. See also Entertainment

Nashua, 16, 74, 77-78, 80
Natural areas
Berlin/Route 16 North area, 337-338
Concord area, 86
Franconia-Bethlehem area, 314-316
Lake Winnipesaukee region, 172
Mt. Washington's Valleys, 273-274, 286-287, 306-307
Peterborough/Keene area, 104-106
Western Lakes region, 207-208
White Mountain National Forest (WMNF), 227-232
see also Green space
Nature centers
Concord area, 86
Hampton/Exeter area, 50
Lake Winnipesaukee region, 166
Mt. Washington's Valleys, 306
Nature preserves. See Natural areas
Nelson, 17, 103, 118
New Boston, 79
Newbury, 211, 219
New Castle, 26, 32-34
New Durham, 187
Newfields, 48, 56
Newington, 26, 32

New Ipswich, 19, 98, 111, 118-119
New London, 19-20, 201, 203-204, 209-214, 217, 222-224
Newmarket, 61
Newport, 203, 205, 209-210, 215, 217, 223-224
Newspapers, 15-16
North Charlestown, 151, 156
North Conway, 7, 12, 236-254, 243
North Country, 327-352
North Hampton, 12, 47-48, 52-53, 55, 57
North Haverhill, 152, 157
North Salem, 66, 75
North Sandwich, 181
North Sutton, 201, 215-216
North Thetford, Vt., 148
North Thornton, 301
Northwood, 6, 88, 92
North Woodstock, 284-288, 290, 293-297
Norwich, Vt., 132, 139-140, 151, 155-157
Nottingham, 48, 75-76

Observatories
Mt. Washington's Valleys, 270
Upper Valley Towns, 138
Orford, 140, 148
Ossipee, 168

Parks, 17-18. See also Green space; Natural areas; State parks
Parsonfield, Me., 195
Pembroke, 87, 92
Peterborough, 6, 15, 20, 95, 98, 105, 107, 109, 112, 119-121, 125, 128-130
Peterborough/Keene area, 94-130
Pick-your-own. See Fruit farms
Piermont, 140, 148, 155-156
Pinkham Notch, 237, 273-275
Pittsburg, 328, 346-349, 351-352
Pittsburg Village, 349
Pittsfield, 92
Plainfield, 150, 156
Planetarium, Concord area, 83-84

Plymouth, 305-309
Portsmouth, 12, 14-17, 20, 22-45
Portsmouth area, 22-45

Quechee, Vt., 141-144, 155-157

Racing
greyhound
Hampton/Exeter area, 53
Peterborough/Keene area, 107
horses, Manchester area, 76
sled dog, 19
stock car
Concord area, 83
Upper Valley Towns, 143
Railroads
Franconia-Bethlehem area, 314
Lake Winnipesaukee region, 166
Mt. Washington's Valleys, 270, 276, 289-290
Randolph, 331
Religious sites
Colebrook/Pittsburg area, 348
Upper Valley Towns, 136
Rental cottages, 18. See also LODGING INDEX
Rest areas, 18
Restaurants. See Eating
Rindge, 106
Rock climbing, Mt. Washington's Valleys, 244
Rock hounding, 18
Rollerblading, Mt. Washington's Valleys, 301
Roxbury, 110
Rumney, 306, 308
Rye, 12, 14, 34-35
Rye Beach, 41

Sailing, Lake Winnipesaukee region, 177
Salem, 75
Sanbornton, 167, 175
Sanbornville, 163, 195, 200
Sandown, 50-51
Sandwich, 5, 168
Scenic drives
Colebrook/Pittsburg area, 348-349

Hampton/Exeter area, 53
Lake Winnipesaukee
    region, 173
Lancaster area, 343
Manchester area, 76
Mt. Washington's Valleys,
    242-243, 256, 271, 287-
    288, 300
North Country/Route 2
    area, 332
White Mountain National
    Forest (WMNF), 227-232
Scuba diving, Lake
    Winnipesaukee region,
    177
Seabrook, 12, 47, 51-53
Seabrook Beach, 47
Seacoast, 21-64
Sharon, 127
Shelburne, 14, 331-335
Shopping
    Concord area, 91
    Durham/Dover area, 63-64
    Franconia-Bethlehem area,
        325-326
    Hampton/Exeter area, 57
    Lake Winnipesaukee
        region, 192-194
    Manchester area, 79
    Mt. Washington's Valleys,
        252-253, 296, 305, 308
    Peterborough/Keene area,
        127-130
    Portsmouth area, 44
    Upper Valley Towns, 154-
        156
    Western Lakes region, 223-
        224
Skiing, 18-19. See also Cross-
    country skiing; Downhill
    skiing
Sled dog races, 19
Sleigh rides, 19
    Lake Winnipesaukee
        region, 197
    Mt. Washington's Valleys,
        258, 291, 302
    Peterborough/Keene area,
        112
    Upper Valley Towns, 144
Snowboarding, Mt.
    Washington's Valleys,
    303
Snowmobiling, 19-20

Berlin/Route 16 North
    area, 339
Colebrook/Pittsburg area,
    350
Franconia-Bethlehem area,
    318-319
Mt. Washington's Valleys,
    279, 291
White Mountain National
    Forest (WMNF), 232
Snowville, 199
Soaring, 20
The Society for the Protection
    of New Hampshire
    Forests (SPNHF), 10
Somersworth, 61, 64
South Conway, 239
South Effingham, 195
South Peterborough, 94
South Sutton, 206, 223
South Wolfeboro, 186-187
Special events. See Annual
    events
Spofford, 110
Springfield, 216-217
Star Island, 32, 34-35
Stark, 341, 345
State beaches
    Hampton/Exeter area, 52
    Lake Winnipesaukee
        region, 173
    Lancaster area, 343
    Portsmouth area, 34
    Western Lakes region, 210
State forests
    Lake Winnipesaukee
        region, 171
    Peterborough/Keene area,
        104, 106
State parks, 17-18
    Berlin/Route 16 North
        area, 338, 340
    Colebrook/Pittsburg area,
        348
    Franconia-Bethlehem area,
        314
    Hampton/Exeter area, 53
    Lake Winnipesaukee
        region, 172
    Manchester area, 75-76
    Mt. Washington's Valleys,
        242, 270, 276-278
    North Country/Route 2
        area, 335

Peterborough/Keene area,
    102, 104-105, 106, 110
Portsmouth area, 34
Western Lakes region, 206-
    207
Stewartstown, 346, 348, 352
Stock car racing
    Concord area, 83
    Upper Valley Towns, 143
Stoddard, 103-105
Stratham, 48, 50, 58
Sugar Hill, 284, 310, 313, 317-
    321, 325
Summer theater, 20. See also
    Entertainment
Sunapee, 203, 213-215, 217,
    220-221
Sunapee Harbor, 204, 208-209,
    220
Surry, 110
Sutton, 210
Sutton Mills, 218
Swanzey, 5, 11, 99-100, 130
Swanzey Center, 129
Swanzey Village, 100
Swimming, 34
    Mt. Washington's Valleys,
        257, 290, 301
    Peterborough/Keene area,
        110
    Upper Valley Towns, 143
    Western Lakes region, 210
    see also State beaches
Tamworth, 20, 168, 171-172,
    179-180, 187-188, 191-192,
    194
Tamworth Village, 167
Taylor City, 195
Temple, 104, 113, 122
Tennis
    Mt. Washington's Valleys,
        290, 301
    Western Lakes region, 210-
        211
Theater, 20. See also Entertain-
    ment
Theme parks
    Lake Winnipesaukee
        region, 171
    Manchester area, 75
    Mt. Washington's Valleys,
        255-256, 286-287
    North Country/Route 2
        area, 331-332

Portsmouth area, 27
Mt. Washington's Valleys,
    242, 286-288
Thetford, Vt., 143, 156-157
Thetford Hill, Vt., 153
Tilton, 169, 185, 191-192
Trails, 20. See also Hiking
Troy, 111-113, 124-125
Twin Mountain, 312, 322

Universities. See Colleges and
    universities
Upper Connecticut River
    Valley, 131-157
Upper Valley Towns, 132-157

Wagon rides, Mt. Washington's
    Valleys, 244
Wakefield, 195, 197
Wakefield Corners, 195
Walks, Upper Valley Towns,
    141. See also Hiking
Walpole, 104, 107, 119
Warner, 12, 217, 222, 224
Warner Village, 205, 221
Warren, 306
Warren Village, 308
Washington, 206
Waterfalls, 20
Water sports
    Lake Winnipesaukee
        region, 177

Western Lakes region, 211
    see also specific sports
Waterville, 300-305
Waterville Valley, 14, 19, 20,
    297-305
Weare, 76, 79
Weirs, 162
Weirs Beach, 9, 160, 167, 171,
    173-175, 182, 192
Wentworth, 307
Wentworth Village, 307
West Alton, 191
West Bethel, 15
West Chesterfield, 20, 113
Western Lakes region, 201-224
Western White Mountains,
    282-309
West Fairlee, Vt., 141
West Hopkinton, 75
West Lebanon, 132, 143, 149,
    152, 154-155
West Milan, 338
Westmoreland, 110, 121, 130
West Ossipee, 181
Westport, 100
West Swanzey, 100
West Thornton, 304
Whale-watching
    Hampton/Exeter area, 52
    Portsmouth area, 34
Whitefield, 20, 341, 343-345
Whitefield Village, 345

White Mountain National
    Forest (WMNF), 17-18,
    226-233
White Mountains, 225-326
White River Junction, Vt., 145,
    152-153, 155-156
Wilder, Vt., 140
Wilderness areas. See Natural
    areas
Wildlife sanctuaries. See
    Natural areas
Wilmot Flat, 205
Wilton, 110, 119, 124
Wilton Center, 20, 128
Wilton Village, 126
Windsor, Vt., 11, 132, 140-141,
    143, 149, 151, 154
Windsurfing
    Lake Winipesaukee region,
        177
    Western Lakes region, 211
Winery, Concord area, 92
Winnisquam, 185-186
WMNF. See White Mountain
    National Forest
Wolfeboro, 7, 160-163, 165-
    166, 168, 171, 173-175,
    177-178, 186-187, 192
Woodstock, 289
Woodsville, 153

Lodging Index

Amber Lights Inn, 304
American Youth Hostel,
    Peterborough, 120
Ames Farm Inn, 186
The Ammonoosuc Inn, 319
The Amos A. Parker House,
    116
The Anchorage, 185-186
Anchorage Inn, 36
Andrew Brook Lodge, 217-218
Antrim Inn, 113
Appalachian Mountain Club
    High Huts, 274-275, 323
Appalachian Mountain Club
    Pinkham Notch Camp,
    274
Appalachian Mountain Club
    Shapleigh Hostel, 280
Applebrook B&B, 335
Apple Gate B&B, 119
Apple Hill Campground, 323
Ashworth By The Sea, 54
Auk's Nest, 119

Back Side Inn, 215
The Balsams Resort, 339-340
The Beal House Inn, 320-321
Bedford Village Inn, 76
The Bells, 321
The Benjamin Prescott Inn,
    117
The Bernerhof, 259
The Birches, 293
The Birchwood Inn, 113
Black Bear Lodge, 303
Black Swan, 185
The Blake House, 262
Blanche's B&B, 321
Blue Goose Inn, 218
The Bradford Inn, 215
The Bretton Arms, 280
Bungay Jar, 321
Burkehaven Motel, 219

The Buttonwood Inn, 246

Candlelite Inn, 218
The Captain Folsom Inn, 37
Cardigan Mountain Lodge
    and Reservation, 219-220
Carlson's Lodge, 322
Carriage Barn Guest House,
    117-118
The Chase House, 147
Chesterfield Inn, 113
The Chieftain Motor Inn, 149
Chocorua View House, 181
Christmas Farm Inn, 259-260
Christmas Island Motel and
    Steak House, 182
Colby Hill Inn, 88
Colebrook Country Club and
    Motel, 351
Colebrook House, 351
Comfort Inn, 36
Corner House Inn, 180
Country House Inn, 61-62
The Country Inn at Bartlett,
    263
Country Options, 184
Covered Bridge House, 262-
    263
Crab Apple Inn, 307
Cranmore Inn, 246-247
Cranmore Mountain Lodge,
    247
Crawford Notch General
    Store and Campground,
    280

Dana Place, 260
The Daniel George House-
    keeping Cottages, 219
Darby Brook Farm, 115-116
The Darby Field Inn and
    Restaurant, 246
The Davenport Inn, 334

Deer Park, 292
Dexter's Inn and Tennis Club,
    213
Dowd's Country Inn, 146-147
Dry River Campground, 280

Eagle Mountain Resort, 258
Eastman, 212-213
Eaton Center, 198-199
1806 House, 218
Ellis River House, 263
The English House, 218
Equestrian Center at Honey
    Lane Farm, 120
Errol Motel, 340
Evergreen Bed & Breakfast,
    321
Evergreen Motel, 335
The Exeter Inn, 54-55

The Fairfield Inn, 77
The Farmhouse, 181
Ferry Point House, 185
The Fitzwilliam Inn, 113-114
Follansbee Inn, 215-216
The Forest Inn, 248
Franconia Inn, 319
Franconia Notch Motel, 293
Fransted Campground, 323
Freedom House B&B, 200

Gale River, 322
The Galway House, 117
The Gilman Tavern, 180
The Glynn House Inn, 184
Goddard Mansion, 148
The Golden Eagle, 303
Goose Pond Guest House, 118
The Gorham House, 334
Gorham Motor Inn, 335
The Gould Farm, 117
Gray's Corner, 119
The Greenfield Inn, 116

Hampton House, 54
Hannah Davis House, 116
The Hanover Inn, 144-145
The Hardie House, 178
Harrisville Squires' Inn, 116-117
Haus Edelweiss, 217
Haverhill Inn, 147
Hedgecroft Inn, 183-184
Hickory Stick Farm, 185
Highlander Inn and Tavern, 76
Highland House, 62
Hilltop Acres, 307
The Hilltop Inn, 321
Hitching Post B&B, 88
Hobson House, 307
Holiday Inn, 36
Home Hill Inn, 147
The Homestead, 321
Horse & Hound Inn, 320
The Hotel Coolidge, 144
Howard Johnson Hotel, 36

Indian Head Resort, 292
The "Inn" on Canaan Street, 216
The Inn at Christian Shore, 36
The Inn at Coit Mountain, 217
The Inn at Crotched Mountain, 114
The Inn at Crystal Lake, 199
The Inn at Danbury, 215
Inn at East Hill Farm, 112-113
Inn at Elmwood Corners, 55
The Inn at Golden Pond, 184
The Inn at Jackson, 263
Inn at Mills Falls, 183
The Inn at New Ipswich, 118-119
The Inn at Strawbery Banke, 37
The Inn at Sunapee, 214
Inn at Thorn Hill, 261

Jack Daniel's Motor Inn, 119-120
Jack O'Lantern Resort, 293
Jackson House, 263
Jacob's Ladder, 217
Jaffrey Manor Restaurant & Inn, 115
The Jefferson Inn, 334
The John Hancock Inn, 114
The Josiah Bellows House, 119
Juniper Hill Inn, 149

Kimball Hill Inn, 344
Kluge's, 145
Kona Mansion, 180

Lafayette Campground, 323
Lake Shore Farm, 88
Lakeview Inn, 178
Lakewood Manor Cottages, 219
Lamplighter Motor Inn, 219
Lantern Motor Inn, 335
Ledgeland Inn and Cottages, 320
The Ledges Hostel, 293
Leighton Inn, 37
Lilac Hill Acres Inn, 117
Loch Lyme Lodge and Cottages, 145
The Lodge at Bretton Woods, 280
Long Island Inn, 181
Lovett's Inn, 319
The Lyme Inn, 146

Madison Carriage House B&B, 200
The Manor on Golden Pond, 182-183
Maple Hedge, 147-148
Maple Hill Farm, 217
Maplewood Inn, 321-322
Margate, 182
Martin Hill Inn, 36-37
Meadowbrook Inn, 36
The Meeting House Inn and Restaurant, 88
Milan Hill State Park, 340
The Mill House Inn, 292
Mittersill, 323
Monadnock B&B, 350-351
The Monadnock Inn, 114-115
Moose Brook State Park, 335
Moose Mountain Lodge, 146
The Mountain Club on Loon, 291-292
The Mountain-Fare Inn, 304
Mountain Lake Inn, 216
Mountain Vale Inn, 249
Mountain Valley Manner, 249
Mt. Laurel Inn, 307
Mt. Washington Cog Railway B&B Chalet, 280
The Mt. Washington Hotel, 279-280

The Mulburn Inn, 322

The Naswa Lakeside Resort, 182
Nereledge Inn and White Horse Pub, 247
Nestlenook Farm, 264
The New England Center, 61
The New England Inn and Resort, 245
New London Inn, 213
Northern Comfort, 351
Northern Zermatt Inn and Motel, 322
The Notchland Inn, 260-261
The Nutmeg Inn, 183

The Occum Inn, 148
Oceanside Hotel, 54
The Old Homestead Bed and Breakfast, 322
Old Mill House, 118
Osgood Inn, 304

Paisley and Parsley, 264
Paquette's Motel and Restaurant, 322
Parade Rest B&B, 185
Partridge Cabins, 351
Partridge House Inn, 322
The Pasquaney Inn, 215
The Patchwork Inn, 218
Philbrook Farm Inn, 333-334
Pick Point Lodges, 178-179
Piermont Inn, 148
Pinestead Farm Lodge, 322-323
Pinky's Place, 62
Pleasant Lake Inn, 214
Powder Horn Lodge and Cabins, 351
Profile Deluxe Motel, 322
Purity Spring Resort, 198

Raynor's Motor Lodge, 322
The Red Coach Inn, 320
Red Hill Inn, 182
Rivagale Inn, 320
Rivergreen Condominiums at The Mill, 292
Riverside Country Inn, 248
Rockhouse Mountain Farm Inn, 198-199
Rutledge Inn & Cottages, 146

Salzburg Inn and Motel, 119
Scottish Lion Inn and
    Restaurant, 245
Seaside Village, 55
Seven Hearths Inn, 214-215
The 1785 Inn, 245
The 1787 Center Chimney
    B&B, 248
The Shaker Inn, 147
Shearton Portsmouth, 36
Sheraton Tara Wayfarer Inn,
    77
Silver Maple Lodge &
    Cottages, 149
Silver Squirrel Inn, 303
The Silver Street Inn, 62
Sise Inn, 36
Six Chimneys, 219
Snowvillage Inn, 199
Snowy Owl Inn, 303
The Spalding Inn Resort, 344
Staffords-in-the-Field, 179
Stag Hollow Inn and Llama
    Keep, 335
Stark Village Inn, 340, 344
Stepping Stones Bed &
    Breakfast, 119
Stone Bridge Inn, 117
The Stone House Inn, 148
Stonehurst Manor, 246
Stone Rest Bed & Breakfast,
    220
Stonewalls Farm, 117
Stonybrook Motor Lodge, 322
Strathaven, 181

Sugar Hill Inn, 321
Suisse Chalet, 77
Sunny Side Inn, 248
The Sunset, 149
Sunset Hill House, 319
Super 8 Motel, 76-77

Tall Timber Lodge, 351
The Tamworth Inn, 179-180
Thatcher Hill Inn, 118
Thayer's Inn, 320
13-Mile Woods Camp-
    grounds, 340
Timberland Lodge and
    Cabins, 351
Tolman Pond, 118
Tourist Village Motel, 335
Town and Country Motor Inn,
    335
The Townhomes at Bretton
    Woods, 280
Trumbull House, 148
Tuckernuck Inn, 184-185
Tuc' Me Inn, 178
Twin Lake Village, 212
289 Court, 118

Umbagog Lake Campground
    and Cottages, 340
Uplands Inn, 116

Valley Inn and Tavern, 303
The Victoria Inn, 55
The Victorian Bed and
    Breakfast, 219

Victorian Harvest Inn, 248
The Village House, 218, 264
The Village of Loon Moun-
    tain, 292
Village at Maplewood, 323

The Wakefield Inn, 200
Wander Inn, 351
Watch Hill B&B, 184
Wayside Inn, 320
Webster Lake Inn, 217
Wentworth Inn and Art
    Gallery, 307
Wentworth Resort Hotel, 258-
    259
West Ossipee House, 181
Westwinds, 116
White Goose Inn, 148
Whitney's Village Inn, 261-262
Wildcat Inn and Tavern, 262
Wilderness Cabins, 249
Wildflowers Guest House,
    248-249
WMNF Campgrounds, Evans
    Notch, 281
WMNF Dolly Copp Camp-
    ground, 275
The Wolfeboro Inn, 178
Wonderwell, 216-217
Woodbound Inn, 113
The Woodstock Inn, 293
Woodwar's Motor Inn, 292-
    293
Wyman Farm, 88

BOOKS ABOUT NEW ENGLAND

Explorer's Guides from The Countryman Press

The alternative to mass-market guides with their homogenized listings. Explorer's Guides focus on independently owned inns, motels, and restaurants as well as on family and cultural activities reflecting the character and unique qualities of the area.

Maine: An Explorer's Guide
  by Christina Tree and Mimi Steadman, $16.95
New Hampshire: An Explore's Guide
  by Christina Tree and Peter Randall, $16.95
Vermont: An Explorer's Guide
  by Christina Tree and Peter Jennison, $16.95

Other Books from The Countryman Press

Classic Regional Humor Books by Keith Jennison:
The Maine Idea, $7.95
Remember Maine, $7.95
Vermont is Where You Find It, $7.95
"Yup. . .Nope" & Other Vermont Dialogues, $7.95
The Humorous Mr. Lincoln, $9.95

Family Resorts of the Northeast
  by Nancy Pappas Metcalf, $12.95
New England's Special Places: A Daytripper's Guide
  by Michael A. Schuman, $12.95
Vermonters
  photographs by Jon Gilbert Fox, text by Donald L. Tinney, $9.95
The Blue Cat of Castletown
A classic Vermont Children's Tale by Catherine Cate Coblentz, $7.95
Maine Memories
by Elizabeth Coatsworth, $10.95
The Earth Shall Blossom: Shaker Herbs and Gardening
  by Galen Beale and Mary Rose Boswell, $18.95
Seasoned with Grace: My Generation of Shaker Cooking
  by Eldress Bertha Lindsay, $11.95
The Story of the Shakers
  by Flo Morse, $6.95

Guidebooks from Backcountry Publications

Written for people of all ages and experience, these quality softbound books feature detailed trail or tour directions, notes on points of interest, maps and photographs.

50 Hikes in Vermont
  by the Green Mountain Club, $11.95
50 Hikes in the White Mountains
  by Dan Doan, $12.95
50 More Hikes in New Hampshire
  by Dan Doan, $12.95
50 Hikes in Northern Maine
  by Cloe Caputo, $10.95
50 Hikes in Southern Maine
  by John Gibson, $10.95
50 Hikes in Massachusetts
  by John Brady and Brian White, $11.95
50 Hikes in Connecticut
  by Gerry and Sue Hardy, $11.95
Walks and Rambles in Rhode Island
  by Ken Weber, $9.95
Walks and Rambles in Westchester and Fairfield Counties: An Nature Lover's Guide to Thirty Parks and Sanctuaries
  by Katherine S. Anderson, $8.95
Walks and Rambles in the Upper CT River Valley
  by Mary L. Kibling, $9.95
25 Bicycle Tours in Vermont
  by John Freidin, $8.95
25 Mountain Bike Tours in Massachusetts
  by Robert S. Morse, $9.95
25 Mountain Bike Tours in Vermont
  by William J. Busha, $9.95
30 Bicycle Tours in New Hampshire
  by Adolphe Bernotas and Tom & Susan Heavey, $10.95
25 Bicycle Tours in Maine
  by Howard Stone, $9.95
25 Ski Tours in New Hampshire
  by Roioli Schweiker, $8.95
25 Ski Tours in Vermont
  by Stan Wass, $8.95
Canoeing Massachusetts, Rhode Island, and Connecticut
  by Ken Weber, $8.96
Canoe Camping Vermont and New Hampshire Rivers
  by Roioli Schweiker, $7.95
Waterfalls of the White Mountains
  by Bruce and Doreen Bolnick, $14.95

We also publish books about bicycling, walking, hiking, canoeing, camping, fishing, and ski touring in New Jersey, New York, Pennsylvania, Maryland, Delaware, Ohio, West Virginia and Virginia. Please write for our catalog.

Out titles are available in bookshops and in many sporting goods stores, or they may be ordered directly from the publisher. Write or call The Countryman Press, P.O. Box 175, Woodstock, Vermont 05091; (802) 457-1049. Please add $2.50 per order for shipping and handling.

READER'S SURVEY

The Countryman Press series of Explorer's Guides reflects our readers' demand for insightful, incisive reporting on the best and most exciting destinations offered in New England. To help us tailor our books even better to your needs, please take a moment to fill out this anonymous (if you wish) questionnaire, returning it to:

The Countryman Press, Inc., P.O. Box 175, Woodstock, Vermont 05091

1. How did you hear about the Countryman Press Explorer's Guides: newspaper, magazine, radio, friends, other (please specify)?

   _____

   _____

2. Please list in order of preference the cities or states (or areas) on which you would like to have a Countryman Press Explorer's Guide, aside from the already existing destinations.

   _____

   _____

3. Do you refer to the Countryman Press guides in your travels or for your own area?

   a. (travels)_____b. (own area)_____c. (both)_____

4. Do you use any guide other than one by Countryman Press?

   If yes, _____

5. Please list, starting with the most preferred, the three features that you like most about the Countryman Press Explorer's guides.

   a._____

   b._____

   c._____

6. What are the features, if any, you dislike about the Countryman Press Explorer's guides?

_____

_____

7. Please list any features you would like to see added to the Countryman Press Explorer's guides.

_____

_____

8. Please list the features you like most about your favorite guidebook series if it is not Countryman Press.

a._____

b._____

c._____

9. How many trips do you make per year for business and for pleasure?

Business: International_____Domestic_____

Pleasure: International_____Domestic_____

10. Is your annual household income over (check appropriate choice)?

$20,000_____$40,000_____$60,000_____

$80,000_____$100,000_____Other (please specify)_____

11. If you have any comments on the Countryman Press Explorer's guides in general, please enclose them on a separate sheet of paper.

We thank you for your interest in the Countryman Press Explorer's guides, and we welcome your remarks and your recommendations about restaurants, hotels, shops, and services.